THE GRACE OF GOD, THE WILL OF MAN

A Case for Arminianism

THE
GRACE
—OF—
GOD,
THE WILL
—OF—
MAN

CLARK H. PINNOCK
General Editor

Academie
Books Grand Rapids, Michigan
Zondervan Publishing House

THE GRACE OF GOD, THE WILL OF MAN
Copyright © 1989 by Clark H. Pinnock

ACADEMIE BOOKS is an imprint of Zondervan Publishing House,
1415 Lake Drive, SE, Grand Rapids, Michigan 49506.

Library of Congress Cataloging-in-Publication Data

The Grace of God, the will of man.

    Includes bibliographies and indexes.
    1. Arminianism. 2. Grace (Theology) 3. Providence and government of God.
4. Election (Theology) 5. Predestination. 6. Free will and determinism.
7. Salvation. I. Pinnock, Clark H., 1937–
BX6195.G68 1989   234'.9   88-22130
ISBN 0-310-51231-X

Printed in the United States of America

90 91 92 93 94 / CH / 10 9 8 7 6 5 4 3 2

CONTENTS

CONTRIBUTORS

William J. Abraham, D.Phil, Oxford University, is professor of evangelism and the philosophy of religion at Perkins School of Theology, Southern Methodist University, Dallas, Texas. Two of his recent books are *An Introduction to the Philosophy of Religion* and *The Coming Great Revival.*

Randall G. Basinger, Ph.D., Northwestern University, is associate professor of philosophy at Messiah College, Grantham, Pennsylvania. With his brother David, he has written *Philosophy and Miracle: The Contemporary Debate* and co-edited *Predestination and Free Will.*

Jack W. Cottrell, Th.D., Princeton Theological Seminary, is professor of theology at Cincinnati Christian Seminary in Ohio, and has written a massive trilogy of books on the doctrine of God: *God the Creator, God the Ruler,* and *God the Redeemer.*

William L. Craig, Ph.D., University of Birmingham, U.K., D.Theol., University of Munich, is associate professor of philosophy and religious studies at Westmont College in Santa Barbara, California. He recently wrote *The Only Wise God: The Compatibility of Divine Foreknowledge and Human Freedom.*

C. Stephen Evans, Ph.D., Yale University, is professor of philosophy and curator of the Hong Kierkegaard Library at St. Olaf College in Northfield, Minnesota. Among other books, he has written *Preserving the Person* and *The Quest for Faith.*

Fritz Guy, Ph.D., University of Chicago, now lectures in theology at Loma Linda University and is a pastor at the University Church of Seventh-day Adventists on campus. He co-edited with Humberto Rasi *Meeting the Secular Mind.,*

William G. MacDonald, Th.D., Southern Baptist Theological Seminary, formerly professor of biblical and theological studies at Gordon College, now does research and lecturing from his home in Virginia. He is author of *Greek Enchiridion: A Concise Handbook of Grammar for Translation and Exegesis.*

I. Howard Marshall, Ph.D., University of Aberdeen, is professor of New Testament exegesis at King's College, University of Aberdeen in Scotland. Among his numerous books are *Kept by the Power of God* and *The Origins of New Testament Christology.*

Terry L. Miethe, Ph.D., St. Louis University, Ph.D., University of Southern California, is Dean of the Oxford Study Centre, Oxford, England, and Managing Editor of Moody Press. He has written *The New Christian's Guide to Following Jesus* and *A Christian's Guide to Faith & Reason,* books on Augustine and Aquinas, and several others.

Grant R. Osborne, Ph.D., University of Aberdeen, is professor of New Testament at Trinity Evangelical Divinity School in Deerfield, Illinois, and has written *The Resurrection Narratives: A Redactional Study* and *Meaning and Significance: The Spiral From Text to Context.*

Clark H. Pinnock, Ph.D., University of Manchester, is professor of theology at McMaster Divinity College in Ontario, author of *The Scripture Principle,* and editor of *Grace Unlimited.*

Bruce R. Reichenbach, Ph.D., Northwestern University, is professor of philosophy at Augsburg College in Minneapolis, Minnesota. Among other books, he has written *The Cosmological Argument* and *Evil and a Good God.*

Richard Rice, Ph.D., University of Chicago, is professor of theology at Loma Linda University and author of *The Reign of God* and *God's Foreknowledge and Man's Free Will.*

John E. Sanders, has an MA in Theology from Wartburg Theological Seminary in Dubuque, Iowa and is an instructor at Oak Hills Bible College in Bemidji, Minnesota.

Jerry L. Walls, Ph.D., University of Notre Dame, teaches philosophy of religion at Asbury Theological Seminary and has published a number of scholarly articles. He recently received his doctorate from the University of Notre Dame in Indiana.

INTRODUCTION

This book, *The Grace of God, the Will of Man* carries on the ancient debate that it shares with its predecessor, *Grace Unlimited* (1975), between proponents of two different evangelical accounts of how God works salvation and relates to his human creatures. The question can be put this way: Is God the absolute Monarch who always gets his way, or is God rather the loving Parent who is sensitive to our needs even when we disappoint him and frustrate some of his plans?

Some readers may be initially surprised to learn that evangelical theology comes in different versions at all. They may have thought that there was just one uncontested set of convictions all real Christians have always held from the beginning. This is a common misunderstanding among us. Although there is a basic grammar of faith including belief in the triune God and the unique salvation in Jesus Christ, in other areas such as the outworking of God's saving purposes there has not been complete agreement. On the contrary, Luther's version of how God works salvation and relates to the world is distinctive and different in some respects from Wesley's and Augustine's versions. They represent different versions of the broad evangelical and Christian tradition. And the differences between them are worth debating and should not always be shoved underneath the rug in a show of unity. For some purposes it makes sense to call a wide variety of Christians "evangelicals" to distinguish them from liberal reductionists for example, but it can also be quite misleading to call them by this adjective if the umbrella term obscures important differences among them which should not be lost sight of.

There are of course some ancient debates among us that might be better forgotten and not continued, such as endless discussions on minute details in eschatology or about the immanent Trinity. They have been pretty much exhausted, and the life has gone out of them. They are beyond our mental powers anyway and do not do the Christian cause much good. But this is not one of those debates. A great deal hangs on whether God is portrayed as an all-determining Power who gets glory even from the damnation of sinners or as a compassionate Lover who enters into the struggles of his significantly free creatures. The writers of this book contend that it makes the difference between having good news or having bad news to offer people whether we start with God's goodness or with his power. Does God love the people next door or has God perhaps excluded them from salvation? Do our choices make any difference or have they been preprogramed from the beginning? Did God devise all the evil in the world or is there something limiting his sovereignty? A lot of theoretical and practical issues hang on our answer to these questions.

We have no particular taste for controversy as such among believers and no desire to hurt anyone. Nor are we even absolutely certain that the debate over divine sovereignty and human freedom is capable of being resolved by human minds. Maybe it is a dialectic or antinomy that cannot be resolved. But we are convinced that the issues involved are important enough to require the debate to go ahead and not be shelved. No one should be surprised that some of us want to carry the debate on; it is more a matter of surprise that more people who are concerned about Christian truth are not involved in it. After all, here is a meaty debate, with weighty issues both theoretical and practical at stake, and in it both sides can appeal to rich scriptural, logical, and experiential data.

There is even reason to hope that progress can be made even at this late date and that we can do more than just rehash old arguments. We think so because the various positions people take are not in fact unchangeable or set in stone. The varieties of evangelical theology are all developing dynamically as everything in history does. Thus there is not one single determinist theology over against one single conditionalist position. There is a spectrum of Calvinisms all the way from supralapsarian to sublapsarian, and a spectrum of Arminianisms from evangelical to rationalistic. Nor do these spectra represent frozen opinions—there is a great deal of movement within them. There is a flexibility and diversity among evangelicals today that gives us grounds for hope. God isn't finished with us yet. The Spirit has more light to give us. So we look ahead to God's leading us forward in our understanding.

This book takes the position that God is a personal being who respects the integrity of the significantly free creatures he made and who relates dynamically with them in the working out of his purposes for the world. We believe that God not only acts but also reacts. God not only influences events in the world but is also influenced by events. God not only has plans for history, but he is also flexible enough to adapt them to the decisions that human beings make. Above all, God is love, and therefore expresses his power, not by having to control everything like an oriental despot, but by giving humanity salvation and eternal life under the conditions of mutuality.

What concerns us is the dual fact that the determinist kind of theology, the type that subordinates God's love to the ideal of absolute power, is both highly influential and exceedingly harmful. On the one hand it enjoys a kind of hegemony in evangelical circles out of all proportion to its popular support and on the other hand inflicts on this community many unpleasant theoretical and practical consequences. Insisting that God's will accounts for everything that happens creates tremendous intellectual and practical difficulties for Christians and almost insurmountable hurdles for seekers to jump over. So we think it is very important that people be made aware of an alternative theology that does not have these effects.

The book begins with a piece of theological autobiography by the editor, who tells the story of how he has wrestled with these issues over some decades, and then it goes on to present fourteen scholarly essays on a variety of specific topics, essays written especially for this volume by an ecumenically diverse and splendid group of evangelical scholars.

The first three chapters after the editor's personal account lay the theological foundation of biblical universalism. Fritz Guy leads off with a well-documented and soundly argued case for the global reach of God's love and care for humankind. Seventh-day Adventists like Fritz Guy and Richard Rice are often shunned by other evangelicals as theologically suspect at certain points. I hope that our readers' discovery of the excellence of their theological insights and convictions will help to bring our communities closer together. Both of these scholars articulate an eloquent and moving plea to place the love of God, rather than omnipotence as such, at the center of our thinking. I. Howard Marshall, a world-renowned New Testament scholar and British Methodist, backs up Fritz Guy's chapter with a careful and irenic study in the Pastoral Epistles about God's universal salvific will and the unconditional good news that is based on it. He refutes the idea of two divine wills, as if we should think that God has a hidden agenda to save only the chosen few while overtly pretending to desire to save everyone. Marshall's first book, *Kept by the Power of God: A Study of Perseverance and Falling Away* (Minneapolis: Bethany, 1969), was an important milestone for some of us in breaking free of this kind of determinist theology. Terry Miethe follows with a vigorous chapter in defense of the universal scope of Christ's atonement, taking issue with J. I. Packer's attempt to defend a limited atonement in the tradition of the Puritan John Owen.

The next three chapters take up the difficult question of the nature of divine sovereignty. Jack Cottrell, who has written a large volume on the subject entitled *God the Ruler* (Joplin, Mo.: College Press, 1984) presents his basic insights in his chapter. Having decided to create a world possessing relative autonomy, God limits his power in relation to it in order to give it room to be. This decision was itself a sovereign choice that was not forced on God from the outside, but God made it in order to facilitate a covenantal relationship between himself and his significantly free human creatures. Cottrell incidentally comes from the tradition simply called the Christian churches or the churches of Christ.

In the course of his presentation, Cottrell raises one of the most fascinating intellectual problems in this book. His view is that God can exercise his governance over all things by means of his exhaustive foreknowledge. Being able to anticipate everything precisely in detail means that God is able to respond to all that happens in a completely wise manner without violating human freedom. It also means that God's plan can be said to include absolutely everything. This has been the classical Arminian position. But Richard Rice follows Cottrell with an essay that questions his approach and offers an alternative viewpoint. Rice believes that if everything were foreknown by God in exhaustive detail, then everything would be as fixed and necessary as if it were actually predetermined. He is concerned that by allowing exhaustive foreknowledge in our thinking we will land right back in the lap of theological determinism, from which we want to escape.

In effect Rice accepts the force of the common Calvinian argument against the Arminian position on precisely this point and therefore presents the case for limited divine foreknowledge in opposition to Cottrell's view. Just as there are things God cannot do though omnipotent, Rice argues, so there are things God cannot know though omniscient, namely future free choices that are not properly objects of knowledge. If human choices are truly free, he reasons, they do not exist to be known in advance by any knower, not even God. And since they cannot be known in advance except speculatively on the basis of existing conditions, it cannot be said that God's knowledge is limited by his not knowing them. Rice has a book on this topic entitled *God's Foreknowledge and Human Freedom* (Minneapolis: Bethany, 1985).

Bill Craig does not agree with Rice against Cottrell and offers us an exposition of the medieval theory of middle knowledge, which he believes will make Rice's move on divine omniscience unnecessary. The theory posits that God knows all contingencies as well as all actualities and therefore can know everything that will come to pass without that knowledge involving the determinist implications that Rice fears. Craig argues that God can know precisely what any individual will do in every situation of life without his foreknowledge implying any loss of human freedom.

Rice refers to the theory of middle knowledge in his own chapter, creating a rudimentary dialogue for us on this point. Craig too has recently written a book on the subject—*The Only Wise God* (Grand Rapids: Baker, 1987).

While the debate about foreknowledge is speculative and not easily resolved, the next three chapters move us back on track in our pursuit of basic principles. John Sanders asks us to compare the absolutist conception of God created by early theologians like Augustine, who were under the influence of Greek thinking, with the dynamic biblical portrayal of God as personal agent. He makes the plea, for the sake of both theological renewal and issues of practical Christian living, that we return to the dynamic biblical portrait of God. His foray into historical theology, showing where the absolutist thinking came from and how it contrasts sharply with biblical teaching, gives his chapter a uniquely valuable thrust in the volume. Stephen Evans follows with a discussion of Søren Kierkegaard and how he saw salvation as an unmerited gift but one freely received and not imposed on us. After Evans, Randall Basinger raises the question of practical outcomes: What difference does it make after all whether one follows the absolutist or the free-will model of theism? He concludes that it makes a good deal of difference and that on this score the Arminians win hands down. Their thinking best explains how we all—even Calvinians—act in the world. To arguments of theoretical reason, Basinger thus adds arguments from practical reason.

Three chapters then follow in the area of biblical and doctrinal theology. Bill MacDonald, a Pentecostal scholar formerly of Gordon College, offers a study of divine election, concentrating particularly on Ephesians 1. Election in the Bible, he claims, is not an arbitrary selection, oriented to the salvation or damnation of individual sinners, but is centered on God's chosen One, Jesus Christ, and is ecclesial or corporate in its application to us. God has chosen a people for his Son and invites all persons to participate in the new solidarity. William Abraham, a Methodist teaching at Perkins School of Theology, follows with a discussion of the assurance of salvation and how we know it. Irenically drawing on Edwards as well as Wesley, he invites us all to ground our Christian assurance in our experience of the Spirit within our hearts and get away from rational speculation in this area. Grant Osborne then takes a candid look at soteriology in the Fourth Gospel. Knowing that the book poses real problems for an Arminian understanding, he wants to investigate the subject. The result is a detailed and scholarly discussion that will be appreciated by all readers.

The last two chapters deal directly with the moral dimension, the point where determinist theology runs into such awful problems and where free-will theism seems to enjoy definite advantages. First Jerry Walls exposes the really outrageous divine-command views of morality held by Luther and Calvin, as if God would still be "good" if he commanded torture and rape, as he in fact does according to some theologies of total sovereignty. Looking to Wesley, Walls urges us to adopt the position of moral reliabilism in ethics. He sees God's commandments as the commands of a loving God, whose will for us takes into account our good and our human nature and reflects God's own character. In a long final chapter, Bruce Reichenbach drives a few more nails into the coffin by showing how determinist theology threatens human moral accountability.

I hope our readers will enjoy the feast set before them. Here is a splendid group of believing scholars, from a generous variety of evangelical traditions, presenting their ideas clearly and forcefully. We do not have the last word, but at least we can keep the ball in play.

FROM AUGUSTINE TO ARMINIUS: A PILGRIMAGE IN THEOLOGY

Clark H. Pinnock

A theological shift is underway among evangelicals as well as other Christians away from determinism as regards the rule and salvation of God and in the direction of an orientation more favorable to a dynamic personal relationship between God, the world, and God's human creatures. The trend began, I believe, because of a fresh and faithful reading of the Bible in dialogue with modern culture, which places emphasis on autonomy, temporality, and historical change. In this chapter I want to tell the story of my pilgrimage and struggle to understand these matters and thus perhaps to give voice to what I suspect is the experience of many others. The account may also serve as a case study about systematic thinking in theology, how it changes and works itself out in a person's life.[1]

WHY A PILGRIMAGE?

The great majority of theologians change their minds quite often. We often refer to their early work and their later work, and sometimes also to the middle stages of their thought. Karl Barth, undoubtedly the greatest theologian of our century, illustrates this very well, and he was not ashamed of changing his mind. It is better to change one's mind than to continue on a wrong path. Of course there are some who do not follow this rule: they refuse to change. Theologians like Bultmann and Van Til, for example, seem to have thought they possessed all the "right" answers from graduate school on and never saw any reason to change them afterward, though many of their readers saw reason to change. But such theologians are the abnormal ones, and it is rather hard for ordinary mortals to identify with them. The reason for this is that in theology we are dealing with great mysteries and intellectually complex problems that can be excruciatingly difficult to sort out and to understand. So almost anyone who seriously tries to resolve them will experience struggle in doing so and changes in his or her understanding. Not only are individual topics like predestination and election remarkably challenging in themselves, but also the interconnections between such themes and other topics in the total grammar of the Christian faith are tricky to establish and maintain in a balanced way.

So I do not apologize for admitting to being on a pilgrimage in theology, as if it were in itself some kind of weakness of intelligence or character. Feeling our way toward the truth is the nature of theological work even with the help of Scripture, tradition, and the community. We are fallible and historically situated creatures, and our best thinking falls far short of the ideal of what our subject matter requires. A pilgrimage, therefore, far from being unusual or slightly dishonorable, is what we would expect theologians who are properly aware of their limitations to experience.

This is particularly true when it comes to our present set of topics: how God relates to his human creatures in history and in redemption. Here the human mind is stretched to its limits and beyond when it dares to inquire how divine sovereignty and human freedom relate to each other. One is almost certain to change one's mind several times over a lifetime on mysteries as deep as these. In speaking of Augustine and Arminius in the title of this chapter, I am using the names of two famous theologians to symbolize two profound ways of structuring the answer—Augustine placing the emphasis on the sovereignty of God and Arminius putting it on significant human freedom. My pilgrimage can be described as a journey from Augustine to Arminius. But I could as easily have spoken of Calvin and Wesley, or Luther and Erasmus. Let us be aware too as I relate the story that it is not a one-way street. Many others, such as R. C. Sproul, will be able to write about their odyssey in the opposite direction. Well-meaning, thoughtful Christians can and do differ in their judgments on these important matters. Therefore, we need to listen to one another, hold back the recriminations, and see what we can learn from one another.[2]

THE CALVINISTIC HEGEMONY IN EVANGELICALISM

Brought up as I was in a liberal church and converted in my teens chiefly through the witness of my grandmother, I was introduced in a natural way during the 1950s to the institutions of what is inexactly called "evangelicalism" in North America, a quasi-denominational world furnished with its own publishers, magazines, conference centers, famous evangelists, youth organi-zations, and the like.[3] Although there is a great and growing diversity theologically and otherwise in this coalition, the domi-nating theology is Reformed or Calvinian. Critics have not exaggerated much when they have wanted to call it "neo-Calvin-ism."[4]

Certainly most of the authors I was introduced to in those early days as theologically "sound" were staunchly Calvinistic: John Murray, Martyn Lloyd-Jones, Cornelius Van Til, Carl Henry, James Packer, Paul Jewett. Theirs were the books that were sold in the Inter-Varsity bookroom I frequented. They were the ones I was told to listen to; sound theology was what they would teach me. A simple fact, which I did not think much about at the time, was that Calvinian theology enjoyed an elitist position of domi-nance within postwar evangelicalism on both sides of the Atlantic. This was due in part to the fact that it was and is also a scholarly and historic system of evangelical theology. Therefore, it is no surprise that I began my theological life as a Calvinist who regarded alternate evangelical interpretations as suspect and at least mildly heretical. I accepted the view I was given that Calvinism was just scriptural evangelicalism in its purest expres-sion, and I did not question it for a long time.

A HOLE IN THE DIKE

I held onto this view until about 1970, when one of the links in the chain of the tight Calvinian logic broke. It had to do with the doctrine of the perseverance of the saints, likely the weakest link in Calvinian logic, scripturally speaking. I was teaching at Trinity Evangelical Divinity School at the time and attending to the doctrine particularly in the book of Hebrews. If in fact believers enjoy the kind of absolute security Calvinism had taught me they do, I found I could not make very good sense of the vigorous exhortations to persevere (e.g., 3:12) or the awesome warnings not to fall away from Christ (e.g., 10:26), which the book addresses to Christians.[5] It began to dawn on me that my security in God was linked to my faith-union with Christ and that God is teaching us here the extreme importance of maintaining and not forsaking this relationship. The exhortations and the warnings could only signify that continuing in the grace of God was something that depended at least in part on the human partner. And once I saw that, the logic of Calvinism was broken in principle, and it was only a matter of time before the larger implications of its breaking would dawn on me. The thread was pulled, and the garment must begin to unravel, as indeed it did.

What had dawned on me was what I had known experiential-ly all along in my walk with the Lord, that there is a profound mutuality in our dealings with God. What happens between us is not simply the product of a set of premundane divine decrees that, written on an everlasting and unchangeable scroll, determine all that takes place in the world. I began to doubt the existence of an all-determining fatalistic blueprint for history and to think of God's having made us significantly free creatures able to accept or reject his purposes for us (Luke 7:30). Even the good news of the grace of God will not benefit us, as Hebrews says, unless "mixed with faith in the hearers." (Heb. 4:2) For the first time I realized theologically that the dimension of reciprocity and conditionality had to be brought into the picture of God's relations with us in creation and redemption and that, once it is brought in, the theological landscape would have to change significantly. The determinist model cannot survive once a person starts down this road, as scripturally I came to see I must.

As a Calvinist of course I had professed to believe in a kind of human freedom, a compatibilist kind that claims that our actions can be both free and determined at the same time. Sometimes I would try to explain it, other times I would give up and call it an antinomy, but deep down I knew there was something amiss. I was faintly aware that an action forever predetermined to be what it will be, however necessitated, whether by external factors or internal motives, did not deserve to be called a "free" action. Now, given my new discovery, I was able to move away from that construction and see the biblical view of human freedom in a different way. God made us "responsible" beings able to respond freely to his word and call. Of the essence of this creature that bears God's own image, marking it off from all the others in this world, is this wonderful capacity to relate or decline to relate to God, to love or not to love him. It was now open to me to regard people not as the product of a timeless decree but as God's covenant partners and real players in the flow and the tapestry of history. I hardly need to add that my reaction to this discovery was one of considerable relief.[6]

THE WIDENING IMPLICATIONS

Driven by Scripture itself as I reflected on it, and not out of rationalist motives as some might unkindly suggest, I found myself having to push ahead and do more rethinking in several other areas of doctrine adjacent to this one in the years that followed during the 1970s. Just as one cannot change the pitch of a single string on the violin without adjusting the others, so one cannot introduce a major new insight into a coherent system like Calvinian theology without having to reconsider many other issues. Let me explain five of the doctrinal moves that logic required and I believed Scripture permitted me to make during this period.

1. The first and the best discovery I made was that there was no "horrible decree" at all. Calvin had used this expression in connection with his belief that God in his sovereign good pleasure had predestined some people to be eternally lost for no fault of theirs (*Institutes*, 3.23). Calvin was compelled to say that because, if one thinks that God determines all that happens in the world (his Augustinian premise) and not all are to be saved in the end (as he believed the Bible taught), there was no way around it. Calvin's logic was impeccable as usual: God wills whatever happens, so if there are to be lost people, God must have willed it. It was as logically necessary as it was morally intolerable.

Of course I had always known how morally loathsome the doctrine of double predestination is and how contradictory it is to the universal biblical texts, but I had not known previously how to avoid it. But now with the insight of reciprocity in hand, which had just surfaced for me in rethinking the doctrine of perseverance, it became possible for me to accept the scriptural teaching of the universal salvific will of God and not feel duty-bound to deny it as before. I was now in a position to rejoice in the truth that God's will is for all to be saved (1 Tim. 2:4), and that God's grace has appeared for the salvation of all people (Titus 2:11).

The dark shadow was lifting; the logic of Calvinism could no longer blind me to these lines of biblical teaching. All mankind has been included in the saving plan of God and in the redemption of Jesus Christ. By the obedience of the Son, there is acquittal and life for all people (Rom. 5:18). Thus the invitation can go out to all sinners, sincerely urging them to repent and believe the good news that offers salvation to everyone without hedging. The banquet of salvation has been set for all people. God has provided plenteous redemption in the work of Christ, sufficient for the salvation of the entire race of sinners. All that remains for any individual to benefit from what was accomplished for him is to respond to the good news and enter into the new relationship with God that has been opened up for all persons.[7]

2. I was then driven back to the Scriptures to reconsider what divine election might mean, if in fact God desires all to be saved and cannot be thought of any longer as selecting some to be saved and placing the others under wrath and reprobation, as in high Calvinism. How shall I understand those texts that I had always assumed said and meant exactly that?

One possibility that presented itself was to think of election as being based on the foreknowledge of God (Rom. 8:29; 1 Peter 1:2). This was the standard Arminian position—one favored by the early Greek fathers—and it would deviate least from the Calvinian idea of the selection of a certain number of specific individuals from before the creation of the world to be saved. It would simply introduce, on the basis of divine omniscience, the element of conditionality into the idea of divine election and thus appear to rescue it from arbitrariness. Although at this time I had not yet come to reconsider the nature of the divine omniscience presupposed in this account, even then I found myself attracted to a second possibility—that election is a corporate category and not oriented to the choice of individuals for salvation. I knew that everyone admitted this to be the case in the Old Testament where the election of Israel is one of a people to be God's servant in a special way. Was it possible that the New Testament texts too could be interpreted along these same lines? Upon reflection I decided that they could indeed be read corporately, election then speaking of a class of people rather than specific individuals. God has chosen a people for his Son, and we are joined and belong to the elect body by faith in Christ (Eph. 1:3–14).

Viewed in this way, election, far from arbitrarily excluding anybody, encompasses them all potentially. As a corporate symbol, election is no longer a dark mystery, but a joyous cause of praise and thanksgiving. Not only so but this model has the distinct advantage of construing election as a divine decision and not the pale notion of God's ratifying our choices as in the standard Arminian interpretation. If election is understood as a corporate category, then it would be God's unconditional decision and be potentially universal as regards all individuals. All are invited to become part of the elect people by personal faith. In addition the idea of corporate election would have had the further advantage of not requiring absolute divine omniscience, which became an issue for me later on.[8]

3. Predestination proved to be less of a problem, surprisingly enough. Familarily with the dynamic character of God's dealing with human beings according to the biblical narrative had prepared me to see predestination in terms of God's setting goals for people rather than forcing them to enact the preprogramed decrees. God predestines us to be conformed to the image of his Son (Rom. 8:29). That is his plan for us, whether or not we choose to go down that path. God's plan for the world and for ourselves does not suppress but rather sustains and includes the spontaneity of significant human decisions. We are co-workers with God, participating with him in what shall be hereafter. The future is not stored up on heavenly video tape, but is the realm of possibilities, many of which have yet to be decided and actualized. Peter gives us a nice illustration of this when he explains the delay of Christ's return as being due to God's desire to see more sinners saved— God actually postponing the near return of Christ for their sakes (2 Peter 3:9).

Previously I had had to swallow hard and accept the

Calvinian antinomy that required me to believe both that God determines all things and that creaturely freedom is real. I made a valiant effort to believe this seeming contradiction on the strength of biblical infallibility, being assured that the Bible actually taught it. So I was relieved to discover that the Bible does not actually teach such an incoherence, and this particular paradox was a result of Calvinian logic, not scriptural dictates.[9] Having created human beings with relative autonomy alongside himself, God voluntarily limits his power to enable them to exist and to share in the divine creativity. God invites humans to share in deciding what the future will be. God does not take it all onto his own shoulders. Does this compromise God's power? No, surely not, for to create such a world in fact requires a divine power of a kind higher than merely coercive.

When predestination is viewed in this light, there is immense relief also in the area of theodicy. The logic of consistent Calvinism makes God the author of evil and casts serious doubt on his goodness. One is compelled to think of God's planning such horrors as Auschwitz, even though none but the most rigorous Calvinians can bring themselves to admit it. But if predestination is thought of as an all-inclusive set of goals and not an all-determining plan, then the difficulty for theodicy is greatly eased. Later, I was to conclude that rethinking the divine omniscience would ease it still more.

Obviously what is happening here is a paradigm shift in my biblical hermeneutics. I am in the process of learning to read the Bible from a new point of view, one that I believe is more truly evangelical and less rationalistic. Looking at it from the vantage point of God's universal salvific will and of significant human freedom, I find that many new verses leap up from the page, while many old familiar ones take on new meaning. In the past I would slip into my reading of the Bible dark assumptions about the nature of God's decrees and intentions. What a relief to be done with them![10]

4. The depth of human sinfulness was another matter that soon demanded my attention. Calvinists, like Augustine himself, if the reader will excuse the anachronism, wanting to leave no room at all to permit any recognition of human freedom in the salvation event, so defined human depravity as total that it would be impossible to imagine any sinner calling upon God to save him. Thus they prevented anyone from thinking about salvation in the Arminian way. Leaving aside the fact that Augustinians themselves often and suspiciously qualify their notion of "total" depravity very considerably and invent the notion of common grace to tone it down, I knew I had to consider how to understand the free will of the sinner in relation to God.

Again, I had a choice of paths to follow. I knew that Wesley had opted for a doctrine of universal prevenient grace by which God enabled the spiritually dead sinner to respond to him in faith. The Fourth Gospel speaks of a universal drawing action of God (John 12:32). This move allowed him to retain his belief in total depravity and still avoid the Calvinistic consequences in terms of particularist election and limited grace.[11] But I also knew that the Bible has no developed doctrine of universal prevenient grace, however convenient it would be for us if it did. Hence, I was drawn instead to question total depravity itself as a possible ambush designed to cut off non-Augustinians at the pass. Was there any evidence that Jesus, for example, regarded people as totally depraved? Does the Bible generally not leave us with the impression that one can progress in sin as in holiness, and that how total one's depravity is varies from person to person and is not a constant? Surely "total" depravity biblically would be the point beyond which it is not possible to go in realizing the full possibilities of sinfulness and not the actual condition of all sinners at the present time. In any case, what became decisive for me was the simple fact that Scripture appeals to people as those who are able and responsible to answer to God (however as we explain it) and not as those incapable of doing so, as Calvinian logic would suggest. The gospel addresses them as free and responsible agents, and I must suppose it does so because that is what they are.

5. I also found I had to think about the atoning work of Christ. The easy part was accepting the obvious fact that contrary to Calvinian logic Jesus died for the sins of the whole world according to the New Testament. Exegesis stands strongly against the system on this point. I had no difficulty with the verses that asserted Christ's death on behalf of the whole race because they fitted so obviously into the doctrine of God's universal salvific will, which I had already come to accept. Even Calvin himself, if not all of his followers, was prepared to concede the universal extent of the atonement and view it as sufficient for the sins of the whole world.

The difficulty arose at the point of the theory that would explain this universal atonement for me. Assuming, as any evangelical would, that the Cross involved some kind of substitution in which Christ bore the guilt of human sin, where then does the human response fit into that? One might easily suppose that all those who were substituted for in the death of Christ would necessarily be saved and have the guilt of their sins automatically removed without any action of theirs entering into it. So if Christ really took away the guilt of the sins of the race, is the whole race then not now justified by virtue of that fact? Has not Christ actually achieved their salvation for them? And would this not lead inexorably either to universal salvation or to the doctrine of limited or particular atonement (neither of which are biblically supported)? What kind of substitution, if unlimited in scope, does not entail absolute universalism in salvation?[12]

Obviously it required me to reduce the precision in which I understood the substitution to take place. Christ's death on behalf of the race evidently did not automatically secure for anyone an actual reconciled relationship with God, but made it possible for people to enter into such a relationship by faith. Gospel invitations in the New Testament alone make this clear. It caused me to look again first at the theory of Anselm and later of Hugo Grotius, both of whom encourage us to view the atonement as an act of judicial demonstration rather than a strict or quantitative substitution as such. Paul's word in Romans 3:25–26 then became more important for me where the apostle himself declares that the cross was a demonstration of the righteousness of God, proving God's holiness even in the merciful justification of sinners.

Later on I became impressed with Barth's version of substitution in terms of a great exchange in which the last Adam proved victorious over sin and Satan by standing in place of the whole human race, bearing the wrath of God against all our sin, and achieving the reconciliation of mankind objectively. My main hesitation lay in the need to place greater stress on the human appropriation of this saving act, because Barth leans too far in the objective direction and needs to be better balanced. Faith after all is the condition for the concrete realization of this salvation in anyone able to respond.[13]

FREE-WILL THEISM

More recently the course of my theological pilgrimage has taken me onto the territory of Christian theism itself. Although I had already come to a fresh understanding of the goodness and power of God, I realized in the early 1980s that there were still more implications to be drawn in the area of the divine attributes. It is understandable that they would dawn on me last rather than first because God who is the mystery of human life is also theology's greatest and most demanding subject. But I could not finally escape rethinking the doctrine of God, however difficult.

The basic problem I had to cope with here is the fact that the classical model of Christian theism, shaped so decisively by Augustine under the influence of Greek philosophy, located the biblical picture of a dynamic personal God in the context of a way of thinking about God that placed high value on the Deity's being timeless, changeless, passionless, unmoved, and unmovable. The resulting synthesis more than subtly altered the biblical picture of God and tended to suppress some important aspects of it. In particular it resisted hearing the Bible's witness to a God who genuinely interacts with the world, responds passionately to what happens in it, and even changes his own plans to fit changing historical circumstances. Augustine's idea that God knows and determines all things in advance and never has to adjust his planning is one that stands in obvious tension with the Bible and yet is deeply fixed in historic Christian thinking. It is due to the accommodation made in classical theism to the Hellenistic culture.

Although the Bible itself presents a very dynamic picture of God and the world, the Greek world in which Christianity moved in the early centuries had a very negative view of historical change and the passage of time and therefore preferred to conceptualize the Deity in terms of pure actuality, changelessness, timelessness, and the like—ideas that negate the value of history and historical change. Curiously in this respect at least modern culture, which values history so much, is closer to the biblical view than classical theism.

I soon realized something would have to be done about the received doctrine of God. I knew I would have to deal with the fact that God has made creatures with relative autonomy alongside himself and that I would have to consider what that implies for the nature and attributes of God.

1. First of all I knew we had to clarify what we meant by the divine immutability. I saw that we have been far too influenced by Plato's idea that a perfect being would not change because, being perfect, it would not need to change—any change would be for the worse. The effect of this piece of Greek natural theology on Christian thinking had been to picture God as virtually incapable of responsiveness. Creatures can relate to God, all right, but God cannot really relate to them. Christian piety has always assumed a reciprocity between God and ourselves of course, but the official theology had tended to undercut the assumption by declaring God to be unconditioned in every aspect of his being.

The way forward, I found, was to speak of specific ways in which the God of the Bible is unchangeable—for example, in his being as God and in his character as personal agent—and also of ways in which God is able to change, as in his personal relationships with us and with the creation. It is not a question of God's changing in the sense of becoming better or worse, but of his pursuing covenant relationship and partnership with his people out of love for them flexibly and creatively. Immutable in his self-existence, the God of the Bible is relational and changeable in his interaction with his creatures. The Word "became" flesh—praise God for his changing unchangeability![14]

2. Although thinking of God as timeless has some apparently positive advantages, I came to believe that it also posed a threat to the basic biblical category of God's personal agency. How could a timeless being deliberate, remember, or anticipate? How could it

plan an action and undertake it? How could it even respond to something that had happened? What kind of a person would a timeless being be? I had known of these philosophical objections to a timeless deity for some time but had not previously given much thought to possible biblical objections. What I came to realize at this stage was how strongly the Bible itself speaks of God as operating from within time and history. He is always presented in the Bible as One who can look back to the past, relate to the present as present, and make plans for what is yet to happen. The alleged timelessness of God does not make a lot of sense to this way of portraying the deity. Of course I do not think God is threatened by time. He is the everlasting God, and his years have no end. But the Bible presents him as operating from within time. God is able to be inside time, and not only outside of it. If he were not able to be within time, he would not be able to be with us on our journey or freely relate to what goes on or make plans and carry them out or experience the joy of victory or the anguish of defeat, as Scripture says God does. Everything would be completely fixed and settled, and novelty would be mere appearance and unreal.[15]

3. Finally I had to rethink the divine omniscience and reluctantly ask whether we ought to think of it as an exhaustive foreknowledge of everything that will ever happen, as even most Arminians do. I found I could not shake off the intuition that such a total omniscience would necessarily mean that everything we will ever choose in the future will have been already spelled out in the divine knowledge register, and consequently the belief that we have truly significant choices to make would seem to be mistaken. I knew the Calvinist argument that exhaustive foreknowledge was tantamount to predestination because it implies the fixity of all things from "eternity past," and I could not shake off its logical force. I feared that, if we view God as timeless and omniscient, we will land back in the camp of theological determinism where these notions naturally belong. It makes no sense to espouse conditionality and then threaten it by other assumptions that we make.

Therefore, I had to ask myself if it was biblically possible to hold that God knows everything that can be known, but that free choices would not be something that can be known even by God because they are not yet settled in reality. Decisions not yet made do not exist anywhere to be known even by God. They are potential—yet to be realized but not yet actual. God can predict a great deal of what we will choose to do, but not all of it, because some of it remains hidden in the mystery of human freedom. Can this conjecture be scriptural?

When I went to the Scriptures with this question in mind, I found more support than I had expected. Evidently the logic of Calvinism had worked effectively to silence some of the biblical data even for me. I began to notice how the prophets in the Old Testament would present God as considering the future as something he did not already know fully. God is presented as saying, "Perhaps they will understand," or "Perhaps they will repent," making it sound as if God is not altogether sure about the future and what he may have to do when it reveals itself (Jer. 3:7; Ezek. 12:3). I also detected a strong conditional element in God's speech; for example, "If you change your ways, I will let you dwell in this place, but if not . . . " (Jer. 7:5–7). These are future possibilities that are seen to hang upon the people's amendment of their ways, and what God will do (and therefore knows) depends on these outcomes. God too faces possibilities in the future, and not only certainties. God too moves into a future not wholly known because not yet fixed. At times God even asks himself questions like "What shall I do with you?" (Hosea 6:4).

Most Bible readers simply pass over this evidence and do not take it seriously. They assume the traditional notion of exhaustive omniscience supported more by the old logic than by the biblical text. Of course the Bible praises God for his detailed knowledge of what will happen and what he himself will do. But it does not teach limitless foreknowledge, because the future will include as-yet-undecided human choices and as-yet-unselected divine responses to them. The God of the Bible displays an openness to the future that the traditional view of omniscience simply cannot accommodate.[16]

Thus it has become increasingly clear to me that we need a "free will" theism, a doctrine of God that treads the middle path between classical theism, which exaggerates God's transcendence of the world, and process theism, which presses for radical immanence.[17]

THE LARGER MOVEMENT

Relating my pilgrimage would not be of much importance if it did not represent the experience of other evangelicals also, but I think it does. It is my strong impression, confirmed to me even by those not pleased by it, that Augustinian thinking is losing its hold on present-day Christians. All the evangelists seem to herald the universal salvific will of God without hedging. The believing masses appear to take for granted a belief in human free will. It is hard to find a Calvinist theologian willing to defend Reformed theology, including the views of both Calvin and Luther, in all its rigorous particulars now that Gordon Clark is no longer with us and John Gerstner is retired. Few have the stomach to tolerate Calvinian theology in its logical purity. The laity seem to gravitate happily to Arminians like C. S. Lewis for their intellectual understanding. So I do not think I stand alone. The drift away from theological determinism is definitely on.

At the same time, however, the Calvinists continue to be major players in the evangelical coalition, even though their dominance has lessened. They pretty well control the teaching of theology in the large evangelical seminaries; they own and operate the largest book-publishing houses; and in large part they manage the inerrancy movement. This means they are strong where it counts—in the area of intellectual leadership and property. Thus one comes to expect evangelical systematic theology to be Reformed as it usually is. The key theological articles in the *Evangelical Dictionary of Theology* (1984) are Calvinian, for example. Although there are many Arminian thinkers in apologetics, missiology, and the practice of ministry, there are only a few evangelical theologians ready to go to bat for non-Augustinian opinions. The Reformed impulse continues to carry great weight in the leadership of the evangelical denominations, though less than it did in the 50s.

Therefore, it was in part a sense of frustration that prompted me initially to edit *Grace Unlimited* in 1975 and the present volume now. I wanted to do something, however modest, to give a louder voice to the silent majority of Arminian evangelicals, to help them understand the theological route they are traveling, and to encourage others to speak up theologically.

WHY IS IT HAPPENING?

Every generation reads the Bible in dialogue with its own vision and cultural presuppositions and has to come to terms with the world view of its day. Augustine did this when he sought to interpret the biblical symbols in terms of the Hellenistic culture and became the first predestinarian in Christian theology. The church fathers before him had denied fatalism, but Augustine out of his experience and intellect devised the system I have been struggling with. Today, like Augustine, we are reading the Bible afresh but in the twentieth-century context and finding new insights we had not noticed before. Just as Augustine came to terms with ancient Greek thinking, so we are making peace with the culture of modernity. Influenced by modern culture, we are experiencing reality as something dynamic and historical and are consequently seeing things in the Bible we never saw before. The time is past when we can be naïve realists in hermeneutics; who we are influences what we see. It is no different now than it was before in this respect. And the rich diversity of biblical doctrine means that changes in orientation are always going to be possible, enabling us to communicate in fresh tones to our contemporary hearers.

I do not think we should feel we have lost something of absolute value when we find ourselves at variance with some of the old so-called orthodox interpretations. There is no need to ruminate darkly about the cause of Arminian thinking being satanic malice or the natural darkness of the human mind.[18] Rather, it is a day of great opportunity for the gospel to be heard in exciting new ways and to become effective as never before. Of course there will be some nostalgia when we leave behind the logically and beautifully tight system of determinist theology. But that will be more than matched and made up for by a sense of liberation from its darker side, which (to be honest) makes hell as much the divine purpose as heaven and the fall into sin as much God's work as salvation is. It is in fact an opportunity to be faithful to the Bible in new ways and to state the truth of the Christian message creatively for the modern generation.

One thing I am asking people to give up is the myth that evangelicals often hold—that there is such a thing as an orthodox systematic theology, equated with what Calvin, for example, taught and which is said to be in full agreement with the Bible. As if theology itself were an immutable system of concepts not relative at all to the historical context in which they are conceived and framed! Granted, the idea holds great appeal for us, not because it is our experience, but because it delivers such a delicious sense of security and gives us such a great platform from which to assail those dreadful liberals who are such historicists. By this means we can try to insulate ourselves from the dizziness one feels when too many concepts are being questioned and called in for review and revision. I guess it is time for evangelicals to grow up and recognize that evangelical theology is not an uncontested body of timeless truth. There are various accounts of it. Augustine got some thing rights, but not everything. How many evangelicals follow him on the matter of the infallible church or the miraculous sacraments? Like it or not, we are embarked on a pilgrimage in theology and cannot determine exactly where will it lead and how it will end.[19]

I have no remedy for those who wish to walk by sight because they find the way of faith too unnerving, or for those who wish to freeze theological development at some arbitrary point in past history. I have no comfort for those who, afraid of missing eternal truth, choose to identify it with some previous theological work and try to impose it unchanged on the present generation or desire to speak out of the past and not to come into contact with the modern situation. I have no answer for those who are frightened to think God may have more light to break forth from his holy Word.

But there is true comfort in the gospel and in the promise of our Lord to preserve his church through time and give to her the

Spirit of truth to guide her in the midst of her struggles. Jesus assured us that the Paraclete would be with us forever and would be guiding us into all the truth. God's people will persist in the truth in spite of all our errors. If an Augustine had the courage to deal with the culture of his day and come up with some dazzling new insights, then we can do the same in our own setting. Just repeating what he said isn't good enough anymore. We have better news to tell than his rendition of the Christian message.

NOTES

[1] I found that telling the story of my pilgrimage in political theology made the issues more vivid and spoke to people in the realm of their own journey. Therefore I am resorting to this genre for a second time. For the other account, see Ron Nash, *Liberation Theology* (Milford, Mich.: Mott Media, 1984).

[2] R. C. Sproul tells his story in *Chosen by God* (Wheaton, Ill.: Tyndale, 1986). Four Evangelicals also debate these matters in David and Randall Basinger, eds. *Predestination and Free Will* (Downers Grove: InterVarsity, 1986).

[3] For an introduction, consult George Marsden, a leading scholar of the subject and the editor of *Evangelicalism and Modern America* (Grand Rapids: Eerdmans, 1984).

[4] See George Marsden again, "Reformed and American," in David F. Wells, editor, *Reformed Theology in America: A History of Its Modern Development* (Grand Rapids: Eerdmans, 1985), 1–12.

[5] I. Howard Marshall called my attention to the same conundrum in the entire New Testament in his book published about that time *Kept by the Power of God: A Study of Perseverance and Falling Away* (London: Epworth, 1969; Minneapolis: Bethany, 1975).

[6] Not the only Calvinist to revise his thinking on this point, I found Hendrikus Berkhof expressing similar convictions: *Christian Faith: An Introduction to the Study of the Faith* (Grand Rapids: Eerdmans, 1979). I have even sensed it in Berkouwer, whose Reformed standing has mattered even more to him.

[7] Paul K. Jewett sees the problem posed by the universal texts and the conditional dimension but sadly does not forsake his Calvinism. (*Election and Predestination* [Grand Rapids: Eerdmans, 1985], 28ff.)

[8] I was helped to see election as corporate particularly by Robert Shank, *Elect in the Son* (Springfield, Mo.: Westcott, 1970).

[9] Sheila G. Davaney explores this issue at length in connection with the work of Barth and Hartshorne in her book *Divine Power: A Study of Karl Barth and Charles Hartshorne* (Philadelphia: Fortress, 1986).

[10] I am of course aware of vigorous efforts to prove these dark assumptions are actually scriptural; for example, John Piper, *The Justification of God: An Exegetical and Theological Study of Romans 9:1–23* (Grand Rapids: Zondervan, 1983). I believe that if Piper had moved forward in Romans beyond Romans 9, he would have encountered Paul's earnest prayer to God that the lost be saved (10:1) and his explanation of how it happens that any are actually included or excluded— through faith or the lack of it (11:20). Romans 9 must be read in the context of the larger context of Romans 9–11.

[11] See Harald Lindstrom, *Wesley and Sanctification* (Grand Rapids: Zondervan, Francis Asbury, 1980), 44–50; Melvin Dieter et al., *Five Views on Sanctification* (Grand Rapids: Zondervan, 1987), 21–25.

[12]In an otherwise marvelous book on the atonement, John Stott evades this question completely. (John R. W. Stott, *The Cross of Christ* [Downers Grove: InterVarsity, 1987]).

[13]Donald G. Bloesch discusses Barth's view of the atonement in *Jesus Is Victor: Karl Barth's Doctrine of Salvation* (Nashville: Abingdon, 1976), chapter 4, registering a similar corrective.

[14]See, for example, Bruce Ware, "An Evangelical Reformulation of the Doctrine of the Immutability of God" *Journal of the Evangelical Theological Society* 29 (1986): 431–46.

[15]On God's eternity see Nelson Pike, *God and Timelessness* (New York: Schocken, 1970).

[16]See Terence E. Fretheim on God's knowledge in *The Suffering of God: An Old Testament Perspective* (Philadelphia: Fortress, 1984), 45–59.

[17]We see the beginnings of this in Ronald Nash, ed., *Process Theology* (Grand Rapids: Baker, 1987).

[18]Packer has written a fine critique of the way of thinking I am defending in his chapter "Arminianisms," in *Through Christ's Word: A Festschrift for P. E. Hughes*, W. Robert Godfrey and Jesse L. Boyd III, eds., (Phillipsburg, N.J.: Presbyterian and Reformed, 1985). He mentions satanic deception as one possible cause for the way Arminians think.

[19]James D. Hunter (*Evangelicalism: The Coming Generation* [Chicago: University of Chicago Press, 1987]) traces the various ways in which the theological boundaries of Evangelicals are presently changing. I am more optimistic than he seems to be in thinking that this represents a movement to maturity on our part, not the beginning of a new liberalism. See also George Marsden, *Reforming Fundamentalism: The Story of Fuller Seminary* (Grand Rapids: Eerdmans, 1988).

THE UNIVERSALITY OF GOD'S LOVE

Fritz Guy

Endeavoring to be faithful and responsive to the totality of the biblical revelation, Christian theology must affirm (among other things) some version of each of the following ideas:

1. Divine love: God wills what is best for every created entity.
2. Divine governance:[1] God is in control of all reality.
3. Divine judgment: God will not forever preserve all of humanity.

These three ideas are all so familiar, so fundamental to Christian understanding, and so thoroughly established in the biblical documents that they are often taken for granted. Consequently they are not always as carefully considered together—that is, "systematically"—as they should be.

Such a consideration, however, immediately confronts a logical difficulty; for the simultaneous and rigorous affirmation of these three ideas results in a three-cornered paradox.[2] It is not easy to see how all three of the ideas can be completely true at the same time. For example, if God truly wills what is best for every created entity (the idea of divine love) and is truly in control of all reality (the idea of divine governance), then why will some of humanity be ultimately destroyed rather than forever preserved (the idea of divine judgment)? Or if God is truly in control, and if some of humanity will truly be forever destroyed, what does it mean to say that God wills "what is best" for every entity? Or if God truly wills what is best, and if some humanity will truly be forever destroyed, what does it mean to say that God is "in control"?

It might of course be claimed that the paradox here cannot be resolved, so that we must simply live with it as a theological "mystery" because the biblical revelation requires that all three ideas be taken seriously and absolutely. Accordingly, it might be argued, if the biblical evidence produces a logical tension, so much the worse for logic; that only demonstrates once again the inability of logic to function as the final judge of religious truth. After all, there are worse things in life than logical dissonance. Physicists, for example, have learned to live with the paradoxical description of light as both wave and particle, even though waves and particles seem to be mutually exclusive as descriptive metaphors. Living with a theological paradox is not in principle illegitimate, much less impossible. In fact, Christian theology does it all the time in affirming the oneness and threeness of God, and the deity and humanity of Jesus the Messiah.

But the assertion of a necessary—that is, an irreducible—paradox must always be a last theological resort. It must come at the end, not the beginning, of the theological enterprise. For if Christianity is to make sense to thoughtful believers (to say nothing of being credible to others by whom they want their religion to be taken seriously), there must be a serious attempt to reduce (if not resolve) the paradox so that there will be as much clarity as possible. And as a matter of fact, few if any Christians have actually claimed that all three of the ideas are absolutely true.

The preferred strategy for resolving (or reducing) the paradox of the divine governance, love, and judgment is to reexamine the ideas themselves to see if they are stated as accurately as possible, and to discover if there is some other, less paradoxical way of understanding the biblical evidence. Since there are three ideas, there are three potential ways of resolving the paradox. All of these approaches have been taken many times in the history of Christian thought, and each has yielded its own ambiguous results—with some success and some remaining perplexity.

The earliest approach to resolving the paradox was to reexamine and revise idea no. 3 about the dual destiny of humanity. This approach, often known as universalism, denies an ultimate duality of human destiny in the light of God's infinite and powerful love, and affirms salvation for all of humanity.[3] The reasoning is simply that if at the end of human existence there is eternal loss for some, then either God is not truly loving (since he evidently does not will what is best—that is, eternal salvation—for all of humanity), or God is not truly sovereign (since in regard to some of humanity the divine will is forever frustrated).[4]

At the opposite end of the theological spectrum, but still comparatively early in Christian theological history, a second approach to the paradox was to revise idea no. 1, regarding a divine love that wills what is best for every created entity—that is, the ultimate good of all things.[5] This approach, predestinarianism, does not deny the reality of the divine love, but makes it relative within a context of divine sovereignty, which from eternity has decided that only some of humanity is to be forever preserved.[6] Again the reasoning is simple and straightforward: if God truly wills the eternal salvation of every human being, then either none of humanity will be lost (since God is in control of reality), or God is not in fact truly sovereign (since his will is frustrated).

It is the argument of this chapter and the premise of this whole book that the best option—best because it is most responsive to the totality of the biblical revelation and hence makes the most theological sense—is the third one, that is, to reinterpret idea no. 2, about the divine governance of all reality. This approach, which has no standard label[7] but might be called "potentialism," claims that in the character of God love is more fundamental than control. Thus the divine love is free, not only to will what is truly good for every created entity but also to create moral freedom with a potential for determining its own relationship to the love that is the character of God. Thus the divine love makes its experience of the world vulnerable to the possible misuse of the moral freedom it creates. This approach affirms the divine will to save all of humanity while acknowledging the dual destiny that humanity is able to determine for itself. The reasoning here is that if God's governance of the world is a matter of absolute control, then either none of humanity will be lost (since that would frustrate the divine will) or God is not truly and completely love (since not all of humanity is ultimately saved).[8]

The route this approach will follow in this chapter is to review some of the most important biblical evidence on the extent and significance of the divine love (idea 1) and then use the results of that review to understand the nature of both the divine governance (idea 2) and the divine judgment (idea 3).

THE PREEMINENCE OF GOD'S LOVE

One of the most serious ways in which the course of Christian theology has been misled by its classical and medieval heritage has been the assumption that the primary fact about God is omnipotent sovereignty and that the evidence of this sovereignty is the exercise of power to control events, including the actions of all of humanity. This assumption has kept a large part of the Christian tradition, both Catholic and Protestant, from hearing the gospel with clarity, because it has misunderstood the character of God.

If Christian theology *really* believes that Jesus the Messiah is the supreme revelation of God, that revelation ought to determine also its understanding of God's governance of the world. To the person who takes seriously Jesus' claim "He who has seen me has seen the Father" (John 14:9) it is obvious that divine power is expressed not by decreeing and controlling (in the fashion of an ancient despot or a feudal lord), but by self-giving and enabling. A great but seldom-recognized irony here is that some Christians who have, in principle, a "high christology" have nevertheless failed to let it guide their understanding of God.

Jesus called his disciples' attention to the radical difference between his own—that is, God's—kind of governance and the kind of governance they had seen in the world around them (Matt. 20:25–28):

> You know that the rulers of the Gentiles lord it over them, and their great men exercise authority over them. It shall not be so among you; but whoever would be great among you must be your servant, and whoever would be first among you must be your slave; even as the Son of man came not to be served but to serve, and to give his life as a ransom for many.

Jesus' recommendation of self-giving service is not merely a useful strategy for successful human relationships. It is also a revelation of the nature of the divine governance of the world. Jesus was the incarnate God who did the work of a servant and washed his disciples' feet, a kind work they refused to do for each other (John 13:1–20). Precisely *that* is the nature of the divine governance.

The same point was made by the apostle Paul as he quoted an early Christian hymn (Phil. 2:5–11):

> Have this mind among yourselves, which you have in Christ Jesus, who, though he was in the form of God, did not count equality with God a thing to be grasped, but emptied himself, taking the form of a servant, being born in the likeness of men. And being found in human form he humbled himself and became obedient unto death, even death on a cross. Therefore God has highly exalted him and bestowed on him the name which is above every name, that at the name of Jesus every knee should bow, in heaven and on earth and under the earth, and every tongue confess that Jesus Christ is Lord, to the glory of God the Father.

The glory of the Father and the honor of Jesus Christ as Lord result from the fact that God himself "took" the form of a servant,"—*this* is the highest revelation of the divine love. This self-identification of God with the need of creation is not an aberration in the existence of God; it is the supreme demonstration in human history of the eternal love of God for the world.

The heart of the Christian gospel is not the existence of God, or the eternity and omnipotence (that is, the ontological independence) of deity, or the triunity of the divine being. The heart of the gospel is the ultimate fact that "God is love" (1 John 4:16). This means that God "exists in love," that is, "constitutes his existence in the event of his love."[9] That is why "love" is the one word that

"the Christian tradition has been willing to apply unqualifiedly to
God." Indeed, "God is the model of love. We learn what love is by
looking at God."[10] Hence Christian theology has sometimes
regarded love, not as a quality or attribute of God, but as the
nature of God.[11] Accordingly, loving may be regarded not simply
as one of a number of divine activities, along with creating,
sustaining, and judging; loving is what *all* of the activities of God
accomplish. Thus there is no "doctrine" of the God's love alongside
the doctrines of creation, humanity, salvation, church, and
ultimate destiny; God's love is the inner content of all the
doctrines of Christianity. It is what they are all *about.*

In the reality of God, love is more fundamental than, and
prior to, justice or power. It is more important for God to give
himself to his creation than to rule the world or to be worshiped
by the whole creation. Divine love is the ground of divine justice,
the motivation of divine power, the character of divine sovereignty. So love does not need to be "balanced" or "kept in check" by
any other attribute or value, such as justice or holiness.[12] It is the
magnificence of the divine love that is the ground and content of
the divine majesty and holiness. It is because of love that sin must
come to an end; for sin is the contradiction and perversion of love.

Recognizing the profound implications of christology for a
proper understanding of the divine sovereignty and power in
terms of love rather than decree and control can result in a
"paradigm shift"[13] in theology. It makes possible a radically
different understanding of God and of created reality as well. In
the first place, it becomes possible to think about "the will of God
as attractive rather than coercive, as a delighting more than a
deciding" and even as "the desire of the lover for the beloved."[14]
It is widely recognized that in the biblical revelation God's "will"
does not necessarily mean "God's specific intention in a given
situation, what he decides shall actually occur," but may in fact
mean "God's general intention, the values with which he is
pleased."[15] Apart from a predestinarian presupposition, it becomes apparent that God's "will" is always to be understood in
terms of intention and desire. "The will of God now becomes, not
the orders of a superior directing what a subordinate must do, but
the longing of a lover for what the beloved is." And it is evident
that "the grandest—and the final—imagery the Bible uses for
[God's] love is precisely that of lover and beloved, bridegroom and
bride. It is the marriage of Christ and the church which is the last
act of the long love affair between God and creation."[16]

In the second place, love is also a fundamental ontological
principle, and as such it stands in radical contradiction to the
ontological principle of competition. In the remarkably candid
(and accurate) explanation provided by the demonic letter-writer
Screwtape:[17]

The whole philosophy of Hell rests on recognition of the axiom that one thing is not another thing, and, specially, that one self is not another self. My good is my good, and your good is yours. What one gains another loses. Even an inanimate object is what it is by excluding all other objects from the space it occupies; if it expands, it does so by thrusting other objects aside or by absorbing them. A self does the same. With beasts the absorption takes the form of eating; for us [devils] it means the sucking of will and freedom out of a weaker self into a stronger. "To be" *means* "to be in competition."

Now, the Enemy's philosophy is nothing more nor less than one continued attempt to evade this very obvious truth. He aims at a contradiction. Things are to be many, yet somehow also one. The good of one self is to be the good of another. This impossibility He calls Love . . . . He introduces into matter that obscene invention the organism, in which the parts are perverted from their natural destiny of competition and made to cooperate.

Thus it becomes clear (although Screwtape does not make the point explicitly) that God and created reality are not in competition for being and power, any more than parents and their children are in competition with each other. For the interests of deity and humanity are ultimately the same. To borrow Screwtape's words, the good of the one is the good of the other. God is "glorified"— that is to say, the divine experience of reality is expanded and enriched—as the humanity created in the divine image experiences more and more of its glorious potential for creativity, understanding, love, and the sheer enjoyment of reality. The best analogy from ordinary experience is the obvious one: the healthy satisfaction that parents derive from the achievements of their children; and the healthy satisfaction of the children themselves does not lessen their appreciation of their parents.[18]

So the divine governance of creation is not a sovereignty that maintains a monopoly of power, nor does God make all the decisions.[19] To the contrary, this sovereignty, unlike any known human government, is a sovereignty in the service of love.[20]

THE SCOPE OF GOD'S LOVE

If the preeminent characteristic of God is love, and if God is the source of all reality, there can be little doubt about the universal scope of God's love. It is unthinkable that the divine love is restricted to a fortunate part of creation and that another (perhaps even larger) part is excluded. In regard to human reality, the divine love includes absolutely all, intending the ultimate good—that is, the eternal salvation—of every person.

Not only is this an inescapable implication of the character of God, but also the biblical revelation emphatically attests the universality of the divine intention in redemption as well as in creation. When the covenant people were in the anguish of their Babylonian exile, there was a divine word: "I have no pleasure in the death of the wicked, but that the wicked turn from his way and live; turn back, turn back from your evil ways; for why will you die, O house of Israel?" (Ezek. 33:11; cf. 18:23). Explaining the parable of the Diligent Shepherd as an illustration of his concern for children, Jesus said, "It is not the will of my Father who is in heaven that one of these little ones should perish" (Matt. 18:14).

The scope of the divine intention for human salvation is, according to the Pauline correspondence, as great as the human need. "God has consigned all men to disobedience, that he may have mercy upon all" (Rom. 11:32). In other words, "as in Adam all die, so in Christ shall all be made alive" (1 Cor. 15:22). So "the grace of God has appeared for the salvation of all men" (Titus 2:11). This means in the first place that God "commands all men everywhere to repent." It means in the second place that God "will judge the world" by Christ, that is, in relation and response to his mission. And it means in the third place that, in regard to the genuineness of the revelation in Christ, God "has given assurance to all men by raising him from the dead" (Acts 17:30–31).

The most familiar sentence in the whole biblical revelation is also the most important, because it is the most succinct and powerful statement of the Christian gospel. The good news is the fact that the whole world of humanity is the object of God's love. "God so loved the world that he gave his only Son, that whoever believes in him should not perish but have eternal life. For God sent the Son into the world . . . that the world might be saved through him" (John 3:16–17). In short, it is the testimony of the Spirit that "the Father has sent his Son as the Savior of the world" (1 John 4:14).

The divine desire is for a unanimous response from humanity. Nothing less than this is the goal of the mission of Christ: "that at the name of Jesus every knee should bow, in heaven and on earth and under the earth, and that every tongue should confess that Jesus Christ is Lord, to the glory of God the Father" (Phil. 2:10–11). God "has made known to us in all wisdom and insight the mystery of his will [θελήματα], according to his purpose which he set forth in Christ as a plan for the fulness of time, to unite all things [τὰ πάντα] in him, things in heaven and things on earth" (Eph. 1:9–10).

The universality of God's intention to save all of humanity is the motivation for Christian concern and service. Prayers for all kinds of persons, including those in high places, are always appropriate because God "desires all men to be saved [πάνταζ ἀνθρώπους θέλει σωθῆναι] and to come to the knowledge of the truth" (1 Tim. 2:4). A diligent, disciplined ministry is inspired by the knowledge that God is "the Savior of all men [πάντων ανθρώπων], especially of those who believe" (4:10).

The fact that the parousia has not come—a fact that has been an object of concern for believers and an occasion of ridicule for unbelievers, can be understood in terms of the fact that God is patient, "not wishing that any should perish [μὴ βουλόμενός τινας ἀπολέσθαι], but that all [πάντας] should reach repentance" (2 Peter 3:9).

Corresponding to the universal scope of God's intention for humanity is the universal potential of his efforts to save. The divine act of atonement "is universal in its outreach and intention but particular in its efficacy." So "all are called to liberation and salvation."[21] The purpose of the incarnation of God in the person of Christ was "to reconcile to himself all things [τὰ πάντα], whether on earth or in heaven, making peace by the blood of his cross" (Col. 1:20). The same point is reiterated in the letter to the Hebrews, which notes that the reason why Jesus "for a little while was made lower than the angels" was "so that by the grace of God he might taste death for every one [ὑπὲρ παντὸς]" (2:9). And all of these passages recall, for any reader familiar with the Old Testament, the prophetic Song of the Suffering Servant: "All we like sheep have gone astray; we have turned everyone to his own way; and the LORD has laid on him the iniquity of us all" (Isa. 53:6).

In the Johannine literature, Jesus is introduced first of all as "the Lamb of God, who takes away the sin of the world [τοῦ κόσμου]!" (John 1:29). In the symbolism of the ancient Hebrew sacrifices, he is "the expiation for our sins, and not for ours only but also for the sins of the whole world [περὶ ὅλου τοῦ κόσμου]" (1 John 2:2). Here the universal significance of the sacrifice is explicitly emphasized. In the Pauline literature, the same point is made in the language of jurisprudence: "As one man's trespass led to condemnation for all men, so one man's act of righteousness leads to acquittal and life for all men [εἰς πάντας ἀνθρώπους]" (Rom. 5:18). For "we are convinced that one has died for all [ὑπὲρ πάντων]. . . . He died for all [ὑπὲρ πάντων], that those who live might live no longer for themselves but for him who for their sake died and was raised" (2 Cor. 5:14–15). In the language of political and economic liberation, Christ Jesus "gave himself as a ransom for all [ὑπὲρ πάντων]" (1 Tim. 2:6). This seems to be a deliberate paraphrase and intensification of Matthew 20:28, in which Jesus explains that the Son of Man came "to give his life as a ransom for many [ἀντὶ πολλῶν]."[22]

As universal as the scope of the divine intention and the divine atonement is, so is the scope of the divine invitation. This is evident in the invitation of the Old Testament: "Ho, every one who thirsts, come to the waters; and he who has no money, come, buy and eat! . . . Let the wicked forsake his way, and the unrighteous man his thoughts; let him return to the Lord, that he may have mercy on him, and to our God, for he will abundantly pardon. . . . " (Isa. 55:1, 7). And it is even more evident in the invitation of Jesus, "Come to me, all [πάντες] who labor and are heavy laden, and I will give you rest" (Matt. 11:28).

The good news of Jesus Christ is good news *for all* of humanity. There is no limit to the scope of the divine love.

THE ACTIVITY OF GOD'S LOVE

The divine love is not just an attitude of good will toward created reality; it is an effective interaction. It is initiatory, vulnerable, responsive, and resourceful.

The initiatory quality of the divine love is the principal meaning of the much misunderstood New Testament language about "foreknowledge" and "predestination."[23] The *locus classicus* is the well-known Pauline statement of assurance (Rom. 8:28–30):

> We know that in everything God works[24] for good with those who love him, who are called according to his purpose. For those whom he foreknew he also predestined to be conformed to the image of his Son, in order that he might be the first-born among many brethren. And those whom he predestined he also called, and those whom he called he also justified; and those whom he justified he also glorified.

So far from describing "God's eternal decree, by which he determined with himself what he willed to become of each man," so that "eternal life is foreordained for some, eternal damnation for others,"[25] the apostle is here declaring that God is effectively present in every situation—not imposing the divine will but *working with* those who have made God's love the functional center of their lives. In fact, the apostle explains, this divine involvement is no afterthought; it is part of the original intention for humanity in general and for every individual in particular.[26]

So in the Pauline language here, "foreknow" (προγινώσκω] means that in every instance "God loves man before man loves God."[27] "Predestine" [προορίζω] means that God takes the initiative to remedy the human predicament. "Call" [καλέω] means that God, through the proclamation of the gospel, invites human beings collectively and individually to participate in the actualization of the divine intention for them. "Justify" [δικαιόω] means that God acts to restore the proper relationship between humanity and deity. "Glorify" [δοξάζω] means that in the process of salvation God transforms human existence in a way that becomes increasingly evident and is ultimately completed.

All of this describes the overall process of salvation, but it is not a precise account of the experience of every human being. Because the love of God is universal and because the divine intention for salvation is likewise universal, all of humanity is "under the sign of predestination, . . . but this predestination takes effect in different ways depending on whether there is a response in faith."[28] At every point the continuation of the process involves a continuing openness to divine grace, which does not force itself on anyone.

Foreknowledge and predestination are valuable ideas in Christian theology; they are significant dimensions of the Christian gospel. They mean that God is aware of all the possibilities (so cannot be caught off guard). They mean that God has a plan that includes all of humanity, and that God has already acted and continues to act. But the biblical revelation clearly indicates that neither the divine will nor the divine activity is coercive. God "may, in the end, overrule men's deeds, but he does so by forgiveness, redemption and grace."[29]

In a particular human representation of the divine love, the prophet Hosea was told, "Go, show your love to your wife again, though she is loved by another and is an adulteress. Love her as the LORD loves the Israelites" (3:1 NIV). And the divine love for the rebellious Israelites is described in a vivid metaphor: "[She] decked herself with rings and jewelry, and went off after her lovers, but me she forgot, declares the LORD. Therefore I am now going to allure her . . . [and] speak tenderly to her. . . . [I] will make the Valley of Trouble a door of hope" (2:13–15 NIVmg.).

The biblical revelation also clearly indicates that the divine love for creation is vulnerable. God does not have to—and does not in fact—get whatever the divine will includes. The vulnerability of divine love means that actualization of the divine will and the effectiveness of the atonement can be limited by humanity.

For grace is never, strictly speaking, "irresistible." Indeed, the term "irresistible grace" looks suspiciously like an oxymoron, like "married bachelor" or "square circle" or "causally determined free action."[30] For grace is the offer of a gift, not the imposition of another's will; and it is in the nature of a gift that it can be rejected. It is the nature of love that it can be ignored or spurned. That is why it made logical (although perhaps not diplomatic) sense for Stephen to say to the leaders of the religious establishment in Jerusalem, "You always resist the Holy Spirit" (Acts 7:51). The New Testament refers specifically to the kind of person who "has spurned the Son of God, and profaned the blood of the covenant by which he was sanctified, and outraged the Spirit of grace" (Heb. 10:29), and to "false teachers among you, who will secretly bring in destructive heresies, even denying the Master

who bought them, bringing upon themselves swift destruction"
(2 Peter 2:1).[31]

The fact is that God is disappointed by the moral failure of
human beings—not only in the first sin, but in every subsequent
sin as well. In the story of Noah, "the Lord saw that the
wickedness of man was great in the earth, and that every
imagination of the thoughts of his heart was only evil continually.
And the Lord was sorry that he had made man on the earth, and it
grieved him to his heart" (Gen. 6:5–6). As the failure of the
covenant people to recognize their Messiah became increasingly
evident to Jesus, he agonized aloud: "O Jerusalem, Jerusalem,
killing the prophets and stoning those who are sent to you! How
often would I have gathered your children together as a hen
gathers her brood under her wings, and you would not!" (Matt.
23:37).

The divine love, though vulnerable to disappointment, is
dynamically responsive. It can weep, but it can do more than
weep. Jeremiah noted that the divine involvement in history
depends not only on the divine intention revealed in prophetic
forecasts, but also on the response of the covenant people to the
possibilities identified in the prophecies. He illustrated both the
conditional nature of prophetic messages and the flexibility of the
divine involvement in human affairs by taking as an analogy the
work of the potter in reworking an object that turned out to be
defective (Jer. 18:7–10):

> If at any time I declare concerning a nation or a kingdom, that
> I will pluck up and break down and destroy it, and if that
> nation, concerning which I have spoken, turns from its evil, I
> will repent of the evil that I intended to do to it. And if at any
> time I declare concerning a nation or a kingdom that I will build
> and plant it, and if it does evil in my sight, not listening to my
> voice, then I will repent of the good which I had intended to do
> to it.

A dramatic example of this interaction of divine and human
activity is the story of Jonah. The message to the citizens of
Nineveh was that the city was destined for devastation, but in the
light of their response the anticipated disaster was averted.

And the divine love is infinitely resourceful. It is not limited
to positive or negative reaction. There are more possibilities of
grace than are immediately apparent either in the analogy of the
potter or in the experience of Jonah. A classic example is the story
of Joseph, whose brothers' treachery became the opportunity for
such an extraordinary career that he could say to them later, "You
meant evil against me; but God meant it for good, to bring it about
that many people should be kept alive" (Gen. 50:20). The divine
love was so resourceful in "working for good" that the whole

scenario seemed programed in advance. Ironically (but under-standably) it was a similar instance of providential resourcefulness in response to human sin that led Augustine to his doctrine of predestination: his selfishness and dishonesty in leaving Carthage began a pilgrimage that brought him eventually to Milan, to Ambrose, and to Christ.[32]

Never coercive, the divine love is always active, always working for the good of the beloved creation.

THE POSSIBILITY OF UNIVERSAL SALVATION

In view of the preeminence, scope, and activity of God's love, it is hardly surprising that the Christian hope is sometimes understood to include a vision of universal salvation. This vision has been eloquently expressed:[33]

> There can be no dual destiny in this hope, if there is to be hope at all. No ultimate division between persons who are sheep and persons who are goats, those who participate in God and those who are condemned to hell, is admissible if the divine power is to be ultimately sovereign and the divine love the ultimate quality of that power.

There are two principal theological grounds for this conviction that rejects the traditional idea of an ultimate division in human destiny. The first is the sense of the moral ambiguity of all humanity, which means the essential moral similarity (if not essential identity) of all humanity, eliminating the possibility of any sort of spiritual elitism:

> Our experience tells that God is related as creative ultimacy to all humans—and to all creatures alike—and that the differ-ences between our responses to this relation—in our being, our loving and our creativity—are at best relative differences. Whether we speak of faith or of works, commitment or love, we can never discover an ultimate division between ourselves and others. Even more, experientially, we be honest, we know unequivocally that together we share tragically in the non-achievements and the waywardness that is characteristic of even the worst of us.

In short: if *I* can be saved, in spite of the moral ambiguity that I know pervades my whole existence, how can I suppose that *anyone* is to be excluded from salvation?

The second reason for denying a dual destiny for humanity is the idea of salvation by God's grace as expressed in the Christian gospel:

> Moreover, the gospel assures us from its side that all alike need mercy at the end if they are to be saved at all, that God's love reaches to the unworthy as well as to the worthy, and so in

principle to all. It would be ironic indeed if the gospel preached a love that transcends all differences, divisions and faults, a mercy that was greater than all sin—and then established a new and more ultimate division between faith and unfaith (unfaith being sin) which the divine love could not overcome.

If salvation is indeed a gift of grace (as all Christians claim), how can it be limited to those who jump high enough behaviorally and through the correct hoops ritually and theologically? Is not God's love in fact so persuasive that its rejection is unthinkable? Cannot the gospel triumph over human perversity? Is it wrong to see additional possibilities of grace in one of Jesus' metaphors?[34]

> To man there remain eternally two ways. And the one that is crowded is still the one that leads to destruction; and many there be that find it. But at some point on that road, be it far or near, each one finds also something, or rather Someone, else. It is a figure, stooping beneath the weight of a cross. 'Lord, where are you going' asks Everyman. And the answer comes: 'I am going to Rome, to Moscow, to New York, to be crucified afresh in your place.' And no man in the end can bear that encounter forever. For it is an encounter with a power than which there can be nothing greater, a meeting with omnipotent Love itself. This love will take no man's choice from him; for it is precisely his choice that it wants. But its will to lordship is inexhaustible and ultimately unendurable; the sinner *must* yield.

A thoughtful Christian must surely be impressed not only by the moral sensitivity and theological force of these arguments, but also by the fact that they can be supported by specific biblical assertions. In any serious consideration of God's extravagant love for his human sons and daughters—the love that, after all, is the essence of the Christian gospel—these assertions cannot be ignored. Elaborating the significance of the resurrection of Jesus, the apostle insisted, "For as in Adam all die, so also in Christ shall all be made alive" (1 Cor. 15:22). That is to say, regarding the crucial act of justification, "as one man's trespass led to condemnation for all men, so one man's act of righteousness leads to acquittal and life for all men' (Rom. 5:18). So ultimately, as a result of Christ's identification with humanity and experiencing the consequences of sin, "at the name of Jesus every knee [shall] bow, in heaven and on earth and under the earth, and every tongue shall confess that Jesus Christ is Lord, to the glory of God the Father" (Phil. 2:10–11).

So even if the idea of universal salvation has had some dubious theological company during the centuries, it must not be dismissed glibly, much less disdainfully. For anyone "who has not felt deeply the attraction of universalism can scarcely have been moved by the greatness of God's love."[35] Its attractiveness is not merely its eschatological optimism, much less its possible seductiveness as a moral opiate, but the seriousness with which it regards both the depth of one's own sinfulness and the power of divine grace. Christianity does not have a vested interest in hell.

Yet the thoughtful Christian must also take account of another, equally strong moral reality and biblical emphasis—namely, the sense of eschatological judgment, a divine activity of judgment that does not in fact *decide* eternal destiny but *discloses* it. In the Torah and the prophets of the Old Testament, and especially in the parables and the letters of the New Testament, the dominant vision is not the one human destiny of universal salvation but the dual destiny of being and nonbeing, eternal life and eternal oblivion. "The hour is coming," Jesus said, "when all who are in the tombs will hear his voice and come forth, those who have done good, to the resurrection of life, and those who have done evil, to the resurrection of judgment" (John 5:28–29). More specifically, in Jesus' scenario of the last judgment, those who refuse to respond to human needs "will go away into eternal punishment, but the righteous into eternal life" (Matt. 25:46).

For the fact is, as Paul wrote, that God "will render to every man according to his works: to those who by patience in well-doing seek for glory and honor and immortality, he will give eternal life; but for those who are factious and do not obey the truth, but obey wickedness, there will be wrath and fury" (Rom. 2:6–8). It is an unfortunate fact of human existence that "the gate is wide and the way is easy, that leads to destruction, and those who enter by it are many," while "the gate is narrow and the way is hard, that leads to life, and those who find it are few" (Matt. 7:13–14). According to the Apocalyptic vision, there will be some who experience the presence of God and some who experience the "second death," some who are finally holy and some who are finally unholy, some who are inside the heavenly city and some who are outside (Rev. 21:7–8; 22:11, 14–15).

Is it possible to regard the judgment language of the biblical revelation as a dramatic and powerful symbolic exhortation rather than a scenario of future events? Might it be intended to point to the twofold fact that on the one hand humanity is held morally responsible and called to account for its behavior,[36] and that on the other hand "God will ultimately succeed in realizing his purposes for history and for all mankind"?[37] If so, the meaning of judgment is not a dual destiny of humanity but the eternal consequences and significance of human decisions and actions.

Yet it remains difficult to escape the conclusion that "as long as we think in the context of love and freedom there are always two possibilities,"[38] and that these possibilities are ultimately ontological as well as existential. Thus every person "in the course of his still ongoing history has to reckon absolutely and up to the very end with the possibility of reaching his end in an absolute rejection of God, and hence in the opposite of salvation."[39] This is the terrible, unthinkable possibility of "definitive destruction."[40] Christian theology cannot ignore "the New Testament insistence that our response to the gospel determines for us the outcome of the final judgment."[41]

Any consideration of these realities, however, must always occur within the context of the ultimate reality of divine love. Just as it is the divine love that intends and wills and works for the salvation of as much of humanity as possible—ideally, all of it— so it is the divine love that respects human freedom, even to the extent of allowing humanity to be utterly irrational and perverse— that is, to reject the love that has created, sustained, and redeemed it. But if it happens, that rejection is recognized and respected by the very love that is rejected.[42]

It is therefore unnecessary to think in terms of a "paradox between God's love and justice" that results from the seemingly conflicting insights that God's love wants all to be saved," while at the same time "God's justice requires all the disobedient to be punished."[43] To reject the grace that sustains one's existence is a monumental ontological blunder; it doesn't have to be "punished" by a new divine act, for its own consequences are intrinsic, inevitable, and decisive. "Hell [however it is conceived] is not a punishment for turning one's back on Christ and choosing the road that leads to destruction. It is where the road goes."[44]

God's passionate love for his creation and his intention to save all of humanity provide a real potential of eternal life for every human being—a *universal possibility of salvation*, which must be logically, at least in some sense, also a *possibility of universal salvation*. This possibility is not, however, the script for an infinitely intricate and complicated puppet show whose every movement is programed in advance by the Ultimate and Omnipotent Puppeteer; and so it can never be proclaimed a reality, but only (at most) a hope. The gracious love that intends salvation for all of humanity also at the same time confronts every person with a genuine choice regarding the meaning of one's present existence and the nature of the ultimate future. For this love loves so extravagantly that it is willing to risk eternal anguish rather than turn its beloved humanity into an object to be controlled by the will of another, even a divine Other.

The rejection and contradiction of God's universal love is the strangest, most inexplicable of all human actions; but it remains a possibility. To the extent that it is actualized, the idea of divine judgment means that some of humanity will not be preserved in eternal life, and the idea of divine governance must be understood to mean that God is not in absolute control of all reality. But the idea of divine love still means what it has always meant: that God wills what is best for every created entity, and salvation for all of humanity.

NOTES

[1] The term *governance* is usually used in this chapter in place of the more familiar *sovereignty* in order to avoid the connotation of theistic determinism that *sovereignty* often carries with it even when it is not intended to do so. That the divine governance involves the dynamic interaction of God and the world will become clear in the course of the chapter.

[2] The paradox is directly analogous to the better-known one involved in the so-called problem of evil (which results from simultaneously affirming the goodness of God, the omnipotence of God, and the reality of evil in the world). Cf. Jack B. Rogers and Forrest Baird, *Introduction to Philosophy: A Case Study Approach* (San Francisco: Harper & Row, 1981), 38–40.

[3] Sometimes identified by a phrase from Acts 3:21, ἀποκαταστάσεως πάντων, and hence known as "the doctrine of apokatastasis," this vision of the ultimate future goes back as far as the brilliant but unorthodox third-century theologian Origen. *On First Principles*, 1.6.2. in *The Ante-Nicene Fathers*, reprint, 10 vols. (Grand Rapids: Eerdmans, 1951), 4:260–61. The doctrine of the ultimate salvation of all humanity was also taught by Gregory of Nyssa and Theodore of Mopsuestia, among others. Later advocates included a few Anabaptists, Cambridge Platonists, and Pietists and the English devotional writer William Law. A brief but comprehensive account of the development of universalism is provided by Richard J. Bauckham, "Universalism: A Historical Survey," *Themelios* 4/2 (1978–79): 48–54.

In modern theology, universalism has been advocated by Friedrich Schleiermacher, *The Christian Faith*, reprint, 2 vols. (New York: Harper & Row, 1960), 2:711–22; Albrecht Ritschl, *The Christian Doctrine of Justification and Reconciliation*, reprint (Clinton, N.J.: Reference Book, 1966), 125–39; and John Baillie, *And the Life Everlasting* (London: Oxford, 1934), 237–45.

Among its proponents in the second half of the twentieth century are John A. T. Robinson, *In the End, God*, 2nd ed. (London: Collier/Fontana, 1968), 108–23; Nels F. S. Ferré, *The Christian Understanding of God* (New York: Harper and Brothers, 1951), 242–49; Paul Tillich, *Systematic Theology*, 3 vols. (Chicago: University of Chicago Press, 1951–63), 3: 406–9, 415–19; John Macquarrie, *Principles of Christian Theology* (New York: Scribner, 1966), 322–23, 325–26; Wolfhart Pannenberg, *Jesus—God and Man* (Philadelphia: Westminster, 1968), 272–73; Gordon D. Kaufman, *Systematic Theology* (New York: Scribner, 1968), 305–6, 459 n., 471–72; John Hick, *Death and Eternal Life* (New York: Harper & Row, 1976), 242–61; *Evil and the God of Love*, rev. ed. (New York: Harper & Row, 1978), 341–45; and Langdon Gilkey, *Reaping the Whirlwind* (New York: Seabury/Crossroad, 1976), 297–99.

The idea that universal salvation remains a hope but cannot be affirmed as a theological conviction has been maintained not only by Karl Barth, *Church Dogmatics*, 4 vols. in 13 (Edinburgh: T. & T. Clarke, 1936–69), 2/2 and 4/1, passim; 4/3: 461–78; *The Humanity of God* (Richmond: John Knox, 1960), 60–62, but also by such diverse post-Barthian figures as Emil Brunner, *Dogmatics*, 3 vols. (Philadelphia: Westminster, 1949–62), 1:334–39, 352–53; 3:415–24; *Eternal Hope* (Philadelphia: Westminster, 1954), 170–84; G. C. Berkouwer, *The Return of Christ* (Grand Rapids: Eerdmans, 1972), 387–423; Karl Rahner, *Foundations of Christian Faith* (New York: Seabury/Crossroad, 1978), 443–44; Helmut Thielicke, *The Evangelical Faith*, 3 vols. (Grand Rapids: Eerdmans, 1974–82), 3:453–56; and Brian Hebblethwaite, *The Christian Hope* (Grand Rapids: Eerdmans, 1984), 192–94, 215–18.

[4] Bauckham, "Universalism," 54.

[5]It might be quibbled that the notion of "the ultimate good of all things" is logically problematic, because some things are *not* good but radically evil (e.g., the devil), so that it is not at all clear what "the ultimate good of something evil" might be. But this objection, while superficially plausible, is not valid. All created reality is essentially good in the sense that it is a result of God's creative activity, however distorted it may actually be. The "ultimate good" of any distorted reality is not nonbeing but a return to its undistorted goodness.

[6]The doctrine of predestination was first formulated by Augustine, certainly the most influential Christian theologian since the apostles; cf. *On the Predestination of the Saints* and *On Grace and Free Will* in *Basic Writings of Saint Augustine*, 2 vols. (New York: Random, 1948), 1:733–74, 777–817; as well as other works.

In the Reformation, predestination was vigorously advocated by Luther, *The Bondage of the Will*, in *Luther and Erasmus: Free Will and Salvation*, ed. E. Gordon Rupp and Philip S. Watson (Philadelphia: Westminster, 1969), 101–334; as well as by Calvin, *Institutes of the Christian Religion*, 3.21–24, 2 vols. (Philadelphia: Westminster, 1960), 920–87, and elsewhere. In the seventeenth century, the doctrine of predestination was enshrined in the Westminster Confession of Faith (1646), ch. 3, in *Creeds of the Churches*, ed. John H. Leith (Garden City, N.Y.: Doubleday/Anchor, 1963), 198–99.

Notable among more recent proponents have been Charles Hodge, *Systematic Theology*, 3 vols. (Grand Rapids: Eerdmans, n.d.), 1:535–49; 2:331–53; Benjamin B. Warfield, "Predestination," in *A Dictionary of the Bible*, ed. James Hastings, 5 vols. (New York: Scribner, 1898–1904), 4:47–63; reprinted in *Biblical and Theological Studies*, ed. Samuel G. Craig (Philadelphia: Presbyterian and Reformed, 1952) 270–333; and Loraine Boettner, *The Reformed Doctrine of Predestination* (Philadelphia: Presbyterian and Reformed, 1932).

Karl Barth has provided a typically creative (and not quite persuasive) revision of the idea of predestination in his notion that Jesus Christ is both the elected and the rejected one, and that in him the whole human race is elected for salvation, though some do not live accordingly. This is elaborated at great length under the title "The Election of God" in *Church Dogmatics*, 2/2:3–506.

In contemporary Reformed theology there is a wide range of views regarding predestination. The idea is presented with philosophical rigor by John Feinberg, "God Ordains All Things," in *Predestination and Free Will*, ed. David Basinger and Randall Basinger (Downers Grove: InterVarsity, 1986), 19–43. A similar view is argued by Millard J. Erickson, *Christian Theology* (Grand Rapids, Baker, 1976), 343–62, 825–41, 907–28, who nevertheless regards the doctrine as "difficult and obscure" (907). Others, like James Montgomery Boice, *Foundations of the Christian Faith* (Downers Grove: InterVarsity, 1986), 511–26, affirm the idea but prefer the rubric of "election."

Still others of the Reformed tradition are critical of the traditional idea of predestination; cf. G. C. Berkouwer, *Divine Election* (Grand Rapids: Eerdmans, 1960); Donald J. Bloesch, *Essentials of Evangelical Theology* (San Francisco: Harper & Row, 1978–79), 1:27–29, 164–69; and Hendrikus Berkhof, *Christian Faith: An Introduction to the Study of the Faith* (Grand Rapids: Eerdmans, 1979, 479–82. Otto Weber, *Foundations of Dogmatics* (Grand Rapids: Eerdmans, 1981–83), gives sustained attention neither to predestination nor to election, much less to "decrees"; the occasional references are almost always descriptive rather than constructive.

A contemporary Baptist, Dale Moody, *The Word of Truth* (Grand Rapids: Eerdmans, 1981), 337–48, decries what he regards as the baneful influence of Augustine and the tendencies of predestinarians to misinterpret Scripture because they are tyrannized by their own tradition.

[7]This view is sometimes called conditionalism because of its association with the idea of conditional immortality as opposed to eternal punishment on the one hand and universal salvation on the other. But while this chapter is entirely

compatible with the idea of conditional immortality, the argument here neither presupposes nor establishes it.

[8]The heritage of this view goes back to Jacob Arminius, "Declaration of Sentiments," in *The Writings of James Arminius* (Grand Rapids: Baker, 1977), 1:247–48; cf. Carl Bangs, *Arminius*, 2nd ed. (Grand Rapids: Zondervan/Asbury, 1985), 340–44, 350–55. Equally important in this tradition is the contribution of John Wesley, "Predestination Calmly Considered," in *John Wesley*, ed. Albert C. Outler (New York: Oxford, 1964), 427–72; cf. "On Working Out Our Own Salvation," in *The Works of John Wesley*, 14 vols. (Grand Rapids: Zondervan, n.d.), 6:506–13. A mid-twentieth-century Nazarene formulation of the Arminian view has been given by H. Orton Wiley, *Christian Theology* (Kansas City, Mo.: Beacon Hill, 1958), 2:295–300.

More recent statements include *Grace Unlimited*, ed. Clark Pinnock (Minneapolis: Bethany, 1975); Stephen H. Travis, *Christian Hope and the Future* (Downers Grove: InterVarsity, 1980), 118–36, and *I Believe in the Second Coming of Jesus* (Grand Rapids: Eerdmans, 1982), 184–208; Hans Schwarz, *On The Way to the Future* (Minneapolis: Augsburg, 1972) 143–50, 214–20; "Eschatology," in *Christian Dogmatics*, ed. Carl E. Braaten and Robert W. Jensen, 2 vols. (Philadelphia: Fortress, 1984), 2:571–79; R. Larry Shelton, "The Redemptive Grace of God in Christ, in *A Contemporary Wesleyan Theology*, 2 vols. (Grand Rapids: Zondervan/Asbury, 1983), 1:473–513; and Bruce Reichenbach, "God Limits His Power," and Clark Pinnock, "God Limits His Knowledge," in *Predestination and Free Will*, 101–24, 143–62.

The argument in this chapter differs somewhat from its tradition by beginning with the preeminence of love in the character of God.

[9]Jürgen Moltmann, *The Crucified God* (New York: Harper & Row, 1974), 244.

[10]Sallie McFague, *Models of God* (Philadelphia: Fortress, 1987), 125.

[11]E.g., Brunner, *Dogmatics*, 1:183–99.

[12]Adrio König, *Here Am I* (Grand Rapids: Eerdmans, 1982), 44.

[13]The phrase was given currency by Thomas S. Kuhn, *The Structure of Scientific Revolutions*, 2nd ed. (Chicago: University of Chicago Press, 1970).

[14]Robert Farrar Capon, *Hunting the Divine Fox* (Minneapolis: Winston/Seabury, 1985), 38. The metaphor of God as love is constructively explored by McFague, *Models of God*, 125–55.

[15]Erickson, *Christian Theology*, 361.

[16]Capon, *Divine Fox*, 39.

[17]C. S. Lewis, Letter 18 in *The Screwtape Letters* (New York: Macmillan, 1962), 81–82.

[18]It is surely a failure to recognize the noncompetitive relationship between God and creation that has enabled predestinarians beginning with Augustine to argue for unconditional election on the ground that to suppose that salvation requires some sort of human acceptance would be to detract from the divine honor. A contemporary example is Boice, *Foundations*, 517: "If we have a part in salvation, then our love for God is diminished by just that amount."

[19]Cf. Capon, *Hunting the Divine Fox*, 38–39, "The will of God may well be, not *his* recipe for my life, but rather his delight in *my* recipe. It may well mean that he loves me in my independence, as any good lover would."

[20]Cf. Bloesch, *Essentials*, 1:27.

[21]Bloesch, *Essentials*, 1:165, 168. Although Erickson's more traditional predestinarianism doesn't allow him to believe that God actually wills the salvation of all humanity, he agrees (385) that "the hypothesis of universal atonement is able to account for a larger segment of the biblical witness with less distortion than is the hypothesis of limited atonement."

[22]Cf. Erickson, *Christian Theology*, 830–31.

[23]Augustine defined predestination as God's will that some of the "condemned mass" (*massa damnata*) of humanity should be saved, and this is entirely a gift of divine grace. Thus there are two categories of humanity: the saved, who

exemplify divine mercy; and the condemned, who exemplify divine justice. There is no injustice, however, in not offering grace to all, for all humanity has sinned (at least seminally in Adam, if not also in every individual's own choice). The New Testament assertion that God "wills all men to be saved" is reinterpreted to mean, not that all are intended to be saved, but that all who are saved are saved by God's will. The divine grace is irresistible, since its effectiveness is not subject to the power of any human being. Grace makes a person a slave to love (caritas) instead of selfish desire (cupiditas). Thus God's will offers more security than the uncertainty of human choice.

24 Or "co-operates," as in the New English Bible; the Greek word is συνεργεῖ.

25 Calvin, Institutes, 3.21.5 (p. 925); cf. Westminster Confession, 3.3. A moderate contemporary statement of Calvinistic predestinarianism is provided by Erickson, 359–60.

26 The assurance of an eternal intention and plan is the point also of another common prooftext for predestinarianism, Ephesians 1:11–12. Also frequently cited is Romans 9:14–26, which, however, is an explanation of God's love for both Gentiles and Jews, not an announcement of a divine determination of the ultimate destiny of individuals; cf. 2 Timothy 2:21.

27 Moody, Word of Truth, 343.

28 Bloesch, Essentials, 168.

29 Brian Hebblethwaite, "Some Reflections on Predestination, Providence and Divine Foreknowledge," Religious Studies 15/4 (December 1979): 437.

30 Cf. John Feinberg, "God Ordains All Things," 24–25: "There is room for a genuine sense of free human action, even though such action is causally determined. . . . This notion of freedom seems reasonable if the agent is causally determined to act as she or he wants to anyway." This view, for which a common philosophical label is "soft determinism" or "compatibilism," is objectionable on a variety of biblical, theological, and experiential as well as logical grounds; but the discussion cannot be pursued here.

31 An interesting pair of Pauline statements even suggests that in some sense it is possible for a person to limit the effectiveness of the atonement for others by failing to respect their religious convictions. "By your knowledge [that eating food offered to idols is not sinful] this weak man is destroyed, the brother for whom Christ died" (1 Cor. 8:11). "Do not let what you eat [of "unclean" food] cause the ruin of one for whom Christ died" (Rom. 14:15). In both cases the results of such religious insensitivity are described in apparent hyperbole.

32 Augustine, The Confessions of St. Augustine, 5:8–15 (Garden City, N.Y.: Doubleday/Image, 1960), 122–32.

33 Gilkey, Reaping the Whirlwind, 298; cf. Tillich, Systematic Theology, 3:408.

34 Robinson, In the End, God, 133.

35 Travis, Christian Hope and the Future, 129–30.

36 Brunner, Dogmatics, 3:418–20.

37 Kaufman, Systematic Theology, 471–72.

38 Moody, Word of Truth, 514.

39 Rahner, Foundations of Christian Faith, 443.

40 Berkouwer, The Return of Christ, 413; citing Albrecht Oepke, "ἀπόλλυμι," in Theological Dictionary of the New Testament, ed. Gerhard Kittel and Gerhard Friedrich, 10 vols. (Grand Rapids: Eerdmans, 1964–76), 1:396.

41 Schwarz, On the Way to the Future, 2:578.

42 Cf. Travis, Christian Hope and the Future, 132.

43 Schwarz, On the Way to the Future.

44 Travis, Christian Hope and the Future, 121.

UNIVERSAL GRACE AND ATONEMENT IN THE PASTORAL EPISTLES

I. Howard Marshall

"God our Savior. . .wants all men to be saved" (1 Tim. 2:3). In the light of this statement it is more than surprising that the earlier volume of essays on *Grace Unlimited* edited by Clark H. Pinnock contains no references to the Pastoral Epistles and to their understanding of grace and salvation. The statements in them about the universal salvific will of God are such that they demand consideration in any discussion of the question of universal or limited atonement.

INTRODUCTION

The problem was highlighted for me shortly before I commenced to write this paper at a conference on "Modern Universalism and the Universality of the Gospel." One of my friends, for whose theological integrity and acumen I have the highest regard, said that, while he could honestly say to any sinner or group of sinners, "God loves you" (John 3:16), he could not say to them, "Christ died for you," since on his view Christ died only for the elect and he could not be sure that his audience belonged to the group of the elect. I think that my friend may have felt that there was something of a tension in his position, since it is precisely because God gave his Son to die that we know the nature of divine love (1 John 4:9). Was he justified in his reservation?

At the same conference it also emerged that one of the reasons why many theologians of a Calvinist persuasion adopt the doctrine of limited atonement[1] is that they are convinced that it is the only real alternative to the "modern universalism" that teaches that all people without exception will ultimately be saved. The theoretical possibility that Christ died for all but that not all will respond to the gospel is thought to be excluded, principally because the efficaciousness of the death of Christ is thought to include the actual redemption of those for whom he died, and also because any other view would suggest that God exacts judgment twice for the same sin, once from Christ and once from those who refuse to accept him as their Savior. Neither of these points is in my view compelling.

At the outset it should be emphasized that in raising the issue I am not concerned to take sides in the Calvinist-Arminian controversy but rather to interpret Scripture correctly. It is sometimes thought that the only alternative to Calvinism is Arminianism, and Calvinists do not find it too difficult to point to problems in Arminianism that make it a less attractive system of thought. But one does not need to be an Arminian to recognize the exegetical difficulties raised by Calvinism and to offer an alternative approach. There are more alternatives to Calvinism than one. Perhaps one should speak of alternatives to "strict Calvinism," since by universal consent Calvin was surely the greatest Protestant theologian, and those of us who question the Calvinist theory of limited atonement would go along with him in much else. The situation is rather that, where strict Calvinism attempts to provide a complete system of theology, in which each element has its ordered place, others of us would want to insist that the Scriptures do not permit us to be so systematic and compel us to recognize the elements of mystery and our sheer lack of knowledge at various points.

The danger in fact is that we proceed to interpret Scripture in the light of a system of doctrine. Calvin himself, of course, was too wise not to recognize that his system must be continually amended in the light of Scripture; the question is whether he and some of his followers let this insight have sufficient influence on their theology.

Reformed theologians have no difficulty in seeing the problems that arise when, for example, the sevenfold dispensational scheme is applied to the interpretation of Scripture and passages are given a meaning other than their obvious one because they must be made to fit in with a given scheme of thought. They can also see that the dispensational type of exegesis often depends on an overly literal interpretation of Scripture—an interpretation they would reject.

The problem is that the Calvinist type of theology and exegesis may suffer from the same kind of approach. There are a number of biblical texts that suggest that Christ died for all mankind, and an unprejudiced exegesis would take these texts at their face value. But there is also teaching in Scripture that could suggest that God's purpose was to choose a limited number of people to be saved and then to carry out an efficacious plan, including the death of his Son, that would lead inevitably to the fulfillment of this purpose. This theory of election then becomes a sort of key for understanding the Scriptures, and the exegete who is persuaded of the harmony and consistency of Scripture must show that texts that apparently run counter to the theory, such as the statements of universal atonement, can in fact be interpreted in harmony with it. This can be done by claiming, for example, that "all" is not to be taken literally but means "all kinds of people," or that the word "save" does not mean "grant spiritual, eternal salvation."

It seems to me, therefore, that we need to ask such questions as these: Are there grounds for believing that, were it not for the prior acceptance of the theory of election (in the form given above), we should interpret the statements of universal atonement literally? Are there reasons for believing that any given biblical author holds to the limited-election theory and that therefore his other statements should be interpreted consistently in the light of it? Is it possible to interpret the election statements in such a way as to be consistent with the universal statements without twisting the meaning of either? Or—another possibility—are there grounds for claiming that both sets of statements must be taken as they stand and that consequently we must reckon with a tension or paradox in Scripture that we must respect rather than try forcibly to remove it?

Naturally as evangelical exegetes and theologians we do assume the harmony of Scripture. That is to say, we reject the idea that it contains doctrinal contradictions, although we recognize that it may contain tensions alongside its fundamental harmony.

But this does raise a question of method. Suppose we find that a given New Testament writer appears to hold to the theory of limited atonement; are we then entitled to assume that this theory is the key to understanding all the other New Testament authors even though there is no evidence in their own writings that they did so? Must we not also ask whether our interpretation of the original author is correct? But in any case must we not examine each author individually, recognizing that there may be individual ways of testifying to the same basic saving truths? Discussions of how to write a theology of the New Testament have emphasized that methodologically we must begin by seeking to establish the theology of each author and then see whether we can construct a total theology of the New Testament.

That the Pastoral Epistles form an identifiable homogeneous group of writings within the New Testament is not disputed. In language, style, and theology they stand together. It is therefore appropriate to regard the contents of any one of the three pastoral letters as throwing light on the others, so that each statement in any given letter can and must be interpreted in the context of the whole corpus.

Now if the object of study was, say, Galatians, it would of course be proper to consider the teaching of that letter in the immediate context of Paul's writings as a whole and in the broader context of the New Testament as a whole (and there are relevant, wider contexts beyond these two). But what about the Pastorals? There is a real scholarly debate about whether they stem directly from the pen of Paul. If they are not by Paul, they form a corpus on their own, and therefore one does not examine their teaching as part of his theology in quite the same way as with Galatians and insist that what Paul says elsewhere may be decisive in interpreting them. If they are by Paul, then we can assume that his theology in general lies behind them—although the way in which scholars, evangelical and other, treat them suggests that they are seen as a separate group within Paul's writings.

The debate is an unsettled one, and there are conservative authors who recognize the difficulty of positing direct Pauline authorship just as there are nonconservatives who accept Pauline authorship. We will have to bear both possibilities in mind. The practical relevance, of course, is the question of how big the immediate context is for arguing that the author of the Pastorals (whom I shall call the Pastor without any prejudice to the question of whether he could also be called Paul) held to any of the theories already referred to. Must the universal statements in the Pastorals be interpreted sharply against the background of Romans 9–11, for example? Few would deny that, even if the Pastorals are not directly from Paul, they do come from an author or "school" standing strongly under his influence. We cannot, therefore, exclude the Pauline corpus of letters from consideration, though limitations of space will require us to concentrate our attention almost exclusively on the Pastorals themselves.

UNIVERSAL GRACE AND ATONEMENT

Our procedure in this paper will be to look first at those passages in the Pastorals that appear to teach universal grace and atonement, and then to consider the passages that appear to teach particular election.

There are four specific texts that appear to be universalist in their teaching, and our principal task will be to examine them in their contexts. They are:

1 Timothy 2:3–4: . . . God our Savior [who] wishes *all* men to be saved and to come to a knowledge of the truth.

1 Timothy 2:5–6: . . . Christ Jesus [who] gave himself as a ransom for *all*.

1 Timothy 4:10: . . . the living God who is the Savior of *all* men, namely of [those who] believe.

Titus 2:11: For there has appeared God's saving grace for *all* men.

These verses appear to teach that God wishes the salvation of all mankind. But is this how they are to be interpreted? I offer eight propositions as to how they are to be understood:

The Word "Save" and Its Cognates Are Used Here in Their Normal Spiritual Sense

There is no reason to take the words "savior," "save," and "saving" in anything other than their full sense. This is clear for 1 Timothy 2:3–4, which is immediately followed in 1 Timothy 2:5–6 by a description of how Jesus acted as a mediator and gave himself as a ransom.[2] The context in Titus 2:11–14 is the same.

Doubts, however, have been raised about 1 Timothy 4:10, where it has sometimes been thought that "save" is used in a broader, nontheological sense. The difficulty has arisen because according to the usual interpretation God is spoken of as "the Savior of all men, *especially* of believers," and commentators have tried to find a meaning for the verb that would fit both "all men" and "believers." However, the context does not favor a broader meaning, such as "preserve alive"; verses 9–10 are a comment on verse 8 where the need for godliness is expressed, and the point is made that it has the promise of life, both the present and future life. This can refer only to spiritual life; nothing suggests that the writer was thinking of length of physical life as the result of godliness. Then verse 10 speaks of the need for spiritual effort and justifies this by saying that the reason why we are prepared for a hard struggle in this world is precisely that we have put our hope in God who saves us.

Further, and this is decisive, the usual translation of the verse is misleading. The possibility exists that we can translate *malista*, not by "especially," but by "namely."[3] The Pastor makes a statement of the character of God as the Savior of all men, and then he makes a necessary qualification: "I mean, of those [among them] who believe." Since this translation gives an excellent sense here, it should be adopted.

The Force of *Thelō* Should Not Be Weakened

Some scholars have drawn attention to the use of the verb *thelō* in 1 Timothy 2:4 and have argued that this verb is weaker than the verb *boulomai* and that it may simply express "the Biblical notion that God does not take pleasure in the death of a sinner

(Ezek. 18:23)."[4] These two conclusions do not stand up to scrutiny, as the following three arguments indicate.

1. To avoid all misconceptions it should be made clear at the outset that the fact that God wishes or wills that all people should be saved does not necessarily imply that all will respond to the gospel and be saved. We must certainly distinguish between what God would like to see happen and what he actually does will to happen, and both of these things can be spoken of as God's will. The question at issue is not whether all will be saved but whether God has made provision in Christ for the salvation of all, provided that they believe, and without limiting the potential scope of the death of Christ merely to those whom God knows will believe.

2. It is an unreasonable weakening of the wording to make it mean simply that God does not take pleasure in the death of the sinner. The Old Testament verse that is cited in favor of this meaning in fact goes on to say that, rather, God is pleased when sinners turn from their ways and live. It is arbitrary to interpret this verse by only the negative half of the Old Testament saying and not to take the positive half into consideration as well.

3. So far as the linguistic problem is concerned, it is true that *thelō* normally expresses a wish or desire, but this does not necessarily mean that it expresses a mere wish as opposed to a real purpose. The range of meaning of the less-commonly used verb *boulomai* is also wide. It can express both an intention and a determination. The closeness of the meanings of the two verbs can be seen by a glance at the associated nouns; both can express the will or purpose of God. For example, Paul says that he is an apostle by the *thelēma* of God. In fact he does not use the noun *boulē* except in 1 Corinthians 4:5 (where it refers to human plans) and in Ephesians 1:11 where it means the plan that issues from God's will (*thelēma*). It appears that the noun *thelēma* can cover the meanings of both verbs, and this suggests that the verbs are close in meaning.

Paul undoubtedly uses *thelō* to express the purposes that God actually carries into effect (Rom. 9:18; 1 Cor. 4:19; 12:18; 15:38; Col. 1:27); it is significant that in 1 Corinthians 12:18 he uses *thelō* in exactly the same way as he uses *boulomai* in 12:11. Surprising as it may seem, Paul never uses *boulomai* of God except in this verse, and the only other New Testament uses are Matthew 11:27 (Luke 10:22); Luke 22:42 (where the use is identical with that of *thelō* in James 4:15); Heb. 6:17; James 1:18; and 2 Peter 3:9.

The last of these texts is especially instructive for our purpose because it declares that God does not will that any should perish but rather that all should come to repentance. Here, in effect, we have a precise parallel in thought to 1 Timothy 2:4 using the stronger word. He, therefore, who contends that it is a weaker verb that is used here must explain why the stronger verb is used to the same effect in 2 Peter. The fact is that, while *thelō* has the wider range of meaning, so that it can on occasion refer to desires and perhaps expresses more the element of personal desire that lies behind the expression of the will, the two verbs are essentially synonymous, and nothing can be built on the fact that one is used rather than the other. Had *boulomai* rather than *thelō* been used in 1 Timothy 2:4, it is difficult to see how the meaning would have been essentially different.

From all this it follows that we cannot weaken the sense of 1 Timothy 2:4 by claiming that the verb has a weak sense. What is expressed is what God genuinely desires to see happen.

There is obviously no possibility of weakening the sense in the case of 1 Timothy 4:10, which asserts that God *is* the savior of all men, or of Titus 2:11, which says that the saving grace of God for all men has appeared.

The Scope of "All" is Not Confined to Men

We must now consider the meaning of the phrase "all men." Although the texts refer to "men," the Greek word used is the one that includes women unless there is specific reason to exclude them (and there is, of course, no such reason here).

The Scope of "All" is Not Confined to Believers

From 1 Timothy 4:10 we have seen that salvation becomes a reality only for believers. There is no indication of a universalism in the Pastorals in the sense that everybody will be saved regardless of faith or that everybody will be brought to faith.

But should the limitation in this verse be carried over to the other verses in the sense that, when they say "all men," they really mean "all believers"?

Certainly this interpretation would make nonsense of 1 Timothy 2:4. Here it is said that God's desire is that all men should be saved *and come to a knowledge of the truth*. It is clear that the two phrases form a pair, so that being saved and coming to know the truth represent the same experience from two different aspects, the one expressing the divine action and the other the corresponding human experience of knowing the truth. But knowing the truth in a context such as this means believing in the truth when it is revealed to us. If now we take "all men" to mean "all believers," we get a statement that would be odd in two ways. First, it would produce a tautology: "God wants 'all believers' to be saved and to believe/come to know the truth." Second, the verse would not fit into its context, which is not concerned with believers but with those who need both a mediator who will offer himself as a ransom on their behalf and an apostle to proclaim the gospel to them.

These difficulties would be surmounted if for "believers" we could substitute "potential believers" or "the elect" (in the sense of the limited group of people whom God has previously destined for salvation). We would then have to take the quite specific term "all men" to mean "all the elect." But absolutely nothing in the context suggests that the phrase should be given this limited meaning. Defenders of a Calvinist position, therefore, have not adopted this interpretation but have attempted to deal with this text in other ways.

There is equally no reason for saying that 1 Timothy 2:6 must be interpreted to mean that Christ gave himself for all the elect or for all potential believers. Similarly, there is no reason to take "all men" in Titus 2:11 in this kind of way.

The Alternation Between "All" and "Us" Does Not Contradict Universality

In numerous places in the Pastorals, as elsewhere in the New Testament, God is described as our Savior or the benefits of Christ's work as said to be for us or for the church. Thus in Titus 2:11–14 the universal statement about God's saving grace for all is followed by the injunction that this grace teaches *us* to live in a godly manner, and it is backed up by the statement that Christ gave himself for *us* that he might redeem *us* to become God's people. In 1 Timothy 2:3 God is spoken of as *our* Saviour. But these and similar statements do not restrict the scope of God's grace shown in Christ. It is natural and inevitable that the Christian Pastor writing as one member of a group of Christians to another representative group of them dwells on their own state of salvation, and from statements that "Christ died for all" he very quickly moves to the logical consequence "Christ died for us." It is difficult for believers to talk about salvation without thinking of what God has done for them personally. When we as believers praise God, we thank him not just for the provision of salvation for all but also for the actual experience that we ourselves enjoy. Likewise, confessional language talks of salvation in terms of personal experience. Such language is not in any way exclusive, so far as the scope of God's mercy is concerned, although it recognizes that not all have come to faith and that many still need to be saved. So equally it is natural to move from the thought of "God our Savior" to the fact that this God does in fact wish others, indeed all men, to be saved as well.

The Term "All" Should Not Be Narrowed
to Refer Only to "the Many"

Scholars agree that 1 Timothy 2:6 is a rewording of the saying of Jesus in Mark 10:45, with "all" replacing the 'many" found in that text. Titus 2:14 is a paraphrase of the same text (with some influence from Ps. 130:8 and Exod. 19:5). A saying of Jesus that tells how the Son of Man came to give his life as a ransom for "many" has been reexpressed using more idiomatic Greek forms of expression. The "many," of course, is an intentional echo of Isaiah 53:11–12. The phrase "for many" used in the versions of the saying over the cup in Mark 14:24 and Matthew 26:28 comes from the same Old Testament source. But in the parallel saying in Luke 22:17 (and in the Lucan and Pauline forms of the saying over the bread) the phrase "for you" is used. It is generally agreed that the actual words of Jesus at the Last Supper have been paraphrased in the course of transmission. And the most probable view is that in the church the change from "many" to "you" was made in order to remind the partakers of the Lord's Supper that they personally were included in the "many"; it was a piece of personal application. The narrowing down in Luke and Paul does not of course restrict the force of the saying to the disciples present at the Last Supper or the partakers of the Lord's Supper; the thought that Christ's death avails for "many" is not lost.

So in Titus 2:14 we have the same change made in a form of words that is a Christian confession of what the Lord has done *for us*. This is an example of the tendency we traced in the preceding section. But in 1 Timothy 2:6 the change is in the opposite direction from "many" to "all." Is this an illegitimate extension of meaning? Or does it mean that "all" really means "many" and must be given a restricted meaning?

It appears to be firmly established that in Hebrew the word for "many" often has the sense of "a great many as opposed to a few," rather than "only some as opposed to all." Thus "all" is the appropriate paraphrase.[5] It is the natural word to use in moving from a crassly literal rendering of the Hebrew to more idiomatic Greek.

We may compare how the words "many" (literally "the many") and "all" alternate in Romans 5. The usage here is instructive:

v. 12 ALL die
        because ALL sinned
v. 15 MANY died,
        grace abounded for MANY
v. 16 MANY transgressions
v. 18 judgment for ALL
        justification for ALL

v. 19 MANY were declared sinners
    MANY will be declared righteous

This chart makes it quite clear that throughout this chapter where Paul is contrasting what the *one* man Adam did with what the *one* person Jesus Christ did, he uses both "many" and "all," each in contrast with "one" to refer to the totality of mankind in sin. Thus "many" is identical with "all" in the sin and death statements. Similarly, both "many" and "all" are synonymous when used with reference to the effects of Christ's righteous act.

One might endeavor to avoid this conclusion by arguing that when Paul uses "all" he simply means "both Jews and Gentiles" as in Romans 3:9. But Romans 3:10–20 shows that, while Paul is arguing that both Jews and Gentiles are sinners, he is also arguing that all people without exception are sinners. There is no reason to suppose that he means his statements in any other sense in Romans 5.

One might also try to show that in 5:15 the "many" who died are specifically the same limited group of "many" for whom God's gift came so abundantly. But it is more natural to take the "many" who died to be identical with the "all" of verse 12. And in any case this objection does nothing to blunt the force of verse 18.

What is happening is that in verse 12 Paul establishes the universal effects of Adam's fall—death came upon all men, and surely nobody will deny that this means "all without exception." But then in verse 15 (cf. 16–17) the contrast is made between "only one" sinner (Adam) and "only one" redeemer (Christ) and the vast number affected by their respective deeds; here the word "all" would be inappropriate for the contrast being made. But then in verse 18 Paul picks up the initial thought of verse 12 and repeats the point about the universality of the effects of Adam's action and (he now adds) of Christ's action. Finally, in verse 19 he recapitulates the contrast between the one and the many again. Thus we see that the rationale of Paul's oscillation in terminology in this section of Romans is the fact that he is emphasising two points: (1) the universal effects of Adam's sin (and of Christ's righteous act); and (2) the contrast between the one who sinned and the many who were affected by his action (and similarly with the One who acted righteously and the many who were affected by his action). Thus "all" and "many" refer to the same groups of people.

There is, of course, a difference. The universality of sin as the actual situation of all people is affirmed: death is known to be a universal fact, and all have sinned (v. 12). But the universality of actual redemption is another matter. The grace of God has been poured out lavishly on all mankind (v. 15), but, as verse 15 indicates, it is those who receive the gift—by faith—who will reign in life, and we may be sure that this condition is in Paul's mind throughout the chapter.

This discussion would appear to demonstrate that Paul uses the terms with the same meaning. We may remind ourselves that Calvin came to the same conclusion. Commenting on Matthew 20:28, he observed: " 'Many' is put, not for a definite number, but for a large number, in that He sets Himself over against all others. And this is its meaning also in Romans verse 15, where Paul is not talking of a part of mankind but of the whole human race."[6]

Finally, it should be observed that in Romans 3:24 Paul writes quite literally: "For all have sinned and fall short of the glory of God, being justified freely by his grace. . . ." Here Paul is capable of declaring that all people are justified, but we can state without any doubt that Paul knew that people are justified only by faith and that not all have faith. He is surely suggesting that, where justification takes place, it is through Christ (and not through the law); the same principle applies for all. So too in Romans 5 the thought must be that justification is by faith and by reception of the gift (5:17).

Thus in Romans 5 the language of "many" and "all" indicates a divine provision of salvation that is as universal as the human state of condemnation because of sin.[7]

"All" Does Not Simply Mean "All Kinds of"

The next point that must be considered is whether there is reason to give "all" a different sense from "all without exception." It is obvious that there are many cases in the New Testament where "all" is used not in the context of the universal set but in the context of a limited set that is either explicitly stated or implicit. For example, when his companions tell Jesus that everybody is seeking him (Mark 1:37), clearly it means "everybody" in the village or neighborhood where he was. This example also reminds us that often we use "everybody" hyperbolically to mean "many" or "a large number" rather than every individual without exception. Further, the word "all" can on occasion mean "all kinds of" rather than "every individual." So much can readily be granted.

But is there any reason to suppose that any such restrictions are implicit in our texts? There is really nothing in the immediate context of any of the texts to suggest that a limited set of people is intended.

It is true that the pastor begins 1 Timothy 2:1 by asking for prayers to be made for all men, and then specifies kings and rulers. The "everyone" of verse 1 clearly cannot be restricted by taking verse 2 to mean "namely, kings and rulers."

There is more to be said for the view that he means "all kinds of people, including (for example) kings and rulers (whom you might have overlooked)." But this leads to a problem. The purpose of the prayer for rulers in verse 2 is "that we might live a peaceable life." It is not a prayer for their salvation (although that is not necessarily excluded), but rather a prayer that non-Christian rulers may live in such a way that Christians will not be molested but be free to live a godly life. But then we have a problem with verses 3–6, which offer a very strange reinforcement for a command to pray so that Christians may lead a quiet life.

It is better to assume that the pastor began to write in verse 1 of prayer for the salvation of all men and then was diverted to mention the particular need to pray for rulers so that Christians might have peace to live a godly life. Admittedly it is strange that the purpose actually expressed for the prayer is not a desire for peace to proclaim the gospel (in the manner of Rom. 15:31–32; 2 Thess. 3:2) but for peace to live godly lives. It seems that the pastor is saying that prayers of all kinds should be made for all people. He mentions in passing the need to include prayers for rulers so that Christians may live in peace, but his main thought is that prayers should be offered for the salvation of all people. The thought in verse 1 is thus taken up in verse 3, and verse 2 is parenthetical. If so, there is no reason to suppose that "all men" means anything other than "all people in the world."

But might the expression in verse 1 still simply mean "all kinds of people," such as kings, rulers, and other categories? Obviously, if the reference is literally to "all men," then "all kinds of men" are implicitly included and intended. But if the reference is to "all kinds of people"—for whom prayer is to be made and whom God desires to be saved—then the pastor is declaring that, since God's saving purpose includes people of all kinds, we must pray for all kinds.

But how does this help the defender of the doctrine of limited atonement? He then has to say that prayer must be offered for "the elect groups within all groups in society"—for example, for elect kings within the group of kings. He at least knows that there will be elect people in every social group, but he is going to have to frame his prayer "for those (limited) numbers of people within each and every group whom God intends to save." There is of course, no point in praying for the salvation of the nonelect, who are not going to be saved; although one might pray that they will not molest Christians (v. 2). And there is the difficulty that one does not know whether particular individuals belong to the elect or not. Presumably one simply prays that God's will to save those who are elect in any and every social group will be accomplished. But this is not in fact what the pastor tells his readers to do; he commands prayer for "all kinds of people" (on this interpretation), not that we should pray that God's will concerning his elect, who will be found among all kinds of people, will be fulfilled. Thus the limited-atonement interpretation has to resort to what looks like twisting the text, and there is in any case nothing in the text to suggest this interpretation rather than the literal one.

A similar interpretation has been offered for Titus 2:11. Here, it is argued, the "all" refers to "all social classes"; the evidence adduced in favor of this suggestion is the references to various social groups earlier in the chapter (older men, older women, younger women, younger men, slaves). Then 2:11 reinforces the fact that commands are given to these various groups by reminding the readers that God's saving purpose applies to all kinds of people and involves living godly lives in the appropriate ways. The difficulty is that it is impossible to see the need for a motivation of this kind. Why should it be necessary to say in effect to some social class in the church, "Of course you must live a godly life in your station because God's saving plan is for people of all stations including your own"? This interpretation simply does not make sense.

But why does the pastor use the word "all" in this context? There are two possibilities that need to be raised. First, there is the possibility that the pastor was dealing with a Gnostic-type heresy that claimed that only certain people possessed the spark of divinity hidden within them and could be saved, the rest of mankind being merely earthly and destined for destruction. The pastor could then be emphasizing that Christian salvation is open to all and not restricted to a predetermined group. But, if this interpretation is correct, it is surely inconceivable that the pastor really meant that in fact salvation was limited to a specific group (the "elect"), the only difference being that this is a different group from the group defined in Gnostic theology.

The second possibility is preferable. Part of the reason undoubtedly is that the word came to him from Christian tradition. As we saw earlier, the pastor knew a tradition containing the saying of Jesus in Mark 10:45, and here the word "all" had replaced the word "many." The alternation of "all" and "many" in Romans 5 may also have been in his mind. But probably his stress on "all" arose out of controversy regarding the place of the Gentiles in the church. The pastor is emphasizing that salvation is for everybody, both Jews and Gentiles. In view of the Jewish character of the heresy that is opposed in the Pastorals, this interpretation has a good deal of plausibility. But it does not help the defender of limited atonement any more than the view that "all" refers to "all kinds of people," for what the pastor is telling his readers to do is to pray for "both Jews and Gentiles," not for "the elect among Jews and Gentiles."

Thus we can find no good grounds for understanding "all" in these texts in any other way than as "all without exception."

The Grace of God Is Identified
With His Saving Act in Christ

It is important to observe next that the expression of God's saving will is inextricably bound up with his action in Christ. The reason why the Pastor can declare in 1 Timothy 2:4 that God wishes all men to be saved is the fact that there is one Mediator, who has given himself as a ransom for all people. The saving will finds expression in the sacrifice of Christ; both are concerned with "all men." How does the pastor know this? Probably he reasons from the wording of Mark 10:45 in which Jesus expresses the saving purpose of his death for "the many," and concludes (rightly) that behind the deed lies the will of God for all mankind.

Similarly, in Titus 2:11–14 the close proximity of verse 11 and verse 14 to each other suggests the same conclusion. But in fact the conclusion emerges from verse 11 on its own. For what the pastor describes in verse 11 is the appearing of God's grace. However we understand grace, the sense can only be that God's gracious purpose found realization and expression in a concrete manifestation—namely, in the appearance of Christ, who is the "epiphany" of the saving purpose of God. Thus the grace is incarnated or incorporated in Jesus, who gave himself as a ransom for us. Thus the grace cannot be separated from the actual coming and the dying of Jesus. Hence it is difficult to see how one might say "God loves you" without at the same time being able to say "Christ died for you," unless the love is understood to be a nonsaving kind of love. It is therefore possible and indeed necessary to affirm both of the two statements with full theological integrity.

ELECTION IN THE PASTORALS

The effect of my argument so far is to suggest that, taken by themselves in their immediate contexts, the "all" sayings in the Pastorals should be understood to teach that the grace of God truly appeared in Christ for all mankind and that behind this manifestation lay the will of God that all mankind should be saved. The offer of salvation is genuinely made to all in the gospel.

The question is now whether there are other statements in the Pastorals that may suggest limited atonement and election, and, if so, we should attempt to see how these are to be understood. We will consider in this connection, first, the use of the term "elect," and, second, the possible presence of the concept of a limited election.

The Use of the Word "Elect"

The adjective "elect" is found in the Pastorals only three times: in 1 Timothy 5:21; 2 Timothy 2:10 and Titus 1:1. The first text contains a reference to "elect angels" and can be ignored for our present purpose.

In Titus 1:1 Paul is said to be an apostle in accordance with the faith of God's elect or to promote the faith of God's elect (ones). Either way, the faith is that shown by the elect. C. Spicq offers in effect two understandings of the word "elect": (1) It refers to "men chosen by God as hearers of his word and beneficiaries of salvation"; (2) the term "elect" was a privileged title for members of the Christian communities in Asia Minor (Eph. 1:4; Col. 3:12; 1 Peter 1:2; cf. John 15:16).[8] These two definitions appear to stand in some tension with each other. The second is weakly based. The term does appear in New Testament material associated with Asia Minor (Col.; 2 Tim.; 1 Peter) but this is a rather narrow basis for the conclusion that it was especially an Asian title for Christians.

The important point that emerges when we examine the word usage is that the term is used throughout the New Testament for Christians, for those who belong to the community consisting of people otherwise called "the saints," the "brothers," the "people of God," etc. They are the group of people whom God has chosen; they have responded to his call and actually belong to the group.

But can the word be used, as Spicq suggests, to refer to those who have been chosen by God before and apart from their response, i.e., to mean "potential believers"? With the possible exception of 2 Timothy 2:10 this use is never found in the New Testament. Moreover, when the verb is used in the New Testament, it is *always* used with reference to people who have responded to the choice with faith and become members of the church.

But what of 2 Timothy 2:10? This verse states that Paul endures everything for the sake of the elect that they may obtain salvation. Spicq takes this phrase to refer to "the Christians who are already justified and sanctified and need to make their calling sure . . . but also the sinners whom God has loved from all eternity (2 Thess. 2:13; Eph. 1:3–5) and whom he calls to salvation (cf. 1 Tim. 1:15f.); the qualification 'which is in Christ' indicates that these people must be converted and enter the church."[9] But this interpretation cannot be upheld. The "salvation" referred to is surely future salvation, since it is coupled with "eternal glory" and since the verse is immediately followed by a "faithful saying," which refers to the attainment of future life and rule with Jesus. Hence the saying can refer only to those who are already Christians and refers to Paul's efforts as a pastor to help them persevere in their salvation. There is nothing in the verse to require us to adopt a meaning for the word other than that found elsewhere in the New Testament.

This conclusion is reinforced by a study of the history of the use of the word. When we inquire whether there is anything in the Old Testament or Judaism to suggest that the word "elect" can refer to "potential members of the people of God," the answer is completely negative. Whenever the term "elect" is used in the LXX with reference to Israel, it is always used of people as God's people, as part of the holy nation. The very fact that the Old Testament does not envisage other people becoming part of Israel naturally leads to this usage. That is to say, the use of the term "the elect" to refer to a group secretly chosen and destined by God for a salvation to which they have not yet responded simply does not exist in biblical thinking. The use of "elect" in this sense is a modern development and it does not correspond to biblical usage.

The Use of the Concept "Elect"

Although the word "elect" is not used to refer to "potential believers already chosen by God," it remains possible that the concept existed and that in these two verses (and possibly elsewhere in the New Testament) the noun could have taken on this meaning.

Are there any indications in the Pastorals that the writer thinks in this way?

1. It is arguable that faith and repentance are the gifts of God, who gives them only to the previously chosen group of the elect. Thus Paul was shown mercy and he received grace "along with the faith and love that are in Christ Jesus" (1 Tim. 1:14).

2. It is God who saved and called us because of his own purpose and grace (2 Tim. 1:9). This grace was given us in Christ before the beginning of time (v. 9). This verse is the strongest statement of a premundane plan of salvation that affects "us." It rightly emphasizes that salvation is entirely of God and does not depend on our works, merit or acceptability but purely on grace. Could this teaching give a basis for the Calvinist view of the "elect" in 2 Timothy 2:10?

3. Similar teaching is found in Titus 1:2–3, where we read that God promised eternal life before the beginning of time and then brought it to light through the preaching of the gospel. And this is in a context referring to the elect!

4. Titus 3:5 might be taken to mean that God gave us the washing of rebirth and renewal by the Spirit and that this then led to our justification and faith.

Two of these passages follow a scheme of thought found elsewhere in the New Testament where the making of God's plan of salvation in the past is placed in contrast with the revelation of his saving action now. The scheme has been discussed by N. A. Dahl, who notes that in Paul it is a contrast between what once was hidden and what has now been revealed (Rom. 16:25–26; 1 Cor. 2:7–10; Eph. 3:4–11; Col. 1:26–27). In the Pastorals and elsewhere the words "mystery" and "hidden" do not appear, and the contrast is between what God gave or promised before the creation of the world and what has now been revealed (2 Tim. 1:9–11; Titus 1:2–3; 1 Peter 1:18–21 (cf. vv. 10–12); 1 John 1:1–3; Ign. Mag. 6:1; Herm. s. 9:12; cf. John 1:1–18).[10] Thus the concept that God planned the work of salvation before creation in eternity is a widespread theological concept in the New Testament.

In Titus 1:2–3 we are told that God promised eternal life before "eternal ages" and that he revealed his word in the gospel. Nothing is said as to whom God made this promise or who were the envisaged objects of it. The point is rather to assert the faithfulness of God in keeping to his eternal purpose. The mention of the "elect" in the context may suggest that they are the implied indirect object or dative of interest with the verb "promised."

In 2 Timothy 1:9–10 God is said to have saved us in accordance with his own purpose and grace, which he gave to us in Christ before eternal ages and which has now been revealed by the epiphany of Christ. The thought of "giving" grace is a familiar one (Rom. 12:3, 6; 15:15; 1 Cor. 3:10; Gal. 2:9; Eph. 3:8; 4:7; James 4:6; 1 Peter 5:5; cf. 2 Cor. 6:1) and means that a person not only is the object of divine love and favor but also receives some kind of spiritual gift or power from God. The problems are (1) In what sense can grace be "given" in eternity past? and (2) Who are the recipients? With regard to the first question, two main types of explanation have been offered: W. Lock argues that the grace was given to us in our ideal, namely Christ, long before we were born; it was contained in the preexistent Christ before the world was created.[11] According to Cajetan, however, the effect of the gift is in time, but the actual giving was in eternity before all times; the reference is not to a material gift but to the loving will of God. Thus the gift was given in the divine predestination, though in effect it is given to us in time.[12] Somewhat similar is the view of J. H. Bernard: "That which is unfalteringly purposed is described as actually given."[13] To the same effect is R. St. J. Parry: "The thought is wholly of the original purpose of God as actualized, so to speak, in . . . the Son contemplated as already incarnate. The grace . . . is described, by a bold hyperbole, as already given to us, though there can be no question of our then existence."[14]

We thus have to decide between two interpretations, the view that the gift was actually given to Christ (in whom we were in effect contained), and the view that the gift was decided in God's purpose and is described hyperbolically as already actually given, though the effect is not seen until Christ comes. The former of these two views seems to be preferable. It links up well with the thought in Ephesians 1:4 that God chose us in Christ before the creation of the world. In the act of determining to send his Son, God intended our salvation and in a sense the decisive gift of grace lay in that purpose that had then to be brought to fulfillment in the concrete reality of the incarnation and atonement. The giving is thus equivalent to the promise in Titus 1:2: Because God cannot lie, when he makes a promise of a gift he has in effect already made the gift.

The "us" to whom the gift is made clearly refers to believers. As in the other verses that speak of election, the viewpoint is that of the members of the saved community. But must we go further and claim that this implies that God had a limited group of "the elect" in mind when he made the gift and the promise? To say this would be to read into the text something that is not there. A purpose of God to create a people consisting of saved sinners, saved entirely by his grace and not by their own efforts, and a purpose to save specified individuals are separable entities, and nothing here compels the view that the second concept must be linked to the first. The gift is given to Christ and to us insofar as we believe in Christ. It is not said that God foreordained specific individuals to salvation.

Rather, the emphasis here, as so often elsewhere, is on the fact that salvation is always and entirely due to God's initiative, which stretches back to eternity, and is not dependent on any works of ours. We cannot save ourselves; we can only receive the gift offered to us.

The statements in Titus 3:4–7 agree with this. Again the emphasis is on God's action as opposed to our works. Commentators may have been misled into thinking that salvation by washing and renewal, justification, and becoming heirs are three temporal stages in the process. But the fact that a purpose clause commences in verse 7 precludes our placing the three processes in a temporal sequence, and the "being justified" in verse 7 can be taken as a recapitulation of verse 6. Faith is not mentioned here, but it is so inseparable from justification elsewhere that it must be assumed. To find here, therefore, a divine regeneration that is prior to and indeed causes our faith is to read more into the text than is permissible. To draw a similar conclusion from 1 Timothy 1:14 would be equally unpermissible.

Against this conclusion it could be argued that the predestination of specific individuals to salvation is found elsewhere in the New Testament, especially in Paul (Rom. 8–11; Eph. 1). The scope of this essay obviously prevents detailed study of these passages. This much must be said: I do not find grounds in these passages for the view that God has purposed to save only a limited number of the elect, and I find nothing to suggest that, if the author of

Romans and Ephesians wrote the Pastorals, then the Pastorals should be interpreted in a different way from that which I have attempted here.

CONCLUSIONS

We have found nothing in the Pastorals that requires that we assume the existence of a "hidden agenda," a secret plan of God to save only the elect, in the light of which the statements of universal grace and unlimited atonement must be given something other than their obvious meaning. We have found that here, as elsewhere in the New Testament, there is a premundane gracious will of God directed to the salvation of a people who will inherit eternal life, and God wills the means to that end. But we are left in the dark as to how that will is worked out in the lives of individuals. What is not obscure, however, is that God has provided in Christ a Savior who is the incarnation of his saving will and purpose for all mankind, and that we can proclaim the offer of salvation to all mankind; those who believe will be saved, and those who do not believe will be lost. But if we ask why some believe and others do not, we can say no more than that this is part of the mystery of evil to which the Pastorals, like the rest of Scripture, can offer no answer.

NOTES

[1] It was pointed out that the French term translated "definite atonement" is a better one.

[2] The possibility that here "save" may mean "preserve, make safe" is discussed by E. K. Simpson (*The Pastoral Epistles*, London, 1954), 41–42, following a suggestion by A. Deissmann, but he cautiously concludes only that it may be the right solution. His caution is justified.

[3] T. C. Skeat, " 'Especially the Parchments': A Note on 2 Tim. 4:13," JTS ns 30 (1979): 173–77.

[4] P. Jones, unpublished paper given at the conference of the Fellowship of European Evangelical Theologians, Altenkirchen, Germany in August 1986, on "To save and to destroy," 13 n. 3.

[5] J. Jeremias, s.v. *polloi*, TDNT 5:536–45.

[6] J. Calvin, *A Harmony of the Gospels* (Edinburgh, 1972), 2:277.

[7] J. Jeremias, *polloi*, 541, discusses other passages where "many" and "all" are interchangeable.

[8] C. Spicq, *Les Epitres Pastorales* (Paris, 1969), 2:592.

[9] Ibid., 747.

[10] N. A. Dahl, "Formgeschichtliche Beobachtungen zur Christusverkündigung in der Gemeindepredigt," in W. Eltester, ed., *Neutestamentliche Studien für Rudolf Bultmann* (Berlin, 1954), 3–9.

[11] W. Lock, *The Pastoral Epistles* (Edinburgh, 1924), 87.

[12] Cajetan, cited by Spicq, *Les Epitres Pastorales*, 2:715.

[13] J. H. Bernard, *The Pastoral Epistles* (Cambridge, 1909), 110.

[14] R. St John Parry, *The Pastoral Epistles* (Cambridge, 1920), 51.

THE UNIVERSAL POWER
OF THE ATONEMENT

Terry L. Miethe

The atonement is that aspect of the work of Christ, particularly his death, that makes possible the restoration of fellowship between God and humankind. The need for the atonement is clear from the fact that man is a sinner (Rom. 3:9–23). The atonement is a "crucial point of the Christian faith." To understand the atonement correctly, it is "essential that our understanding of God the Father and of his Son be correct, and that our conception of the nature of man and his spiritual condition be accurate." Again, as Millard J. Erickson has written:

> The doctrine of the atonement is the most critical for us, because it is the point of transition . . . from the objective to the subjective aspects of Christian theology. Here we shift our focus from the nature of Christ to his active work in our behalf; here systematic theology has direct application to our lives. The atonement has made our salvation possible.[1]

It is also clear that it was God's will to bring salvation through the life, death, resurrection, and ascension of his Son, Jesus. "For God so loved the world that he gave his one and only Son, that whoever believes in him shall not perish but have eternal life"[2] (John 3:16; see also Rom. 5:8–10; 2 Cor. 5:19).

> The New Testament does not put forward *a theory of atonement.* . . . There are several indications of the principle on which atonement is effected: . . . the perfect sacrifice of Christ (Heb. 9:26; 10:5–10). Christ paid sin's due penalty (Rom. 3:25–26; 6:23; Gal. 3:13). He redeemed us (Eph. 1:7), paying the price that sets us free (1 Cor. 6:20; Gal. 5:1). He made a new covenant (Heb. 9:15). He won the victory (1 Cor. 15:55–57). He effected the propitiation that turns away the wrath of God (Rom. 3:25), made the reconciliation that turns enemies into friends (Eph.

2:16). His love and his patient endurance of suffering set an
example (1 Peter 2:21); we are to take up our cross (Luke 9:23).
But however [salvation] is viewed, Christ has taken our place,
doing for us what we could not do for ourselves. Our part is
simply to respond in repentance, faith, and selfless living
(emphasis added).[3]

God's plan, the scheme of redemption, was to offer salvation
through the very life and death of his Only Begotten One: "This is
love: not that we loved God, but that he loved us and sent his Son
as an atoning sacrifice for our sins." (1 John 4:10).

To the everyday "reader of the New Testament, the universal
significance of Christ's death and resurrection . . . seems too
obvious even to question."[4] But it is in fact questioned. The
doctrine of the atonement is very complex. Space does not allow a
complete examination of the historic theories of the atonement,[5]
or the nature of the atonement,[6] or even the question "For what
did Christ die?"[7] The purpose of this chapter is to examine only
the classical issue: for *whom* did Christ die? Did Jesus die for the
sins of everyone in the entire world, or only for the sins of a select
group chosen by God, the elect? Who can be recipients of *his*
saving grace? The first view is called the "unlimited atonement" or
"general redemption." The second view is referred to as "limited
atonement" or "particular redemption."

Even this more limited question, "For whom did Christ die?"
cannot be dealt with in a thorough fashion here.[8] However, in the
context of that question this chapter will address arguments for
limited atonement [considered and answered]; arguments for
limited atonement [considered and expanded]; and J. I. Packer's
introductory essay, Calvin on the Atonement, and draw some
conclusions. The position defended in this chapter is that "*the
redemptive events in the life of Jesus provided a salvation so extensive and
so broad as to potentially include the whole of humanity past, present, and
future!*"[9]

ARGUMENTS FOR LIMITED ATONEMENT

The idea that Jesus died for the elect only, but not for the sins
of everyone, arose as the implications of the doctrine of election
and the satisfaction theory of the atonement were developed
immediately following the Reformation. What is now referred to
as the "Five-Points of Calvinism' or T U L I P[10] was formulated at
the Synod of Dort, convened in 1618, and represented counter-
affirmations to the Remonstrance of 1610 in which followers of
Jacob Arminius (1560–1609) rejected the major Calvinistic dogma.
Most Calvinists, though certainly not all,[11] believe in a limited
atonement.

1. Scripture limits the extent of the atonement

"In the Bible there is a qualification as to who will benefit by the death of Christ, thus limiting its effect."[12] Calvinists argue that Scriptures that say Jesus died for "his sheep" (John 10:11, 15), "his church" (Acts 20:28; Eph. 5:25); "the elect" (Rom. 8:32–35); "his people" (Matt. 1:21); "us" (Titus 2:14), show that the Bible teaches a limited atonement. But when the Bible talks about Christ dying for "us," for "our" sins, and for his "church" the limitation is only in relation to the personalized language. "A particular body of people is being addressed, in the grammatical form of first person plural. To say to any [particular] audience, 'Christ died for us!' does not [logically] imply 'for us and no one else.' "[13]

In regard to Romans 8:32, for example, the context of the whole chapter centers on Christians—i.e., "on the elect *who have believed* (vv. 1, 4, 5, 9, 10, 11, 12, 14, 15, 16, 17, 23, 26, 27)." We see in verse 33 that their justification is "effected through faith (Rom. 5:1)."

> Consequently, Rom. 8:32 refers not to the elect *as such*, but . . . it refers to them *as Christians*. Since the entire chapter has to do with Christians, it was perfectly natural for the Apostle, in speaking of Christ's death, to speak of it merely in relation to *them*. There was no least reason for him, on reaching this point, to contemplate, in a negative way, those who were not Christians. Consequently, to construe Paul as deliberately leaving out the non-elect is quite unwarranted. To read him as meaning that God delivered Christ for all of us who believe *and for none else*, is injecting into the words what is not there.[14]

Hence, this amounts to an argument from silence. One cannot argue in positive support of a point when what is being argued is simply not in the grammar, language, or structure of the text.

2. Scripture teaches that not everyone will be saved

The argument goes like this: "God's designs are always efficacious (having the power to produce a desired effect) and can never be frustrated by man. Had God intended all men to be saved by the death of Christ, then all would be saved. It is clear that not everyone is saved . . . " They argue that "because the Bible clearly teaches that those who reject Christ are lost . . . it stands to reason that Christ could not have died for everyone, because not everyone is saved." If Christ died for everyone, then everyone must be saved. But if they are not saved, then "God's saving will" is not efficacious; it is limited in its power.

This is an incredible argument that misunderstands not only the nature of God but also the nature of man as created in God's image. First, it misunderstands the nature of God because it makes God's sovereignty contradictory to any possibility of human freedom. But this is simply—and clearly—not so! The problem would be with a god who could not create free creatures, or a god who had to force people to do his will. Surely this "god" would not be sovereign.

Human freedom is no restriction on God's power. Exactly the opposite is in fact true: "If God had to negate man's freedom and force him to choose in the proper way, then his omnipotence truly would be compromised."[15] Freedom in man is "delegated sovereignty" freely given by God to man because we are created in His image.[16] God, by unlimited authentic power, can produce independently existing creatures who share in the "liberty of deity" and can "become co-creators with Him in their own measure." This is true *power*, both for God and for man! God is freedom and Love, and he imparts these qualities to his creatures because it is his very nature to do so.[17]

The second problem with this argument comes from the idea that "God's designs . . . can never be frustrated by man." Again, this is obviously not so. How do we account for the fact of sin in that case? Do we want to opt for the solution that the Holy Spirit turned His back on Adam and Eve and allowed them to sin?[18] If that is true, then there is no possible way to avoid saying that God was originally, at least in his permissive will, responsible for sin. And then, of course, there is the problem that Christians, "the elect" who are born again, also continue to frustrate the will of God, or sin. You cannot have it both ways: either God is so in control that man cannot frustrate his power; therefore, sin is ultimately the result of God's permissive will, or man is free, and therefore can choose to accept God's gracious gift of salvation, and he, man, is responsible for sin.

3. If the atonement is unlimited, hell is unjust

"If Christ died for everyone, God would be unfair in sending people to hell for their own sins. No law court allows payment to be exacted twice for the same crime, and God will not do that either." Thus the atonement cannot be unlimited unless his plan is that everyone be saved. "Christ paid for the sins of the elect; the lost pay for their own sins."

This argument suffers, in part, from the same error as the one above it. It assumes that because Christ's death was "sufficient" to save all for whom he died, then it must save all for whom he died. It ignores again both the nature of God and the nature of man as created in God's image. There is certainly no logical contradiction in saying that Jesus' suffering and death were universal [in quality], but that free, responsible individuals have to accept his free gift [quantity]. There is no double payment! Only Jesus could pay the penalty for anyone or everyone, but each individual must still accept that free gift.

Those who follow this argument commit a rather basic error:

> . . . in speaking of Christ's death in terms of *quantity*. The *divine* Christ is infinite; his suffering was infinite. Quantitative speculations are out of place, because the effects or benefits of Christ's death are potentially *unlimited*, infinite. This is true simply because of *who* Christ is: the Son of God.[19]

It is clear in the Bible that Christ's death is universal in sufficiency and intention, but it is limited in its application. This limitation is imposed not by God but by man. The individual human being, created in the image of God with free will, must accept the benefits of the atonement.

4. Unlimited atonement leads to universalism

"To say that Christ died for everyone logically leads to universalism." However, not all who believe in an unlimited atonement believe in universalism. "If they were consistent they would, because they are arguing that Christ paid for everyone's sins, thus saving them."

This, again, makes the same mistake as the above arguments. To say that Christ died for everyone "logically" leads to universalism only if his death is viewed in terms of "quantity" and not in terms of "quality." It leads to universalism only if God's sovereignty means that every act of God must be "efficacious" and "cannot be frustrated by man" (in the sense of the second argument above), thereby negating any possible human freedom as being consistent with divine sovereignty.

5. If the atonement is unlimited,
it is possible that no one will be saved

"Christ died not just to make salvation possible, but actually to save. To argue that Christ died only to provide the possibility of salvation is to leave open the question of whether *anyone* is saved." The Bible certainly "teaches that the death of Jesus actually secures salvation . . . , thus making it a certainty and limiting the atonement (Matt. 18:11 [for which there are manuscript problems]; Rom. 5:10; 2 Cor. 5:21; Gal. 1:4; 3:13; Eph. 1:7)."

Certainly, we receive reconciliation through our Lord Jesus Christ (Rom. 5:11). No Christian doubts this. But the real question here is the logic of the above argument. It surely makes *as much sense* to argue (as we will see in Isa. 53:6; John 3:16; 1 Tim. 2:6, 4:10; Titus 2:11; Heb. 2:9; 2 Peter 3:9; 1 John 2:2) (1) the Bible unquestionably teaches an unlimited atonement; (2) the Bible also teaches that some will be saved; (3) therefore some individuals *will* accept the free gift of God's grace and will in fact be saved. (And, if the above-mentioned passages do teach an unlimited atonement, then this second argument is logically undeniable.) Doesn't the Calvinist argument above, which *declares* a limited atonement, really say that the Holy Spirit is powerless in his working in the world to convict sinners of sin? Surely there is a great difference between saying that something is effective for some, given free will, and saying it might not be effective for any.

In regard to 2 Corinthians 5:18–20, for example, which says in part "that God was reconciling the world to himself in Christ, not counting men's sins against them," the question here is, Does this somehow teach a limited atonement? Certainly not! Douty correctly says, "All the Greek lexicons I have consulted (Robinson, Grimm-Thayer, Arndt-Gingrich, Abbott-Smith and Kittel) say that "world" here means "mankind."[20]

6. The atonement is limited and faith is a gift of God

"Because there are no conditions to be met in order to be saved [i.e., salvation is by grace and not by works, even an act of faith], both repentance and faith are *secured* for those for whom Christ died" (emphasis added). It is argued that "if the design of the atonement were for everyone, then all would receive repentance and faith, but this is clearly false." Therefore, the death of Jesus was intended only for the elect.

The first part is not an argument. It is a simple assertion, one the Scripture does not teach. The second part, the argument that "if the . . . atonement were for everyone, then all would receive repentance and faith" simply assumes that the first part is true, i.e., that faith is both a work and a gift of God.

Faith is not a "work."

How can one construe the response of a human to the call of the Holy Spirit a "work"? Is it a work to respond to the loving call of God? A "work" is something a person does because he believes that in so doing he will earn "credit" or "merit" toward something. Simply responding to a free gift can in no way be considered a "work" or a "merit" *earned* by the recipient.

Someone walks up to my door. I answer the door. She says, "Here is a free Mercedes. Take it if you wish." If I take it, *I* have done nothing to secure or merit or work for the free gift. Now if she says, "If you accept it, then you must do certain things; e.g. take care of it, fill it up with gas if you want to use it, be a good steward of the gift, etc.," my acceptance still has nothing to do with "earning" or "meriting" the free gift. In the same way James tells us quite clearly that our faith must be seen in our works, that "faith" and "works" are not contradictory but must go hand in hand (James 2:14–26).

Faith is not a gift of God.

The classic text, used by Calvinists, to support the assertion that even faith must be given to men by God is Ephesians 2:8, which says, "For it is by grace you have been saved, through faith—and this not from yourselves, it is the gift of God." But in the Greek text of this passage there is only one pronoun, not two; and that pronoun does not agree grammatically with the word "faith." The pronoun is neuter in gender, while the word "faith" is feminine. According to all grammatical rules, the gift cannot be faith! What is referred to in this passage is God's gracious gift of salvation, which none can merit.

7. "World" really means "the elect"

"The passages that speak of Christ's death for 'the world' have been misunderstood (John 1:29; 3:16, et al.). The word 'world' really means the world of the elect, the world of believers, the church, . . . "

Again, this is an important assertion. The question is Where does the burden of proof lie? Douty mentions the following works: Trench's *Synonyms of the New Testament*, Kittel's *Theological Dictionary of the New Testament*, Vine's *Expository Dictionary of New Testament Words*, Vincent's *Word Studies in the New Testament*, Robinson's *A Greek and English Lexicon of the New Testament*, Thayer's *Greek-English Lexicon of the New Testament*, Souter's *Pocket Lexicon of the Greek New Testament*, Berry's *Interlinear Greek-English New Testament*, Arndt-Gingrich's *A Greek-English Lexicon of the New Testament*, Abbott-Smith's *Manual Greek Lexicon of the New Testament*, *The New Schaff-Herzog Encyclopedia of Religious Knowledge*, Hastings' *Bible Dictionary* and *Dictionary of the Apostolic church*, the *International Standard Bible Encyclopedia*, Tasker's *New Bible Dictionary*, Everett F. Harrison in Baker's *Dictionary of Theology*, and John D. Davis in his *Dictionary of the Bible* (both Harrison and Davis list John 3:16 as referring to mankind, though both are Presbyterians). Then Douty says,

> But amid all the divisions and sub-divisions listed, the word [for world] is never said to denote "the elect." These lexicons know nothing of such a use of *kosmos* in the New Testament, under which to tabulate John 1:29; 3:16–18; 4:42; 6:33, 51; 12:47; 14:31; 16:8–11; 17:21, 23; 2 Cor. 5:19; 1 John 2:2; 4:14.

Douty goes on to say:

All of this is disastrous for the advocates of Limited Atonement. They have ventured to set themselves above the combined scholarship of our lexicons, encyclopedias and dictionaries, when they have ascribed a further signification to the word *kosmos*, which will support their theological system.[21]

8. "All" means only "all classes" of people

"The passages that say Christ died for all men have also been misunderstood. The word 'all' means 'all classes' of men, not everyone" (Rom. 5:18–19; 1 Cor. 15:22).

On Romans 5:18 John Calvin said,

He makes this favor common to all, because it is propoundable to all, and not because it is in reality extended to all (i.e., in their experience); for though Christ suffered for the sins of the whole world, and is offered through God's benignity indiscriminately to all, yet all do not receive Him.[22]

Thus Calvin held that Romans 5:18 taught a general redemption. In this chapter in Romans, the apostle Paul contrasts the sin and condemnation that was brought into the world by Adam, with the grace and salvation brought in by the Second Adam, Jesus. Calvin says, "Consequently, just as the result of one trespass was condemnation for all men, so also the result of one act of righteousness was justification *that brings life for all men*" (emphasis added). The intent of the text is clear. Just as no one stands outside of Adam's sinful heritage; so all people stand under the grace and salvation extended by the Second Adam.

As Lake says, "It is this fact that makes verse 18 . . . even more potent: *Then as one man's trespass led to condemnation for all men, so one man's act of righteousness leads to acquittal and life for all men.*" It is true that there is a shifting between "all" and "many" here, but Paul can hardly mean anything different from the "all men" of verse 12. Here the contrast is not many versus all, but many versus one. (See also Mark 10:45; Heb. 9:28).[23] The fact remains that there is just no evidence that when the text says "all" it means anything else but "all."

ARGUMENTS FOR UNLIMITED ATONEMENT

The idea that the death of Christ was designed to include all humankind but is applied only to those who accept it, believe in Jesus as Lord and Savior, is referred to as the "unlimited" or "general" atonement. There are *many* passages in the Bible that clearly teach this idea. Among the more important are Isaiah 53:6; Matthew 11:28; John 3:16–17; 1 Timothy 2:6; 4:10; Titus 2:11; Hebrews 2:9; 2 Peter 3:9; 1 John 2:2; Revelation 22:17. There are those who equate the idea of an unlimited atonement with a new "heresy," Arminianism, as contrasted with what they call the "old gospel," meaning biblical Christianity.[24] But this is simply not true.

1. Unlimited atonement is the historic position

Even Presbyterian Walter Elwell admits:

> Those who defend general redemption begin by pointing out that it is the historic view of the church, being held by the vast majority of theologians, reformers, evangelists, and fathers from the beginning of the church until the present day, including virtually all the writers before the Reformation, with the *possible exception*[25] of Augustine. Among the Reformers the doctrine is found in Luther, Melanchthon, Bullinger, Latimer, Cranmer, Coverdale, and even Calvin in some of his commentaries (emphasis added).[26]

In fact, the following also held to an unlimited atonement: Clement of Alexandria (150–220), Eusebius (c. 260–340), Athanasius (c. 293–373), Cyril of Jerusalem (c. 315–386), Gregory Nazianzen (324–389), Basil (c. 330–379), Ambrose (c. 340–407), Cyril of Alexandria (376–444), Richard Hocker (1553–1600), James Ussher (1581–1656), Richard Baxter (1615–1691), John Bunyan (1628–1688), John Newton (1725–1807), Alfred Edersheim (b. 1825), B. F. Westcott (1825–1901), J. B. Lightfoot (b. 1828), Augustus H. Strong (1836–1921), A. T. Robertson (b. 1863), and many others.[27]

The following "Confessions of the Reformation Age" also teach an unlimited atonement: The Augsburg Confession (1530), First Confession of Helvetia (1536), Confession of Saxony (1551), Articles of the Church of England (1553), Heidelberg Catechism (1563), Latter Confession of Helvetia (1566), and others.[28] *If this be heresy, it is certainly not a new one!*

2. Scripture teaches an unlimited atonement

"When the Bible says Christ died for all, it means just that. The word ought to be taken in its normal sense unless some compelling reason exists to take it otherwise, and no such reason exists." Isaiah 53:6 says, "We all, like sheep, have gone astray, each of us has turned to his own way; and the Lord [Yahweh] has laid on him [Jesus] the iniquity [the punishment] of us all." This is a statement to the people of Israel with prophetic import. "The people of Israel are to be taken, as in Romans 3:19, as representative of all mankind."[29] It is clear that the atonement—the suffering—of Christ is said to be on behalf of all.

In 1 Timothy 2:1–6; 4:10 we read, in part: "This is good, and pleases God our Savior, who wants *all men to be saved* and to come

to a knowledge of the truth" (vv. 3–4) and "God" gave Christ
Jesus "as a ranson for *all men*" (v. 6). In 4:9–10 Paul writes, "This
is a trustworthy saying that deserves full acceptance (and for this
we labor and strive), that we have put our hope in the living God,
who is the Savior of all men, and *especially of those who believe*"
(emphases added).

In verse one of the 1 Timothy passage, Paul exhorts that
"requests, prayers, intercession and thanksgiving be made for
everyone" (" . . . on behalf of all men" NASB). Calvin says this
means "not only for believers, but for all mankind."[30] But does
"all" in verse 6 mean less than "all men" in verses 1 and 4? F. F.
Bruce says:

> To say that He died for His people is certainly Scriptural . . . but
> it is equally Scriptural to say that He died for all. . . . And when
> Scripture says "all" in a context like this, it means "all." Some
> readers who are not sure of this statement may find it profitable
> to consider certain exegetical comments of John Calvin. On
> Matt. 26:28 and Mark 14:24 ("Which is shed for many") he says:
> "By the word *many* he means not a part of the world only, but
> the whole human race." . . . . [again quoting from Calvin]
> "Paul makes grace common to all men, not because in fact it
> extends to all, but because it is offered to all."[31]

In relation to 1 Timothy 4:10, " . . . who is the Savior of all
men, and especially those who believe," Erickson says: "This is a
particularly interesting and significant verse, since it brackets as
being saved by God both believers and others, but indicates that a
greater degree of salvation attaches to the former group."[32] Now
certainly those who do not believe are not saved. The Scripture is
completely clear on this. Thus, quite obviously, this verse is
saying that although Christ died for *all men*—i.e., the free gift was
extended to all—it is finally effective only for those who accept it.

3. "World" really means "world"

"The Bible says Christ takes away the sin of the world and is
the Savior of the world. A study of the word 'world'—especially
in John, where it is used seventy-eight times—shows that the
world is God-hating, Christ-rejecting, and Satan-dominated."
Elwell goes on to say, as well as it can be said: "Yet that is the
world for which Christ died. There is not one place in the entire
New Testament where 'world' means 'church' or 'the elect.' " This
was the unequivocal force of the evidence above in answer 7
under Arguments for Limited Atonement, where it is shown there
is absolutely no logical reason to deny that when the text says
"world" it means "world."

4. An unlimited atonement does not lead to universalism

"The several arguments that reduce to a charge of universalism are special pleading. Just because one believes that Christ died for all does not mean all are saved," or that one believes in universalism. All Christian theologians agree that a person must have faith in Jesus to be saved, "so the fact that Christ died for the world apparently does not secure the salvation of all. Paul had no trouble saying that God could be the Savior of all, in one sense, and of those who believe, in another. . . . (1 Tim. 4:10)." To argue that the death of Christ was intended to be for everyone because Scripture surely teaches this and that each person must accept this free gift in no way logically leads to universalism. (See the answers to arguments 2 and 4 above in "Arguments for Limited Atonement.")

5. God is fair only on the view of unlimited atonement

"God is not unfair in condemning those who reject the offer of salvation. He is not exacting judgment twice. Because the nonbeliever refuses to accept the death of Christ as his own, the benefits of Christ's death are not applied to him." The unbeliever is condemned, "not because Christ did not die for him (nor because Christ's death is somehow not enough), but because he refuses God's offer of forgiveness." (See the answers to argument 3 above in Arguments for Limited Atonement.)

Further, what does the reasoning that Christ died only for the elect, that Christ paid for the sins of the elect and the lost pay for their own sins, and that God must give this select few even the ability to believe (i.e., faith) and the ability to be sorry (i.e., repentance) really say about the "Being" so represented? Certainly, this "God" would either be (1) grossly unfair because he chose "before the foundations of the world" some to be saved and some to be damned, therefore never really giving anyone a chance, or (2) a respecter of persons because he chose some and not others, or at least (3) very arbitrary in his choosing, because we are never told on what basis he chooses. It certainly could not be on the basis that some are less guilty than others, or he would, again, be a respecter of individual people, and their actions would make a difference. (And if individual people and their actions can make a difference, then surely responding to the free offer, believing on Christ, and truly repenting of sins are the factors that make individual salvation "fair" to God and for men.) Or, (4) he is very limited in his power because he cannot create truly free creatures. He is not powerful enough to create people really in his own image, as the Bible says he did.

But none of these are true of God as represented in the

Scripture. The "god" spoken of above surely would not be worthy
of worship and certainly would not be the Christian God. In what
sense can it be said that "The Lord [God] is not slow in keeping
his promise, as some understand slowness. He is patient with
you, *not wanting anyone to perish, but everyone to come to repentance*"
(2 Peter 3:9), if Christ did not die for all? Again, in 1 Timothy 2:4,
we are told that God "wants *all men to be saved* and to come to a
knowledge of the truth" (emphasis added).

6. Christ did not die only for the elect

"It is true that the benefits of Christ's death are referred to as
belonging to the elect, his sheep, his people, but it would have to
be shown that Christ died *only* for them." Yet as has been seen,
the Scripture teaches exactly the opposite—i.e., that Christ died
for all men. No Christian denies that Christ died for the church or
for his sheep. It is only denied that Christ died exclusively for
them. As we have seen above in the answer to the first of the
"Arguments for Limited Atonement," it does not follow, logically
or necessarily, from these verses that others are excluded from the
effect of Christ's death.

7. Jesus died for sinners, not just for the elect

"The Bible teaches that Christ died for 'sinners' (Rom. 5:6–8;
1 Tim. 1:15). The word 'sinner' nowhere means 'church' or 'the
elect,' but simply all of lost mankind."

> Are we to suppose that the elect are the only ones who labor
> and are heavy laden and that they are thus the only ones to
> whom the invitation of Jesus is issued (Matt. 11:28) or that the
> elect are the only ones who are invited to take the water of life
> without price (Rev. 22:17)? Do not these invitations [made to all
> sinners] presuppose that the free response of man, though not
> meriting salvation, is nevertheless the condition upon which
> the benefits of the atonement are dispensed? Moreover, there
> are clear assertions in Scripture that Christ died for all (II Cor.
> 5:14), that he gave himself a ransom for all (I Tim. 2:6), that he is
> the expiation of the sins of the whole world (I John 2:2; cf. also I
> Tim. 4:10; Tit. 2:11), and that he tasted death for every man
> (Heb. 2:9).[33]

In 1 John 2:2 we read, "He is the atoning sacrifice for our sins,
and not only for ours but also for the sins of the whole world."
How could it be put any plainer! The contrast here is clear. Jesus *is*
the "atoning sacrifice" for the sins of the church, but "not only for
ours": Jesus paid the price of sin for all people. John Owen's
dogmatic polemic simply will not do here.[34] As Douty points out
so clearly, quoting in part from Alvah Hovey:

[Hovey] presents three reasons why the expression "the whole world" must here signify all mankind: first, because *world*, "used of men, naturally includes all, unless its meaning is, in some way, restricted;" secondly, because "our" and "world" are here contrasted—"the one referring to Christians, and the other to all men;" and thirdly, "because the adjective *whole* is manifestly emphatic." I [Douty] would add a fourth reason, namely, because the same expression, "the whole world," is used in ch. 5:19 ("the whole world lieth in the evil one") to denote all unsaved persons. Thus the Apostle declares that Christ is the propitiation for all mankind. But faith is necessary to enter into the good of this gracious provision.[35]

Douty goes on to say that every Greek lexicon he has consulted lists 1 John 2:2 as "denoting mankind: Robinson, Grimm-Thayer, Arndt-Gingrich and Kittel."[36]

8. God's offer extends to all

"God sincerely offers the gospel to everyone to believe, not just the elect. How could this be true if Christ did not actually die for everyone? God would know very well that some people could never be saved because he did not allow Christ to pay for their sins."

J. I. Packer tries to argue that even though it is a limited atonement, God's invitation is still given to all people:

These invitations are *universal*; Christ addresses them to sinners, as such, and every man, as he believes God to be true, is bound to treat them as God's words to him personally and to accept the universal assurance which accompanies them, that all who come to Christ will be received. Again, these invitations are *real*; Christ genuinely offers Himself to all who hear the gospel, and is in truth a perfect Saviour to all who trust Him. The question of the extent of the atonement does not arise in evangelistic preaching. . . . [37]

What incredible double talk! What possible sense can this statement make? Who is the "every man, as he believes God to be true"?

Certainly Packer has not forgotten how he defined points 1 and 2 of the five points of Calvinism:

Fallen man in his natural state *lacks all power to believe the gospel*. . . despite all external inducements that may be extended to him. . . . God's election is a free, sovereign, unconditional choice of sinners, as sinners, to be redeemed by Christ, *given faith* and brought to glory (emphasis added).[38]

Packer has not forgotten, according to his theology, that man is so lost, so wretched, that God has to give him the power even to

believe or repent. Then by what possible logic does it make sense
to say that the "invitations are *universal*" or that "the question of
the extent of the atonement does not arise in evangelistic
preaching." This is ridiculous! Of course it does. For, according to
Packer's theology, the same sinner—whether he hears the
preaching or not—is still predestined to be saved or to be
damned, and *nothing*, no "external inducements," can change
that.

Of course the case for limited atonement is not so certain and
the evidence for the alternative position is not so totally lacking as
extreme dogmatic Calvinists like Packer, and others, would have
us think. Even Louis Berkhof, a Calvinist scholar and staunch
defender of limited atonement, willingly admits, "It need not be
denied that there is a real difficulty at this point," in regard to
what he calls "a bona fide calling." He goes on to say:

> . . . it should be borne in mind that God does not offer sinners
> the forgiveness of sins and eternal life unconditionally, but only
> in the way of faith and conversion; and that the righteousness
> of Christ, though not intended for all, is yet sufficient for all.[39]

Of course, "the forgiveness of sins and eternal life" are not offered
unconditionally.

The question is, What is the nature of God and the nature of
man as created in God's image? Does the Bible teach that Jesus
died for the sins of mankind? Does the Bible teach that man,
created in God's image, can [i.e., is free to] and must respond to
God's free gracious offer of salvation? I answer that the Scriptures
clearly teach that Jesus died for the sins of all people, and man can
and must respond to the free offer of salvation. Any other position
is (1) *logically contradictory* to the clear teaching of Scripture; (2)
theologically repugnant, for it misunderstands the nature of God and
of man; and (3) *philosophically deficient*, for as Thompson has said
so very well:

> That man is free we may be confident, as confident as we are
> that man is capable of knowing. For unless man is free, capable
> of some kind of genuine creative act, then he cannot know. He
> can only react, and his supposed awareness that he can react is
> only another reaction, and so on endlessly . . . "Determinism is
> not, and never was, a working philosophy of life. One can
> conceivably die by it; no one ever consistently lived by it. If
> people would reflect more simply and sincerely on their actual
> experience of living they would be less vulnerable to a great
> deal of academic nonsense, and philosophy would be the
> gainer. In essence determinism [philosophical or theological] is
> one of those theories which, as Professor Broad said of
> behaviorism, "are so preposterously silly that only very learned
> men could have thought of them." Whether or not we are in
> fact free is a question only for those who wish to play games

with concepts. Once we see what the question is we see that the very possibility of considering it *as a question to which true or false answers may be given* presupposes the fact of freedom.[40]

And if man is free because he is created in God's image and even the fall did not erase that, then he certainly can respond to the love of God.

J. I. PACKER'S "INTRODUCTORY ESSAY"

Although some comments have already been made about Packer's famous "Introductory Essay" to John Owen's *The Death of Death in the Death of Christ*, perhaps now we should look to the essay itself.[41] The content and structure of J. I. Packer's essay prompt me to say that it is the finest piece of polemics mixed with little argument I have ever read. Packer's essay amounts to no less a polemic, in the negative sense, than Owen's own book, which it introduces. Packer starts his essay by saying of Owen's book:

> [It] is a polemical work, designed to show . . . that the doctrine of universal redemption is unscriptural and destructive of the gospel. There are many, therefore, to whom it is not likely to be of interest. Those who see no need for doctrinal exactness and have no time for theological debates which show up divisions between so-called Evangelicals may well regret its reappearance. Some may find the very sound of Owen's thesis so shocking that they will refuse to read his book at all; so passionate a thing is prejudice, and so proud are we of our theological shibboleths. [p. 1]

Packer goes on to equate his and Owen's position with the biblical gospel. He calls his position the "old gospel." He says:

> The new gospel conspicuously fails to produce deep reverence, deep repentance, deep humility, a spirit of worship, a concern for the church. Why? We would suggest that the reason lies in its own character and content. It fails to make men God-centered in their thoughts and God-fearing in their hearts. . . . One way of stating the difference between it and the old gospel is to say that it is too exclusively concerned to be "helpful" to man—to bring peace, comfort, happiness, satisfaction—and too little concerned to glorify God. The old gospel['s] . . . first concern was always to give glory to God. [pp. 1–2]

Packer further says this new gospel is "a half-truth masquerading as the whole truth [which] becomes a complete untruth." [p. 2]

Well, what is this new gospel, this heresy that is "masquerading as the . . . truth"? It is the idea that the atonement was unlimited, an idea that Packer equates with the heresy of Arminianism. But [as we have seen earlier in this chapter], many moderate Calvinists hold to an unlimited atonement, as it seems

Calvin himself did. Certainly (again, as we have seen) this was the position of most theologians from the very early days of the church.

One is tempted to say immediately, "Professor Packer, it seems that you protest too strongly. If there is such clear evidence that so many teachers of the church, perhaps even Jesus and Paul, as well as many from at least the second century down through church history, felt the Bible taught a universal atonement, then how can you say so dogmatically that your position is synonymous with the 'old gospel'? And if a 'half-truth masquerading as the truth becomes a complete untruth,' does not this apply to your claim as well?"

So what exactly are Packer's problems with this so-called new gospel? It rejects "the themes of man's natural inability to believe, of God's free election being the ultimate cause of salvation, and of Christ dying specifically for His sheep." These "are not preached." [p. 2] But aren't these claims exactly what is at issue? Take each "theme" as such: (1) "Man's natural inability to believe," (it has been shown) is not taught, at least in Ephesians 2:8, and (I would argue) not in the rest of Scripture either. (2) Concerning "God's free election being the ultimate cause of salvation," there is some great misunderstanding of the so-called Arminian position. God's free election *is* the ultimate cause of salvation! The question is who is elect? And does the fact that man can respond to God's offer make God less sovereign or Christ's death less necessary? The answer is (as we have seen): clearly not! (3) Yes, the Bible teaches that Christ died for his sheep, but there is no grammatical or logical reason why this means that he did not die for others as well.

Later Packer says in regard to the Remonstrance and the Arminian position:

> The theology which it contained . . . stemmed from two philosophical principles: first, that divine sovereignty is not compatible with human freedom, nor therefore with human responsibility. . . . [p. 3][42]

I have argued repeatedly above that divine sovereignty *is* compatible with human freedom. In fact, a strong case can be made that divine sovereignty and human freedom are analogical aspects of the relationship of God to man, of Creator to that which was created in his image. On the other hand, it is extreme Calvinism that teaches that the sovereignty of God is not compatible with human freedom. Some doctrine of human freedom is essential, both philosophically and theologically, to any meaningful theory of human responsibility!

At any rate, Packer goes on to say:

From these principles, the Arminians draw two deductions:
first, that since the Bible regards faith as a free and responsible
human act, it cannot be caused by God, but is exercised
independently of Him; second, that since the Bible regards faith
as obligatory on the part of all who hear the gospel, ability to
believe must be universal. [p. 3]

I have tried to show above the idea that divine sovereignty and
human freedom, and responsibility, are the clear teaching of the
Bible, theologically undeniable because of the nature and character
of God and his relationship to man, and philosophically necessary
as is seen in any clear analysis of thought or reason. It is certainly
true that Arminians drew the two conclusions stated by Packer.
They drew these conclusions *because of the clear teaching of the Bible*
that (1) faith is a free and responsible human act and (2) faith is
taught to be obligatory on the part of the hearer. If, and I only say
"if" for sake of argument, these two things are taught by the
Scripture (as clearly they are), then Packer's last statement,
"ability to believe must be universal" is logically undeniable.

After Packer summarizes the five points of Calvinism, he goes
on to say, "The difference between them is not primarily one of
emphasis, but of content. One [Calvinism] proclaims a God who
saves; the other [Arminianism] speaks of a God who enables man
to save himself." [p. 4] Again, this is simply not true! I certainly
do not believe, nor does any Arminian I know, believe that man
saves himself. There is absolutely no reason to draw from a belief
in divine sovereignty that truly honors God as so great, so
absolute, that he can create in the free and responsible beings
made in his image any notion that man saves himself.

Packer goes on to say:

In the first place, Calvinism is something much broader than
the "five points" indicate. Calvinism is a whole world-view,
stemming from a clear vision of God as the whole world's
Maker and King. Calvinism is the consistent endeavour to
acknowledge the Creator as the Lord, working all things after
the counsel of His will. Calvinism is a theocentric way of
thinking about all life under the direction and control of God's
own Word. Calvinism, in other words, is the theology of the
Bible viewed from the perspective of the Bible—the God-
centered outlook which sees the Creator as the source, and
means, and end, of everything that is, both in nature and in
grace. Calvinism is thus theism (belief in God as the ground of
all things), religion (dependence on God as the given of all
things), and evangelicalism (trust in God through Christ for all
things), all in their purest and most highly developed form.
[p. 5]

This is a clear example of a simple assertion, which in logic
amounts to nothing more than the fallacy of *petitio principii*

(begging the question).[43] At best this is a rather naïve statement that simply, ipso facto, equates Calvinism with the gospel: Calvinism, we are told, equals "The Gospel"! The gospel equals Calvinism! Actually, this is exactly what is at question here. Every time Packer uses the word *Calvinism* one could simply replace it with almost any other type of Christian theology that claims to be biblical and he would have the same result. In fact, if we take the word *Calvinism* out of Packer's statement and replaced it with the word *Arminianism*, I do not know of a single Arminian who would disagree with a single statement.

From this point we get little more than the same as Packer tries to assert the five points of Calvinism. We are told that "the Calvinist is the Christian who confesses before men in his theology just what he believes in his heart before God when he prays," and "Calvinism is what the Christian church has always held and taught when its mind has not been distracted by controversy and false traditions from attending to what Scripture actually says. . . . " [p. 10][44]

One last comment of interest. In the thirty-nine Articles of Faith of the Anglican Church, Article 31 reads: "The offering of Christ, once made, is the perfect redemption, propitiation, and satisfaction for the sins of the whole world, both original and actual."[45] As far as I know, Jim Packer still considers himself an Anglican minister. At any rate, I have had the definite *privilege* of kneeling by his side at services on a Sunday in the Anglican church where he regularly worshiped. One has to wonder how Article 31 squares with the doctrine of a limited atonement?

CALVIN ON THE ATONEMENT

What was the position of the great "patron saint" of Calvinism, John Calvin (1509–1564), on the atonement?[46] Without question Calvin was a great biblical expositor. His commentaries on the Bible are rich with important material for us yet today. It is also frequently said that some of John Calvin's statements have been an embarrassment to "Calvinists" for more than three hundred years. I had a Calvinist professor [he was quite proud that he was a solid "five pointer"] in seminary who used to quip that "Calvin wouldn't accept all of the five points of Calvinism." The professor was undoubtedly correct.

We have already seen (in argument no. 8 of the "Arguments for Limited Atonement") that on Romans 5:18 Calvin said, "Christ suffered for the sins of the whole world." Calvin held that this verse taught a general redemption. Elwell says that "even Calvin in some of his commentaries" defends "general redemption" or an unlimited atonement:

For example Calvin says regarding Col. 1:14, "This redemption was procured through the blood of Christ, for by the sacrifice of his death, all the sins of the world have been expiated"; and on Mark 14:24, *"which is shed for many.* By the word "many" he means not a part of the world only, but the whole human race."[47]

Clear references in Calvin show that he interpreted these passages to teach that Christ died for the "whole human race." Other Scriptures, also were seen by Calvin to teach that Christ suffered for the sins of the world. Of John 1:29 he says:

> And when he says *the sin OF THE WORLD, he extends this favour indiscriminately to the whole human race,* that the Jews might not think that he had been sent to them alone. But hence we infer that the whole *world* is involved in the same condemnation; and that as all men without exception are guilty of unrighteousness before God, they need to be reconciled to him. John the Baptist, therefore, by speaking generally *of the sin of the world,* intended to impress upon us the conviction of our own misery and exhort us to seek the remedy [emphasis added].[48]

And again in his comments on Galatians 5:12 he writes:

> *Would that they were even cut off.* His indignation proceeds still farther, and he prays for destruction on the imposters by whom the Galatians had been deceived. The word "cut off" appears to be employed in allusion to the circumcision which they pressed. "They tear the Church for the sake of circumcision: wish they were cut entirely off." Chrysostom favours this opinion. But how can such an imprecation be reconciled with the mildness of an apostle, *who ought to wish that all should be saved and therefore that not one should perish.* So far as men are concerned, I admit the force of this argument; *for it is the will of God that we should seek the salvation of all men without exception, as Christ suffered for the sins of the whole world* [emphasis added].[49]

Thus it is quite clear that Calvin repeatedly saw the atonement of Christ as for the sins of the whole human race, the entire world (see also Calvin in *Institutes* 3.1.1; *Eternal Predestination of God,* 9.5 and commentaries on Isa. 53:12; Rom. 5:15; Col. 1:15).

While it is clear that Calvin thought the atonement was limited in *effect* (only some men, the elect, will be saved: see his comments in *Institutes* 3.1.1, 3.24.17; *The Mystery of Godliness,* p. 83; and in his commentaries on Hebrews 4:9; 1 John 2:2), it is also clear that he saw that in principle no people were barred from salvation:

> He had commanded Timothy that prayers should be regularly offered up in the church for kings and princes; but as it seemed somewhat absurd that prayer should be offered up for a class of men who were almost hopeless (all of them being not only

aliens from the body of Christ, but doing their utmost to
overthrow his kingdom), he adds, that it was acceptable to God,
who will have all men to be saved. *By this he assuredly means
nothing more than that the way of salvation was not shut against any
order of men; that, on the contrary, he had manifested his mercy in
such a way, that he would have none debarred from it* (emphasis
added).[50]

Quite a strong statement! For Calvin, unbelief was the reason that
some people do not receive the benefits of Christ's atonement:

To bear, or, take away sins, is to free from guilt by his
satisfaction those who have sinned. He says the sins of *many,
that is, of all,* as in Rom. v.15. It is yet certain that all receive no
benefit from the death of Christ; *but this happens, because their
unbelief prevents them* (emphasis added).[51]

See also Calvin's comment on John 12:46.

Donald M. Lake, in discussing whether Calvin held to a
limited atonement, says:

What is important . . . is the fact that the issue of *limited
atonement* does not appear in Calvin, but belongs to second
generation Calvinists. Yet, it must be emphasized that Calvin
himself lays little stress, if any, upon the universal significance
of the atonement. Where the subject does come to light in his
Institutes is in Book III where he responds to criticisms about his
view of God's sovereignty. But it must be emphasized that the
question of the extent of Christ's redemptive grace had received
no real examination by Calvin. For him the question is rather:
does God will to save all men? That is a question of election, not
of the atonement. This fact is all the more surprising, since
Calvin is one of the Church's greatest exegetical theologians.[52]

The evidence is quite strong. Calvin did not teach that the
Scriptures taught a limited atonement! Thus Calvinists who hold
to the doctrine of the limited atonement must go elsewhere to
support their position.

CONCLUSIONS

As Walter A. Elwell admits:

Both points of view are trying to preserve something of
theological importance. The defenders of limited atonement are
stressing the certainty of God's salvation and the initiative he
took in offering it to man. . . . The defenders of general
redemption are attempting to preserve the fairness of God and
what to them is the clear teaching of Scripture. Salvation is no
less certain because Christ died for all.[53]

While I do not deny that the Calvinists think they are preserving
"the certainty of God's salvation" and God's "initiative . . . in

offering it to man," I do not know any Arminian who is not defending the same. It does, however, seem quite impossible to preserve "the fairness of God" and "the clear teaching of Scripture" if one holds to a limited atonement.

Elwell simply *ends his essay* by quoting E. A. Litton's attempt to "mediate the two views":

> And thus the combatants may not be in reality so much at variance as they had supposed. The most extreme Calvinist may grant that there is room for all if they will come in; the most extreme Arminian must grant that redemption, in its full Scriptural meaning, is not the privilege of all men.[54]

This is a most naïve statement! If nothing else, 369 years have shown this rather conclusively. In my experience "the most extreme Calvinist" will not, cannot if he is true to his theology, grant that there is room for all if they will come in." For this is exactly what people cannot do—i.e., come in. They *must* be brought in. They have no choice, nor do the ones who will *not be brought in* have a choice! The Arminian, on the other hand, would never have a problem with the *fact* that "redemption . . . is not the privilege of all men," for they freely acknowledge that the Scriptures teach that not all *will* be saved.

No, the differences are quite major! They are really the most severe differences possible (J. I. Packer is quite right about this) philosophically, perhaps ultimately also psychologically, about the nature of God, the nature of man, the teaching of Scripture, and (many times) man's responsibility to his fellow man. While I would not want to make light of these important differences, I do not want to make more of them than I should. In some sense this *is*, for the most part, an "in-house" fight *between members of the same family*. I am certainly more than willing to grant that "fire breathing" five-point Calvinists are my brothers in Christ. I can only hope that they will extend me the same acknowledgment (though I must add I have often found this not to be the case.) I would much rather sit down with Calvinists, begin with prayer, and then start discussing our family differences in an attitude of peace, love, and respect than fighting hand to hand or across the field of battle. I would much rather start with what we agree on and work toward the points on which we disagree.

Finally, what then of the atonement: is it "limited or unlimited"? I think it is impossible to explain away the clear teaching of Scripture. As Millard J. Erickson so aptly says:

> We find that some of the verses which teach a universal atonement simply cannot be ignored. Among the most impressive is I Timothy 4:10, which affirms that the living God "is the Savior of all men, especially of those who believe." Apparently the Savior has done something for all persons, though it is less

in degree than what he has done for those who believe. Among the other texts which argue for the universality of Christ's saving work and cannot be ignored are I John 2:2 and Isaiah 53:6. In addition, we must consider statements like 2 Peter 2:1, which affirms that some for whom Christ died do perish.[55]

If Christ died for all men, "there is no problem in asserting that he died for a specific part of the whole." To make passages that say he died for "his sheep," "his people," etc., "normative or determinative" is a *clear* contradiction of the *clearly* universal passages and is logically incorrect. Erickson goes on to say, "We conclude that the hypothesis of universal atonement is able to account for a larger segment of the biblical witness with less distortion than is the hypothesis of limited atonement."[56]

The Scriptures clearly teach that Jesus died for the sins of all people, and man can—and must—respond to the free offer of salvation. First, the doctrine of limited atonement is *logically contradictory* to the clear teaching of passage after passage of Scripture—e.g., those mentioned throughout this chapter, specifically in the paragraph above. Second, it is *theologically repugnant*, for it misunderstands the nature of God and of man. The divine sovereignty of God and human freedom are analogical aspects of the relationship of God to man—of the Creator to that which was created in his image. Third, it is *philosophically deficient*, for the very existence of reason, or the ability to know, shows that man is capable of choice. Some doctrine of human freedom is essential to any meaningful theory of human responsibility.

NOTES

[1]Millard J. Erickson, *Christian Theology*, vol. 2 (Grand Rapids: Baker, 1984), 781.

[2]John 3:16 is often referred to, and rightly so, as "the Gospel in miniature."

[3]Leon Morris, "Atonement" in *Evangelical Dictionary of Theology*, ed. Walter A. Elwell (Grand Rapids: Baker, 1984), 97.

[4]Donald M. Lake, "He Died for All: The Universal Dimensions of the Atonement," in Clark H. Pinnock ed., *Grace Unlimited* (Minneapolis: Bethany, 1975), 31.

[5]For a more complete discussion of the historic theories of the atonement see: Erickson, *Christian Theology*, 781–800; Archibald A. Hodge, *The Atonement* (Philadelphia: Presbyterian Board of Publication, 1867), 440 pages; Laurence W. Grensted, *The Atonement in History and in Life* (London: Society for Promoting Christian Knowledge, 1929), 340 pages; idem, *A Short History of the Doctrine of the Atonement* (London: Longmans, Green, 1920), 376 pages; and Robert Mackintosh, *Historic Theories of Atonement: With Comments* (London: Hodder and Stoughton, 1920), 319 pages.

[6]Erickson, *Christian Theology*, 801–23.

[7]Erickson, *Christian Theology*, 825, says that in regard to the extent of the atonement there are two issues. I have been addressing the first, the "classical,"

issue in this chapter. "The second is an issue that has attained some prominence in the twentieth century—namely, for what did Christ die? Was the purpose of his death solely to deliver us from our sins, from spiritual evils? Or did he die to deliver us from sickness as well? That is, did he die to remove physical as well as spiritual evils?"

8For a more complete treatment of the idea of (1) **limited** atonement, see Rienk B. Kuiper, *For Whom Did Christ Die?* (Grand Rapids: Eerdmans, 1959); John Owen, *Death of Death in the Death of Christ: A Treatise in Which the Whole Controversy About Universal Redemption Is Fully Discussed,* with a foreword by J. I. Packer (London: Banner of Truth, 1959), 312 pages; (2) **unlimited** atonement, see Norman F. Douty, *The Death of Christ: Did Christ Die Only for the Elect?* (Irving, Texas: William & Watrous, 1978), 180 pages; Robert P. Lightner, *The Death Christ Died: A Case for Unlimited Atonement* (Des Plains, Ill.: Regular Baptist Press, 1967), 151 pages.

9Lake, "He Died for All."

10J. I. Packer in his "Introductory Essay" to John Owen's book, *Death of Death,* 4, summarizes the five points as follows: (1) Fallen man in his natural state lacks all power to believe the gospel, just as he lacks all power to believe the law, despite all external inducements that maybe extended to him (this is known as Total depravity). (2) God's election is a free, sovereign, unconditional choice of sinners, as sinners, to be redeemed by Christ, given faith and brought to glory (Unconditional election). (3) The redeeming work of Christ had as its end and goal the salvation of the elect (Limited atonement). (4) The work of the Holy Spirit in bringing people to faith never fails to achieve its object (Irresistible grace). (5) Believers are kept in faith and grace by the unconquerable power of God till they come to glory (Preservation of the saints).

11See, for instance, Douty, *Death of Christ.* Douty who accepts the other four of the five points, but very strongly believes that the Bible does not teach a limited atonement. Also Calvinists Moise Amyraut, Richard Baxter, John Bunyan, John Newton, John Brown, and many others accepted a generalism called hypothetical universalism.

12Numerous arguments are used to defend the idea of a limited atonement, but some of the more frequently used are recorded in Walter A. Elwell's, "Atonement, Extent of the," in *Evangelical Dictionary of Theology* (Grand Rapids: Baker, 1984), 98–100. I will use the eight arguments for and the eight arguments against limited atonement that are listed in this introductory essay (by a first-rate conservative Presbyterian scholar) and expand on each.

13Jack Cottrell, *Basic Theology Syllabus,* 65.

14Douty, *Death of Christ,* 92.

15Samuel M. Thompson, *A Modern Philosophy of Religion* (Chicago: Regnery, 1955), 503.

16Terry L. Miethe, *A Christian's Guide to Faith and Reason* (Minneapolis: Bethany, 1987), chap. 4.

17Terry L. Miethe, *The Metaphysics of Leonard James Eslick: His Philosophy of God* (Ann Arbor: University Microfilms, 1976), 171.

18This seems to be the position that Jonathan Edwards is left with, in spite of all his protestations to the contrary, in his *Freedom of the Will,* ed. Paul Ramsey (New Haven: Yale University Press, 1957), 404–5. Specifically Edwards states, "On the whole, it is manifest, that God may be . . . the order and disposer of that event [sin], which in the inherent subject and agent is moral evil; and yet his so doing may be no moral evil. He may will the disposal of such an event, and its coming to pass for good ends, and his will not be an immoral or sinful will, but a perfectly holy will" (p. 406).

19Cottrell, *Basic Theological Syllabus,* 65.

20Douty, *Death of Christ,* 106; see through 110.

21Ibid., 41–45.

22John Calvin, *Commentary on Romans* (Grand Rapids: Baker, 1979), 211. See Douty, *Death of Christ,* 90–91; Lake, "He Died for All," 32–33.

23 Lake, "He Died for All," 32–33; C. K. Barrett, *Harpers New Testament Commentaries: The Epistle to the Romans* (New York: Harper & Row, 1957), 114; the *Interpreter's Bible*, 9:466; and the *New International Dictionary of New Testament Theology*, 1:94ff.

24 As we will see in his "Introductory Essay," J. I. Packer continually makes the mistaken claim that the doctrine of limited atonement is synonymous with the "old gospel" and that the doctrine of the unlimited atonement is a new heresy brought about by Arminianism. See Packer, "Introductory Essay," 2ff.

25 Of Augustine (354–430), Douty, *Death of Christ*, 137–38, says, "I am aware that Owen and Smeaton claim the Bishop of Hippo as an advocate of Particular Redemption, but I submit that Davenant, who was deeply versed in the Fathers, demonstrates that he [Augustine] sometimes advocated the opposite view. In a part of his exposition of Ps. 95, which is quoted by Smeaton himself, Augustine says: "The Redeemer came and gave the price, shed His blood, and bought the world. Do you ask what He bought? See what He gave, and find what He bought. The blood of Christ is the price: what is of so great worth? What, but the whole world? What, but all nations?" Is this the doctrine of Particular Redemption? No, indeed. In his tractate no. 92 on John's Gospel, he [Augustine] says: "The blood of Christ was shed for the remission of all sins."

26 Elwell, "Atonement," 99.

27 Douty, *Death of Christ*, 136–63. Douty lists "over 70 of the Church's leading teachers—from the early centuries to the present one."

28 Ibid, 142–43.

29 Ibid., 72–73.

30 Calvin, *Commentary on the First Epistle to Timothy*, (Grand Rapids: Baker, 1979), 50.

31 F. F. Bruce, *Answers to Questions* (Grand Rapids: Zondervan, 1972), 197.

32 Erickson, *Christian Theology*, 830.

33 Robert H. Culpepper, *Interpreting the Atonement* (Grand Rapids: Eerdmans, 1966), 125.

34 Owen, *Death of Death*, 219–20; see also Douty, *Death of Christ*, 122–23.

35 Alvah Hovey, *Manual of Systematic Theology* (Boston, 1877), 228–29; Douty, *Death of Christ*, 125.

36 Douty, *Death of Christ*, has a rather interesting observation in regard to "B. B. Warfield's rather pretentious explanation" of 1 John 2 (Benjamin B. Warfield, *Shorter Writings* [Nutley, N.J.: Presbyterian and Reformed, 1970] vol. 1, chap. 23): "Here the former president of Princeton Seminary puts forth an altogether novel view of John's words, but with all the assurance in the world. Even a great scholar is not warranted in advancing an interpretation never heard of without some diffidence. He tells us that the Apostle was not an 'each and every' universalist (that Christ is the propitiation for the sins of all human beings), but that he was an 'eschatological' universalist (that, in the end, Christ will have a saved world to present to the Father, when the Gospel shall have subdued it)."

37 Packer, "Introductory Essay," 18–19.

38 Ibid., 4.

39 Louis Berkhof, *Systematic Theology* (Grand Rapids: Eerdmans, 1941), 462.

40 Thompson, *Modern Philosophy of Religion*, 178–79; Miethe, *Christian's Guide*, chap. 4.

41 At the beginning, I want to make it clear that I consider Jim Packer to be one of the *very finest Christian gentlemen* I have ever had the privilege of meeting or of kneeling beside in worship! I have nothing but the highest regard for Dr. Packer. He has contributed an essay to a volume I edited: *Did Jesus Rise From the Dead: The Resurrection Debate* (San Francisco: Harper & Row, 1987), 143–50. (This was the seminal debate primarily between Gary Habermas and Antony Flew.)

I also want to give Prof. Packer the benefit of the doubt. His "Introductory Essay" was written in 1958. While I have no reason to doubt that he still holds as strongly to the doctrine of a limited atonement, I certainly hope that he has softened the dogmatism of his polemic regarding it. Certainly there are very fine Christians on both sides of this argument and there are passages from Scripture that seem to teach both positions.

42 I have read this statement of Jim Packer on page 3 several times. It is difficult for me to believe that Packer intended to say this. He is usually quite careful in regard to historical statement. I seriously doubt that the Remonstrance teaches that "divine sovereignty is *not* compatible with human freedom." And certainly this is not part of any historic Arminian position I have ever known. As I have said, just the opposite is true.

43 Irving M. Copi, *Introduction to Logic*, 7the ed. (New York: Macmillan, 1986), 89, says, "Logicians use the term [fallacy] in the narrower sense of an error in reasoning or in argument"; and on page 101: "In attempting to establish the truth of a proposition, one often cases about for acceptable premises from which the proposition in question can be inferred as conclusion. If one assumes as a premise for an argument the very conclusion it is intended to prove, the fallacy committed is that of *petitio principii*, or begging the question."

44 I realize I have really only covered five of the twenty-five pages of Packer's "Introductory Essay" in any sort of thorough way. I have addressed some other pages in my arguments earlier in the chapter. I was asked by my editor and publisher to "address" Packer's introduction and perhaps I have spent too much time on it now. A fuller treatment would certainly continue to show the same, and more, inconsistencies in his essay.

45 Douty, *Death of Christ*, 174–45 also quotes the following from the Anglican Church:

"The Order for the Administration of the Lord's Supper or Holy Communion," which is to be read every Sunday in the Church of England, speaks of Christ's "one oblation of Himself once offered," as being "a full, perfect, and sufficient sacrifice, oblation, and satisfaction, for the sins of the whole world." In the General Thanksgiving we read, "We bless Thee for our creation, preservation, and all the blessings of this life; but, above all, for Thine inestimable love in the redemption of the world by our Lord Jesus Christ." Also in the "Catechism," the question is asked, "What dost thou chiefly learn in these Articles of thy Belief?" and the answer given is "First, I learn to believe in God the Father, Who hath made me, and all the world. Secondly, in God the Son, Who hath redeemed me, and all mankind. Thirdly, in God the Holy Spirit, who sanctifieth me, and all the people of God." The circle narrows from "all the world" (the universe) to "all mankind," and then to "all the people of God."

46 It should be stated clearly that the fight over the extent of the atonement and the doctrine of the atonement did not develop historically until *after* the life of John Calvin. Calvin died in 1564; the Remonstrance was not written until 1610, forty-six years after his death, and the Synod of Dort was not convened until 1618. Thus it is really not possible to say exactly how Calvin would have aligned himself on the new systematic argument. I was reminded of this by a fine Calvinist scholar and valued colleague, Lee W. Hähnlen. It is possible, however, to see what Calvin actually said in regard to the texts that are used to support a limited or unlimited atonement. From these texts one can see if Calvin supported the premises that "Christ died for all mankind" or not.

47 Elwell, "Atonement," 99. For the original source see John Calvin *Commentary on the Epistle to the Colossians* (Grand Rapids: Baker, 1979), 148; *Commentary on a Harmony of the Evangelists* (Grand Rapids: Baker, 1979); 3:214.

48 John Calvin, *Commentary on the Gospel According to John* (Grand Rapids: Baker, 1979), 64–65.

49 John Calvin, *Commentaries on the Epistles of Paul to the Galatians and Ephesians* (Grand Rapids: Baker, 1979).

50 John Calvin, *The Institutes of the Christian Religion*, Library of Christian Classics. Translated by Ford Lewis Battles. Edited by John T. McNeill. 2 vols. (Philadelphia: Westminster, 1960), 3.24.16.

[51] John Calvin, *Commentary on the Epistle of Paul the Apostle to the Hebrews* (Grand Rapids: Baker, 1979), 220.

[52] Lake, "He Died for All," 33.

[53] Elwell, "Atonement," 99–100.

[54] Edward A. Litton, *Introduction to Dogmatic Theology,* new ed., ed. Phillip E. Hughes (London: James Clarke, 1960), 236.

[55] Erickson, *Christian Theology,* 834.

[56] Ibid., 835.

THE NATURE OF THE DIVINE SOVEREIGNTY

Jack W. Cottrell

Although the doctrine of divine sovereignty is most often associated with Calvinism, it is important to non-Calvinists, too. The disagreement is not over its *significance*, but over its *definition*. The question of the meaning or essence of sovereignty divides these two viewpoints even more decisively than the TULIP doctrines. What is its *sine qua non*? That God must be the ultimate cause or determiner of all things? That he must be in constant and complete control of all things? That he must be free to do whatever he wishes at any time? That he must be able to carry out his plans and purposes without anything thwarting them? That he must be absolutely unlimited in his nature and actions? That all his decisions and deeds must be totally unconditioned by anything outside himself?

The issue is usually stated in terms of the relation between divine sovereignty and human free will. In what sense do human beings have free will or free agency? How do their free decisions and actions relate to divine sovereignty? Do some concepts of free will limit or even negate sovereignty? As Carson puts it, "If God is absolutely sovereign, in what sense can we meaningfully speak of human choice, of human will? . . . Must God be reduced to accommodate the freedom of human choice?"[1]

The specific focus of this chapter is the meaning of divine sovereignty. The purpose is to examine the typically Calvinistic view of sovereignty and to suggest an alternative that is more nearly biblical. My thesis is first that consistent Calvinism has a deterministic view of sovereignty that sees the unconditioned will or decree of God as the only true cause of every event without exception, with the corollary that the human will is not truly free. Although most Calvinists would repudiate determinism and affirm some form of free will, I contend that this is inconsistent with the view of an unconditioned decree, which all Calvinists seem to include in the essence of sovereignty. The other part of my thesis is that true biblical sovereignty includes conditional elements, thus avoiding determinism and allowing for truly free will for human beings.

CALVINISM AND DIVINE SOVEREIGNTY

Within Calvinism the problem of sovereignty and free will is usually addressed on two distinct levels. First, in the context of soteriology, the necessity of sovereign grace is argued from the premise of universal total depravity. The inability of any sinner to respond to the gospel requires the unconditionality of God's sovereignty in the bestowing of salvation. Second, in the context of the doctrine of God (theology proper), sovereignty is posited as a characteristic of all of God's works in reference to creation and to man as such (not just as sinner). Here the issue is to maintain the honor of God by defending the integrity of divine sovereignty against all human claims to self-determination and autonomy. Our concern in this essay is only with this second issue.

Calvinistic discussions of this problem are laced with words like *paradox, antinomy, contradiction,* and *mystery.* As Klooster says, "Divine sovereignty and human responsibility are paradoxical and beyond human comprehension."[2] Despite this rather agnostic attitude, Calvinists have spent much time and energy trying to explain the unexplainable. The rest of this section is an attempt to analyze their efforts in this direction.

Consistent Calvinism

My contention is that consistent Calvinism is a genuine determinism. As John Feinberg observes, "Calvinists are usually deterministic."[3] This determinism is inherent in the doctrine that is the most significant embodiment of divine sovereignty for consistent and inconsistent Calvinists alike, namely, God's eternal decree (purpose, plan, or will).[4] It is called eternal because it was made in eternity past, before the creation and existence of anything outside of God. It is also called comprehensive or universal, embracing "whatsoever comes to pass," as the Westminster Confession of Faith (III:1) says. As Zanchius put it, "All beings whatever, from the highest angel to the meanest reptile, and from the meanest reptile to the minutest atom, are the objects of God's eternal decrees."[5] Toplady affirms concerning the sparrow that God's "all-wise Providence hath before appointed what bough it shall pitch on, what grains it shall pick up, where it shall lodge, and where it shall build; on what it shall live, and when it shall die." Also, God guides the movements of the "motes and atoms wandering up and down in a sun-beam." Indeed, "*not a dust flies in a beaten road but God raiseth it, conducts* its uncertain motion, and by His particular care, *conveys* it to the certain place He had *before appointed* for it" (italics his).[6] The "all-embracing decree," says Boettner, includes everything in the course of nature and "the course of history even down to its minutest details."[7] This includes all human decisions, even sinful ones.

To say that God has an eternal plan that includes "whatsoever comes to pass" is not in itself objectionable. What makes the concept of the decree distinctively Calvinistic and deterministic is the addition of two other qualifiers, namely, that it is both efficacious and unconditional. To say that the decree is efficacious means that whatever happens happens by virtue of the fact that it was included in the decree. It is the effect of "the totally efficacious word of the divine will."[8] Murray speaks of God's "all-pervasive and efficient sovereignty," which "he exercises with omnipotent and irresistible efficiency."[9] Sproul says, "What we mean by the sovereign or efficacious will of God is that determination by which God sovereignly wills something to come to pass which, therefore, indeed does come to pass through the sheer efficacy, force, or power of that will."[10] Thus, in Bavinck's words, "The final answer to the question why a thing is and why it is as it is must ever remain: 'God willed it,' according to his absolute sovereignty."[11] Thus to the degree the decree is said to be efficacious, it is also deterministic.

The other deterministic element in the decree is its unconditionality. This means that nothing in the decree has been conditioned by anything outside of God; God did not include anything in the decree as a response to or reaction to something. "God initiates all things;"[12] what he decrees and does in no way depends upon the creature. "A conditional decree would subvert the sovereignty of God and make him . . . dependent upon the uncontrollable actions of his own creatures," says A. A. Hodge.[13]

When all of these factors are taken together—i.e., when the eternal and comprehensive decree is also said to be efficacious and unconditional—the only possible result is a theistic determinism. Consistent Calvinists acknowledge this and accept its implications, even to the point of denying human free will. They freely affirm with Storms that "human free will is a myth."[14]

Inconsistent Calvinism

Most Calvinists, however, have faltered when it comes to drawing the conclusions consistent with their concept of an efficacious, unconditional decree. They want to deny that God has caused the Fall and other human sins. To this end they also want to defend some concept of free will or free agency. Most eschew the label "determinism," though some accept it while defending a view of free will they feel is compatible with it.

Both Unconditional Decrees and Human Freedom

Those who argue for both determinism and free will are sometimes called compatibilists (after the idea that determinism is *compatible* with free will). An example is John Feinberg, who argues for "a view of freedom which is deterministic in nature." All free human actions, including sin, are "causally determined."[15]

Most Calvinists, however, reject the determinist label while still using its language and sounding quite deterministic. For example, Geisler rejects Feinberg's view as "a strong Calvinistic determinism,"[16] yet himself says that God predetermines all things, even our future free-will choices. He says, for example, that "God *determined* that Judas would *freely* betray Christ." Indeed, "the future can be absolutely determined and yet some events can be totally free."[17] Berkhof says, "Reformed theology stresses the sovereignty of God in virtue of which He has sovereignly determined from all eternity whatsoever will come to pass."[18]

While defending a kind of free will, these Calvinists still ascribe to the divine decree the same attributes characteristic of determinism, namely, unconditionality and efficacy (though the latter is somewhat modified). Charles Hodge affirms that God's decrees are free, meaning they are "in no case conditional"; and they are "certainly efficacious, that is, they render certain the occurrence of what He decrees."[19] Shedd and Berkhof likewise speak of the decree as unconditional and efficacious.[20]

Means of Attempted Harmonization

Now we may ask, How can such Calvinists continue to speak of this kind of sovereign decree while at the same time defending human free will? In their explanations we find at least three concepts or devices used specifically in the effort to reconcile these two ideas.

The first such device is a redefinition of free will in order to make it compatible with a determining decree. One idea rejected by almost every Calvinist is that freedom must include the power of contrary choice, or the ability to choose between options or opposites. Rather, the preferred definition is that freedom is the ability to choose voluntarily and without coercion as influenced by one's desires and inner motivation. In short, a person is free as long as he is able to do what he *wants* to do. Of course, what a person wants to do in any given situation is *determined* by outward circumstances and inner motivations. Feinberg explains that such conditions function as decisive and sufficient causes, inclining the will toward the one and only choice that it will make in that situation. Nevertheless the will is still free since it is not conscious of being caused or compelled to make that choice. The person is only doing what he wants to do, even though he "could not have done otherwise, given the prevailing causal influences."[21]

The key words here are *desire* and *motive*. One is free as long as he is able to choose according to his desires and motives. As Sproul explains it, "To have free will is to be able to choose according to our desires." Our strongest desire at any moment will determine what we choose, but the choice will be free because we will be choosing what we want.[22] But how does this definition of free will enable the Calvinist to maintain his deterministic view of sovereignty? The answer is simple enough: Although I freely make choices in accord with the desires and motives of my heart, it is God who determines what desires and motives will prevail at any given time. His decree includes not only his chosen ends (my specific decisions), but also the necessary means to those ends. "Such means include whatever circumstances and factors are necessary to convince an individual (without constraint) that the act God has decreed is the act she or he wants to do. And, given the sufficient conditions, the person will do the act," says Feinberg.[23] Boettner puts it thus: "God so governs the inward feelings, external environment, habits, desires, motives, etc., of men that they freely do what he purposes."[24]

The second device used by Calvinists to harmonize God's efficacious, unconditional decree with human free will is the idea of second causes. When applied to the acts of moral creatures, it means that every human act has two causes, a primary cause that is God himself and a secondary cause that is the person's own will. These are not two *partial* causes; each cause is *wholly* responsible for an action. As Berkhof says, "Each deed is in its entirety both a deed of God and a deed of the creature."[25]

Since both causes operate simultaneously to produce an act, God remains sovereign in the sense of universal causation, and man is still responsible for the deed. But since God's causation is *primary* and man's only *secondary*, man's will can never operate independently of God but works only as moved by God. "In every instance the impulse to action and movement proceeds from God," who "enables and prompts His rational creatures, as second causes, to function, and that not merely by endowing them with energy in a general way, but by energizing them to certain specific acts."[26]

The third device used by Calvinists to harmonize sovereignty and free will is the concept of divine permission—i.e., God

sovereignly permits man to will and to do certain things. This in
effect modifies the concept of the efficacious decree. Although in
general the decree is efficacious, there is *one* area where it is only
permissive. That one area is sin. God does not efficaciously decree
sin, but only permissively decrees it.

Examples of an appeal to a permissive element in the decree
are abundant. Toplady says, "In His decree God resolved, within
Himself, what He would do and what He would permit to be
done."[27] "The Divine decrees are divided into efficacious and
permissive," says Shedd.[28] It is generally agreed, however, that
the permissive decree is limited only to *sinful* actions. "The
permissive decrees embrace only moral features which are evil,"
says Chafer.[29] In Shedd's words, "The permissive decree relates
only to moral evil. Sin is the sole and solitary object of this species
of decree."[30] In this way God would appear to be relieved of the
actual responsibility for sinful acts.

In this section we are discussing inconsistent Calvinism, or
Calvinists who hold to the notion of an unconditional, efficacious
decree (which logically entails determinism, which logically
excludes free will), but who at the same time defend human free
will. Now that we have explained the ways in which they try to
avoid the logical implications of this kind of decree, another task
yet remains—i.e., to show just *why* this approach is inconsistent
and why all Calvinists must logically embrace determinism to the
exclusion of any significant notion of free will.

Why This View Is Inconsistent

I believe the Calvinistic effort to reconcile sovereignty with
free will must fail as long as the concept of unconditionality is
maintained. No matter how "free will" is redefined and the
efficacy of the decree is qualified, Calvinism is still a theology of
determinism as long as it declares that nothing God does can be
conditioned by man or can be a reaction to something in the
world.

This idea that a sovereign God must always *act* and never *react*
is a point on which almost all Calvinists seem to agree. As Daane
says, "How pervasively this view has penetrated and shaped
Reformed theology! Here is the theological bottom from which has
arisen what is often regarded as the correct Reformed understanding of God's immutability and of sovereignty."[31] Erickson sees the
terms *conditional* and *unconditional* as typifying the contrast between Arminianism and Calvinism. "In the Calvinistic view," he
says, "God's plan is unconditional."[32] In his book defending
"pure" Calvinism, Shedd opposes sovereignty and conditionality.[33] So does John Murray, who also parallels sovereignty and

unconditionality.[34] "God's actions would be unjust if they were responses conditioned by the creature," says Beale.[35]

Reformed theologians agree that the eternal decree is unconditional or absolute. "The decrees of God are in no case conditional," says Charles Hodge flatly.[36] This means they are dependent on nothing outside of God or outside of the decree itself. "Decretal theology" decrees that "God cannot be affected by, nor respond to, anything external to him," says Daane.[37]

One implication of this is that the decree is in no way conditioned by or dependent on God's foreknowledge of future free-will choices or events. It is always the other way around: God's foreknowledge is conditioned on his decree. As Boettner says, God's eternal purpose is "unconditioned by any subsequent fact or change in time. Hence it is represented as being the basis of the divine foreknowledge of all future events, and not conditioned by that foreknowledge or by anything originated by the events themselves."[38] The idea that God makes certain decisions based on his foreknowledge of men's actions "places God in the unworthy position of being dependent upon His creatures," says Chafer.[39]

In short, Calvinists *must* embrace unqualified unconditionality because their concept of sovereignty demands it. A. A. Hodge says it clearly: "A conditional decree would subvert the sovereignty of God."[40] Ness is even more emphatic: "A conditional decree makes a conditional God, and plainly *ungods* Him."[41]

Now, my firm conviction is that this idea of unconditionality completely rules out any meaningful notion of human freedom. Those Calvinists who continue to hold to both are simply inconsistent, and the devices by which they hope to rescue rationality—redefined free will, second causes, and permission—quickly lose their integrity within the confines of unconditionality.

This is especially true of the Calvinist's redefined notion of free will, i.e., that the will is free as long as a person is able to choose voluntarily or to do what he wants to do, as influenced by his motives and desires. But we will remember that Calvinists also say that God is the one who determines the desires and motives that underlie all choices. Hence God determines specific choices by sovereignly determining the situations, motives, and desires that will infallibly cause those choices. Every human decision is exactly as God decreed it would be; it could not be otherwise.

Calvinists call this true freedom. It is, says Feinberg, "a genuine sense of free human action, even though such action is causally determined."[42]

In my judgment, however, the mere ability to act in accord with one's desires is not a sufficient criterion of freedom. This can be demonstrated even in nontheistic contexts, where hypnotic suggestion and brain-washing can determine actions even though in their own consciousness people are doing what they want to do. Thus I agree with Geisler, who says that in reality this view "amounts to a denial of human free choice and, thus, would make God responsible for evil." The view "really reduces to a strong Calvinistic determinism in which we are not actually free at all."[43]

The reason for this confusion again is the idea of unconditionality. Calvinists are rightly concerned to maintain free will, but at the same time they will not allow God to react to anything in man. But these two thoughts are simply incompatible. If man's action is truly free, then God does not cause it but responds to it. If he cannot respond to it, then he must cause it. The latter is the only alternative consistent with an unconditional decree.

Another ambiguity of the unconditional decree is the concept of second causes. It is introduced into the system mainly to provide some plausibility to the idea of free will. The concept is vague, however, even to Calvinists. In answer to the question of the relationship between secondary causality and primary causality, Sproul replies, "I do not know. I have not a clue!" He says he asked the same question of his college professors, of John Gerstner and of G. C. Berkouwer; and they each replied, "I don't know."[44]

I am not surprised at these answers, because in my judgment the Calvinistic idea of second causes is incoherent. In an unconditional, nonreactive decree, the "second cause" is not a true cause. When applied to persons, the term *cause* is meaningful only if the second cause operates *alongside* the first cause, not when it is an *instrument* of the first cause. As an analogy, we may think of a man who tries but fails to move a large rock. He asks someone to help him, and both of them working together move the rock. Each is a genuine cause. But if the man uses a lever instead of his friend to help him move the rock, the lever is not a true second cause but is only an instrument of the real cause of the movement. Despite protestations to the contrary, in an unconditional decree only the latter model can apply. Man is a second cause only in the sense of being an instrument used by God. Such second "causes" are themselves caused by God. They do not operate alongside God even in a secondary role; but rather they operate in sequence (logical if not chronological). The first cause causes the second cause to cause X, as a man causes a lever to move a rock.

Such an analysis seems justified in view of A. A. Hodge's statement that "the foreordination of God does include the free actions" of moral agents, wherein "men and nations are the mere instruments . . . in the hand of God to do his will."[45] Toplady says, "God is the supreme, independent first Cause, of whom all secondary and inferior causes are no more than the effects, else proper originality [i.e., unconditionality] and absolute wisdom, unlimited supremacy and almighty power cease to be attributes of

Deity."[46] Berkhof's thinking is similar: "In every instance the impulse to action and movement proceeds from God. . . . So God also enables and prompts His rational creatures, as second causes, to function, and that not merely by endowing them with energy in a general way, but by energizing them to certain specific acts."[47]

In my judgment the concept of cause has no real significance when used in this sense. In such a system man contributes only what has been predetermined and "fed into him" by the First Cause. Berkouwer speaks of the "interweaving" and "interlacing" of divine and human acts,[48] but this is not a meaningful analogy within an unconditional decree. None of the threads in the pattern really comes from man—not even the sinful ones; they all come from the unconditional decree, some being placed into the pattern directly and some indirectly through man as means. The result, as Miner Raymond notes, is that "the divine will is the sole agent in the universe—all that is not God acts only as acted upon."[49]

The third device adjoined to the unconditional decree in an effort to uphold human freedom is the concept of permission, which is introduced only to explain God's relation to sinful acts and to relieve him of responsibility for sin. Now, we agree that divine permission is taught in the Bible, but we contend that it is incompatible with an unconditional decree, simply because the very notion of permission is *conditional*; it is a reactive response.

Although this is not necessarily the case regarding a general class of actions ("I am allowing you to do whatever you please"), it is certainly true regarding specific acts. One in authority can allow a specific act to take place only if he foreknows it as planned and forthcoming, in which case the permission is a *response* to a plan or an intention known in advance. Now, for the Calvinist God's permission is not general but specific, since it applies selectively to sins and not to good acts. Thus the permission of sin is very much a reaction to an anticipated human act. But as such it is inconsistent with God's unconditional decree. So how can the decree be unconditional and permissive at the same time?

It is no wonder that many Calvinists feel uneasy about the concept of permission, as did Calvin himself.[50] This uneasiness usually does not lead to a total rejection of the concept, but a rejection of something called "the figment of bare permission."[51] Berkouwer notes that Reformed theology has never intended the idea of permission to denote any kind of restriction on God's active participation in man's deeds. It is used only to signal man's own freedom and responsibility with regard to sin. "But the idea of permission is always qualified as being active in nature, and as forming no limitation to God's purposeful activity. Divine permission is, in fact, meant by Reformed theology as a work of Divine majesty."[52]

It is no wonder, then, that Calvinists give God's permissive decree a connotation that sounds much more like determination than true permission. Zanchius speaks of God's "efficacious permission," or "his determining will of permission."[53] No formula is more strained than this, that God "peremptorily ordained to suffer the fall of Adam," says Jewett.[54] In view of such statements, we are not surprised at Carson's remarks: "Distinctions between permissive will and decretive will appear desperately artificial when applied to an omniscient and omnipotent being. . . . Wherein then does this permission differ from decree?"[55]

Another inconsistency is the willingness to apply the concept of permission to evil but not to good acts. Why is it not applied to good acts? Because this would negate God's sovereignty. However, Shedd says the permissive decree is quite adequate with respect to sin, for it maintains the divine sovereignty.[56] But if it is adequate for one, why not the other? And if it is unacceptable for one, why not the other?

In view of all the problems and inconsistencies involved in trying to mix permission with an unconditional decree, why was it ever introduced into Calvinism in the first place? Only because it seems to exonerate God from the responsibility for sin. Indeed it does so when sovereignty includes conditionality; but as long as sovereignty is defined in terms of unconditionality, permission is incompatible with it, and God remains responsible for sin.

The conclusion to this section is that Calvinism is a true determinism and has no place for genuinely free will. Efforts to make a place for free will by redefining it and by introducing the concepts of second causes and permission are not successful, because they break down when examined in the light of the Calvinistic *sine qua non*, the unconditional decree. The only way to arrive at a real alternative to determinism is to abandon the notion of unconditionality as essential to the definition of divine sovereignty. The next section will present such an alternative.

THE BIBLICAL ALTERNATIVE

Although he was speaking within another context, John Frame has well said that "we must use greater care in formulating our concept of divine sovereignty than has sometimes been shown among theologians." Sovereignty, he says, "is a more complex concept than we often imagine. Use of it requires some careful thinking rather than jumping to conclusions that seem intuitive." This is a problem because "intuition misleads us."[57] I could not agree more fully. It is my conviction that the Calvinistic view of sovereignty described above was formulated in a rather intuitive manner, with certain assumptions being made as to what must be the case if God is sovereign—i.e., omnicausality and unconditionality. What I am proposing in this section is a biblical model of sovereignty that omits these assumptions and can be held without resorting either to determinism or to inconsistency.

The Sovereign Decree

Calvinism says that if the decree is conditional in any way, God cannot be sovereign. This is simply not the case. Now, we agree that God's original and primary purpose for creation is unconditional. Nothing outside of God influenced or conditioned his original motivating purpose for making this world and for making it the kind of world it is. We disagree, though, that the eternal decree included a specific purpose for every specific moment in the existence of every specific particle of the creation.

In other words the sovereign decree contains both conditional and unconditional elements. Regarding the latter, we can say that God has a *specific* purpose for the whole of creation *in general:* to glorify himself and to share his goodness. This could be stated in just the opposite way, namely, that God has a *general* purpose for every *specific part* of his creation (again, to glorify himself and to share his goodness). This and other general elements of the decree are unconditional. But God does not have a specific, unconditional purpose for each discrete particle, object, person, and event within the creation. Most of God's dealings with the specific parts of the universe are conditioned: his foreknowledge is conditioned on the actual occurrence of events themselves (as foreknown); the entire plan of redemption, with all its many elements from Genesis to Revelation, is conditioned on (is a response to) man's sin; acts of judgment and wrath, including hell, are likewise conditioned by sin; answers to prayer are conditioned by the prayers themselves (as foreknown). But in all of this God is *no less sovereign* than if he had unconditionally predetermined each specific component of the whole.

In many ways this reduces to a disagreement not over the basic nature of God, but over the basic nature of the *creation.* What kind of *creation* did God purpose to make? One that has no capability of acting independently of God in any way whatsoever? One in which he must predetermine every specific motion, no matter how minute? Or one that has been freely endowed with a measure of freedom concerning individual movements, decisions, and actions? I, along with most non-Calvinists, have opted for this latter model. But if this was the kind of world God decided to make, then this *was* his decree, and it was a *sovereign* decree. This is the kind of world he wanted; so this is the kind of world he decreed and made.

To be sure, God's choice to make this kind of world involved the choice to impose limitations on himself. Some bristle at the very idea of limitations on a sovereign God, as if sovereignty were inconsistent with limitations as such. "It seems impossible to ascribe limitations of any nature to the Absolute Being, for limitation of any character implies imperfection," Warburton says.[58] But such an idea is an *a priori* assumption, and is not very well thought out. Frame refers to it as one of those premature "intuitions" that, upon reflection, turn out to be incorrect. "Sovereignty cannot be taken to mean an absence of all . . . limitations," he says. "There is, therefore, no *carte blanche* sovereignty, sovereignty without any 'limitation' at all." Rather, we must use sound theological thinking "to tell us what *kinds* of 'limitations' are inappropriate to divine sovereignty—i.e., what sorts of 'limitations' would *really* be limitations."[59]

First, some limitations are inherent in the very nature of God. As Frame says, "Most theology books, even by Calvinists, recognize that God is 'bound,' at least by His own character—by, e.g., His goodness, rationality, and transcendent greatness; God *cannot* be evil, stupid, or weak."[60]

But more significant for our purposes here is the fact that some limitations are not inherent but are the result of God's own sovereign choices. For example, Frame notes that "in Scripture, God makes covenant promises, by which He *binds Himself*."[61] In fact, any statement of intention on God's part binds him to carry out his stated plan. Also, creation itself is a self-limitation for God. Although his decision to create was free and sovereign, by allowing other beings to exist alongside him he limits himself. "The idea of the divine self-limitation is included in that of the creation of a world which is not God," says Brunner.[62]

Now for the main point: God limits himself not only by creating a world as such, but also and even further by the *kind* of world he chose to create. That is, he chose to make a world that is *relatively independent* of him. On the one hand, this applies to nature and natural laws. In the very beginning God endowed his creatures with built-in forces or animal instincts enabling them to function without his having to determine their every move.[63] On the other hand, the concept of relative independence applies to the free-will creatures God made to inhabit his universe. This means that God has created human beings as persons with an innate power to initiate actions. That is, man is free to act without his acts having been predetermined by God and without the simultaneous and efficacious coaction of God. Ordinarily man is allowed to exercise his power of free choice without interference, coercion, or foreordination. By not intervening in their decisions *unless* his special purposes require it, God respects both the integrity of the freedom he gave to human beings and the integrity of his own sovereign choice to make free creatures in the first place.[64]

This creation of free beings is indeed a true form of self-limitation for God, especially in the fact that this God-given freedom includes human freedom to rebel and to sin against the Creator himself. By creating a world in which sin was possible, God thereby bound himself to *react* in certain specific ways should sin become a reality. To be specific, should sin occur, God's love was bound to express itself in *grace*, involving a plan of redemption centered around his own incarnation and the offer of forgiveness for all who would accept it. In the face of sin his love could not do otherwise; his nature would require it. At the same time, should sin occur, God's holiness was bound to express itself in *wrath*, determining the very nature of the required redemption and ultimately requiring the eternal punishment of hell for unrepentant sinners. In the fact of sin his holiness could not do otherwise; his nature would thus require it.[65]

This understanding of God's decision to create a universe inhabited by free-will creatures able to sin against him helps us avoid some serious yet common errors. On the one hand, some say it is not *necessary* for God to express his wrath against sinners; he could simply *will* not to do so. This idea is extended by some to exclude the necessity for a substitutionary atonement. The issue is sovereignty, we are told: "We limit God's sovereignty if we envisage him as complying, even complying reluctantly, with the demands of justice, or of law."[66] But such thinking applies the concept of sovereignty at the wrong place. The freedom of his sovereignty applies to his act of *creation*. That is to say, God did not have to create, nor did he have to create moral beings who might sin. That he did so was his own free choice. But once he freely chose to create moral beings, his nature was *bound* to react in wrath if they chose to sin. This does not limit his sovereignty, because he freely and knowingly put himself into this position through his sovereign decree to create this kind of world.[67]

At this point we must emphasize that this same reasoning applies to Calvinists' "sovereign grace." They try to justify unconditional election with the idea that a sovereign God is free to love or not to love whomever he pleases, that he is free to give grace or to withhold it as he pleases. Thus God has a choosing or electing love, a preferential love, a distinguishing grace. Again the issue is sovereignty. Love must be sovereign, says Pink, since "God Himself is sovereign, under obligations to none, a law unto Himself, acting always according to His own imperial pleasure. Since God be sovereign, and since He be love, it necessarily follows that His love is sovereign. Because God is God, He does as He pleases; because God is love, He loves whom He pleases."[68] In response to this idea, we affirm from the standpoint of the sinner grace is certainly free, for the sinner has no claim on it and can in no way compensate God for it. But it is a most serious error to

think that grace is free (i.e., *optional*) from God's standpoint, as if
he were free to show grace to some and not to others. To say this
is to say that God can act against his own nature. The problem
here is the same as in the last paragraph: the concept of
sovereignty is applied in the wrong place. God's free choice was
exercised at the *creation*. He did not have to create free-will beings;
but when he did so, he *bound* himself to react with grace if those
creatures chose to sin. His nature would not allow him to react in
any other way! But again this does not limit his sovereignty,
because he freely and knowingly put himself into this position
through his sovereign decree to create this kind of world.[69]

Such limitations as these in no way contradict God's sovereignty, simply because they are *self*-limitations. They are a *part* of
the sovereign decree, not a violation of it. If they were limitations
imposed on God from outside God, then his sovereignty would
indeed be compromised. But they are *God's own choice*, and as such
are not the negation of sovereignty but the very expression of it.
The sovereign God is free to do as he pleases, and this includes
the freedom to limit himself.

In the final analysis what is at stake here is not just man's
freedom but God's freedom also. A sovereign God is a God who is
free to limit himself with regard to his works, a God who is free to
decide *not* to determine if he so chooses, a God who is free to
bestow the gift of relative independence on his creatures. Such
freedom does not diminish God's sovereignty; it magnifies it.

What, then, of the sovereign decree? It is still eternal and
universal, but it is not totally unconditional and efficacious. All
things are embraced within it, but not all things are determined or
caused by it. As Reichenbach says, "God's sovereignty does not
necessitate that every human or nonhuman action is predetermined, a part of his plan, or even desired."[70] This is true
especially of actions that occur as the result of relative independence; such actions occur because God unconditionally decreed
that his creatures should have the ability to initiate them. It is his
unconditional purpose and will for man to have freedom of
choice.

Although the *fact* of free will is an unconditional element in
the decree, the *specific choices* of individual free wills are conditional as far as the decree is concerned. That is, their presence in the
decree is conditioned by their actual future occurrence as foreknown and permitted by God. Here is the role of God's
permissive will.[71] Unless his specific purposes call for something
different from what the laws of nature or human free choices will
bring about, God simply allows these agents to produce what they
will. This is true permission, i.e., not efficaciousness but noninter-
ference. God permits men and women to carry out their plans
(1 Cor. 16:7; Heb. 6:3; James 4:15), or else he intervenes and

prevents them. This is true even when such plans go against his preceptive will (Acts 14:16). Both the permission and the prevention are conditional in that they are God's reaction to what he sees and knows in the hearts of his creatures.

What enables God to monitor people's plans and include such permission in his eternal decree? The answer is his foreknowledge. While acknowledging that non-Calvinists disagree on this point, I affirm that God has a true foreknowledge of future free-will choices without himself being the agent that causes them or renders them certain.[72] Such foreknowledge is grounded in—and is thus conditioned by—the choices themselves as foreknown.[73] This is how God maintains sovereign control over the whole of his creation, despite the freedom he has given his creatures.

Sovereign Control

This leads us into a more detailed yet concise explanation of the nature of God's sovereignty over his creation. In the last section we saw that God's eternal decree did not include an unconditional predetermination of every specific event that would ever occur. In this section my point is that such detailed foreordination or causation is not necessary, since there are other ways for God to maintain sovereign control over his world.

The key word in this context is *control*. Calvinists often use this word in reference to sovereignty; but in consistent Calvinism *controlled* means "caused" or "determined." This is an unnecessary extreme, however, since God's control of his world does not depend on detailed determination. Of course many things *are* directly determined by God, but most occur according to his permissive will or through his nondeterminative influence. Nevertheless God remains *completely in control of everything*. We must not think that God's control varies according to the degree that he causes things or the degree of freedom bestowed on his creatures. Unless God is in *total* control, he is not sovereign. The issue is whether such total control requires a predetermination or causation of all things. I contend that it does not; God's sovereignty is *greater* than that! As Raymond rightly says, "We assume that God is competent to govern an infinite number of morally responsible beings, persons who have power within limits of determining what they will do; and we insist upon it that this concept of a divine government is incomparably superior to that of our opponents."[74]

Now our question is, *How* does God maintain such control over a relatively free world? The answer is, through his *foreknowledge* and through his *intervention* in creaturely affairs whenever this is necessary to accomplish his purposes. Here I am referring to true foreknowledge, which is conditioned by the actual events that are foreknown.[75] Even before the creation God foreknew every free-will act, even every *planned* free-will act, since he knows human hearts, plans, and intentions. These are not uncertainties for God; he does not have to wait for them to occur before he can know them with certainty. Nothing takes God by surprise.

What is the advantage of such foreknowledge? Simply this: through it God knew, even before creation, when and how he would have to intervene in his world to accomplish his purposes. Even though he bestowed relative independence on his creatures, as Creator he reserved the right to intervene if necessary. Thus he is able not only to *permit* human actions to occur, but also to *prevent* them from occurring if he so chooses (Prov. 19:21; James 4:15). In addition, God's foreknowledge also enables him to plan his own responses to and uses of human choices even before they are made. Thus he remains in complete control and is able to carry out his purposes, especially regarding redemption.

We may classify God's sovereign control (or providence) over his creation under three main headings.[76] The first is *general providence,* by which God governs the world through his permissive will. This includes the realm of nature and refers to God's work of preserving the universe in existence and directing its natural processes in the predictable patterns we call the "laws of nature." It also includes most free-will actions, especially sinful ones. The basic mark of general providence is God's nonintervention; it is the sphere of activity in which he allows his creatures the full integrity of their relative independence.

The second sphere is *special providence,* the category of actions and events resulting from God's nonmiraculous intervention into his creation. These are the times when God sovereignly intervenes in order to accomplish his purposes or to answer prayer, but without violating either natural laws or free will. Still, through the subtle manipulation of such laws and of mental states, God is able to produce variations in nature and bring about free-will decisions that would not have occurred otherwise. The result is something similar to determinism's redefined notion of free will, as discussed above and dismissed as not being truly free. That is, I am granting here that through his special providence God brings about sets of circumstances calculated to influence people to make particular decisions that will serve his purposes.

There are two significant ways in which this view of special providence differs from deterministic "free will," however. One, the manipulated circumstances do not infallibly produce the desired result; because the individual's will is truly free, he can resist and act to the contrary. This is the very situation described in Amos 4:6–11 and Haggai 1:5–11. Here the prophets indicate that in his special providence God sent such things as drought, locusts, and plagues on his people to influence them to a particular decision; but their resistance is lamented in Amos' refrain, " 'Yet you have not returned to me,' declares the LORD" (Amos 4:6, 8–11).

Second, this differs from the determinists' view in that such special intervention and influence are the exception and not the rule; in the total scope of providence they are relatively rare. The Bible certainly speaks of God's ability to turn a person's heart and actions (e.g., Prov. 16:1; 21:1), and it gives many examples (e.g., Gen. 50:20; Exod. 10:20; Ezra 1:1). The Calvinistic fallacy, however, is to generalize from these particulars and to assume that they are paradigms for the way God works in every decision without exception.[77] But this is totally unwarranted. That God worked in such a way in connection with Israel in Old Testament times is to be expected, since the people of Israel were the focal point of God's purpose in that era. Hence it is natural that the Old Testament teems with accounts of special providence. But we have no reason to assume that God was working in Australia and South America in such ways at the same time; the bulk of history still falls under God's general control or general providence.

The third category of God's sovereign control over creation is *miracle*, which is his most intense and least used form of control. It refers to those occasions in which God intervenes in history in a way that violates natural law and even free will if necessary.[78] Tangential to this category are those supernatural acts that are outside natural law but are not evidential in purpose, such as inspiration and regeneration. I do not believe that miracles are a point of dispute in the present debate; all would agree that God works them in a causative or determinative way.

What I have presented here is a model of divine government that includes both a God who is completely sovereign and in total control of his creation and moral beings who have a truly free will. It involves no dishonoring of God and no elevating of the creature above the Creator. The time has come to consider seriously whether such an "Arminian" view does in fact offer a concept of God's sovereignty that is attractive, unqualified, coherent, consistent, and true to Scripture. I believe that the view I have presented here (and explained and documented in much more detail in *God the Ruler*) is just such a view.

Scriptural Considerations

This leads to the final section of this chapter, namely, a brief look at a few biblical passages that through constant misreading have pointed many toward the Calvinistic view of sovereignty. The first is Romans 9–11.[79] This is commonly interpreted (especially chapter 9) as meaning that God unconditionally decides who will be saved and who will be lost; this then becomes the paradigm for sovereignty in general, i.e., a comprehensive unconditionality. Both of these assumptions, however, must be challenged.

It is true that the passage teaches that God makes some unconditional choices: "Therefore God has mercy on whom he wants to have mercy, and he hardens whom he wants to harden" (Rom. 9:18). The best understanding of this, however, is that God unconditionally chooses individuals and nations for temporal roles in his plan of redemption. That is, he chooses whom he pleases for service, not salvation. The main point of the section is Paul's defense of God's right to reject the Jews as his chosen people. This issue has been raised by the material in Romans 1–8, where Paul teaches that anyone who believes in Christ is a true Jew (2:25–29) and a true child of Abraham (4:9–16). But if this is so, then national Israel is no longer something special in God's plan. Would this not mean that God is somehow breaking faith with his chosen people?

Paul's answer to this question is that a sovereign God can choose whomever he wants to serve him and to help him work out his purpose of making grace available through Jesus Christ. He can also sovereignly reject whomever he pleases. If he wants to choose Isaac over Ishmael for this purpose, that is his prerogative. This is the way it was with his initial choice of Israel; the same applies to his decision to set them aside. It is his right to do so. Besides, it is not as if he were rejecting them individually for salvation; he is simply setting them aside collectively—as a nation—as far as their service of preparation is concerned.

But even if it be granted that Paul is talking about an unconditional choice for service, would this not indicate that God is a God whose decrees are unconditional with regard to everything? Certainly not, as Paul clearly shows in this very section. In fact, Paul affirms the *conditionality* of the main thing Calvinists want to view *unconditionally*, namely, salvation! This is clear from his discussion of the eternal destiny of individual Jews. Any who are rejected as far as salvation is concerned are rejected because of personal unbelief (Rom. 9:32; 11:20). Likewise, any Jew can be saved by accepting Jesus as the Messiah (10:13–17; 11:23–24). In fact God is pictured as constantly pleading with Israel to come to him, but they remain disobedient and obstinate (10:21).

In summary, Romans 9–11 shows that God's election and rejection of the Jews as a nation with regard to their role of service was a matter of God's sovereign choice, while his acceptance or rejection of individual Jews with regard to their salvation is conditioned on their belief or unbelief.

A second passage that needs clarification is Exodus 33:19, "I will have mercy on whom I will have mercy, and I will have compassion on whom I will have compassion."[80] This is important not only as it stands in Exodus but also as it is quoted in Romans 9:15, where it is interpreted to substantiate the view that Paul is there speaking of unconditional election to salvation. One reason for this is that the Hebrew word (*chanan*) used in Exodus 33:19 is usually translated "to be gracious, to have mercy." These English words usually connote saving grace. But this is not the basic meaning of the Hebrew word, which is more general than this. It means "to be favorable or act favorable toward, to bless, to come to one's aid," especially in response to a request or prayer, and usually with regard to temporal blessings. When an Old Testament saint prayed, "Be gracious to me," he was simply asking God to hear and answer the prayer that was about to follow. He was saying, in effect, "God, I pray that you think well enough of me to answer this prayer." Thus the word refers to God's favorable attitude that moves him to bless and to answer prayer. In Exodus 33:19 God is not speaking of saving grace in the New Testament sense, but of his sovereignty in deciding whom he will bless and whom he will not bless. In response to Moses' strong petitions to know God more intimately (Exod. 33:12–18), God says, "All right, I will grant your request, but remember: I am still in charge. I still decide what prayers I will answer and whom I will bless."

When this is quoted in Romans 9:15 as "I will have mercy on whom I have mercy," it retains its nonsoteriological connotation. It is not saving mercy, but the mercy of temporal blessings—i.e., the blessing of choosing certain ones for the privileges of service. Paul often refers to his selection as an apostle (a role of service) as an act of grace and mercy on God's part (see Rom. 15:15–16; 1 Cor. 3:10; 7:25; 15:10; 2 Cor. 4:1; Gal. 2:9; Eph. 3:7–8). We must not read more into Romans 9:15 than is meant by the Hebrew term.

A final passage used to prove an efficacious, unconditional decree is Ephesians 1:11, which speaks of the one "who works all things after the counsel of His will" (NASB).[81] Like many others, Feinberg sees this verse as "perhaps the clearest expression" of deterministic sovereignty.[82] We agree that the passage would give considerable support to Calvinism *if* the term *all things* (*panta*) were intended to be absolute. Most likely, however, it is *not* absolute but rather must be understood within the limitations imposed by the context.

It is not unusual for the term *panta* to be used in a limited, noninclusive sense. Examples are John 19:28; Acts 17:25; Romans 8:32; 1 Corinthians 6:12; 12:6; and Ephesians 6:21. Especially important is 1 Corinthians 12:6, where the language is exactly parallel to Ephesians 1:11. The former verse says literally that God works all things (*panta*) in all men, yet the context (see 12:11) specifically limits the *panta* to the Spirit's gifts. In the same way, the context of Ephesians 1:11 does not allow us to think of *panta* in an absolute sense but limits us to a specific focus. This focus is "the mystery of his will" (1:9), which is the uniting of Jews and Gentiles together into one body, the church (3:6). To say that God works all things after the counsel of his will means that he does whatever is necessary to accomplish this purpose—i.e., the gathering together of Jews and Gentiles under one head, Jesus Christ (cf. 1:10). Thus the *panta* in Ephesians 1:11 does not have a universal reference, but refers to "all things" required for uniting Jews and Gentiles under one Head in one body.[83]

This concludes our brief study of divine sovereignty. It is of course only a framework for more detailed study, but it is enough to show that there is a reasonable, consistent, and biblical alternative to Calvinism's unconditional and therefore deterministic decree.

NOTES

[1] D. A. Carson, *Divine Sovereignty and Human Responsibility* (Atlanta: John Knox, 1981), 1.

[2] F. H. Klooster, "Sovereignty of God," *Evangelical Dictionary of Theology*, ed. Walter A. Elwell (Grand Rapids: Baker, 1984), 1039.

[3] John S. Feinberg, "God Ordains All Things," *Predestination and Free Will*, ed. David Basinger and Randall Basinger (Downers Grove: InterVarsity, 1986), 20.

[4] See Charles Hodge, *Systematic Theology*, 3 vols. (Grand Rapids: Eerdmans, n.d.), 1:535ff.; Louis Berkhof, *Systematic Theology* (London: Banner of Truth Trust, 1939), 102–8; Jack Cottrell, *What the Bible Says About God the Ruler* (Joplin, Mo.: College Press, 1984), 169–82.

[5] Jerom Zanchius, *The Doctrine of Absolute Predestination*, trans. Augustus Toplady (London: Sovereign Grace Union, 1930), 82–83.

[6] Augustus Toplady, foreword, Zanchius, *Absolute Predestination*, 14. This is part of a quotation from Bishop Hopkins' "Sermon upon Providence, from Matt. x. 29, 30."

[7] Loraine Boettner, *The Reformed Doctrine of Predestination* (Grand Rapids: Eerdmans, 1932), 13.

[8] Philip E. Hughes, "The Sovereignty of God—Has God Lost Control?" in *Soli Deo Gloria: Essays in Reformed Theology*, ed. R. C. Sproul (Phillipsburg, N.J.: Presbyterian and Reformed, 1976), 30.

[9] John Murray, *The Sovereignty of God*, rev. ed., "Tracts for Today," no. 5 (Philadelphia: Committee on Christian Education, The Orthodox Presbyterian Church, n.d.), 11.

[10] R. C. Sproul, "Discerning the Will of God," *Our Sovereign God*, ed. James M. Boice (Grand Rapids: Baker, 1977), 105.

[11] Herman Bavinck, *The Doctrine of God*, ed. and tr. William Hendriksen (Grand Rapids: Eerdmans, 1951), 371.

[12] A. W. Pink, *The Sovereignty of God*, rev. ed. (London: Banner of Truth Trust, 1961), 158.

[13] Archibald Alexander Hodge, *Outlines of Theology* (New York: Robert Carter, 1876), 168.

[14] C. Samuel Storms, *The Grandeur of God* (Grand Rapids: Baker, 1984), 80.

[15] Feinberg, "God Ordains All Things," 19, 24.

16 Norman Geisler, "Response" to Feinberg, *Predestination and Free Will*, ed. David Basinger and Randall Basinger (Downers Grove: InterVarsity, 1986), 47.

17 Norman Geisler, "God Knows All Things," *Predestination and Free Will*, ed. David Basinger and Randall Basinger (Downers Grove: InterVarsity, 1986), 72–73.

18 Berkhof, *Systematic Theology*, 100. Pink asserts, "He has determined in Himself from all eternity everything which will be" (*Sovereignty of God*, 74).

19 Charles Hodge, *Systematic Theology*, 1:540–41.

20 William G. T. Shedd, *Dogmatic Theology*, 3 vols. (Grand Rapids: Zondervan, 1969), 1888; reprint ed., I:404–5; Berkhof, *Systematic Theology*, 104–5.

21 Feinberg, "God Ordains All Things," 21.

22 R. C. Sproul, *Chosen by God* (Wheaton: Tyndale, 1986), 54. See also Millard J. Erickson, *Christian Theology*, 3 vols. (Grand Rapids: Baker, 1983–85), 1:357–59.

23 Feinberg, "God Ordains All Things," 26.

24 Boettner, *Reformed Doctrine of Predestination*, 214; see also 215; Erickson *Christian Theology*, 1:357–59; Lewis S. Chafer, *Systematic Theology*, 8 vols. (Dallas: Seminary Press, 1947), 1:241.

25 Berkhof, *Systematic Theology*, 172.

26 Ibid., 173. See also Archibald Alexander Hodge, *Popular Lectures on Theological Themes* (Philadelphia: Presbyterian Board of Publication, 1887), 49; Herman Bavinck, *Our Reasonable Faith*, trans. Henry Zylstra (Grand Rapids: Eerdmans, 1956), 181–82.

27 Toplady, preface, 22.

28 Shedd, *Dogmatic Theology*, 1:405. Charles Hodge concurs: "Some things He purposes to do, others He decrees to permit to be done" (*Systematic Theology*, 1:541). See also Boettner, *Reformed Doctrine of Predestination*, 14; Sproul, *Chosen by God*, 26.

29 Chafer, *Systematic Theology*, 1:236.

30 Shedd, *Dogmatic Theology*, 1:406. See also Charles Hodge, *Systematic Theology*, 1:541; Berkhof, *Systematic Theology*, 105.

31 James Daane, *The Freedom of God: A Study of Election and Pulpit* (Grand Rapids: Eerdmans, 1973), 159–60.

32 Erickson, *Christian Theology*, 1:355.

33 William G. T. Shedd, *Calvinism: Pure and Mixed* (New York: Scribner, 1893), 4.

34 Murray, *Sovereignty*, 18, 27.

35 G. K. Beale, "An Exegetical and Theological Consideration of the Hardening of Pharaoh's Heart in Exodus 4–14 and Romans 9," *Trinity Journal* 5 NS, no. 2 (Autumn 1984): 152.

36 Hodge, *Systematic Theology*, 1:540.

37 Daane, *The Freedom of God*, 160.

38 Boettner, *Reformed Doctrine of Predestination*, 14. See Feinberg, "God Ordains All Things," 29–30.

39 Chafer, *Systematic Theology*, 1:230.

40 A. A. Hodge, *Outlines of Theology,* 168.

41 Christopher Ness, *An Antidote to Arminianism* (Millersville, Pa.: Classic-A-Month Books, 1964), 14–15. See Zanchius, *Absolute Predestination*, 51.

42 Feinberg, "God Ordains All Things," 24.

43 Geisler, "Response," 46–47. In their responses to Feinberg in the same volume, Bruce Reichenbach and Clark Pinnock say the same thing. "The freedom asserted by Feinberg is an illusion," says Reichenbach (p. 51). "What Feinberg is pleased to call *freedom* does not deserve the name," says Pinnock (p. 59).

44 R. C. Sproul, "Prayer and God's Sovereignty," in James M. Boice, ed., *Our Sovereign God* (Grand Rapids: Baker, 1977), 135–36.

45 A. A. Hodge, *Popular Lectures*, 147.

46 Toplady, "Preface," 21.

47 Berkhof, *Systematic Theology*, 173. See G. C. Berkouwer, *The Providence of God*, trans. Lewis B. Smedes (Grand Rapids: Eerdmans, 1952), 130.

⁴⁸Berkouwer, *Providence of God*, 93, 95.

⁴⁹Miner Raymond, *Systematic Theology*, 3 vols. (Cincinnati: Walden and Stowe, 1877), 1:496.

⁵⁰John Calvin, *Institutes of the Christian Religion*, I.18.1, ed. John T. McNeill, trans. Ford Lewis Battles, "The Library of Christian Classics," vols. 20–21 (Philadelphia: Westminster, 1950), 1:229. See ibid., I.18.2; II.4.3. See also Gordon H. Clark, *Biblical Predestination* (Nutley, N.J.: Presbyterian and Reformed, 1969), 53; Carl F. H. Henry, *God, Revelation and Authority*, 6 vols. (Waco: Word, 1983), 4:86.

⁵¹Calvin, *Institutes*, I.18.1.

⁵²Berkouwer, *Providence of God*, 137–38.

⁵³Zanchius, *Absolute Predestination*, 54–55; cf. 106–7. Cf. Bavinck, *Doctrine of God*, 386, 388.

⁵⁴Paul K. Jewett, *Election and Predestination* (Grand Rapids: Eerdmans, 1985), 96, n. 63. The comment is from Zanchius, *Absolute Predestination*, 84 (footnote). Jewett attributes the footnote and thus the statement to Toplady.

⁵⁵Carson, *Divine Sovereignty*, 213–14; cf. 220.

⁵⁶Shedd, *Dogmatic Theology*, 1:407.

⁵⁷John M. Frame, "The Spirit and the Scriptures," in D. A. Carson and John D. Woodbridge, eds., *Hermeneutics, Authority, and Canon* (Grand Rapids: Zondervan, 1986), 223–24.

⁵⁸Ben A. Warburton, *Calvinism* (Grand Rapids: Eerdmans, 1955), 64.

⁵⁹Frame, "The Spirit and the Scriptures," 224.

⁶⁰Ibid. Even Warburton recognizes that God must be "consistent with His character" (*Calvinism*, 64).

⁶¹Frame, "The Spirit and the Scriptures," 223.

⁶²Emil Brunner, *The Christian Doctrine of Creation and Redemption: Dogmatics, vol. 2*, trans. Olive Wyon (Philadelphia: Westminster, 1952), 173.

⁶³See Cottrell, *God the Ruler*, 105–13.

⁶⁴Ibid., 187–95. Bruce Reichenbach says, "It is not inconsistent with God's omnipotence that he limit himself or his activity. In particular, God limits himself in the creation of individuals who are free" ("God Limits His Power" in David Basinger and Randall Basinger, eds. *Predestination and Free Will*, [Downers Grove: InterVarsity, 1986], 108).

⁶⁵See Jack Cottrell, *What the Bible Says About God the Redeemer* (Joplin, Mo.: College Press, 1987), chs. 5–6.

⁶⁶R. P. C. Hanson, *The Attractiveness of God: Essays in Christian Doctrine* (Richmond: John Knox, 1973), 148–50.

⁶⁷See Cottrell, *God the Redeemer*, 314–18.

⁶⁸Arthur W. Pink, *The Attributes of God* (Swengel, Pa.: Reiner, 1968), 72.

⁶⁹See Cottrell, *God the Redeemer*, 381–89.

⁷⁰Reichenbach, "God Limits His Power," 119.

⁷¹See Cottrell, *God the Ruler*, 314–16.

⁷²See Jack Cottrell, *What the Bible Says About God the Creator* (Joplin, Mo.: College Press, 1983), 279ff.; idem, *God the Ruler*, 208–9, 214–16.

⁷³See Reichenbach, "Response" to Feinberg, 53.

⁷⁴Raymond, *Systematic Theology*, 1:505–6.

⁷⁵Unconditional foreknowledge is possible only within determinism and is not true foreknowledge. See Cottrell, *God the Ruler*, 224–26.

⁷⁶These are treated in detail in ibid., chs. 3–6.

⁷⁷Cf. Charles Hodge, *Systematic Theology*, 1:544: "What is true of the history of Joseph, is true of all history."

⁷⁸See my defense of this concept of miracle in *God the Ruler*, 244–61. For the parallel idea that God may "violate" free will, see ibid., 196.

⁷⁹For a fuller discussion see ibid., 204–7.

⁸⁰See the fuller discussion in Cottrell, *God the Redeemer*, 361–65.

⁸¹See Cottrell, *God the Ruler*, 306–8.

⁸²Feinberg, "God Ordains All Things," 29.

[83]Calvinists surely will not complain about giving the word *all* a limited scope. They do it regularly in such passages as John 12:32; 1 Timothy 2:4; and 2 Peter 3:9. See G. C. Berkouwer, *Divine Election*, trans. Hugo Bekker (Grand Rapids: Eerdmans, 1960), 237; Jewett, *Election and Predestination*, 104–5.

DIVINE FOREKNOWLEDGE AND FREE-WILL THEISM

Richard Rice

All Christians agree that omniscience, or perfect knowledge, is an essential attribute of God, but there are perplexing questions as to what perfect knowledge involves. The traditional view is that God knows all reality—past, present, and future. No one denies that God knows the past and the present. In fact, some people maintain that God's knowledge of the past is what gives it reality. The questions concern God's knowledge of the future. Again, however, no one denies that God knows a good deal about the future. The question is whether God's knowledge of the future is exhaustive. Specifically, it is the question of whether or not God knows the content of future free decisions.

The purpose of the discussion in this chapter is to formulate an Arminian interpretation of divine foreknowledge. The topic is essential to any doctrine of God, but it poses a particular challenge to Arminian theologians because of the importance they attach to human freedom. To set the stage for this endeavor let us review the positions of Calvin and Arminius themselves on the topic.

Calvin's reply to the question of divine foreknowledge is clear and consistent: God knows the future exhaustively; his foreknowledge is absolute. In Calvin's words:

> When we attribute foreknowledge to God, we mean that all things always were and perpetually remain, under his eyes, so that to his knowledge there is nothing future or past, but all things are present. And they are present in such a way that he not only conceives them through ideas, as we have before us those things which our minds remember, but he truly looks upon them and discerns them as things placed before him. And his foreknowledge is extended throughout the universe to every creature.[1]

For Calvin there is a close relation between divine foreknowledge and predestination—"God's eternal decree, by which he compacted with himself what he willed to become of each man."[2] Calvin rejects the idea that God's election is based on his foreknowledge of merit.[3] Instead, he maintains, it is the other way around: God's foreknowledge is based on election. In other words, God knows all things precisely because he has determined all things. Calvin admits that foreknowledge alone would not impose necessity on the future. But since God "foresees future events only by reason of the fact that he decreed that they take place," "it is clear that all things take place . . . by his determination and bidding."[4]

Like Calvin, Arminius affirms God's absolute foreknowledge, but unlike Calvin, he has no coherent explanation for it. "The knowledge of God," he states, "is eternal, immutable and infinite, and . . . extends to all things, both necessary and contingent. . . . But I do not understand the mode in which He knows future contingencies, and especially those which belong to the free-will of creatures. . . ."[5]

One explanation is that all things, including contingent events, are present to God and coexist with him in "the infinite Now of eternity, which embraces all time." Arminius finds this helpful, for if there are no future contingencies, as far as God is concerned, but only present ones, the difficulties involved in the notion of "certain knowledge of future contingencies" evaporate.[6] This approach is incomplete, however, for it fails to account for God's knowledge of contingent nonexistents—"those things which may happen, but never do."[7] Since they never exist, they cannot coexist with God in the Now of eternity.

Arminius also sees no way to account for God's knowledge of future contingencies that depend on free choice. Clearly, God can know future contingent events if the contingent causes of these events are "complete and not hindered in their operation"—in other words, if their conditions are all fulfilled. But what if a contingent event depends on free choice? How can its conditions be complete if the free will, even at the moment of choice, is free not to choose, or to choose something else?[8]

Because he affirms creaturely freedom, Arminius insists that both God's knowledge and his will are responsive to creaturely actions. This makes it necessary to attribute different types of knowledge to God. All God's knowledge is "eternal," he maintains, but it is "not equally so in reference to all objects of knowledge."[9] God's knowledge of himself and all possibilities is "absolutely eternal." But his knowledge of beings that will exist is eternal only in duration; in nature it is subsequent to some act of divine will, and, in some cases, even subsequent to some foreseen act of the human will.

God's will is also responsive to human activity. God wills some things, Arminius observes, that he would not will if a certain human volition did not precede. These include his will to remove Saul from the throne of Israel, to destroy the Sodomites and their neighbors, to give his Son to redeem sinners, and to condemn Judas.[10]

Whether Calvin and Arminius are the best representatives of Calvinism and Arminianism is debatable, of course. But their divergent views of omniscience are characteristic of these two theological perspectives. For Calvinists, God knows the future exhaustively because he planned it, down to the last detail. And nothing could be other than it is, because his sovereign will is immutable.

Arminians characteristically affirm God's absolute foreknowledge, too. But they have difficulty accounting for it because they also affirm creaturely freedom. Instead of attributing everything that happens to the sovereign will of God, Arminians insist that human beings have a capacity for genuine choice and self-determination. In particular, they are free to accept or reject God's offer of salvation. The obvious question for Arminians is how God can foresee the content of such choices. If human beings are really free, and their actions are not determined by God, how can he know in advance everything they are going to do? To put the question in its most familiar form, how can we reconcile human freedom and divine foreknowledge?

The literature that has accumulated around this question over the centuries is vast and complicated, and contemporary scholars have pursued it with impressive vigor. It would take a sizable book just to survey the current discussion, so my objectives here will be quite modest. I will review some representative treatments of God's foreknowledge and then outline a position that "consistent Arminianism" suggests.

Among contemporary Evangelicals, the Calvinist position that God's foreknowledge rests on predestination exerts considerable influence. Carl F. H. Henry, for one, supports the doctrine that "God foreordains the entire course of world and human events."[11] This does not eliminate freedom, however, because human beings still have "rational self-determination." "To be morally responsible," Henry asserts, "man needs only the capacity for choice, not the freedom of contrary choice."[12] In other words, a person is free as long as she acts in harmony with her nature or disposition. She need not have the ability to do otherwise.

Most philosophers and theologians today reject the Calvinist account of absolute foreknowledge in favor of explanations that preserve a stronger sense of human freedom. A familiar alternative is the concept advocated by Boethius, Augustine, Thomas

Aquinas, and may others, including C. S. Lewis, that God stands outside time and therefore views past, present, and future all together in one eternal moment. To quote Boethius,

> Since God lives in the eternal present, His knowledge transcends all movement of time and abides in the simplicity of its immediate present. It encompasses the infinite sweep of past and future, and regards all things in its simple comprehension as if they were now taking place.[13]

This understanding of divine knowledge preserves both divine necessity and creaturely freedom, the argument goes. "God sees as present those future things which result from free will," and these things are necessary "from the standpoint of divine knowledge," states Boethius. "But considered only in themselves, they lose nothing of the absolute freedom of their own natures." In other words, God's knowledge of future free actions is necessary, but the actions themselves are not. Indeed, God's foreknowledge does not depend on future events. Instead, he knows them "from the simplicity of his own nature."[14]

Another alternative to Calvinism that advocates absolute foreknowledge is the medieval concept of "middle knowledge," or "Molinism," which is currently enjoying a revival of sorts. Its advocates distinguish three forms of divine knowledge. God knows all pure possibilities and all actualities, but besides, or "between," these two forms of knowledge, so to speak, God also knows all "conditional future contingent events."[15] In other words, he knows the content of future free decisions.

The concept involves a distinction between what *could* happen and what *would* happen. Because he knows all possibilities, God knows what every conceivable individual *could* do. But through middle knowledge he knows something else as well: he knows what every individual *would* do in all conceivable circumstances.[16] That is to say, he knows precisely what free choices an individual would make in any specific situation.

The idea of middle knowledge is sometimes expressed in terms of "possible worlds." God knows all possible worlds, and he knows what the free choices of each individual would be in every one of them. He also knows which of these possible worlds is actual, because he created it. Consequently, he knows what all the future free decisions of the creatures in the actual world will be. In this way God's foreknowledge is absolute, while future decisions remain genuinely free.

Like Calvinism and eternalism, this concept affirms God's exhaustive knowledge of the future. But unlike these other views it introduces an element of contingency into God's knowledge. What God knows about the future depends on which of all possible worlds is the actual one. So it seems to avoid the difficulties involved in maintaining that God's knowledge of the world is entirely necessary, while the world itself is contingent.

Another response to the question of divine foreknowledge and human freedom is to deny that it really requires an answer. The strategy of some thinkers is to argue that the various objections people have to the concept that God can foreknow free decisions do not succeed. And since no one has shown conclusively that the idea is absurd, Christians are entitled to believe it, whether or not they can somehow explain the phenomenon. Thus, Stephen Davis attributes "future vision" to God—"He simply sees the future," without trying to account for it.[17] And William Lane Craig, while he warmly embraces the concept of middle knowledge, insists that all a Christian has to show is that God's foreknowledge of future free decisions "has not been proved to be impossible, that there is no good reason to reject it."[18]

Supporters of this view insist that God's foreknowledge in no sense causes what he foreknows will happen. True, God's knowledge of the future is infallible, so what he foreknows cannot but take place. But from his foreknowledge it only follows that something *will* take place, not that it *must* take place. The fact that Christ foreknew in 1888 and before what I will do in 1988 does not mean that my decisions now are not free. It only means that whatever I freely choose, God knew it in advance. Certain aspects of human knowledge provide an analogy. We know events that happened in the past, and this doesn't mean that these events were necessary rather than contingent. So why should God's knowledge of creaturely actions that will happen in the future make them necessary rather than contingent?

Theologians and philosophers have raised serious objections to all these accounts of divine foreknowledge. From a theological standpoint, as Arminius illustrates, the principal target in Calvinism has been its view of divine election rather than foreknowledge. If God determines the ultimate destiny of every human being, indeed, the entire course of human history, then there is nothing left for men and women to decide. They merely fulfill their preassigned roles.

This view of things may be compatible with certain concepts of freedom, but it leaves many thinkers unconvinced. For human beings to be genuinely free, it seems, they must not only be able to do what they choose, they must also be able to choose otherwise. But each attempt to demonstrate that absolute foreknowledge is compatible with a libertarian notion of freedom also has problems.

The idea that God sees the entire future because he stands outside time and thus views all reality in a single eternal moment, raises many questions. One interesting objection is that a timeless being cannot be omniscient, because there are certain things no timeless being could know. Specifically, a timeless being could never know what time it is now.[19] In a well-known essay, Norman Kretzmann argues that "an omniscient being must know not only the entire scheme of contingent events from beginning to end at once, but also *at what stage of realization that scheme now is.*"[20] But a being who always knows what time it is is subject to change, while a timeless being must be changeless. Consequently, Kretzmann argues, the concept of God as both omniscient and immutable is incoherent.

Many thinkers agree that an utterly changeless being could not have perfect knowledge of a changing reality. In recent years, a number of evangelicals have taken the position that God must be thought of as changing in certain respects. In *The Concept of God*, Ronald Nash argues that immutability is one of the classic theistic attributes that needs to be reinterpreted.[21] In the opening chapter of his book *The Logic of God*, Stephen Davis straightforwardly asserts that God is "a temporal being. Past, present and future are real to him. . . . "[22] And a couple of chapters later he states that we need not attribute to God "immutability in the sense of immunity to all genuine change."[23]

At the same time both Nash and Davis adhere to the idea of absolute divine foreknowledge. In effect, their position is that the creaturely world changes and God's experience of the creaturely world changes, but God's knowledge of the future is exhaustive and therefore unchanging. There are considerable difficulties in this position. For one thing, it is hard to understand how God's experience of the world could change if his knowledge of the future is exhaustive. If God knows absolutely everything that will happen, then he not only knows what his creatures will do, he also knows what all his reactions to their actions and decisions will be. Consequently, there is nothing left for him to find out from the actual occurrence of events. But in that case, what sense does it make to say that he changes in response to changes in the world? To know everything that an experience involves, which absolute foreknowledge requires, is more than to anticipate the experience; it is already to have it.

In a similar way the concept of absolute foreknowledge renders meaningless any notion of divine freedom and therefore of divine decision.[24] To know exactly what you are going to decide is to have made the decision already. There is nothing left to be decided. Consequently, it makes no sense to speak of divine decisions if we attribute absolute foreknowledge to God, for he must know everything that he is ever going to decide. It is equally impossible to imagine a time before which God had decided to do something—to create, for example. For if he had absolute foreknowledge of his future actions, he had already made the decision. So, it seems, there is no coherent way to think of God as changing, if we hold to the notion of absolute foreknowledge. The concept of middle knowledge is supposed to provide an explanation of divine foreknowledge that preserves creaturely freedom, but on close inspection it, too, fails to deliver. God knows what each creature will freely do in all possible worlds, the reasoning goes. And he knows which of these possible worlds is the actual present world, since he created it. So, he knows what all the future free decisions of this world's inhabitants will be. Both premises of the argument are objectionable.

The first presupposes that a free decision is so related to the circumstances surrounding its occurrence that a knowledge of the circumstances yields knowledge of the decision. In the words of one supporter, "God knows what every possible creature *would* do (not just *could* do) in any possible set of circumstances."[25] But this cannot be true if one is genuinely free "to do otherwise." On this notion of freedom, an agent in a specific set of circumstances may do more than one thing, so knowing the circumstances does not provide a knowledge of the choice.

The second premise raises a related objection. The claim that God knows everything that will happen in the actual world because he selected and created it out of all the possible worlds he knows attributes the entire state of affairs to God's creative decision. But if God's creatures have genuine freedom, which possible world is actualized depends on their decisions as well as on God's. As Richard Creel puts it, "The flaw in this theory is its assumption that God can know which possible world is the actual world." The appeal to middle knowledge, he argues, fails to distinguish between "knowledge of all logically possible worlds, i.e., all worlds that are self-consistent or internally coherent," and "knowledge of all creatable worlds, i.e., all worlds that would come to pass were they willed by God."[26] So the course of a world containing free creatures cannot be known in advance. It is not merely the product of God's creative power but also owes its content to God-and-the-creatures.

In view of the difficulties involved in appeals to eternalism and middle knowledge to account for divine foreknowledge, the apparently simple assertion that God just "knows" future free decisions because he is God and is therefore omniscient may seem attractive. But this position, too, has serious problems. In spite of assertions that absolute foreknowledge does not eliminate freedom, intuition tells us otherwise. If God's foreknowledge is infallible, then what he sees cannot fail to happen. This means that the course of future events is fixed, however we explain what actually causes it. And if the future is inevitable, then the apparent experience of free choice is an illusion.

Jonathan Edwards gave this point pellucid expression in his

treatise on freedom of the will. Edwards, of course, was a staunch predestinarian, but he recognized that absolute foreknowledge by itself excludes free choice, whether one accepts a strong doctrine of predestination or not. "Whether prescience be the thing that *makes* the event necessary or no," Edwards insists, "it alters not the case. Infallible foreknowledge may *prove* the necessity of the event foreknown, and yet not be the thing which *causes* the necessity" (italics his).[27] Other theologians make the same observation, and, like Edwards, turn it against Arminians. Carl F. H. Henry, for example, insists that we have no reason to reject foreordination as incompatible with freedom if we accept absolute foreknowledge, since either concept renders the future completely certain. "Foreknowledge, in the sense of prior knowledge, marks future events as certain no less than does predestination."[28]

From this brief review it is evident that attempts to show the compatibility of genuine human freedom with absolute divine foreknowledge have serious problems. They cannot dislodge the conviction that we really decide nothing if the entire future is known to God in advance. Traditional Calvinists have a strong case when they argue that absolute foreknowledge excludes the freedom to do anything other than what God knows will occur. To avoid the difficulties involved in trying to reconcile creaturely freedom with absolute divine foreknowledge, a number of thinkers propose revisionary interpretations of omniscience.

One interesting approach is to develop a definition of omniscience that is parallel to the generally accepted definition of omnipotence. Nearly all philosophers and theologians maintain that omnipotence should be understood not as "power to do anything," but as "power to do anything logically possible." Perfect knowledge, like perfect power, must be defined coherently. Accordingly, we should not say, "An omniscient being knows everything," period. Instead, we should say, "An omniscient being knows everything logically knowable."

Charles Hartshorne is well known for supporting such a view of omniscience.[29] Hartshorne's concept of God is closely related to his process metaphysics. According to process philosophy, reality consists of a successive multiplicity of self-creative occasions of experience whose identity is never fully determined until they become actual. Consequently, their content is by definition unknowable until they come into existence. Being omniscient, God knows all reality, but because reality is constantly developing, God's knowledge is constantly increasing. Richard Taylor shows how this concept applies to human decisions:

> An omniscient being . . . knows everything that it is possible to know. There can, however, be no antecedent truth with respect to particular future free actions of men other than that they

might and might not occur. God, accordingly, cannot know whether they will be performed until the time for the performance arrives. He is nevertheless omniscient, since only those things that are inherently unknowable are unknown to him.[30]

Process philosophers are not the only ones to take this approach to omniscience. Richard Swinburne also suggests a view of omniscience that he describes as "modified," "limited," and "attenuated."[31] Since omnipotence is not just "power to do anything," but "power to do what is logically possible," he argues, we should define omniscience, "not as knowledge of everything true, but . . . as knowledge of everything true which it is logically possible to know."[32] Consequently, "if propositions about the future actions of agents are neither true nor false until the agents do the actions," then an omniscient person need not know them until the actions occur.[33]

The crucial question here is whether creaturely decisions are genuinely creative. Do they introduce something into reality that was not there before? If not, then God must know them in advance if he is truly omniscient. But if so, it implies no deficiency in divine knowledge to say that God does not know them until they occur. Indeed, to say that God is ignorant of future creaturely decisions is like saying that God is deaf to silence. It makes no sense, because before they exist such decisions are nothing for God to be ignorant of.

This definition of omniscience calls for a new approach to the question of divine foreknowledge and creaturely freedom. Appropriately phrased, the primary question is not "Does God know future free decisions?" but "Are future free decisions knowable?" "Are they logically possible objects of knowledge?" A negative answer to the first formulation implies that there is something God does not know, and this seems incompatible with omniscience. But a negative answer to the second formulation does not detract from perfect knowledge, it simply clarifies what perfect knowledge means.

This revisionary interpretation of omniscience also calls for a new description of God's relation to the future. Those who believe that our future free decisions are not known to God are often referred to as advocating "limited foreknowledge," in contrast, of course, to those who espouse the traditional concept of "unlimited," or "comprehensive," foreknowledge. This choice of terms reflects a deep-seated bias in favor of the traditional view. The very idea that God's knowledge is limited in any sense strikes us as objectionable—both religiously and philosophically. A being of limited knowledge would be unworthy of worship, and limited knowledge would be inconsistent with perfection. But the revisionary interpretation of omniscience does not impose limits on

God's knowledge. It fully accepts the claims that God's knowledge is perfect and that perfect knowledge involves knowing everything there is to know. It departs from the tradition only in calling for careful attention to what it means to be an object of knowledge.

We have noted three general approaches to the question of human freedom and divine foreknowledge. Calvinists affirm absolute divine foreknowledge on the basis of predestination, a concept that excludes genuine creaturely freedom. Traditional Arminians affirm both absolute divine foreknowledge and creaturely freedom and strive to demonstrate their compatibility. Several recent thinkers redefine omniscience in order to allow for a strong sense of creaturely freedom.

It is tempting to enter this discussion by arguing in favor of one of these positions or some variation of it. But arguments on the question of freedom and foreknowledge typically reflect a more fundamental theological position, which their proponents assume to be valid. Consequently, instead of pursuing the question further along the lines we have been following, it may be more illuminating for us to examine the theological substructure that lies beneath the contrasting approaches to this issue.

The conflict between Arminian and Calvinist views of divine foreknowledge involves more than the question of human freedom. On a deeper level, these divergent theological perspectives reflect contrasting views of God's relation to the world. Their "root metaphors" or "basic portraits" of God are notably different.

Calvinism presents a magnificent portrait of divine majesty. Its basic metaphor for God is that of an absolute monarch. His most impressive characteristics are power, sovereignty, and control. For Calvinism, God sits enthroned above the rough and tumble of human events, serenely presiding over the course of history. He decides, he decrees, and his purposes are inevitably fulfilled. Nothing can resist his will. The basic portrait of God, or the root metaphor, which Arminianism suggests is that of a loving parent. If power, control, and sovereignty are the preeminent divine qualities according to Calvinism, then love, sensitivity, and openness, as well as reliability and authority, are the essential qualities of God for Arminians.

There are important similarities in these two views of God. Both affirm God's sovereignty over creation and his interest in human affairs. The essential distinction between them concerns the nature of creaturely agency. In Calvinism, God assigns each creature its destiny, and its fulfillment of God's will is inevitable. In Arminianism, the fulfillment of God's will is not inevitable. To an extent, God's plans call for the voluntary cooperation of his creatures. This means that the course of history is not decided unilaterally by God. Human decisions make a genuine contribution to the scheme of things, and God respects the integrity of our choices, whether or not they please him. For Arminianism, then, there is an aspect of reality determined by creaturely decision rather than divine will, and the possibility exists that God may be disappointed. For Calvinism, of course, the notion of divine disappointment is meaningless, since everything is as God plans it to be.

This basic difference is apparent in the familiar contrast between Calvinist and Arminian views of salvation. For Calvinism it is entirely up to God whether we are saved or lost. Our eternal destiny is something he assigns to us. For Arminianism, salvation is conditional upon human response. We have the option of accepting or rejecting God's grace.

Every view of God has its characteristic strengths and weaknesses. And every view of God should be evaluated in light of three criteria: the biblical evidence for it, the logical evidence that supports it, and its implications for personal religious experience. Let us apply these criteria to our two portraits of God.

There is impressive biblical evidence to support the Calvinist view of God. The opening chapter of the Bible establishes his status as creator of heaven and earth. And biblical descriptions of divine power and glory are too numerous to mention. The Bible also affirms the changelessness, or immutability, of God in verses like Malachi 3:6 ("For I the Lord do not change") and James 1:17 (in the father of lights "there is no variation nor shadow due to change").

The Calvinist view of God enjoys logical support as well. If God is omnipotent, then he must be able to bring about whatever he wills. And if God decides everything, then he knows everything, including all human actions and decisions—past, present, and future. In addition, God's perfection means that he is incapable of change. Since he is the "greatest conceivable being," to use Anselm's definition, he could not change for the better. So if he were to change at all, it could only be for the worse.

The needs of personal experience also lend support to the Calvinist view of God. If God is completely reliable, then his power must be irresistible and his experience unchanging. Otherwise, how could we trust him? How could we place in him our unreserved commitment? People often find comfort in the thought that God is in absolute control of their lives. They believe that everything that happens to them is part of God's specific plan for them. He not only surrounds us with blessings, he also permits tragedy and disappointment with our welfare in mind. We can face the future confident that God knows utterly everything that lies ahead and that everything that comes to us is for the best.

It is not hard to see why the Calvinist view of God has exerted great influence in Christian thought. This magisterial divine portrait gives us a great deal to admire. But it also presents us with a number of serious problems.

First, it is difficult to reconcile the Calvinist view of God with a number of important biblical themes, including affirmations of God's desire to save all people (e.g., 1 Tim. 2:4; 2 Peter 3:9), numerous calls to repentance (e.g., Ezek. 33:11; Matt. 3:2; Acts 2:38; 17:30), warnings about falling away (e.g., 1 Cor. 10:12; Heb. 6:4–6; 2 Peter 2:20–21), and the general emphasis on human responsibility.

On the logical level, God's omnicausality involves omniresponsibility. If everything happens just the way God plans it, then God is responsible for everything. This excludes creaturely freedom, and it seems to make God responsible for all the evil in the world.

On a personal level as well, the Calvinist view of God poses problems. It is difficult to understand how we could have a personal relationship with a being who is absolutely changeless. If God is love, and love involves sensitivity, then God should be infinitely sensitive to our daily experiences. But the God of Calvinism is impervious to change. In any respect he cannot be other than exactly what he is.

A sense of God's dynamic interaction with the world lies at the heart of the Arminian portrait of God. Arminian thought emphasizes God's respect for the integrity of creaturely freedom and God's responsiveness and sensitivity to creaturely experiences. Let us examine this view of God in light of the three criteria I mentioned earlier.

From beginning to end the Bible supports the view that God's relation to human beings is one of the dynamic interaction. When God saw the wickedness that preceded the flood, Genesis records, he "was sorry that he had made man on the earth, and it grieved him to his heart" (6:6). In the long accounts of Israel's history, we see God as an active participant in the play and counterplay of events. According to the prophets, he responded to changes in Israel's fortunes with various emotions, including pain, disappointment, revulsion, and longing: "I hate, I despise your feasts, and I take no delight in your solemn assemblies" (Amos 5:21); "How can I give you up, O Ephraim! How can I hand you over, O Israel! . . . My heart recoils within me, my compassion grows warm and tender" (Hosea 11:8).

Jeremiah describes God as adapting his plans to human decisions. God promises to "repent of the evil that [he] intended to do" if a nation turns from its evil, and to "repent of the good which [he] had intended to do" if a nation does evil in his sight (Jer. 18:7–10). Such passages indicate that human behavior has a profound effect on God. God not only influences the events of this world, but the events of this world influence him, too.

The Gospels reinforce the idea that God is highly responsive to human decisions. Jesus' most famous parables teach that God responds with joy and enthusiasm when sinners accept his gracious offer of salvation (Luke 15:7, 10). And they imply that he is genuinely grieved when they refuse it.

On a conceptual, or logical, level the portrait of God as a loving parent finds strong support as well. For one thing, it gives integrity to creaturely freedom. To the extent that we are genuinely free, our decisions make a real contribution to the scheme of things. The content of our choices is not something God decides for us. A strong affirmation of creaturely freedom makes it possible to relieve God of responsibility for evil, and this is one of the principal strengths of Arminian theology. Evil originated in the misuse of creaturely freedom. It is not attributable to a defect in God's original design for the world.

The Arminian portrait of God can also incorporate much of what is positive in the Calvinist portrait, while avoiding many of the latter's difficulties. On the Arminian view of God, as on the Calvinist view, we can affirm that God is utterly changeless in the essential qualities of divinity—in his existence and his nature and in his fundamental disposition toward his creatures. At the same time, we can acknowledge that God changes in certain respects. Specifically, he experiences the events of this world on a momentary basis. Each event contributes something to his experience precisely as it happens.

With these two portraits of God in mind, let us return to the question of divine foreknowledge. We observed above that people tend to answer this question on the basis of their fundamental view of God. And in the earlier part of this discussion we noticed the considerable difficulties encountered by those who seek to reconcile the concept of absolute divine foreknowledge with an affirmation of creaturely freedom. Now we can identify the basic cause of these problems. They arise from the attempt to combine contradictory elements from different views of God, specifically from the attempt to incorporate elements of the Calvinist view of God within the Arminian model.

There is a severe tension within traditional Arminianism, and it is evident in Arminius' own writings. The concept of absolute foreknowledge retained from Calvinism is incompatible with the dynamic portrait of God that is basic to Arminianism. Absolute foreknowledge—the idea that God sees the entire future in advance—is incompatible with the concept that God interacts with his creatures on a momentary basis. If God knows everything that will ever happen, including all our future decisions, then the actual occurrence of events contributes nothing to his experience. He already enjoys whatever value they have, along with that of his reaction to them.

Recent developments in evangelical thought indicate that support is growing for the Arminian view of God. As we mentioned, a number of evangelical theologians have abandoned the traditional view of divine immutability. They recognize the impossibility of attributing personal relationships to a changeless being. Some evangelical writers straightforwardly attribute emotional experience to God.[34] But we cannot make such changes in our concept of God coherently while clinging to the traditional concept of divine foreknowledge. To be consistent, we must reformulate our understanding of omniscience. Let us conclude this discussion by suggesting the interpretation of foreknowledge that "consistent Arminianism" requires.

The idea that God interacts with a world where there is genuine creaturely freedom does not require us to deny divine foreknowledge. It requires only that we define the scope of foreknowledge with care. In some respects the future is knowable, in others it is not. God knows a great deal about what will happen. He knows everything that will ever happen as the direct result of factors that already exist. He knows infallibly the content of his own future actions, to the extent that they are not related to human choices. Since God knows all possibilities, he knows everything that could happen and what he can do in response to each eventuality. And he knows the ultimate outcome to which he is guiding the course of history. All that God does not know is the content of future free decisions, and this is because decisions are not there to know until they occur.

This view of divine foreknowledge gives integrity to a number of biblical descriptions of God. As we have seen, the Bible speaks of God as repenting, as grieving, and as rejoicing. The concept of absolute divine foreknowledge requires us to interpret such descriptions as so many anthropomorphisms and robs them of their evocative power. But on the view that the future is genuinely open to God, statements like these can retain their natural meaning. They indicate that God appreciates and responds to the events in our lives as they happen.

The understanding of divine foreknowledge just described also requires us to reinterpret some important aspects of the Christian doctrine of God. But in each case the effect is to enrich, rather than detract from, the idea involved. Two such concepts are prophecy and providence.[35]

There is no question that prophecy figures prominently in the biblical view of God. But just what role it plays and what relation between God and the future it presents are not as clearly understood. As it actually functions in the Bible, prophecy is primarily an expression, not of divine knowledge, but of divine agency. Its major purpose is not to provide information about the future, although it may indeed do that. Rather, its major purpose is to express God's intentions to act in certain ways and to assure people that God is directly involved in their lives. Accordingly, when God makes a prediction, his perspective is not that of a passive observer, but of an active participant. He states that certain things will happen because he intends to bring them about.

A biblical statement often cited in discussions of divine foreknowledge illustrates this point: "I am God, and there is no other; I am God and there is none like me. I make known the end from the beginning, from ancient times, what is still to come" (Isa. 46:9–10). Many quotations of this passage stop with these words, but the following assertions are equally important: "My purpose will stand, and I will do all that I please. . . . What I have said, that will I bring about; what I have planned, that will I do" (vv. 10–11). According to these statements, the basis of divine predictions is God's intention to do certain things in human history. This understanding of prophecy fits nicely with the view that God is dynamically involved in the creaturely world.

Not all prophecies express God's intention to act, of course. In certain cases there are rather precise descriptions of what human beings will do. Some well-known examples are the warning to Moses that Pharaoh would refuse his request to release the Israelites (Exod. 4:21), Isaiah's account of Cyrus' future decision to repatriate the Jews (Isa. 44:28–45:4), and Jesus' statements that Judas would betray him (Matt. 26:20–25; Mark 14:43–45; Luke 22:47, 48; John 18:2–5) and that Peter would deny him (Matt. 26:34; Mark 14:66–72; Luke 22:54–62; John 18:17–27).

There are several ways to explain such predictions that allow them to be compatible with the view of foreknowledge proposed here. It is possible that all the necessary conditions for a particular occurrence were fulfilled at the time of its prediction. Since God knows the present exhaustively, he also knows everything that will happen as the inevitable consequence of past and present factors. This would be particularly applicable where the predicted event lay in the relatively near future. This might explain the accurate accounts of Pharaoh's actions, along with those of Judas' and Peter's behavior. Knowing their characters as intimately as God knows, one could accurately predict what they would do in certain situations. Genuine freedom excludes the concept that all human actions are predictable in this way, but it allows that some of them may be.

This explanation is not helpful in cases where individuals do not yet exist, of course. So, in the case of a prophecy like the one concerning Cyrus, we must look elsewhere. Two possibilities present themselves. One is that such a prophecy is conditional; its fulfillment depends on the actions of human beings.[36] We typically apply the category of conditional prophecy to unfulfilled predictions, such as Jonah's announcement that Nineveh would be destroyed. But it also applies to certain fulfilled predictions.[37]

Another possibility is that God sometimes takes direct action to bring about the fulfillment of a prophecy. In view of the general latitude that God allows for human freedom, such acts of intervention would be highly exceptional. But this does not mean that they are inconceivable from a perspective that emphasizes freedom. It is important to remember that occasional divine intervention is compatible with the affirmation of genuine creaturely freedom, while absolute foreknowledge is not.

At any rate, it is not necessary to provide a precise explanation for each particular prophecy. That would be known only to God. It is sufficient to show that prophecy is compatible with the view that future free decisions are not knowable in advance.

Perhaps the most important implications of the view of foreknowledge proposed here lie in the area of divine providence. On the Arminian portrait of God, providence is not the inexorable outworking of an invariant plan established in eternity. It is God's creative response to events as they happen, based on his perfect anticipation of the future and his infinite capacity to work for good in every situation.

This understanding of providence requires a higher kind of power than does a Calvinistic view. It takes greater resourcefulness for God to accomplish his purposes when he must respond to the actions of his creatures, than if he planned in advance everything that happens. Similarly, it takes greater resourcefulness for God to achieve his purposes if the future course of history is not entirely known to him than it would if it were.

This notion of providence also has important practical implications. Instead of viewing the negative experiences of life as things that God specifically plans for us to endure, for reasons usually known only to him, this concept of providence allows us to acknowledge that some things are not good and cannot be what God has intended for us. At the same time, however, it assures us that God is acutely aware of our suffering, that he shares in it to the fullest, and most important, that he will work for good in response to it, no matter how tragic it may be (see Rom. 8:28).

Further evidence for the portrait of God as a loving parent comes from its impact on personal religious experience. It provides us with a view of God who is genuinely personal and lovable. It presents us with a God who is vulnerable, who can take risks and make sacrifices, a God who is momentarily delighted and disappointed, depending on our response to his love.

It is evident, then, that a consistently Arminian concept of God's relation to the future has a lot more going for it than the fact that it resolves the old problem of freedom and foreknowledge. It is part of a comprehensive view of God that is essentially positive rather than negative. Instead of removing from God's experience something that conceivably belongs there, it attributes to God a range of experience that absolute foreknowledge excludes. When we cease to insist that God already knows the entire course of the future, we can affirm God's genuine interaction with the creaturely world. And the dynamic view of God that emerges is superior to the traditional view by every relevant criterion. It renders more faithfully the biblical descriptions of God, it makes more sense logically, and it meets the needs of personal religious experience.[38]

There is a final point worth pondering. The standard criticism against those who reject absolute foreknowledge is that their view detracts from God's power. But those who maintain that a denial of absolute foreknowledge imposes an unacceptable limit on God face an interesting question. Is it within God's power to create a world whose future he would not know completely in advance? Can he create beings with a capacity to surprise and delight him, as well as disappoint him, as they choose, and not know in advance what all their choices will be? If he cannot, then there is something significant that God cannot do. And this means that his power is limited. Either that, or the very idea of such a world is incoherent, and this is by no means obvious. But if, on the other hand, God can create such a world, just how would that world differ from the one that now exists? From all indications, not only does God have the power to create a world whose future is open, but this is exactly the kind of world he did create.

However we respond to the question of divine foreknowledge, our answer will have important implications, both for the doctrine of God and for theology in general. The view of God's knowledge briefly presented here has much to recommend it. It has strong support from the Bible, from philosophy, and from personal religious experience. It deserves careful consideration from those who wish to bring their understanding of foreknowledge into harmony with an Arminian portrait of God.

NOTES

[1] John Calvin, *Institutes of the Christian Religion*, 3.21.5, trans. Ford Lewis Battles (Philadelphia: Westminster, 1960), 2:926.

[2] Ibid. It seems that Calvin's doctrine of divine decrees was not as prominent in his own theological system as it was for later Calvinism (see, for example, the Westminster Confession). But both Calvin and his successors affirmed the position we have identified as absolute divine foreknowledge and justify it on the basis of divine election.

[3] *Institutes*, 3.21.1–6.

4 Ibid., 3.23.6; 2:954–55.

5 "A Discussion on the Subject of Predestination, Between James Arminius, D.D., Minister at Amsterdam, and Francis Junius, D.D., Professor of Divinity at Leyden," in *The Writings of James Arminius*, trans. James Nichols and W. R. Bagnall, 3 vols. (Grand Rapids: Baker, 1956), 3:66.

6 Ibid.

7 Ibid. Arminius cites 1 Samuel 23:12, which indicates that God knew that the citizens of Keilah would have delivered David into the hands of Saul, had David not escaped in time.

8 Ibid., 66.

9 Ibid., 67.

10 "An Examination of the Treatise of William Perkins Concerning the Order and Mode of Predestination," in *The Writings of James Arminius*, 3:479.

11 *God, Revelation and Authority*, vol. 6 (Waco: Word, 1983), 84.

12 Ibid., p. 85.

13 Boethius, *The Consolation of Philosophy*, trans. Richard Green (Indianapolis: Bobbs-Merrill, 1962), 116.

14 Ibid., 118–19.

15 John A. Mourant, "Scientia Media and Molinism," in *Encyclopedia of Philosophy*, ed. Paul Edwards, 8 vols. (New York: Macmillan, 1967), 7:338.

16 "By his middle knowledge God knows all the various possible worlds that he could create and what every free creature would do in all the various circumstances of those possible worlds" (William Lane Craig, *The Only Wise God: The Compatibility of Divine Foreknowledge and Human Freedom* [Grand Rapids: Baker, 1987], 133).

17 Stephen T. Davis, *Logic and the Nature of God* (Grand Rapids: Eerdmans, n.d.) 65–66.

18 Craig, *The Only Wise God*, 119.

19 "Omniscience and Immutability," in Baruch A. Brody, ed., *Readings in the Philosophy of Religion: An Analytic Approach* (Englewood Cliffs, N.J.: Prentice-Hall, 1974), 366–76. The essay originally appeared in *The Journal of Philosophy* 63 (1966).

20 Ibid., 370–71; emphasis his.

21 Ronald H. Nash, *The Concept of God* (Grand Rapids: Zondervan, 1983), 99–105, 114.

22 Davis, *Logic of God*, 23.

23 Ibid., 51.

24 In the words of Richard Swinburne, "It seems doubtful whether it is logically possible that there be both an omniscient person and also free men: but . . . it is definitely logically impossible that there be an omniscient person who is himself perfectly free" (*The Coherence of Theism* [Oxford: Clarendon, 1977], 172).

25 Craig, *The Only Wise God*, 130.

26 Richard E. Creel, *Divine Impassibility: An Essay in Philosophical Theology* (Cambridge: Cambridge University Press, 1986), 90. This distinction is essentially the one involved in the familiar free-will defense. This theodicy maintains that the events of the actual world are the joint issue of God's decisions and those of free creatures, some of whom misused their freedom to rebel. God is not responsible for evil, because he cannot create beings who are free and at the same time guarantee what they do with their freedom. In other words, God alone does not, and logically cannot, determine what the actual world will be, if in fact some of its inhabitants are free. If God creates morally free creatures, it is logically possible for them to remain loyal to him and logically possible for them to rebel. But which of these becomes the actual course of events is something God alone cannot determine. So we cannot assume that God can create every possible world. There are some possible worlds which only God-and-the-creatures can make.

27 Jonathan Edwards, *Freedom of the Will*, ed. Paul Ramsey (New Haven and London: Hale University Press, 1957), 263; italics his.

28 *God, Revelation and Authority*, 6:85.

[29] Hartshorne's enormously productive philosophical career is now in its seventh decade. His most important books on God are *Man's Vision of God and the Logic of Theism* (Chicago: Willett, Clark, 1941; reprint, Hamden, Conn.: Archon, 1964); *The Divine Relativity* (New Haven and London: Yale University Press, 1948); and *A Natural Theology for Our Time* (LaSalle, Ill.: Open Court, 1967). For a recent and readable expression of his views, see *Omnipotence and Other Theological Mistakes*, especially chapter 1 (Albany, N.Y.: State University of New York Press, 1984).

[30] Richard Taylor, "Determinism," *Encyclopedia of Philosophy*, ed. Paul Edwards, 8 vols. (New York: Macmillan, 1967), 2:363.

[31] *The Coherence of Theism*, 172–78.

[32] Ibid., 175.

[33] Ibid., 174.

[34] Gordon Lewis and Bruce Demarest, *Integrative Theology*, vol. 1 (Grand Rapids: Zondervan, 1987), 191–92, 237.

[35] For more extensive discussion of the following points, see my book *God's Foreknowledge and Man's Free Will* (Minneapolis: Bethany, 1985). See also Pinnock's advocacy of this view of omniscience in Basinger and Basinger pp. 143–62 as well as in the present volume.

[36] The clearest description of conditional prophecy is found in Jeremiah 18:7–10.

[37] An example is Jeremiah's prophecy of Jerusalem's destruction by the Babylonians (Jer. 32:4; cf. 38:17–18; 52:12–14). In fact, Jesus' predictions of Judas' betrayal and Peter's denial may have been conditional prophecies. It is possible that Jesus was seeking to warn them of what could (and ultimately did) happen in hopes that they would change their ways in time to avert the tragedies that followed.

[38] The respective effects of the concept of absolute foreknowledge and the alternative proposed here on the doctrine of God are described in two little known nineteenth-century works by Lorenzo D. McCabe, *Divine Nescience of Future Contingencies a Necessity* (New York: Phillips and Hunt, 1882), and *The Foreknowledge of God and Cognate Themes in Theology and Philosophy* (Cincinnati: Walden & Stowe, 1882). The first is particularly helpful in showing how a denial of absolute foreknowledge enhances our understanding of God. William McGuire King discusses McCabe's theory in "God's Nescience of Future Contingents: A Nineteenth-Century Theory," *Process Studies* 9 (1979): 105–15.

MIDDLE KNOWLEDGE
A CALVINIST-ARMINIAN
RAPPROCHEMENT?

William L. Craig

INTRODUCTION

Writing in the aftermath of the Protestant Reformation and the Council of Trent, the Spanish Jesuit Luis Molina (1535–1600) formulated a doctrine of divine omniscience, which he called *scientia media* (middle knowledge). By means of this doctrine he proposed to avoid the Protestant error of denying genuine human freedom, yet without thereby sacrificing the sovereignty of God. It is a sad note of history that in Molina's perception, the *main point* of the Protestant Reformation was that man lacks true freedom in virtue of God's knowledge and sovereignty.

The Council of Trent in its decree on justification (1547) had declared that the initiative in the process of justification is God's unmerited, prevenient grace, which stirs and solicits the will of man, but which may be either accepted or resisted by the human will. Anyone who denies either prevenient grace or human freedom is summarily condemned. Firmly persuaded of these truths, Molina opposed himself to what he perceived to be the central teaching of the Reformation: the denial of human freedom. He thereby tragically missed the Reformers' most vital teaching of justification by faith alone and adhered to what Gerard Smith has himself as one of the "constant assertions of Catholic dogma": that salvation is the work of God and man–God provides unmerited grace to man, who makes good use of it to perform supernatural acts, which in turn go to merit his glorification.[1] But we should be short-sighted, indeed, if our repugnance at Molina's soteriology blinded us to his insights in resolving the tension between the doctrines of divine sovereignty and human freedom. He claimed to be able to affirm both these doctrines, and he boldly asserted that had the doctrine of middle knowledge been known in the early church, then neither Pelagianism nor Lutheranism would have arisen.[2] The resolution of the tension between God's sovereignty and man's freedom is an admirable objective that ought to interest any Christian. Molina therefore deserves to be given a fair hearing, for who knows whether through the doctrine of *scientia media* we might not achieve the desirable goal of a Calvinist-Arminian *rapprochement*?

Molina's doctrine of middle knowledge is perhaps best understood against the backdrop of the Reformers' views on human freedom.[3] Here it must be admitted that Molina's perception of their teaching was clear-sighted: the principal Reformers did deny to man significant freedom, at least in his dealings with God. Luther and Calvin were prepared to grant to man only spontaneity of choice and voluntariness of will, not the ability to choose otherwise in the circumstances in which an agent finds himself.

Luther's denial of freedom of the will was predicated on what he perceived to be the incompatibility of such freedom with God's foreknowledge and omnipotence. According to Luther, since God's foreknowledge is certain and infallible and since God can bring about whatever he wills, it follows that whatever he foreknows and wills happens necessarily. Luther explains,

> . . . God knows nothing contingently, but . . . he foresees and purposes and does all things by his immutable, eternal, and infallible will. . . . If he foreknows as he wills, then his will is eternal and unchanging (because it belongs to his nature), and if he wills as he foreknows, then his knowledge is eternal and unchanging (because it belongs to his nature).
>
> From this it follows irrefutably that everything we do, everything that happens, even if it seems to us to happen mutably and contingently, happens in fact nonetheless necessarily and immutably, if you have regard to the will of God. For the will of God is effectual and cannot be hindered . . . ; moreover it is wise, so that it cannot be deceived. Now if his will is not hindered, nothing can prevent the work itself from being done, in the place, time, manner, and measure that he himself both foresees and wills.[4]

In short, "God's foreknowledge and omnipotence are diametrically opposed to our free choice."[5] Thus Luther does not draw back from asserting that Judas betrayed Christ necessarily.[6] The only freedom of the will that remains is that the will chooses voluntarily, that is to say, it is not coerced; but the fact remains that what it chooses it chooses necessarily. Curiously—and inconsistently—Luther seemed to consider exempting natural choices in worldly dealings from this necessity, claiming that we might treat man as free in things below but bound in things above.[7] But as other proponents of theological fatalism have clearly seen, since God's foreknowledge embraces all future contingents, the argument, if sound, would apply equally to human choices concerning worldly affairs as well as to choices concerning divine affairs. Everything that happens does so necessarily.

Calvin, on the other hand, did not argue that in virtue of divine prescience everything happens necessarily. Rather, his denial of human freedom grew out of his doctrine of divine providence. In Calvin's view, God's providence is universal and total, so that nothing can happen but that God has decreed and willed it. Calvin writes:

> . . . what is called providence describes God, not as idly beholding from heaven the transactions which happen in the world, but as holding the helm of the universe, and regulating all events. Thus it belongs no less to his hands than to his eyes. When Abraham said to his son, "God will provide," he intended not only to assert his prescience of a future event, but to leave the care of an unknown thing to the will of him who frequently puts an end to circumstances of perplexity and confusion. Whence it follows that providence consists in action; for it is ignorant trifling to talk of mere prescience.[8]

> Those who wish to bring an odium on this doctrine, calumniate it as the same with the opinion of the Stoics concerning fate, with which Augustine also was formerly reproached. Though we are averse to all contentions about words, yet we admit not the term *fate;* both because it is of that novel and profane kind which Paul teaches us to avoid, and because they endeavour to load the truth of God with the odium attached to it. But that dogma is falsely and maliciously charged upon us. For we do not, with the Stoics, imagine a necessity arising from a perpetual concatenation and intricate series of causes, contained in nature; but we make God the Arbiter and Governor of all things, who, in his own wisdom, has, from the remotest eternity, decreed what he would do, and now, by his own power, executes what he has decreed. Whence we assert, that not only the heaven and the earth, and inanimate creatures, but also the deliberations and volitions of men, are so governed by his providence, as to be directed to the end appointed by it. What then? you will say; does nothing happen fortuitously or contingently? I answer . . . that *fortune* and *chance* are words of the heathen, with the signification of which the minds of the pious ought not to be occupied. For if all success be the benediction of God, and calamity and adversity his malediction, there is no room left in human affairs for fortune or chance. . . . And though [Augustine] elsewhere decides, that all things are conducted partly by the free will of man, partly by the providence of God, yet he just after shows that men are subject to it and governed by it, assuming as a

principle that nothing could be more absurd, than for any thing
to happen independently of the ordination of God; because it
would happen at random. By this reasoning he excludes also
any contingence dependent on the human will. . . . But in what
sense *permission* ought to be understood, whenever it is
mentioned by him, will appear from one passage; where he
proves that the will of God is the supreme and first cause of all
things, because nothing happens but by his command or
permission. He certainly does not suppose God to remain an
idle spectator, determining to permit any thing; there is an
intervention of actual volition, if I may be allowed the expression, which otherwise could never be considered as a cause.[9]

His view of human freedom is in the end the same as Luther's: the
liberty of spontaneity.[10] God's complete sovereignty excludes any
genuine possibility of man's choosing in any circumstances other
than as he does choose.

Thus, according to the Protestant Reformers, in virtue of
God's prescience and providence, everything that occurs in the
world does so necessarily. Human choice is voluntary and
spontaneous, but the will is not free to choose other than as it
does. Now to Molina, such a doctrine was quite simply heretical.
He could not see how mere spontaneity of choice sufficed to make
a human being a responsible moral agent nor how the Reformers'
view would not lead to making God the cause of man's sinful acts
and, hence, the author of evil. He was therefore deeply exercised
to formulate a strong doctrine of divine prescience, providence,
and predestination that would be wholly compatible with genuine
human freedom, and he believed that in *scientia media* he had
found the key.

THE DOCTRINE OF MIDDLE KNOWLEDGE

According to Molina's understanding of God's omniscience,
the divine ideas present to God not only all *possibilia* but also all
futuribilia—that is, states of affairs that not only *could* obtain but in
fact *would* obtain under the hypothesis that certain other states of
affairs already obtained. By choosing to actualize a certain order of
hypothetical states, God thus knows what further states will be
actual as a consequence. Molina explains:

It is not simply because things exist outside their causes in
eternity that God knows future contingents with certainty;
rather, before (in our way of conceiving it, but with a basis in
reality) He creates anything at all, He comprehends in Himself—because of the depth of His knowledge—all things
which, as a result of all the secondary causes possible in virtue
of His omnipotence, would contingently or simply freely come
to be on the hypothesis that He should will to establish these or
those orders of things with these or those circumstances; and by

the very fact that through His free will He established in being that order of things and causes which He in fact established, He comprehended in His very self and in that very decree of His all the things which were in fact freely or contingently going to be or not going to be as a result of secondary causes—and He comprehended this not only prior to anything's existing in time, but even prior (in our way of conceiving it, with a basis in reality) to any created thing's existing in the duration of eternity.[11]

Several notions in this account merit comment. The notion of a sort of conceptual, atemporal priority within the knowledge of God is nothing new. Scotus had posited three moments in God's timeless knowledge of future contingents: (1) God's knowledge of contradictory pairs of all logically contingent propositions, (2) God's decision to actualize the state of affairs described in one disjunct of each contradictory pair, and (3) God's knowledge of all logically contingent propositions that as a result are in fact true.[12] Similarly, Aquinas had posited three logically consecutive aspects of God's timeless act of knowledge: (1) *scientia simplicis intelligentiae*, by which God knows all the possibles; (2) *scientia approbationis*, by which God decides to create certain of the possibles; and (3) *scientia visionis*, by which God knows what exists at any time in the actual world.[13] Molina, too, posits three logically consecutive moments in God's knowledge of the actual world. He holds the relation of priority among them to be conceptual (*nostro modo intelligendi*); we are not to admit of any temporal priority or succession in God's knowledge. On the other hand, this relation of priority is not therefore a mere figment of the imagination (*cum fundamento in re*). What Molina had in mind, I think, is a relation of conditionship between the various aspects of God's knowledge; God can have a certain sort of knowledge only on the condition of his having a certain other type of knowledge. The latter sort is thus in a sense prior to the former.

Natural vs. Free Knowledge

Now Molina's first and third sorts of divine knowledge correspond with Thomas' *scientia simplicis intelligentiae* and *scientia visionis*, and Molina agrees that between these a decision of the divine will interposes. Precisely in virtue of this act of divine will, Molina prefers to call God's knowledge prior to his decision "natural knowledge" and his knowledge subsequent to that decision "free knowledge." God's natural knowledge comprises not only all the possibilities taken as individual entities but also all possible complexes of such entities and their actions:

Through this type of knowledge He knew all the things to which the divine power extended either immediately or by the mediation of secondary causes, including not only the natures of individuals and the necessary states of affairs composed of them, but also the contingent states of affairs—through this knowledge He knew, to be sure, not that the latter were or were not going to obtain determinately, but rather that they were able to obtain and able not to obtain, a feature which belongs to them necessarily and thus also falls under God's natural knowledge.[14]

God's natural knowledge thus affords him a knowledge of every contingent state of affairs that could hypothetically obtain: " . . . the divine ideas represent to God *naturally*, before any free determination of his will, every future contingent state of affairs *under that hypothesis and condition*."[15] A central feature of God's natural knowledge is that the content of this knowledge is essential to God; indeed, this is why such knowledge is natural. It does not depend on God's will, but necessarily belongs to God's omnipotence.

On the other hand, God's free knowledge is the aspect of his omniscience that comprises his knowledge of this existent, contingent world. This knowledge is posterior to the free decision of God's will to create, to instantiate one of the possible orders known by his natural knowledge. In Molina's words:

> The second type is purely *free* knowledge, by which, after the free act of his will, God knew *absolutely* and *determinately*, *without any condition or hypothesis*, which ones from among all the contingent states of affairs were *in fact* going to obtain and, likewise, which ones were not going to obtain.[16]

Since this knowledge is posterior to the decision of God's will and since God's decision to create this world is free, it follows that the content of free knowledge is not essential to divine omniscience but is contingent on which world God in fact creates. Had God created different worlds or even no world at all, the content of his free knowledge would have been different.[17] So while it is essential to God to have free knowledge, the content of what he freely knows is contingent on which world he chooses to create.

Now between these two moments of divine knowledge is interposed the act of the divine will, which Aquinas denominated *scientia approbationis*. According to Molina, God's act of will reflects "an absolutely complete and unlimited deliberation"[18] and results in one contingent order being freely instantiated by God rather than some other. But for Molina the act of God's will to create a world is not itself a type of knowledge. Hence, he denies that God's knowledge is a cause of things, except insofar as God's natural knowledge serves as a sort of exemplary cause on which creatures are patterned and insofar as his third type of knowledge, discussed below, delimits which possible orders of things God is able to bring into existence.[19] Since God's willing to create some world is not itself a type of knowledge, Thomas' three types of divine knowledge reduce to two: natural and free knowledge.

Middle Knowledge

But now Molina suggests that there is in fact a third type of knowledge in God that stands between natural and free knowledge; for want of a better name, Molina calls it simply middle knowledge. Middle knowledge is the aspect of divine omniscience that comprises God's knowledge, prior to any determination of the divine will, of which contingent events would occur under any hypothetical set of circumstances. Molina writes:

> . . . the third type is *middle* knowledge, by which, in virtue of the most profound and inscrutable comprehension of each free will, He saw in his own essence what each such will would do with its innate freedom were it to be placed in this or that or, indeed, in infinitely many orders of things—even though it would really be able, if it so willed, to do the opposite. . . .[20]

Thus, whereas by his natural knowledge God knows that, say, Peter when placed under a certain set of circumstances *could* either deny Christ or not deny Christ, being free to do either under identical circumstances,[21] by his middle knowledge God knows what Peter *would* do if placed under those circumstances.

According to Molina, middle knowledge cannot be reduced to either natural knowledge or free knowledge but shares features of each. It cannot be reduced to free knowledge because (1) it is prior to any free decree of God's will and (2) the content of divine middle knowledge does not lie within the scope of his power, so that he cannot control what he knows via such knowledge.

These two features of middle knowledge are extremely important. The first implies that God's knowledge of what contingent events would take place under any set of circumstances is a prerequisite for God's knowledge of what will in fact occur in the world. Both God's willing to create a world and his consequent knowledge of what will in fact be actual presuppose and depend on his knowing what would occur under any given set of circumstances. He did not, for example, first know what Peter would do in the actual circumstances that would exist and then on this basis know what Peter would have done had he been placed in some other set of circumstances. Rather the opposite is true: prior to God's decision to create any set of circumstances, he knew what Peter would do within any possible order of circumstances; then, given the decision of his will to bring about a certain set of circumstances, God knew what Peter would in fact do. The second feature of middle knowledge follows from the first. Since middle knowledge is prior to the divine will, its content is independent of the divine will and, hence, outside the pale of God's omnipotence. Just as God's knowledge of logical truths is outside his control and is simply given, so, too, his knowledge of what would be the free decisions of created wills under certain circumstances is simply given and outside his control. Of course, God may easily prevent a creature's free decision by not creating that creature at all or by altering the circumstances in such a way as to bring it about that the creature freely decides to do something else; but God cannot annul the fact that if a free creature *were* to be placed in a certain set of circumstances, he *would* choose to do a certain act. Thus, for example, God could prevent Peter's denial of Christ by not creating Peter at all while creating many of the same extra-Petrine circumstances or else by creating a different set of circumstances under which Peter would not have denied Christ. But God cannot control the fact that were he to bring about a specific set of circumstances, then Peter would freely deny Christ. Since the content of divine middle knowledge thus depends on what the creatures themselves would do, God cannot control what he knows by his middle knowledge.

On the other hand, neither can middle knowledge be reduced to natural knowledge, though Molina at first introduces it as a sort of natural knowledge.[22] For whereas the content of God's natural knowledge is essential to him, clearly the content of his middle knowledge is not, since creatures are free under certain sets of circumstances to refrain from doing what they would do. While it is essential to God's nature that he have middle knowledge, the content of that knowledge is contingent because creatures could act differently under identical circumstances. But if their decisions were to be different, then the content of God's middle knowledge would be different. As Molina explains, "If created free choice were going to do the opposite, as indeed it can, then God would have known that very thing through this same type of knowledge, and not what he in fact knows. Therefore, it is no more natural for God to know through this sort of knowledge one part of a contradiction that depends on created free choice than it is for him to know the opposite part."[23]

Middle knowledge, then, may be said to be like natural knowledge in that it is prior to the decision of the divine will and outside God's power, but to be like free knowledge in that such knowledge depends on a decision of free will (in this case, however, creatures', not God's) that could be different.

As Molina's original explanation cited above indicates, it is God's middle knowledge that thus supplies the basis for God's foreknowledge of contingent events in the actual world. By knowing what every possible creature would do under any possible circumstances, God knows what will in fact take place in the world. Molina explains,

> All contingent states of affairs are . . . represented to God *naturally, before* any act or free determination of the divine will; and they are represented not only as being *possible* but also as being *future*—not *absolutely future,* but *future under the condition and on the hypothesis* that God should decide to create this or that order of things and causes with these or those circumstances. However, once the determination of the divine will is added . . . God knows all the contingent states of affairs with certainty as being future *simply* and *absolutely,* and now *without any hypothesis or condition.*[24]

For Molina an order of things and causes constitutes a possible world that God instantiates progressively in time, while sets of circumstances are less than maximal states of affairs within the world. By knowing what free creatures would do under any possible circumstances, God is, so to speak, able to construct a possible world containing (1) circumstances caused directly by God, (2) decisions wrought by the free creatures whom God wills to create, and (3) further circumstances brought about by the free decisions of such creatures. By means of his middle knowledge, God is able to construct a possible world that is both within his power to actualize and is consonant with his will. By taking into account the free decisions of creatures in his planning, God in willing to actualize a certain world does not violate the freedom of creatures in that world, though he knows with certainty what they will do:

> . . . the explanation for God's knowing with certainty which part of any contradiction among those contingent states of affairs dependent on free created choice is going to obtain is not a determination of the divine will by which God turns and determines created free choice to one or the other part, but is instead a free determination by which God decides to create free choice in this or that order of things and circumstances. Nor do we believe that this determination is *by itself* a *sufficient* explanation for God's knowing with certainty which part of each contradiction among those states of affairs is going to obtain; rather the sufficient explanation is the determination of the divine will *along with* God's comprehension in his essence of each created free will through his natural [i.e., middle] knowledge, a comprehension by means of which He knows with certainty, before the determination of his will, what such and such a free will would do in its freedom on the hypothesis and condition that God should create it and situate it in this particular order of things—even though it could, if it so willed, do the opposite, and even though if it were going to do the opposite, as it is able to, then God would have known *this* in his essence through that very same knowledge and comprehen-

sion, and *not* what He *in fact* knows is going to be done by that free will.[25]

By positing middle knowledge in God, Molina is thus able to offer an innovative and provocative account of how it is that God foreknows future contingents.

Now it might be asked how it is that by knowing his own essence alone God is able to have middle knowledge concerning what free creatures would do in any situation. Molina and his compatriot and fellow Jesuit, Francisco Suarez, differed in their responses to this question. Molina's answer is alluded to in the words of the initial citation above: "because of the depth of his knowledge." According to Molina, God not only knows in his own essence all possible creatures, but his intellect infinitely surpasses the capabilities of finite free wills so that he understands them so thoroughly that he knows not only what they *could* choose under any set of circumstances, but what they *would* choose.[26] In another place Molina speaks of "his immense and altogether unlimited *knowledge,* by which he comprehends in the deepest and most eminent way whatever falls under his omnipotence, *to penetrate created free choice* in such a way as to discern and intuit with certainty which part it is going to turn itself to by its own innate freedom."[27] Because his intellect is infinite, whereas a free creature is finite, God's insight into the will of a free creature is of such a surpassing quality that God knows exactly what the free creature would do were God to place him in a certain set of circumstances.

Suarez, on the other hand, argues that God must have knowledge of *furtura conditionata* because the conditional propositions concerning such events are bivalent.[28] To the extent that such propositions are true, they are knowable; for all truth is as such knowable, since truth as truth is the proper object of the intellect and of knowledge. Since God is all-knowing, he must therefore know such conditional propositions. Suarez compares God's omniscience to his omnipotence: just as his power extends to all things possible, so God's knowledge extends to all things knowable. The whole dispute therefore devolves down to the question of whether such conditional propositions have determinate truth and falsity. Since, on Suarez's view, such propositions are true or false, God knows essentially and immediately all such true propositions.

In summary, then, divine omniscience, though eternal and complete, can be conceptually differentiated into three types of knowledge, which are ordered according to a sort of conditional priority. Most fundamental is God's unconditional natural knowledge, which includes his knowledge of all logically possible states of affairs and possible maximal orders. Posterior to this is God's middle knowledge, which serves to delimit the possible states of affairs to those that would become actual through the free decisions of creatures, should God choose to actualize certain sets of circumstances that include them, and to those maximal orders that could obtain, should God freely decide to act in one way or other. God then deliberates which order he will instantiate, including what decisions he will take and what decisions he would take under other circumstances, and freely chooses to create a certain world order. Finally, then, on the basis of his decision to create some world order, God knows every detail about that order, not only the circumstances he will directly bring about and the decisions he will make, but also the free decisions that creatures will make and the contingent circumstances that will result in consequence of those decisions.

PRESCIENCE, PROVIDENCE, AND PREDESTINATION

One of the principal motivations behind Molina's theory of *scientia media* is the theological capital he thought stood to be gained from such a conception in reconciling divine sovereignty and human freedom, especially in light of Protestant errors. I am convinced that a Molinist theory of middle knowledge can go a long way toward reconciling Calvinist and Arminian views, affirming with the Calvinist a strong doctrine of divine sovereignty and insisting with the Arminian on genuine human freedom. Let us look more closely, then, at the implications of middle knowledge for prescience, providence, and predestination.

Prescience

Little more needs to be said of the value of *media scientia* for the doctrine of divine foreknowledge. If Molina is correct, he has furnished a remarkably ingenious basis for God's knowledge of the future. By knowing what every possible free creature would do in any possible situation, God can by bringing about that situation know what the creature will freely do. Of course, the situation itself may depend on the conspiration of previous contingent causes, so that God would have to know what even earlier circumstances to bring about in order to get precisely the situation he desires. And that situation may constitute part of the circumstances for still further free decisions that God would foreknow. These sets of circumstances combine to form world orders from which God, by willing his own free actions, including the decision to create, selects one to bring into actuality. Thus he foreknows with certainty everything that happens in the world.

Moreover, God's infallible foreknowledge is not incompatible with the contingency of future events, for were some event to occur in a different way from the way it will in fact occur, God's middle knowledge would have been different, and, hence, God would have foreknown differently than he in fact does. Molina dares even to assert the temporal necessity of God's beliefs and volitions and to deny any power whatsoever over the past; for since he holds that neither temporal necessity nor power is transmitted by logical entailment, a state of affairs that is necessary and outside our control may entail another state of affairs that is nonetheless contingent and within our control. While it is impossible in the composed sense, given God's foreknowledge, for anything to happen differently from the way it will, this sense is irrelevant to contingency and freedom. In the relevant, divided sense we are as perfectly free in our decisions and actions as if God's foreknowledge did not exist.[29] Middle knowledge therefore supplies not only the basis for divine foreknowledge, but also the means of reconciling that foreknowledge with creaturely freedom and contingency.

Providence

The world view of the Bible involves a very strong conception of divine sovereignty, even as it presupposes human freedom and responsibility.[30] Reconciling these two doctrines without compromising either has proven extraordinarily difficult. But Molina's theory of middle knowledge furnishes a startling solution to this enigma. Since God knows prior to his decision to create what any possible creature would do in any possible circumstances, God in deciding what creatures to create and which circumstances to bring about or permit ultimately controls and directs the course of world history to his desired ends, yet without violating in any way the freedom of his creatures.

Molina defines providence as the ordering of things to their ends either directly by God himself or mediately through secondary causes.[31] But here one must distinguish between God's absolute and conditional intentions concerning creatures. It is, for example, God's absolute intention that no creature should ever sin and that all should reach beatitude. But we have seen that it is not within God's power to determine what decisions creatures would freely take under various circumstances. In certain circumstances, creatures will freely sin, despite the fact that it is God's will that they not sin. If then God, for whatever reason, wants to bring them precisely those circumstances, he has no choice but to allow the creature to sin, though that is not his absolute intention. God's absolute intentions are thus often frustrated by sinful creatures, though his conditional intention, which takes into account the creature's free action, is always fulfilled. Now obviously in this world it is the plan of providence to permit sin to occur. But even sin serves God's conditional intentions in that it manifests his overflowing goodness in the Incarnation for the purpose of rescuing man from sin, his power in his redeeming man from sin, and his justice in punishing sin.

While God's providence, then, extends to everything that happens, it does not follow that God wills positively everything that happens.[32] God wills positively every good creaturely decision, but evil decisions he does not will, but merely permits. Molina explains,

> . . . all *good* things, whether produced by causes acting from a necessity of nature or by free causes, depend upon divine predestination . . . and providence in such a way that each is *specifically intended* by God through His predetermination and providence, whereas the *evil* acts of the created will are subject as well to divine predetermination and providence to the extent that the causes from which they emanate and the general concurrence on God's part required to elicit them are granted through divine predetermination and providence—though not in order that *these particular acts* should emanate from them, but rather in order that *other, far different, acts* might come to be, and that in order that the innate freedom of the things endowed with a will might be preserved for their maximum benefit; in addition evil acts are subject to that same divine predetermination and providence to the extent that they cannot exist in particular unless God by His providence *permits them in particular* in the service of some greater good. It clearly follows from the above that all things without exception are *individually* subject to God's will and providence, which intend certain of them *as particulars* and permit the rest *as particulars*. Thus, the leaf hanging from the tree does not fall, nor does either of the two sparrows sold for a farthing fall to the ground, nor does anything else whatever happen without God's providence and will either *intending* it *as a particular* or *permitting* it *as a particular*.[33]

Everything that happens, therefore, occurs either by God's will or permission, and thus falls under his providence.

This serves to bring into focus Molina's doctrine of simultaneous concurrence, which together with middle knowledge supplies the underpinnings of his doctrine of providence.[34] Since God is the first cause, Christian theology traditionally held that God not only conserves the universe in being, but that he also concurs with the operation of every secondary cause in the universe so that he is quite literally the cause of everything that happens.

Aquinas interpreted the notion of divine concurrence to mean that God not only supplies and conserves the power of operation in every secondary cause, but that he also acts on the secondary causes to produce their actual operations, a view that came to be known as the doctrine of premotion. With regard to contingent acts of the will, this doctrine meant that the free decisions of creatures are produced by God's causing the will to turn itself this way or that. The doctrine of premotion has thus a very strong conception of divine sovereignty, but its proponents insist that human freedom is not thereby annulled, since God causes the finite will to turn itself *freely* to one or the other part of a contradiction. Molina, however, rejects the interpretation of divine concurrence in terms of premotion as in reality utterly deterministic and incompatible with the existence of sin.[35] Lutherans and Calvinists seem to agree with Molina with regard, at least, to determinism, since they, quite consistently it seems, recognize that God's turning the will this way or that is incompatible with human liberty of indifference. But Molina does not adopt the Reformers' determinism; instead, he proposes to regard divine concurrence as simultaneous concurrence; that is to say, God acts, not *on,* but *with* the secondary cause to produce its effect. "God's general concurrence . . . is *not* an influence of God's *on the cause* so that the cause might act after having been previously moved and applied to its act by that influence, but is instead an influence *along with the cause directly on the effect.*"[36]

He compares divine concurrence with secondary causes to two men pulling a boat: there are two causes cooperating to produce a single, total effect. Thus when a man wills to produce some effect, God concurs with the man's decision by also acting to produce that effect; but he does not act on the man's will to move it to its decision. "This concurrence is not a motion of God's *on* the will by which He moves, applies, and determines the will either to precisely *that* act . . . or even to *an* act . . . ; instead it is an influence *along with* the will which depends for its existence on the influence and cooperation of the will itself. . . ."[37] In sinful decisions, God concurs by acting to produce the effect, but he is not to be held responsible for the sinfulness of the act, since he did not move the finite will to do it, but only out of his determination to allow human freedom, he permitted the decision to be made.[38] In either willing or permitting everything that happens, therefore, God acts to produce every event in the actual world.

In reconciling divine sovereignty and human freedom, Molina thus appeals both to middle knowledge and simultaneous concurrence. By his middle knowledge God knows an infinity of orders that he could instantiate because he knows how the creatures in them would in fact respond given the various circumstances. He then decides by a free act of his will how he would respond in these various circumstances and simultaneously wills to bring about one of these orders. He directly causes certain circumstances to come into being and others indirectly by causally determined secondary causes. Free creatures, however, he allows to act as he knew they would when placed in such circumstances, and he concurs with their decisions in producing in being the effects they desire. Some of these effects God desires unconditionally and so wills positively that they occur, but others he does not unconditionally desire, but nevertheless permits them because of his overriding desire to allow creaturely freedom and knowing that even these sinful acts will fit into the overall scheme of things so that God's ultimate ends in human history will be accomplished.[39]

God has thus providentially arranged for everything that happens by either willing or permitting it, and he causes everything that does happen, yet in such a way as to preserve freedom and contingency. For God's providential order is not necessary: given the effects produced by God in the world either directly or else indirectly via deterministic causes, things could go vastly differently were the creatures simply to choose differently, as they are free to do. But, of course, were they to so choose, God would have possessed different middle knowledge than he does and so would have chosen a different providential plan to bring about his ends. Although creatures are free, God's ends will certainly be achieved, since the infallibility of middle knowledge guarantees that God's providential plan cannot fail. Divine sovereignty and human freedom are, therefore, entirely compatible, given middle knowledge and simultaneous concurrence.

Predestination

If Molina's reconciliation of divine providence and human freedom is stunning, his reconciliation of predestination and freedom is even more ingenious. According to Molina, prior to Augustine the church fathers typically based predestination on divine foreknowledge: God predestined those to be saved whom he foreknew would freely place their faith in Christ. With the advent of Pelagianism, however, Augustine showed the need of God's prevenient grace if any person was to come to faith. Lost in sin, people would never on their own initiative come to Christ; hence, God must first stir their wills by his unmerited grace to move them to saving faith. Predestination thus became the arbitrary gift of God, unrelated to his foreknowledge. Hence, in the absence of a doctrine of middle knowledge, one seemingly has to hold either that predestination is based on the foreknowledge of human merits or else that predestination is wholly wrought by God without any consideration of human free decision. It is this dilemma that Molina seeks to resolve by means of the theory of middle knowledge.

In Molina's view, predestination is merely that aspect of providence that pertains to eternal salvation. Predestination is the

concept of the order and the means by which God ensures that
some free creature attains eternal life.[40] It has its basis in (1) the
divine middle knowledge, through which God knows that a
certain creature will freely assent, given certain circumstances, to
God's gifts of grace, and (2) the divine will, which chooses to
actualize such an order of circumstances and gifts. In the final
analysis, the act of predestination is simply God's instantiating
one of the world orders known to him via his middle knowledge.

Molina rejects as Calvinistic and heretical the view of Bañez
that God gratuitously chooses certain persons to be saved and
others to be damned and then premoves each elect person's will to
produce saving faith while leaving the nonelect in sin, so that the
elect are subjects of predestination while the nonelect are subjects
of reprobation.[41] At the same time, Molina rejects as Pelagian the
view of Lessius that predestination consists in God's creating
certain persons because he knew that they would freely make
good use of the grace God would give them and so be saved.
Rather, Molina held that God's choosing to create certain persons
has nothing to do with how they would respond to his grace; he
simply chose to create the world order he wanted to, and no
rationale for this choice is to be sought other than the divine will
itself. In this sense, predestination is for Molina wholly gratuitous,
the result of the divine will, and in no way based on the merits or
demerits of creatures.[42]

Persons in the world order that God has chosen to create who
are not predestined to salvation cannot complain of injustice on
God's part, because God in his goodness provides sufficient grace
for salvation to all people in the world, and the only reason they
are not predestined is that they freely ignore or reject the divine
helps that God provides. Their damnation is therefore entirely
their own fault. This is so even though if they had been put in
different circumstances or given other helps, they would freely
have responded to God's grace and been predestined to salvation.
(Similarly, those who are predestined to salvation, if placed in
different circumstances or given different helps, might not have
responded and so been lost.) For the fact remains that God desires
all people to be saved and has provided gracious helps sufficient
for every person to have faith and be saved, if only the person so
wills. That is not to say that according to Molina it is simply up to
us to be predestined or not, as Van Steenberghe reminds us,

This is not to say that predestination depends on the individual,
since it consists in the choice made by God of an order of things
in which He foresaw that this individual will arrive at salvation.
Precisely there is the delicate point, "the unfathomable depths
of God's designs": God knew an infinite of providential orders
in which the non-predestined would freely arrive at eternal life
and thus would have been predestined; He knew as well an

infinity of providential orders in which the predestined would have freely lost beatitude and would have been reprobate; and yet He chose for the one and for the other the order of providence in which He foresaw that the one would be saved and the other not. He did this by his will alone and without consideration of their acts, but without injustice, since He has provided them all the means of arriving at eternal life.[43]

In Molina's view, we might say that it is up to God whether we find ourselves in a world in which we are predestined, but that it is up to us whether we are predestined in the world in which we find ourselves.[44]

This serves to bring into focus Molina's doctrine of grace. As a Catholic Counter-Reformer, Molina did not profit from Luther's insight into the nature of grace as the unmerited favor of God, but instead thought of grace as a sort of divine assistance or power given to people to enable them to perform certain acts, which they in their corrupted natural state could not do, that lead in turn to their meriting salvation. Although man's unassisted will can produce a sort of natural faith that is not salvific, justifying faith is a supernatural act that requires God's prevenient and exciting grace to solicit and rouse the will. The action of prevenient grace is followed by a response of the human will, either assenting to or dissenting from the operation of grace. Prevenient grace is wholly unmerited, but is given gratuitously by God to all people, even to those who have no natural faith or desire for salvation. If the will assents to the action of prevenient grace, this same grace becomes cooperating grace simply in view of the will's decision to cooperate with it. God infuses into the assenting person a *habitus fidei supernaturalis*, whereby the believer from then on makes the act of faith with only God's general concurrence and so multiplies good works meriting salvation. The action of prevenient grace, which is a particular concurrence of God, differs from God's general concurrence in that his particular concurrence acts *on* the will, not *with* it, to render it capable of responding freely to God's initiative, and particular concurrence is not simultaneous, but precedes in time or nature the operation of the will. The will remains free to resist the action of prevenient grace, thus aborting the process of justification.

Obviously, then, for Molina grace is not intrinsically efficacious, but only extrinsically efficacious; that is to say, the difference between sufficient grace and efficacious grace lies not in the quality or magnitude of the grace itself, but in the response of the human will to that grace.[45] Sufficient grace for salvation is accorded to all people; for those who assent to its operation this same grace is efficacious in procuring their justification. God desires and has given grace sufficient that all people should be saved. If some believe and others do not, it is not because some received prevenient grace and calling while others did not. Rather, the efficacy of God's grace in our lives is up to us, and every person, however unconducive his circumstances, is called and moved by God in a measure sufficient for salvation. The reconciliation of predestination with free will is accomplished by means of God's middle knowledge. Prior to the determination of the divine will, God knows how every possible free creature would respond in all possible circumstances, including the offer of certain gracious helps that God might provide. In choosing to create a certain order God commits himself, out of his goodness, to offering various graces to all people—graces that are sufficient for their salvation. He knows, however, that many will in fact freely reject his aids and be lost. But those who assent to his grace render it efficacious in procuring their salvation. Given God's immutable determination to create a certain order, those who God knew would respond to his grace are predestined to be saved. It is absolutely certain that they will respond to and persevere in God's grace; and, indeed, in the composite sense it is impossible that they should be lost. Nevertheless, in the divided sense they are entirely free to reject God's grace; but were they to do so, then God would have had different middle knowledge than he does and so they would not be predestined.

In Molina's view, then, predestination involves God's willing that aspect of the world comprising the natural circumstances and supernatural gifts of grace that form the milieu in which a person freely responds to God's gracious initiatives and is saved. Since God chooses to create any world he wishes without respect to how any given person would respond to his grace, predestination is unmerited and gratuitous. God in his mercy has decided to grant all people grace sufficient for salvation, even those he knew would reject it, but grace becomes efficacious only for those who assent to it. A person who assents to and continues in God's grace is predestined in virtue of the temporal necessity of God's creative will and act. But he remains free not to respond; only were he not to respond, then he would not be predestined, and God would have known that that person would respond differently under the same circumstances and given the same graces than the way in which he would in fact respond. Thus predestination and freedom are entirely compatible.

Now while Molina's doctrine of justification can only be regarded as heinous by any biblical Christian, this doctrine is not entailed by his theory of middle knowledge. Therefore it remains open to one to accept Molina's reconciliation of predestination and human freedom based on God's middle knowledge of who would freely respond to his gracious initiatives without also accepting Molina's doctrine of justification. Through the doctrine of middle knowledge, Molina is able to preserve human freedom even while affirming God's selection of certain persons to be saved.

In fact, through this same doctrine, Molina's successor Suarez came so close to Calvinism that it is scarcely possible to distinguish their doctrines of predestination; yet Suarez did not sacrifice human freedom. The difference between Molina and Suarez on this score can be best appreciated by comparing them to theologians of opposing viewpoints. According to Thomists like Bañez and Alvarez, God predestines persons to heaven or hell logically prior to any prevision of human merits. God gives or withholds the efficacious grace without which the accomplishment of acts leading to salvation is impossible. God wills to permit the fall of man into sin and the damnation of the reprobate in order to manifest his justice. At the other extreme stands a theologian like Vasquez, who held that predestination and reprobation are based on prevision of merits and demerits. Grace is not intrinsically efficacious, but becomes so when a person cooperates with it. Between these two views, Molina and Suarez take their respective positions. Molina stands closer to Vasquez's end of the spectrum, Suarez to Bañez'.

Distinguishing between election (appointment to beatitude) and predestination (decree not only of eternal salvation but also of the means to arrive at it), Suarez emphasizes more strongly than Molina the wholly gratuitous character of God's election.[46] According to Suarez, God gratuitously chooses some individual to be saved. Then, on the basis of his middle knowledge, he discovers what graces would be efficacious in winning the free consent of that individual to God's offer of salvation. Such graces are called by Suarez congruent grace (*gratia congrua*). Congruent grace consists of the divine gifts and aids that will be efficacious in eliciting the response desired by God, but without coercion. No grace is intrinsically efficacious; but congruent grace is always in fact efficacious because it is so perfectly suited to the creature's temperament, circumstances, desires, and so forth, as to win his free and affirmative response. Such suitability is not the whole story, however; otherwise those who are not accorded such grace would not have a truly sufficient grace. Rather, Suarez explains,

> The efficacy of this call consists in this, that God, in his infinite wisdom foreseeing what each cause or will shall do in every event and occasion, if placed in it, also knows when and to which vocation each will shall give assent if [the call] is given. Therefore, when He wills to convert a man He wills also to call him at that time and in that way in which He knows he will consent, and such a vocation is called efficacious because although of itself it does not have an infallible effect, yet inasmuch as it is subject to such divine knowledge it shall infallibly have it.[47]

   The efficacy of the grace is not to be found in the call itself, but in its coming from a God who possesses infallible middle knowledge. God gives congruent grace to the elect and thus predestines them to salvation. Because the grace is congruent, there is no chance that the elect will fall away; nevertheless, they are perfectly free to do so. As for the nonelect, the grace given to them is sufficient for salvation, but they freely reject it because it is somehow incongruent for them. Grace is thus extrinsically efficacious; otherwise one would be forced to say that God does not give sufficient grace to all men. But in that case, he, in commanding them to have faith, would be demanding the impossible and then condemning them for failing to do it.[48] Theodore de Regnon contrasts the views of Molina and Suarez:

> According to Molina, God first gives to Peter a grace *capable* of obtaining a virtuous act. He then foresees that Peter will either consent or resist. Consequently He knows whether the grace will be efficacious or sufficient. On God's part, there is thus nothing which distinguishes efficacious grace from sufficient grace. Their difference derives wholly from human acceptance or rejection. . . .
>
>   According to Suarez, God first decides by an *absolute pre-definition* that a certain act of virtue will be done by Peter. God then *chooses*, from the treasury of His gifts, a grace which His middle knowledge has shown Him will be accepted by Peter. Consequently He gives this grace precisely because He foresees it to be efficacious. It is congruent grace. . . . [49]

We might ask whether there is in Suarez' opinion a congruent grace for every person whom God could create or whether some individuals are so incorrigible that regardless of the graces accorded them by God, they would always reject God's salvation. Suarez seems to affirm that God can win the free response of any possible creature to his grace; but in response to the objection that it is logically possible that someone should resist every grace, Suarez inconsistently concedes that this is true but adds that God could still achieve such a person's salvation by overpowering his will.[50] It is simply a mystery why God chose this order of things rather than another.

   It is an interesting historical note that Congruism soon supplanted Molina's own views among the theologians of the Society of Jesus, being proclaimed on December 14, 1613, to be the official doctrine of Jesuits by Aquaviva, then the head of the order. Congruists typically distinguished between a *predestination to glory* and a *predestination to grace*. The former is the gratuitous decree of God by which God selects an individual to share in eternal salvation. It is gratuitous because it is prior to any prevision of human merits, actual or conditional. This decree is infallible because God operates infallibly to bring about what he decrees.

The latter is the decree of God to grant the elect a series of congruent graces to win their free response to God's offer of salvation. It is infallible because it is based on God's middle knowledge of what a person would do when offered certain of God's helps. Regnon provides this convenient synopsis of the positions of Thomism, Congruism, and Molinism:[51]

Thomism	Congruism	Molinism
1. God decides absolutely and gratuitously to predestine S to glory.	1. God decides absolutely and gratuitously to predestine S to glory.	1. God decides absolutely and gratuitously to give sufficient grace to every person he creates.
2. God then decides to give S a series of intrinsically efficacious graces to cause his free assent to God's offer of salvation. Those not included in (1) are reprobate.	2. On the basis of his middle knowledge, God chooses those graces to which he knows S would freely respond, if he were given them. These graces are therefore efficacious for S. Those not included in (1) are reprobate.	2. On the basis of his middle knowledge, God knows whether S would respond if given sufficient grace. If so, then in creating S, God predestines S to glory, and his grace becomes efficacious. If not, then S is not predestined, and God's grace remains merely sufficient.

In Congruism, I think we can clearly see how closely Arminianism and Calvinism can be brought by a doctrine of middle knowledge. For Lutheranism/Calvinism is (with respect to the issue at hand) simply a more consistent Thomism, and Congruism gives the Thomist everything he could desire in terms of God's gratuitous and sovereign election and yet, unlike Thomism, consistently maintains human freedom. With Luther, one could affirm God's infallible foreknowledge of future contingents and, with Calvin, God's sovereign providence over the universe and yet not thereby sacrifice genuine human freedom. Middle knowledge does not entail Congruism, of course, and Arminians are not apt to go so far in affirming the gratuity of election and the efficacy of God's gracious initiatives; but the point remains that by laying a common foundation of a doctrine of middle knowledge, Calvinists and Arminians could reduce the chasm that now separates them to the small divide that serves to distinguish Molina from Suarez, and this would be a monumental and laudable achievement.[52]

NOTES

¹Gerard Smith, *Freedom in Molina* (Chicago: Loyola University Press, 1966), viii.

²Ludovici Molina, *Liberi arbitrii cum gratiae donis, divina praescientia, providentia, praedestinatione et reprobatione concordia*, 7.4et5. 1. membr.ult.

³For a fine discussion, see Smith, *Freedom in Molina*, chapters 1 and 2. I have left out a discussion of Aquinas' view, which Smith summarizes in chapter 3, in view of the audience of this volume. Aquinas held that God determines everything that comes to pass, even the volitions of the human will, but that this does not remove genuine freedom. Dominicans vehemently opposed Molinism and instigated a papal inquiry that dragged on in Rome for nearly a decade. During the *"de auxiliis"* disputes in Rome, Molina's case was ably defended by Francisco Suarez in two *opuscula* (1594–97). In the end the pope declared that just as the Dominicans could not be condemned as Calvinists, since they affirmed human freedom, neither could the Molinists be condemned as Pelagians, since they insisted on the necessity of prevenient grace. It seems to me that the Reformers were at least more consistent than Aquinas because they recognized that if God determines the volitions of the will, then the will cannot be said to be truly free.

⁴Translation adapted from Martin Luther, "The Bondage of the Will," trans. P. S. Watson, in *Luther's Works*, vol. 33: *Career of the Reformer III*, ed. Philip S. Watson (Philadelphia: Fortress, 1972), 37–38.

⁵Ibid., 189. Cf. "I admit that the question is difficult, indeed impossible, if you wish to maintain at the same time both God's foreknowledge and man's freedom" (ibid., 188).

⁶Ibid., 192–95.

⁷Ibid., 70.

⁸John Calvin, *Institutes of the Christian Religion* 1.16.4. Translation adapted from the 8th rev. American ed., trans. John Allen, 2 vols. (Grand Rapids: Eerdmans, 1949).

⁹Ibid., 1.16.8.

¹⁰See Ioannis Calvini, *De areterna Dei praedestinatione*, in *Opera*, vol. 8: *Tractatus theologici minores*, 249–366. Corpus Reformatorum 36: John Calvin, *Concerning the Eternal Predestination of God*, trans. with an intro. by J. K. S. Reid (Greenwood, S.C.: Attic, 1961).

¹¹Molina *Concordia* 4.49.8. Translation is from Luis Molina, *Molina on Divine Foreknowledge*, trans. with an Introduction and Notes by Alfred J. Freddoso (forthcoming).

¹²John Duns Scotus *Ordinatio* 1.39–39.23. For a discussion of Scotus' view, see my book *The Problem of Divine Foreknowledge and Human Freedom from Aristotle to Suarez* (Leiden: Brill, 1980), chap. 5.

¹³Thomas Aquinas *Summa contra Gentiles* 1.66.4; idem *Summa theologiae* 1a.14.8. On Aquinas' doctrine, see Craig, *Foreknowledge and Freedom*, chapter 4.

¹⁴Molina *Concordia* 4.52.9.

¹⁵Ibid., 4.50.17.

¹⁶Ibid., 4.52.9.

¹⁷Molina notes that even in the case in which God decides not to create, he would have free knowledge, though it would be comprised of negative propositions; e.g., "Creatures do not exist," "The Son will not become incarnate," etc. (ibid., 4.53.4.3.)

¹⁸Ibid., 4.52.13.

¹⁹In responding to the Thomistic doctrine that God's knowledge is the cause of things, Molina agrees that God's natural and middle knowledge are a cause of future contingents, but he denies that they are the total cause, since the free will of creatures is also part of the cause of which world obtains. (ibid., 4.52.31.)

²⁰Ibid., 4.52.9.

[21] Molina rejects any analysis of freedom in terms of spontaneity, for even animals, children, and the demented possess the latter. True liberty must entail the ability to do or refrain from an act or to do the opposite of an act under identical causal conditions. This liberty of indifference is a fact of experience, is theologically presupposed by the existence of sin, and is taught by the Scriptures and the church fathers. The ultimate source of contingency in the world is God's own free will, but the immediate source is the free will of men and angels, as well as a sort of vestige of freedom in certain animals. Were these removed from the world, then, barring divine miracles, the universe would be totally deterministic and contingency would have no place in it. For more on Molina's view of free will, see Blaise Roymeyer, "Libre arbitre et concours selon Molina," *Gregorianum* 23 (1942): 7.

[22] Molina *Concordia* 4.49.13.

[23] Ibid., 4.52.10.

[24] Ibid., 4.50.15.

[25] Ibid.

[26] Ibid., 4.49.11.

[27] Ibid., 4.50.15.

[28] R. P. Francisco Suarez, *Opera omnia*, ed. Carolo Berton (Parisiis: Ludovicum Vives, 1856–78), vol. 2: *opuscula sex inedita*, 2: *De scientia Dei futurorum contingentium* 2.5; idem, *Opera*, vol. 7: *Tractatus de gratia Dei: Prolegomenon* 2.8.1.

[29] In a proposition taken in the composite sense, the modal operator governs the proposition as a whole; e.g., "Necessarily, if God sees Socrates sitting, he is sitting." When the proposition is taken in the divided sense, the modal operator modifies only a component of the proposition; e.g., "If God sees Socrates sitting, he is necessarily sitting." In our example, the proposition is true *in sensu composito* and false *in sensu diviso*.

[30] See Donald Carson, *Divine Sovereignty and Human Responsibility*, New Foundations Theological Library (Atlanta: John Knox, 1981), 24–35.

[31] Molina *Concordia* 6.1.1.

[32] Ibid., 4.53.3.14.

[33] Ibid., 4.53.3.17.

[34] Ibid., 2.25–26. See also Romeyer, "Libre arbitre et concours," 177–88; *Dictionnaire de théologie catholique*, s.v. "Molinisme," by E. Van Steenberghe, vol. 10.2., cols. 2109–16.

[35] See his devastating critique in *Concordia* 4.53.2.

[36] Ibid., 4.53.3.2.

[37] Ibid., 4.53.3.7.

[38] Ibid., 4.53.3.9. Van Steenberghe comments, "Thus, our evil acts lie outside the end for which God has given us freedom and His general concurrence. He does not will them, neither as the author of nature nor as legislator, since He forbids them and seeks to turn us from them; He would will that they not exist if we ourselves were to so will, but He permits them in light of a greater good; the normal exercise of our free will. As for our good works, He wills them first with a conditional will, if we ourselves will them freely: thus it is that He wills the salvation of all men; but foreseeing what shall emanate from our free will, He consents to them and wills them with an absolute will." (*Dictionnaire de théologie catholique*, s.v. "Molinisme," by Vansteenberghe, 10.2., col. 2112.)

[39] On the way in which sins contribute to the eventual realization of God's purposes, see the powerful statement in *Concordia* 4.53.2.15.

[40] Ibid., 7.1.; 2.1.8.

[41] For a good statement see ibid., 4.50.9.

[42] Ibid., 7.4, 5; 1.11.7–16; 4.53.4.12. Whitacre notes that subsequent Molinist theories of predestination distinguished two alternative views of predestination: (1) *post praevisa merita*: God predestines those whom he knows will make good use of his grace; (2) *ante praevisa merita*: God gratuitously elects whom he wants to save and then predestines them. But Molina's own view bursts these categories, since he held predestination to be gratuitous and yet *post praevisa merita*, since the

decision of the divine will is posterior to middle knowledge. (*Hasting's Encyclopedia of Religion and Ethics*, s.v. "Molinism," by Alfred Whitacre.) On Molina's view predestination did not occur prior to God's middle knowledge of what every creature would do under any set of circumstances, yet his choice of a world with its predestined was not chosen on the basis of the fact that those individuals would be saved. Hence, it would be best to say that on Molina's view, predestination is *post praevisa merita, sed non propter praevisa merita*.

[43] *Dictionnaire de théologie catholique*, s.v. "Molinisme," by Vansteenberghe, 10.2., cols. 1028–29.

[44] See the provocative series of contrasts in Théodore Regnon, *Bannesianisme et Molinisme* (Paris: Retaux-Bray, 1890), p. 48.

[45] Molina, *Concordia* 3.40; 4.53.2.25, 30.

[46] See Suarez, *Opera*, vol. 10: *Appendix prior: Tractatus de vera intelligentia auxilii efficacis, ejusque concordia cum libertate voluntarii consensus* 1, 12, 13, 14; idem *Opuscula*, 1: *De consursu et efficaci auxilio Dei ad actus libri arbitrii necessario* 3.6, 14, 16, 17, 20. See also discussion in *Dictionnaire de théologie catholique*, s.v. "Congruisme," by H. Quilliet, vol. 3.1, cols. 1120–38; *Dictionnaire de théologie catholique*, s.v. "Suarez, Francois," by R. Brouillard, vol. 14, cols. 2687–90; *Hasting's Encyclopaedia of Religion and Ethics*, s.v. "Molinism," by Whitacre, Léon Mahieu, *François Suarez: sa philosophie et les rapports qu'elle a avec sa theologie* (Paris: Desclée de Brouwer, 1921), 233–46; Thomas V. Mullaney, "The Basis of the Suarezian Teaching on Human Freedom," *Thomist* 11 (1948): 448–502.

[47] Suarez *De Concursu et auxilio Dei* 3.14.9.

[48] Ibid., 3.15–17.

[49] Th. de Regnon, *Bañes et Molina* (Paris: Oudin, 1883), 126.

[50] Suarez *De scientia Dei* 2.6.9; idem, *De concursu et auxilio Dei* 3.14.16.

[51] Regnon, *Bañes et Molina*, 157–58. I have revised it slightly.

[52] Of course, the doctrine of middle knowledge is a matter of great dispute. But I have attempted to rebut both philosophical and theological objections to it in my popular-level book *The Only Wise God* (Grand Rapids: Baker, 1987), 138–52, and in a scholarly level forthcoming book. See also Alvin Plantinga, "Reply to Robert Adams," in *Alvin Plantinga*, ed. James Tomberlin and Peter Van Inwagen, Profiles 5 (Dordrecht, Holland: D. Reidel, 1985), 371–82.

GOD AS PERSONAL

John E. Sanders

"It looks like God was wrong," Ken blurted out. The class momentarily was shocked into silence; then small pockets of murmurs could be heard as the class waited to see how I would answer such an accusation. We were discussing Jeremiah 3:7, 19–20 where God expresses disappointment in Israel's lack of faith:

> "I thought that after she had done all this she would return to me but she did not, and her unfaithful sister Judah saw it. . . . I myself said, How gladly would I treat you like sons and give you a desirable land, the most beautiful inheritance of any nation. I thought you would call me 'Father' and not turn away from following me. But like a woman unfaithful to her husband, so you have been unfaithful to me, O house of Israel," declares the LORD.

"So you think God was mistaken, Ken?" I asked trying to soften his remark.

"Well, the text says God thought they would respond in faith, but they didn't; so God was wrong," he replied.

"Is it possible," I inquired, "for God to be mistaken about anything?"

To this several students immediately said, "No!"

"Why not?" I asked.

Diane raised her hand. "Because God is omniscient."

"Please explain," I said.

"Omniscience means," she continued, "that God knows everything. God knows all that has happened and all that will happen. So God couldn't possibly be wrong about anything."

"And how long has God had this knowledge," I asked.

"From all eternity," answered Dean. "God is timeless and has known everything before anything was created."

Ken retorted, "But the text says that what God thought would happen didn't happen."

"How are we going to explain these passages?" I asked. From the back of the room Mark said, "I think God is just speaking from a human perspective so we can understand it. God really knew all along what would happen; it's just an anthropomorphic way of speaking."

"So the text doesn't mean what it seems to mean," I suggested. This point made the class a bit uneasy so I continued. "What does the text mean then?"

After the long silence Lori spoke up. "I believe it might mean that God is just expressing his feelings toward Israel."

"But God doesn't have feelings," said Bill. "God is impassible, so he is not affected by emotions. Besides, God is immutable, which means he can't change in any way."

"Of course God has feelings," Virginia said passionately.

Sensing a verbal brawl was about to ensue I interjected, "If Bill is correct about God being impassible and immutable then what does the text mean?"

"I'm not sure what it means," answered Kevin. "But it has to mean something completely different from what it seems to mean."

"Perhaps some other passages will help us solve this problem," I said. "Turn to Exodus 32:7–14. In this passage God informs Moses about the golden calf and asks Moses to leave him alone so he can destroy the people. But Moses doesn't like the idea, so he intercedes for the people and asks God to relent of the decision. In response God changes his mind and allows them to live as Moses requested. Did God actually change his mind?"

Diane and Bill both raised their hands. "Since God is omniscient, God always knew what he would do; so he didn't change his mind."

"Besides," added Bill, "God can't change, since he is immutable."

"Then what does the passage mean?" I asked.

"It was just for Moses' benefit," said Diane. "God was testing Moses to see if he loved the people. It's just like Mark said, it's an anthropomorphism, so we can understand it."

"Furthermore," said Bill, "1 Samuel 15:29 says clearly that God does not change his mind."

"But Exodus 32:14 and 1 Samuel 15:11, 35 all clearly say God did change his mind," replied Ken. "So which verses are right?"

"It has to be 1 Samuel 15:29," answered Bill, "because we know God is omniscient, eternal, and immutable."

"How do we know what God is like?" I asked.

"Exodus 34:6–7," said Rebecca, "says God is compassionate, gracious, patient, loving, faithful, and forgiving. Deuteronomy

10:17–18 says God is the God of gods who won't show partiality nor take a bribe. It also says he loves the widows, orphans, and aliens."

"But," said Ken, "if the verses that say God repents or God was mistaken don't mean what they seem to mean, then maybe the verses that say God is loving, just, and forgiving don't mean what they seem to mean! Perhaps God only seems to care for widows and orphans. Maybe they are just anthropomorphisms also. How do we decide which texts mean what they say and which ones only seem to mean what they say?"

Indeed, how do we decide? The above (largely true) account of a class discussion reflects the tensions within evangelicalism between a *prima facie* reading of the text and a theologically controlled reading of the text. Many believe that prayer may truly change God's mind, whereas traditional theology has, since the early Fathers, taught us to believe that we cannot change God's mind, since God is omniscient and immutable. Ideas like *immutable, impassible,* and *timeless* function as "control beliefs" governing our reading of the text.

This raises some serious issues. Should control beliefs govern exegesis? If so, which control beliefs should be used? How do we know what God is really like? Greek philosophers like Plato and Aristotle speculated about the nature of God without the aid of biblical revelation. Many of the conclusions they reached, however, were seen as complimentary, not contrary to the biblical description of God by the early Fathers. When texts of the Bible contradicted the speculative view of God, the Bible was not judged to be wrong but merely incorrectly interpreted. The Fathers, following Plato,[1] viewed any biblical references to God's emotions, repentance, etc. as "mere" anthropomorphisms. They were for the benefit of the many (*hoi polloi*), those who could not comprehend the true nature of God.

This placing of (what I shall call) the "absolutistic" conception of God derived from Greek philosophy above the "personalistic" conception presented in the Bible has, in the history of the church, led to many problems. These problems include the general topic of this book. It would be nice if the debate between those who hold, generally speaking, to Calvinistic and Arminian perspectives could be settled by simply appealing to Scripture. But both sides use the same Bible, often even the same text against each other. It is the contention of this chapter that the doctrines of soteriology (especially election), and anthropology (especially faith), are discussed within the framework of the doctrine of God. Our view of God is deeply influenced by the control beliefs we bring to the Scripture. These control beliefs are, to a large extent, the result of a synthesis of Greek and biblical thought.[2] The remainder of this chapter will fall into three sections: the nature of control beliefs, a description of the absolutistic conception of God and some problems with it, and finally a discussion of the personalistic conception of God.

CONTROL BELIEFS

Control beliefs are those ideas and values that are used as paradigms and ultimate presuppositions to interpret our experiences, recognize problems, and organize information.[3] They are the branches on which we sit. From these branches we act and try to make sense of life; hence, we must not saw them off until we have a new branch to sit on. Because we do not normally look at the branch we sit on, it is usually easier to see the control beliefs of those with whom we disagree than our own.[4] We usually do not take time to examine our own presuppositions critically and thus often fail to realize that the reason another person seems so "unreasonable" to us is that the points of departure—our control beliefs—are different. These paradigms are quite significant, because they influence our other beliefs, values, and actions. In the case of interpretation, we should not be surprised to find "in" Scripture an absolutistic God if in our exegesis we use control beliefs about the nature of God derived from Greek philosophy.

Having control beliefs is part of the human experience. Thiselton writes, "No one expounds the Bible to himself or to anyone else without bringing to the task his own prior frame of reference, his own pattern of assumptions which derives from sources outside the Bible."[5] In interpreting Scripture we also bring different learning styles, different perceptual expectations, and different traditions that shape our questions and frame of reference.[6] Examples of such beliefs are inerrancy, dispensationalism, the deity of Christ, and the law of noncontradiction. We use these, or other beliefs, depending on our background, to collect Scriptures that support our position and to interpret those passages that seem to be against our views. Augustine used the practice of infant baptism as a control belief to argue for the validity of his view of original sin.[7] Augustine also used the concept that "the will of the Omnipotent is always undefeated" to control his view of predestination and election.[8] Arminians typically use the doctrine of unlimited atonement as a control belief for their views of predestination and election.

Often our control beliefs revolve around or hinge on a few metaphors from the Bible that serve as keys to unlock the doors of interpretation to all other passages.[9] The images we choose to emphasize are crucial, for they shape our life of faith and structure the way we relate to God. The images of God and of the nature of our relationship with God that the Bible uses function like analogies, explaining the unknown in terms of the known. When

God is described as parent or spouse, we immediately know something of what is being spoken about. Care must be taken, however, to ask what kind of husband or father is being described, since the meaning of these terms will vary from one individual or culture to the next. Two extremes are to be avoided: (1) there is no essential relationship between the metaphor and God and (2) there is a literal correspondence in all respects. Many scholars, since the early Fathers, have tended to depreciate the anthropomorphic metaphors used of God in the Bible. This is not wise, as Terence Fretheim writes:

> The metaphor does in fact describe God, though it is not fully descriptive. The metaphor does contain information about God. The metaphor does not stand over against the literal. Though the *use* of the metaphor is not literal, there is literalness intended in the relationship to which the metaphor has reference.[10]

Without the biblical metaphors we would lose the divinely revealed nature of God. Yet, it is sometimes assumed that the early biblical writers were naïve in their use of anthropomorphisms and that progressive revelation corrected this problem. This assumption is incorrect, as some images for describing God were ruled out in the Old Testament (e.g., sexual). The biblical writers were well aware of what they were doing. Besides, the New Testament is replete with many of the same images and metaphors about God as is the Old Testament.

In the history of the church, guidelines were developed, often unwittingly, for interpreting biblical metaphors.[11] The guidelines, once established, functioned like axioms in geometry, taking on incontestable certitude. They were formulated under the belief that the Greek philosophical way of speaking of God (impassible, immutable, timeless, etc.) was superior to the anthropomorphic way (father, changeable, suffering, etc.). The church has followed this path for so long that we now take this way of thinking for granted. We now find it difficult to critically examine our control beliefs about the nature of God. If we desire to be faithful to the Bible, we must make the effort, however difficult or painful, to examine the absolutistic lenses in our glasses to discover if the image of God we see through them is actually the same as the biblical portrait.[12]

GOD AS ABSOLUTISTIC

Perhaps the most dominating metaphors used to justify this view of God are that of king and author. God's kingship involves him in all that happens in the universe. But God is more than merely involved. J. I. Packer believes that as the King, God "orders and controls all things, human actions among them, in accordance with His own eternal purpose."[13] God is in some respects like a human king in that he works through others (secondary causes). But God controls (in a strict sense), absolutely *everything* that happens within the kingdom from the actions of princes and paupers to the deaths of men and mules. The other metaphor, often used to further the kingly image, is that of God as author. God is the playwright or novelist, and we are the characters in the story. Since God has written the story, nothing ever happens that is contrary to the will of God.

Yet even these metaphors may be a bit deceiving, for we might imagine God's thinking out the plot or making plans about the characters as a human author would. But God, in the absolutistic conception, is totally unconditioned; nothing (knowledge, power, feelings, etc.), can affect God in any way. It is not correct to say God "plans" or "thinks," since God "knows" everything all at once. Planning and thinking imply that the future is as yet undetermined, that courses of action remain undecided. The future is *closed* for an omniscient God with total foreknowledge of all future events.

Another concept often incorporated into the images of King and Author is omnipotence. Since God has literally all the power in the universe, God will get whatever he wants. This unlimited power effectually brings about whatever God knows.

Plato and Aristotle were among the first to develop these notions of God.[14] Using the method of natural theology, they began with the human concept of perfection and simply deduced the implications. Because God is perfect (without lack), he cannot change, as that would only be change for the worse. Therefore God is immutable. God's immutability applies to every aspect of his being: knowledge, power, will, etc. Since emotions fluctuate and adversely affect the reason, God must be impassible. God is a timeless (experiencing no duration) pure mind totally unaffected by all other forms of being. Most of these ideas were transmitted to the early Fathers through Philo. Early apologists like Athenagoras set the course we still follow today when he defined God as "one God, uncreated, eternal, invisible, impassible, incomprehensible, illimitable, who is apprehended by the understanding only and the reason, who is encompassed by light, and beauty, and spirit, and power ineffable."[15] Augustine, in his *Confessions* (12.15), described God's will as immutable, and he closely connected it with timelessness in the *City of God* (11.21). A timeless being cannot change, because change implies duration.

The concepts of timelessness, immutability, impassibility, omniscience, and omnipotence are all closely related and interconnected. They flow easily out of the Platonic ideal of the perfect, static, unchangeable forms. The early Fathers, desiring to relate the Christian message to their age, naturally used the terms and concepts familiar to them and to their audiences to establish the credibility of the faith. Thus the concept of *Dignum Deo,* that which is fitting for God to be, came to play a significant role as a control belief in the interpretation of the Bible.[16] It was thought fitting for God to be timeless, immutable, impassible, etc. The biblical references to God's mutability, experience of duration, and emotions were viewed as mere anthropomorphisms. They could not mean what they seemed to mean, since it had already been determined what the nature of God was like according to the *Dignum Deo.*

Augustine, accepting the absolutistic view of God, clearly understood the implications of this view of God in explaining the nature of the covenant relationship between God and humanity. Because God is totally unconditioned, he cannot "respond" to a person's faith. God is not dependent on a human decision for the decree of who will or will not be saved. God has always known who would be saved and who would be damned. Furthermore, God does not decide who will be saved based on foreknowledge of future human decisions because God is immutable. Basing election on any sort of human activity would imply conditionality and mutability in God. God is thus the sole cause of salvation and damnation. God is, in fact, the sole cause of everything (he is omnicausal) if he is unconditioned by anything external to Godself. If God does not cause all events, then he has ceased to be God.[17] God has simply decreed all that happens, just as a novelist does.

In this system grace was conceived of as a material force acting irresistibly on the object of God's benevolence. Grace cannot be resisted, as this would mean that God's will could be resisted, and this would imply conditionality in God. We may describe the plan of salvation by the analogy of a pool table.[18] God pushes the cue stick of power (efficient cause), striking the cue ball of irresistible grace (instrumental cause), which implants faith in the eight ball so that it rolls across the table (material cause) into the pocket (final cause). Since God never misses a shot, we have eternal security that the ball will end up in the pocket as God unconditionally elected from all eternity it should do. It is no accident that the doctrines of unconditional election, limited atonement, and irresistible grace developed. They are all logical corollaries with the absolutistic conception of God.[19] The soteriological doctrines of Augustine and Calvin are quite correct if God actually is as the absolutistic view claims he is. The covenant has to be seen as unilateral on God's part. There can be no reciprocity or conditionality to it. The working out of the covenant is necessarily monergistic: faith is a solely divine work in us.

But is God really like this? Does God actually operate in this way? Is classical theism with its synthesis of Greek philosophic natural theology and biblical theology synonymous with biblical theism? Despite the logical consistency of the view and the renown of those who have taught it, the perspective has many fatal flaws. Space permits only a brief review of three of them.[20] The first and foremost (since the others derive from it) difficulty with the absolutistic conception of God is that it logically entails monism or theopanism.[21] God is actually the only actor; humans are but characters in the novel. Bruce Reichenbach explains,

> All the participants in the storyline do exactly what the author determines. All have their traits laid out by and have no existence apart from the author. The plot moves inexorably to the end determined by the author. What he desires is precisely what occurs; there can be no variation.[22]

Western theology in general and Reformed theology in particular have ventured furthest in the absolutistic direction by viewing the relationship between God and humanity in terms of a subject-object scheme.[23] God is the sole subject (cause) of all events; humans are but objects of God's actions (instrumental causes). All our inclinations and impressions result from the prime mover. God is the archer, and we the arrows. The arrows may *seem* self-directed but they are not. Augustine, and Calvin after him, argued that even though God is the cause of everything, humans are still responsible since we are secondary causes. But to say that God works *through* secondary causes misses the point, since it is still *God* doing the acting, and this is monistic.

This brings us to the second major flaw—determinism. If the characters do only what the novelist determines, then the novelist is responsible for what happens. Both Augustine and Calvin acknowledged this to be the case, and both attempted to argue for a form of soft-determinism or compatibilism (human freedom and divine determinism are not contradictory), by making a distinction between remote and proximate causes.[24] They thought that if God was only the remote cause, then humans are still free and responsible as the proximate causes. The problem is that the proximate cause only does what the remote cause determines it should do. Soft-determinism is actually a determinism in freewill clothing.[25]

The third major problem that absolutism entails is that it robs the biblical language about God of genuine meaning by denigrating it to the status of *mere* anthropomorphism. After all, how can a timelessly immutable Being plan, anticipate, remember, respond, punish, warn, or forgive, since all such acts involve temporality and mutability.[26] A timelessly immutable God cannot "answer" prayer, as this would imply that God "responds" to our prayer. The absolutistic God only *seems*, from a human perspective to answer prayer.[27] In fact, our view of prayer must include the idea that God decrees the very prayer we pray not just the answer.[28] The meaning of the common activity of praying for unsaved persons must be radically altered also. Our prayer can of course have no impact on God's decision whether to elect or damn an individual since God has known from all eternity what he will do with that person. If we pray and that person is saved, his being saved will not be because of our prayer but because God decreed both our prayer and the person's salvation.

Furthermore, absolutism calls into question the integrity of God's invitations to repentance and the resulting options of blessings and curses. With an omnicausal God there are no "options." The calls for repentance are presented in a straightforward and literal manner in the Bible, but the absolutistic view makes a sham of them and of all the interpersonal language about the relationship between God and human persons if God already knew what the response would be and had in fact determined that response. Why do we think that the biblical way of speaking about God is merely a human and consequently inferior form of speech? Why do we believe God to be so different from the biblical witness and that he is accurately described only in Greek philosophical terms? Could not such terms have been used by the biblical writers and understood by the people? The absolutistic view leads to so many forced readings of the text, with no justification in the texts themselves, that it ends up "placing the *integrity* and coherence of all God's words in jeopardy: does God really mean what is said or not?"[29]

If God is absolutistic, then even the meaning of statements about God's love become suspect, since God does not love as we are commanded to love. We are commanded to love our enemies and seek their eternal welfare. But God does not do this, since God does not love the nonelect with the same redeeming love that is poured out on the elect.[30] Consequently, most of the biblical language regarding God's relationship with the world is misleading if not deceptive, to the common reader.

Those who prefer to speak of God in Greek philosophic terms fail to realize that those terms are just as anthropomorphic as the metaphors in the Bible. There is one crucial difference, however: the Bible is inspired. In the final analysis, the attempt to describe God in absolutistic categories, imposed on the biblical revelation, "ends inevitably in the use of terms which are not supra-personal but sub-personal."[31] It is like buttoning your coat; once you begin with the wrong button you never manage to get buttoned up.

GOD AS PERSONAL

One of the key control beliefs for the personal view of God is that the biblical metaphors about God are the best sources to discover who God *really* is. From these metaphors we see a God revealed who may be more than, but never less than or contrary to, a personal being. In the Bible God is not an abstract concept of "being" but a concrete personal being who reveals his personal name, "Yahweh,"[32] implying vulnerability, accessibility, and intimacy.[33] In the use of the term *personal* care must be taken again not to imbue it with Greek philosophic overtones.[34] A person is not primarily an isolated *cogito* but an agent who acts, wills, plans, loves, creates, and values in relation to other persons. As Trinity, the Godhead is the model of loving interpersonal relationships. As Creator, Yahweh freely enters into dynamic interpersonal relations with the world. Fretheim summarizes this so clearly that he deserves to be quoted at length.

> The world is not only affected by God; God is affected by the world in both positive and negative ways. God is sovereign over the world, yet not unqualifiedly so, as considerable power and freedom have been given to the creatures. God is the transcendent Lord; but God is transcendent not in isolation from the world, but in relationship to the world. God knows all there is to know about the world, yet there is a future which does not yet exist to be known even by God. God is Lord of time and history, yet God has chosen to be bound up in the time and history of the world and to be limited thereby. God is unchangeable with respect to the steadfastness of his love and his salvific will for all creatures, yet God does change in the light of what happens in the interaction between God and the world.[35]

The metaphors of marriage, childrearing, and adoption tend to be the dominating biblical metaphors used to convey the personalistic nature of Yahweh. In raising children, Yahweh's goal is to preserve and increase the value in his children's lives. In this activity Yahweh desires the children to participate in their own development. He does not do everything for them nor protect them from all suffering and failure. To change the metaphor, lovers do not change each other's lives by taking over the other persons being and controlling it. Rather, the lover seeks to nurture a multitude of factors to a point where the beloved willingly turns from his self-destructive ways. When my wife decided that we should eat more nutritiously, she did not force me into health foods. She cultured my taste buds and educated me to change my values. Now I admit that I forced myself to eat my first whole-wheat-and-bran birthday cake with a smile so as not to offend her. But after years of patient nurture on her part, I have eaten, and enjoyed(!), mountains of healthy food. To have forced me into this situation would have harmed the kind of love relationship she desired. The same is true of the teacher-student realtionship. The best teachers do not force themselves on the students, but rather attempt to create an environment within which the students feel free to respond and request additional help and instruction from the teacher. If the students are willing to have the teacher become a decisive factor in their lives, then the teacher may give "special grace" to them without destroying the integrity of the relationship. The risk of failure will always be present as long as the integrity of the relationship is maintained, since the only way the teacher can guarantee the students will not fail is to do their work for them. But then the students would not really "succeed" either, for they would not have done the work. Yahweh uses such "anthropomorphic" metaphors as these to communicate the true nature of his relationship to us. When the biblical metaphors are allowed to speak within a personalistic conception of God, then a quite different image emerges than the one seen through absolutistic lenses.

The background of the picture is Yahweh's relatedness to his creation and to humanity in particular. This basic relatedness undergirds all the rest of the metaphors. Yahweh expends so much concern and so much focused attention on humans that he could be described as "anthropotropic."[36] Yahweh chooses to be related to humanity in such a way that humans become a factor in his life. Our love and obedience give him joy, while our faithlessness grieves him. Yahweh could, of course, have chosen not to be so related. But he has freely decided to find pain in our unfaithfulness and joy in our love.

Since Yahweh in his sovereignty resolved to put himself in such a position, we should see him as the *defenseless superior power*.[37] As sovereign he is omnicompetent in his affairs with the world, but not omnicausal. Yahweh is the creator and sustainer of the world. As creator he established the rules by which the game of life operates. Yet in this superiority Yahweh saw fit to create and bind himself to rules whereby he would be "defenseless" or vulnerable. Yahweh freely allows this vulnerability by sharing his powers with his creatures. Both creative and destructive powers were given to the creatures (Gen. 1:28; 4:8). Because of this sharing of powers Yahweh has made it possible that his will may not be done; that he may not accomplish everything he desires. In Judges 5:13–23[38] the will of Yahweh was for all the tribes of Israel to band together against their enemies but this did not occur. The rejection of Yahweh's will by Israel caused great pain in his life. Yahweh's great patience endures the suffering until judgment and destruction are long overdue. Yet even the decision to destroy Israel, which would carry out the promised curses, caused suffering to Yahweh. Hosea, after announcing judgment, then describes the turmoil[39] within Yahweh's own heart:

> How can I give you up, Ephraim? How can I hand you over, Israel? . . . My heart is changed within me; all my compassion is aroused. I will not carry out my fierce anger, nor will I turn and devastate Ephraim. For I am God, and not man (11:8–9).

A human would have destroyed the people, but Yahweh is different, he can change his mind due to his steadfast love. The Bible is replete with references to the vulnerability and suffering of Yahweh. In his almightiness he makes himself defenseless before his creatures, even to the point of being crucified.

Yet Yahweh is not overwhelmed by these emotions, as we are apt to be; instead, he continues in his *changeable faithfulness*[40] towards us. Yahweh is faithful in bringing about his salvific plan despite our rejection. This constant love has demonstrated Yahweh's dependability. But dependability must not be construed to mean immutability. Yahweh changes in the way he feels, plans, and acts in response to our response to him. There are almost forty texts that speak of Yahweh repenting or changing his mind (e.g., Exod. 32:14; 33:14; Num. 14:12; Jer. 26:19), but these passages have often been robbed of their meaning by two verses that say he does not repent (Num. 23:19; 1 Sam. 15:29). This is quite strange since the meaning of the last two passages is simply that Yahweh does not lie.[41] Yahweh is free to alter his plans to accommodate human actions, since the future is open for both parties.[42] This should cause us no anxiety, though, for Yahweh is never capricious or fickle but has promised to be faithful to his salvific will. Consequently, whatever changes Yahweh makes will be in the best interest of the covenant relationship.

Openness in the covenant relationship is required because of Yahweh's creation of minicreators whom he made "respondable." The response we make to Yahweh's love is not always what he desires, for we often spurn it. Whatever our response, however, it is not Yahweh's "echo." Our response is, in a real sense, *ex nihilo*, since it originates within us and is not merely the effect of divine causation. He has set up the game rules in such a way that there is a genuine and dynamic openness between divine and human persons. Yahweh's wrath can change to kindness, his power to defenselessness, and judgment to forgiveness because he is the *living personal God*.

When these ideas are applied to the covenant relationship between Yahweh and humanity, then it is clear that it must be seen as a dynamic, open I-Thou arrangement. The Scriptures do not portray the future as something that comes about as the result of a meticulous divine decree but as the interplay between the covenant parties. The salvific goals of Yahweh have been established, but the detailed outworkings towards their achievement are open to change because both parties are creating the future.

The dynamic aspect of the covenant relationship is seen in the pattern of withdrawal and return between Yahweh and Israel. Just as a mother withdraws after interacting with the child with the intention of allowing the child to respond and develop, so Yahweh grants periods of more intense input and then withdraws to see how we will react. Enough "space" is given so we are free to respond positively or negatively to Yahweh's gracious activity. In this process the same kind of "mutual choosing" can be observed as occurs between wives and husbands, parents and children, and teachers and students.[43] Divine election functions more like a love affair between persons than a preprogrammed computer operation. Just as when a woman and a man mutually choose each other for marriage, so we enter into a covenant relationship with Yahweh by his election of us and our election of him as Lord. In this process of election humans are solely receptive but are not mere passive objects with no voice in the marriage decision. We are solely receptive because it is Yahweh's grace that takes the initiative and provides for the possibility of the marriage. Yet the grace is not manipulative nor overpowering (like the cologne advertisements), since we are able to accept or refuse it. Grace functions in ways appropriate to personhood rather than to billiard balls. It is neither all Yahweh and nothing of us nor part Yahweh and part us, but all Yahweh and all us; it is truly an interpersonal relationship.

Because it is a genuine interpersonal covenant, it is open to change as the parties involved respond to each other. Yahweh relates to us within the framework of conditionality. Judgment is announced, but if repentance ensues, then forgiveness may be obtained. Jonah, of course, did not appreciate such conditionality; he preferred an unconditional decree. This openness gives humanity the power to significantly affect the life of Yahweh.[44] We are not mere characters doing whatever the cosmic novelist determined we should do. Instead, Yahweh is part of the drama with us in a live extemporaneous performance.

The performance is not "staged," for it is truly an I-Thou relationship. Yahweh desires to be the Lord our God not a *Deus absolutus*. That is, he wants to be the Lord "of" not just "over" humanity. Yahweh does not force us to love him; enforced love is not love at all.

The covenant relationship is not unilateral nor bilateral but *monopluristic*. Konig writes, "the covenant is 'monopluristic' in the sense that it is one-sidedly ('mono'-) established by the Lord, but involves obligations on the part of both the Lord and his people ('pluralistic')."[45] The covenant arises from Yahweh's free love and gracious provision. We are not equal covenant partners, however, since the encounter is based on and precipitated by God's initiative. Yahweh, out of grace, provides us with the opportunity to become involved in a genuine covenant that encompasses real responsibilities and contributions to the relationship on our part. The Scriptures witness to the fact that Yahweh seems to desire nothing else than to be our covenant partner.

There are many advantages to viewing the relationship between Yahweh and humans as personal rather than absolutistic, but space permits the mention of only five.[46] First, the relationship is a genuine dialogue, not a monologue, so monism is avoided. Second, because Yahweh's will is not always accomplished, he is not the cause of all that happens. This means that Yahweh is not responsible for human sin. We are solely responsible, and this is good news since sin is forgivable but causation is not. Third, our biblical views of prayer are indeed meaningful. Yahweh is not a coercive parent manipulating us into making a request. We are free to ask and possibly change Yahweh's plans should he consider it prudent. Fourth, not only are human beings free but *Yahweh is free* to respond to prayer, to love in changing ways, and to experience joy and pain because he is not bound by inexorable knowledge or an immutable will. Finally, the prima facie meanings of the biblical text are allowed to stand without having to measure up to Greek philosophic standards.

CONCLUSION

The Bible is best interpreted through personalistic lenses. With these lenses we see clearly that the love relationship that Yahweh provides for us is dynamic, open, and personal. The living personal God invites us to the heart of our calling: to be desperately in love with him. After all, the Bible ends with quite a show, not a show of raw power but a romance, in which we are called to be the bride of the Lamb (Rev. 21).

NOTES

[1] David Clines, "Yahweh and the God of Christian Theology," *Theology,* 83 (1980): 325.

[2] Adrio Konig, *Here Am I* (Grand Rapids: Eerdmans, 1982), 111.

[3] For a full discussion see Nicholas Wolterstorff, *Reason Within the Bounds of Religion* (Grand Rapids: Eerdmans, 1976).

[4] Loraine Boettner thinks himself free from all control beliefs. *Reformed Doctrine of Predestination* (Philadelphia: Presbyterian and Reformed, 1965), 53.

[5] Anthony Thiselton, *The Two Horizons* (Grand Rapids: Eerdmans, 1980), 114.

[6] See Cedric Johnson, *The Psychology of Biblical Interpretation* (Grand Rapids: Zondervan, 1983).

[7] Jaroslav Pelikan, *The Emergence of the Catholic Tradition* (Chicago: University of Chicago Press, 1971), 316ff.

[8] Augustine, *Enchiridion,* 26.102.

[9] Especially helpful here is Terence Fretheim, *The Suffering of God* (Philadelphia: Fortress, 1984), chap. 1.

[10] Ibid., p. 7.

[11] Lester Kuyper, "The Suffering and Repentance of God," *Scottish Journal of Theology,* 22 (1969): 258.

[12] Since, of course, this cannot be achieved in this chapter, the reader is encouraged to see the rest of this book as an attempt to present a cumulative case for its defense.

[13] J. I. Packer, *Evangelism and the Sovereignty of God* (Downers Grove: InterVarsity, 1961), 22.

[14] See Plato: *Philebus* 33, 60c; *Republic* II, 380–81; *Timaeus* 28c; *Symposium* 200–3; and Aristotle: *De Generatione* 324b; *Metaphysics* 1071b, 1074–75; *Nico. Ethics* 1178b.

[15] Athenagoras, *Plea,* 10, in A. Roberts and J. Donaldson eds., *The Ante-Nicene Fathers,* vol. 2 (New York: Christian Literature, 1893), 133.

[16] See Konig, *Here Am I,* 62ff.

[17] So says Gordon Clark, "The Sovereignty of God," *The Trinity Review* (November 1982), 4.

[18] The illustration is from Ralph Quere, *Evangelical Witness* (Minneapolis: Augsburg, 1975), 89.

[19] Many Arminians do hold to an absolutistic view of God but try to escape the soteriological implications. In my view they are not successful in this attempt. Spinoza, Schleiermacher, and Tillich are examples of those who follow the absolutistic conception of God to somewhat different, but consistent, conclusions.

[20] For further discussion of the absolutistic conception see Stephen Davis, *Logic and the Nature of God* (Grand Rapids: Eerdmans, 1983); Emil Brunner, *The Christian Doctrine of God* (Philadelphia: Westminster, 1949); Jack Cottrell, *What the Bible Says About God the Ruler* (Joplin, Mo.: College Press, 1984); Rem Edwards, "The Pagan Dogma of the Absolute Unchangeableness of God," *Religious Studies* 14 (1978); J. K. Mozley, *The Impassibility of God* (Cambridge: Cambridge University Press, 1936); Wolfhart Pannenberg, *Basic Questions in Theology* 2 vols. (Philadelphia: Fortress, 1971), ch. 5; and Arthur Lovejoy, *The Great Chain of Being* (Cambridge, Mass.: Harvard University Press, 1964).

[21] See Brunner, *Doctrine of God,* 249.

[22] Bruce Reichenbach, "God Limits His Power," in *Predestination and Free Will,* ed. D. and R. Bassinger (Downers Grove: InterVarsity, 1986), 106.

[23] See Hendrikus Berkhof, *Christian Faith,* trans. Sierd Woudstra (Grand Rapids: Eerdmans, 1979), 198, 216ff.

[24] See Calvin, *Concerning the Eternal Predestination of God,* trans. J. Reid (London: James Clarke, 1961), 181.

[25] For the problems of soft-determinism see William Hasker, *Metaphysics* (Downers Grove: InterVarsity, 1983), 33ff.

[26] Davis, *Logic and the Nature of God,* 14ff.

[27] At this point many try to escape to "mystery" or "paradox" to avoid admitting a contradiction. Concerning the invalidity of this tactic see *ibid.,* 16, 78, 140ff.

[28] W. G. T. Shedd, cited by Cottrell, *What the Bible Says,* 172.

[29] Fretheim, *The Suffering of God,* 47.

[30] See Thomas Talbott, "On Predestination, Reprobation, and the Love of God," *Reformed Journal* (February 1983), 11ff.

[31] T. E. Pollard, "The Impassibility of God," *Scottish Journal of Theology,* 8 (1955): 361.

[32] On the importance of using God's personal name see Clines, "Yahweh."

[33]See the following for thorough discussions on the personalistic view of God: Fretheim, *The Suffering of God;* Konig, *Here Am I;* Berkhof, *Christian Faith;* and Abraham Heschel, *The Prophets,* 2 vols. (New York: Harper & Row, 1962).

[34]For especially helpful treatments of the nature of personhood see John Macmurray, published in two vols., *The Self as Agent* and *Persons in Relation* (London: Faber, 1956), and Peter Bertocci, *The Person God Is* (New York: Humanities, 1970).

[35]Fretheim, *The Suffering of God,* 35.

[36]The term is Heschel's, *The Prophets,* II, 219.

[37]The term is Berkhof's, *Christian Faith,* 133.

[38]Verses used in this section are not intended as prooftexts but as illustrations. See the works already cited by Konig, Fretheim, and Heschel for the biblical substantiation of the claims made in this chapter.

[39]Classical theism sought to remove all tensions from within the Godhead, but in so doing it depersonalized God.

[40]The phrase is Berkhof's, *Christian Faith,* 140.

[41]For a discussion of passages that have been interpreted as referring to God's immutability, see Konig, *Here Am I,* 66ff.

[42]See Ezekiel 12:1–3; Jeremiah 3:7, 19; and Fretheim, *The Suffering of God,* 45ff.

[43]See the suggestive article by Augustine Shutte, "Indwelling, Intersubjectivity and God," *Scottish Journal of Theology* 32 (1979), 201–16.

[44]That God experiences time and is affected by his creatures is documented from the Scriptures by Fretheim, *The Suffering of God,* 40ff.

[45]Konig, *Here Am I,* 128.

[46]A sixth advantage would be that it avoids the polar errors of the absolutistic and process views of God.

SALVATION, SIN, AND HUMAN FREEDOM IN KIERKEGAARD

C. Stephen Evans

It is biblically and theologically correct to ascribe human salvation to God and not ourselves. Salvation is not earned or merited by human effort. Søren Kierkegaard, raised in a Lutheran home, understood this as well as anyone:

> This is the law of the relations between God and man in the God-relationship. . . .
>
> There is an infinite, radical, qualitative difference between God and man.
>
> This means, or the expression for this is: the human person achieves absolutely nothing; it is God who gives everything; it is he who brings forth a person's faith, etc.
>
> This is grace, and this is Christianity's major premise.[1]

However, Kierkegaard also held, just as emphatically, that salvation must somehow be seen as requiring a free human action:

> There is a pious suspicion about subjectivity, that as soon as the least concession is made to it it will promptly become something meritorious—this is why objectivity must be emphasized.
>
> Fine. In order to constrain subjectivity, we are quite properly taught that no one is saved by works, but by grace—and corresponding to that—by faith. Fine.
>
> But am I therefore unable to do something myself with regard to becoming a believer? Either we must answer this with an unconditioned "no," and then we have fatalistic election by grace, or we must make a little concession. The point is this— subjectivity is always under suspicion, and when it is established that we are saved by faith, there is immediately the suspicion that too much has been conceded here. So an addition

is made: But no one can give himself faith; it is a gift of God I must pray for.

Fine, but then I myself can pray, or must we go farther and say: No, praying (consequently praying for faith) is a gift of God which no man can give to himself; it must be given to him. . . .

There are many, many envelopes—but there must still be one point or another where there is a halt at subjectivity. Making the scale so large, so difficult, can be commendable as a majestic expression for God's infinity, but subjectivity cannot be excluded, unless we want to have fatalism.[2]

Of course some would say that what Kierkegaard here calls theological fatalism is simply the truth of the matter, because it is what the Scriptures teach. Perhaps the term *theological fatalism* is objectionable but if the question concerns who is to be saved and who is not, the biblical answer is simply that God and God alone decides.

Such an answer would surely be too quick, however. Although there are certainly passages that seem to teach such a doctrine of "unconditional election," there are surely many others that imply that the decisions humans make have eternal consequences and that they are free to choose and are held accountable for their choices.

In the passage quoted, Kierkegaard obviously does not refute what he terms theological fatalism, nor does he even attempt to do so. Someone who wishes to hold to a strict doctrine of unconditional election and double predestination will probably reject the term Kierkegaard uses for the view but will fail to see any reason why "subjectivity" should be given a valid role in the economy of salvation. However, to anyone who is uncomfortable with the idea that salvation is something that happens to a person independently of any free choice the person may make, Kierkegaard's remarks are interesting. He points out a significant—and in itself praiseworthy—motive for moving in the direction of a doctrine of unconditional election, namely, to honor God. It is natural and right for the redeemed to ascribe their redemption to God and to wish no merit to be ascribed to themselves. What Kierkegaard wants to do is satisfy this theological demand without resorting to what one of his pseudonyms call "the desperate presumptuousness of predestination." If he is successful, then a significant part of the motivation for theological fatalism will be undermined.

Kierkegaard's strategy for accomplishing this goal is neither unique nor specially original, but it is clearly thought out and articulated. The crucial move consists in separating the question of merit from the question of free, subjective participation on the part of the individual. It is crucial that at some point in the process of salvation, the individual have some role to play that is due to free choice, but it is not necessary to see this role as giving the individual any merit. The choice of the individual is in no way directed toward earning salvation.

SALVATION IN *PHILOSOPHICAL FRAGMENTS*

Kierkegaard's pseudonym Johannes Climacus gives an excellent illustration of the characteristic Kierkegaardian view of salvation in *Philosophical Fragments*. This work is directed toward a crucial comparison of Christianity with philosophical idealism. The major differences are clear: philosophical idealism presupposes that the truth (the essential truth, which if possessed is equivalent to salvation) is present at bottom in every individual; Christianity asserts that this essential truth must be brought to human beings in an authoritative revelation. Philosophical idealism assumes that since all humans have the truth, the most one human being can do for another when it comes to discovering the essential truth about life is to be a Socratic teacher who helps the individual discover the truth buried within. The teacher is only an "occasion," a Socratic mid-wife. Christianity asserts that since individuals are caught in sin, God himself must become the teacher, and that only if God entered history as a human being could the truth be grasped by human beings. In this case the teacher must also be a savior, who not only brings the truth but transforms humans so they can receive that truth.

It is clear that this Christian view gives God the glory and sharply checks human pride and presumption. Indeed, Climacus stresses that Christianity will be offensive to prideful humans if they insist that their autonomous reason is sufficient to enable them to reach the truth. One would think that this view would incline Climacus toward a doctrine of unconditional election. The essential difference between Christianity and idealism is simply that idealism assumes that the ability to attain salvation is within human beings, while Christianity insists that this condition is totally lacking. What then, from a Christian perspective, can the individual do? Climacus' answer is simply that the individual can only recognize his inability to do anything. When the God becomes our teacher, the one point of analogy between the God and the Socratic teacher is the discovery of our *un*truth. On this point and this point alone, the God serves as an occasion for us to "recollect" a truth from within.[3] The one thing a person can do for his or her own salvation is to recognize his or her own sinfulness.

Strictly speaking, the person cannot even do this without divine assistance. It is a consistent theme in Kierkegaard's writings that sin-consciousness, which must be contrasted with mere guilt-consciousness, can be achieved only by divine revelation. It is only when God reveals true holiness to me that I perceive my true sinfulness. However, although God's revelation makes possible the consciousness of sin, it does not make it necessary. My sinfulness is still something I must freely recognize.

The means by which Climacus here preserves a legitimate role for human freedom, while at the same time giving God full credit for human salvation, also allows him to save a legitimate role for human reason. Kierkegaard is often read as an irrationalist, and a superficial reading of *Philosophical Fragments* supports that reading. Since human reason cannot by itself attain the truth that is equivalent to salvation, Climacus insists that faith requires that reason be "set aside" in favor of a truth that human reason cannot comprehend, a truth that is a paradox.

What must be added to this picture is Kierkegaard's understanding of sin. God's incarnation to become our teacher and savior is a paradox to human reason because human reason is sinful.[4] If a person recognizes his or her sinfulness, then the offensiveness of the idea of God becoming a human being actually can be seen to be a mark of its truth.[5] If reason is willing to recognize its own bankruptcy, then the appropriateness of a revelation that transcends reason can be seen. When reason is permeated by a consciousness of sin, then reason and the paradox can embrace in the happy passion that Climacus calls faith. Reason can remain on "good terms" with revelation, because reason "sets *itself* aside."[6]

Climacus can therefore consistently reject unconditional election while at the same time denying that salvation is the result of a human act of will,[7] and denying that salvation is due to a human intellectual act.[8] Faith is a gift of God offered to human beings, and whether a person accepts the gift depends on whether the requisite sin-consciousness is present in that individual. That consciousness is itself something the individual is powerless to develop by himself, since it is possible only when God reveals himself to the person. But the self-understanding that God offers is one that the individual is free to accept or reject. The acceptance of this consciousness is hardly meritorious for the individual, since it consists precisely in the individual's recognition that there is no merit present within him or her at all. The one thing people can do toward their own salvation is to recognize their own inability to do anything toward their own salvation. Even this they can do only with God's help, but in Kierkegaard's view, this is enough of a concession to subjectivity to eliminate the need for theological fatalism.

BIBLICAL FREEDOM AND BONDAGE TO SIN

Any view of salvation that gives a role to human free choice must face the objection that human freedom is an unbiblical concept. Many have urged that the idea of human free will is the product of Greek or perhaps Enlightenment thinking, a prideful exaltation of human capacities. Surely, thinks this sort of critic, the Bible teaches that people are not free, that they are slaves to sin. What I must do in response to this charge is to show that the kind of freedom Kierkegaard needs to assume for his view of salvation is consistent with biblical teachings, particularly teachings about human bondage to sin.

I believe it is helpful to begin by distinguishing two kinds of freedom: formal and material. Formal freedom is the "freedom of the will," which is the usual subject of philosophical inquiry. To say that a person is free in the formal sense is to say that on some occasions he has the ability to choose from more than one alternative. No causal chain determines that the person will choose one inevitable outcome. Material freedom is the ability to be the kind of person God is calling an individual to be. It is the ability of a person to choose what God wishes her to choose, in the manner God wishes the choice to be made.

It is clear that a person can be free in the formal sense and still be limited in all sorts of ways. First, the number of occasions on which I possess the ability to choose may be limited. Second, on those occasions in which I do possess alternatives, the number and character of those alternatives may be limited. Third, in those situations in which I do possess alternatives there may exist powerful tendencies to choose one alternative, and this means that other alternatives can be chosen only if a great effort of will is exerted. Not all of the possibilities may be live; even some of those that are live may be barely alive.

It is because formal freedom can be limited in this way that a person can be formally free and materially unfree. I take it that the biblical doctrine that the natural man is a "slave to sin" and that freedom from this bondage is found through Christ should be understood in the following way. Because of sin the number of situations in which a person has a genuine choice is limited, the number of alternatives the person has in those situations is limited, and some of those alternatives may be nearly impossible to resist. The cumulative effect of these limitations is to make it impossible for the individual to live a godly life; although the person may on some occasions make a right choice, the overall pattern is squarely against God's intentions.

Of course the reason this is so is that the individual is sinful, and sin must be understood primarily as the condition of someone who has rebelled against God and broken the relationship with God. God's primary intention for every individual is that they live in conscious dependence and communication with himself. Someone who has chosen not to do that severely restricts the possibilities for his life because he is going against the structures of the created order. He frequently sins because his life as a whole can be seen as sin. Sin is not merely found in his actions, but in his being.

This view of sin and freedom can be clearly seen in Kierkegaard. Although no one defends the reality and significance of human freedom more vigorously than Kierkegaard, he completely rejects any philosophical account of freedom that makes the human will into a pure, disinterested chooser uncontaminated by its history:

> That abstract freedom of choice (*liberum arbitrium*) is a phantasy, as if a human being at every moment of his life stood continually in this abstract possibility, so that consequently he never moves from the spot, as if freedom were not also an historical condition—this has been pointed out by Augustine and many moderns.
>
> It seems to me that the matter can be illuminated simply in the following way. Take a weight, even the most accurate gold weight—when it has been used only a week it already has a history. The owner knows this history, for example, that it leans towards off-balance one way or other, etc. This history continues with use.
>
> So it is with the will. It has a history, a continually progressive history. A person can go so far that he finally loses even the capacity of being able to choose. With this, however, the history is not concluded, for, as Augustine rightly says, this condition is the punishment of sin—and is again sin.[9]

As Johannes Climacus puts it in *Philosophical Fragments,* freedom is real, but the consequences of genuine freedom may include the loss of freedom, without any loss of responsibility. Drawing on Aristotle, Climacus points out that a man may be free to throw a stone or not to throw a stone, but he is not free to recall the stone once it is thrown.[10]

FREEDOM AND ORIGINAL SIN

The critic may feel at this point that Kierkegaard's view is still not cleared of the taint of Pelagianism. Even if the historical character of freedom allows us to see how human beings can be formally free yet materially slaves to sin, a question may arise as to whether formal freedom is consistent with *original* sin. How can the notion that human beings freely choose and are responsible for sin be squared with the belief that all human beings are sinners because of Adam's sin?

It is evident, I think, that the church has been wise in rejecting Pelagianism. The Pelagian view that sin is only environmentally transmitted and that people would be good if it were not for their environment is neither biblically nor experientially adequate. Our own honest self-awareness does not square with the assumption that the wrong choices and orientation of our lives can be completely pinned on the external environment. So it seems to me that it is right to extend our understanding of the historical character of freedom to the race as well as to the individual. Sinful choices affect not only our own wills but also those of our fellow human beings, and Adam's choice was one with tragic consequences for the race.

The principle that must be steadfastly maintained here is that there is a substantial unity to the human race. In some sense all human beings "sinned in Adam." The trick is not to interpret this in a mechanical manner, as if Adam sinned and then his sin was somehow biologically transmitted to the race as if sin were an inheritable disease. Rather, as Kierkegaard says in *The Concept of Anxiety*, which contains his fullest treatment of this problem, "Every individual is both himself and the race."[11] This is true of Adam but it is also true of every subsequent individual.

In concrete terms this means that Adam freely chose to sin. This sin has consequences, certainly environmental ones that Pelagians emphasize, and perhaps even genetic changes of the sort at which the traditional theory of "inherited sin" is aiming. On Kierkegaard's view (as expressed by his pseudonym Vigilius Haufniensis) these consequences mean that the individual who is born after Adam is both internally and externally different from Adam *quantitatively*.[12] The forces that tend to produce evil are much stronger than they were for Adam. People are truly born in sin; both they and their world are shaped by sin.

All this is compatible with regarding the person as a free, responsible agent. The individual's sin cannot lie simply in what befalls him or her, as if falling into sin were like catching measles or being born with spina bifida. Rather, the individual's choice to be the sinful person his genetic and environmental heritage has produced is the *choice* to be a sinner. This choice is quantitatively different from Adam's but qualitatively it is the same. In sinning, the individual recapitulates Adam's decision and consciously identifies with the fallen race that Adam initiated and represents.

That every human person makes such a choice is indeed mysterious, but it is neither more nor less mysterious than Adam's original choice. Why did Adam sin? We can say that the reason was his desire "to be as a god," but that reason cannot be seen as a determining cause. Adam simply chose to sin. In the same way each member of the human race except Jesus recapitulates Adam's choice, affirming his unity with Adam and the race.

Kierkegaard expresses this by claiming that sin is psychologically inexplicable.[13] No science can really explain sin and to try to do so always alters the concept of sin and makes it something else.

One must simply say that "sin came into the world by a sin."[14] This is true for Adam and every other human being.

SALVATION AND THE LEAP

I have dwelt at some length on Kierkegaard's understanding of sin. I have done this partly to clarify his understanding of human freedom and partly to defend his view from the charge that it is Pelagian. However, it also illuminates his view of salvation itself. Sin is a qualitative leap that has irreparable consequences both for the individual and for the race. Human beings are unable to repair the damage by their own efforts. One can even go so far as to say that human beings cannot repair the damage even with God's help. It is truer to say that God alone can repair the damage. What is possible for the individual, with God's help, is to recognize the necessity of giving up his futile expressions of autonomy and self-sufficiency. He must allow God to step in.

Corresponding to the qualitative leap from innocence to sin is the qualitative leap from the condition of sin to that of faith. In Kierkegaard's view faith is a life-transforming passion that transforms the individual, a passion that the individual cannot produce in himself, but is produced in him by God when the individual encounters Christ in the right way. The encounter itself makes possible that "right way," by making it possible for the individual to recognize his sinfulness. Nevertheless that recognition is forced on no one. Faith and the sin-consciousness that is its precondition cannot be produced by an act of will, but they are not produced in the individual unless the individual wills it. Kierkegaard highlights the significance of this change in the individual and the role of the individual's freedom by calling the transition a leap. The leap of faith is neither blind nor arbitrary; it is truly a gift of God, but it is not a gift mechanically imposed on the individual by an external power.

Kierkegaard says in his *Journals and Papers*, "That God could create beings free over against himself is the cross which philosophy could not bear but upon which it has remained hanging."[15] He could just as easily have said the same about some theologies, which have been, if anything, even less comfortable with human freedom. The chief reason is that human freedom has been seen as an incitement to human pride and an expression of human autonomy, as well as a threat to divine omnipotence and sovereignty. Kierkegaard views both worries as misplaced.

Freedom is not a threat to divine omnipotence, but the crowning achievement of omnipotence. The greatest good one person can do for another is to make that other person free.[16] No human person can do this fully and completely because "the one

who has power is himself captive in having it and therefore
continually has a wrong relationship to the one whom he wants to
make free."[17] In attempting to help another person become free I
inevitably acquire a certain power over that person and thus
defeat my goal. God's ability to make free beings is a sign of his
superiority and his ultimate control over all things. "Therefore if
man had the slightest independence over against God (with
regard to *materia*), then God could not make him free. Creation out
of nothing is once again the Almighty's expression for being able
to make independent. He to whom I owe absolutely everything,
although he still absolutely controls everything, has in fact made
me independent. If in creating man God himself lost a little of his
power, then precisely what he could not do would be to make
man independent."[18]

Nor does Kierkegaard think that the "concession" to human
subjectivity that he believes God has made in any way provides a
basis for human pride and autonomy: "The most tremendous
thing conceded to man is—choice, freedom. If you want to rescue
and keep it, there is only one way—in the very same second
unconditionally in full attachment give it back to God and yourself
along with it. If the sight of what is conceded to you tempts you, if
you surrender to the temptation and look with selfish craving at
freedom of choice, then you lose your freedom."[19]

NOTES

[1] *Søren Kierkegaard's Journals and Papers*, vols. 1–7, ed. and trans. Howard V.
and Edna H. Hong (Bloomington, Indiana: Indiana University Press, 1967–78).
Entry 1381, 3:113.
[2] *Journals and Papers*, entry 4551, 4:352.
[3] *Philosophical Fragments*, ed. and trans. Howard V. and Edna H. Hong
(Princeton: Princeton Univesity Press, 1985), 14.
[4] Ibid., 47.
[5] Ibid., 49–54.
[6] Ibid., 47–48.
[7] Ibid., 62–63.
[8] Ibid., 62.
[9] *Journals and Papers*, entry 1268, 1:73.
[10] *Philosophical Fragments*, 16–17n.
[11] *The Concept of Anxiety*, ed. and trans. by Reidar Thomte in collaboration
with Albert Anderson (Princeton: Princeton University Press, 1980), 28.
[12] Ibid., 30–34, 53–54.
[13] Ibid., 14–23.
[14] Ibid., 32.
[15] *Journals and Papers*, entry 1237, 2:58.
[16] Ibid., entry 1251, 2:62–63.
[17] Ibid.
[18] Ibid.
[19] Ibid., entry 1261, 2:69.

EXHAUSTIVE DIVINE SOVEREIGNTY: A PRACTICAL CRITIQUE

Randall G. Basinger

To what extent do the events in the world flow from God's will? Although this question is simple and straightforward, there is no concensus in the Christian community over how this question is best answered. And it is precisely this question that drives a wedge between the theological traditions of Calvinism and Arminianism.

According to the Calvinist, God has unilaterally and freely decreed—down to the very last detail—the actual course this world will take. All events are consequent and hence subservient to the will of God. Hence the Calvinist speaks of an eternal, immutable, and exhaustive divine plan. The script of cosmic history has one Author. In a word, God is totally sovereign.

The Arminian denies that there is an exhaustive divine plan for this world. While the Arminian God has unilaterally brought this world with its basic structures into existence, he does not exhaustively determine the actual course of the world. As the Arminian sees it, in creating free persons God in effect created co-creators. Hence, the script of cosmic history is to an extent co-authored with his creature-creators. In a word, God's exhaustive sovereignty is denied.

The battle between these rival positions is fought on many fronts. The basic philosophical issues are as difficult as they are well-known: the Calvinist must reconcile God's exhaustive sovereign will with human freedom and explain how a God who wills the events in this world can be perfect in goodness and how a God who decreed what each person will do can hold them accountable for what they in fact do. The Arminian, in contrast, must explain how a God whose control over the world is limited can be considered perfect in power.

In view of the fact that these issues presuppose some of the most thorny and devisive metaphysical issues (e.g., freedom and determinism), it is not surprising that consensus is not easy to come by. And of course there are epistemological issues that complicate things even further. While Calvinists and Arminians agree that any view of God must be true to the biblical material, they disagree on what the biblical text teaches. And beyond this there is disagreement on the extent to which we can and should seek a rationally coherent view of God. Thus the age-old faith/reason debate is never far below the surface.

And so the debate goes on, as well it should. For what is at stake is nothing less than how we view God and the God/world relationship. However, these theoretical issues, important as they may be, will not be the primary focus of this essay. My focus will be on the practical implications these rival views of God have for our lives. The questions we will explore are these: (1) What practical difference does it make if one is a Calvinist or an Arminian? And (2) does this difference tilt the evaluative scale toward either of these rival views?

THE PRIMA FACIE DIFFERENCE

Calvinists and Arminians see different worlds and speak different languages. The Calvinist sees every event as having been willed by God for a purpose. Nothing can occur that falls outside God's eternal, immutable plan. Arminians see a world in which things occur that cannot be attributed to God's unilateral determination. Similarly, Calvinists and Arminians have a different language available for describing and explaining what occurs in the world. Calvinists can talk about events being ordained by God or occurring for a purpose in a way that is simply not available to the Arminian. More specifically, Calvinists often argue the words "chance" or "luck" can have no place in the Christian's vocabulary.[1] And of course we should not be surprised when such terms manage to find their way into the Arminian's vocabulary.

But to what extent do these differences affect the way Calvinists and Arminians behave—i.e. deliberate, make decisions and act? One way to begin answering this question is with examples of how Christians do sometimes theologically reflect on events in their lives and, more importantly, how this reflection affects how they live.[2] Consider the following cases:

Mary's application to graduate school has just been rejected. Her pastor feels that God is "closing the door" to graduate school and leading her into another career area. "After all," he reasons, "if God would have wanted you in graduate school, he would have got you in." One of Mary's friends, however, feels that Mary should not simply resign herself to the rejection. "After all," her friend reasons, "just because something happens does not mean it should have or had to have happened." And Mary's friend encourages her to try to figure out *why* she was rejected. Was it because of her grades? How did the interview go? What is the school's track record for admitting women? How many are admitted on their second attempt? Were all her admission materials in order? "Only after you get a handle on *why* you were rejected," the friend argues, "can you decide on some meaningful strategy of action."

Or consider the Christian college that, after launching a capital improvement campaign, is finding it difficult to raise the needed money. Some administrators might conclude that there is no need for drastic action because if God wants the new buildings to go up, *God* will supply the money. If God does not supply the money and the campaign fails, these administrators can rest in the confidence that God must have a purpose for the failure. In contrast, other administrators might conclude that there needs to be a change in development office personnel and hire an outside firm to develop a new, comprehensive fund-raising strategy. Or these administrators, feeling that no one could have predicted the current dip in the economy, might decide to simply wait out the current recession.

Finally, consider a couple one of whom carries a genetic defect. Some couples might choose to have children, believing that if God wants them to have a healthy baby, they will have one; if he does not, then they will joyfully accept their child as a special gift from God. After all, they reason, God has the whole world— including their reproductive lives—in his hands. Other couples might argue that, in view of the high probability that their child will inherit the genetic defect, the responsible thing would be to either adopt children, pursue some alternative reproductive technology, or simply choose to remain childless.

How Christians act in given situations is often determined, as the above examples suggest, by their understanding of the God/world relationship. Some, assuming that God is in control, act as if events in the world are the way they must be and should be. As a result, the human factor is seemingly left out of their understanding of the situation and hence out of their subsequent actions. Others, assuming that humans are responsible for what occurs in the world, act as if events in the world could be or should be different. As a result they seek explanations and predictions based on natural and human causes and act accordingly, and God is seemingly left out of the deliberations. It appears, at first glance at least, that whether or not we affirm God's exhaustive sovereignty—whether or not one is a Calvinist or a Arminian—does make a difference in how we live.

THE ARMINIAN'S CHALLENGE

Who, in the above examples, is speaking and, most important, acting in the most appropriate way? To answer these questions, let's take a closer look at our hypothetical administrator. While it may be possible in isolation to affirm and act on the basis of divine sovereignty, it certainly cannot be and in fact should not be our normal way of living. An administrator who deduces from her belief in God's sovereignty that the current failure of a capital campaign is God's will and thereby passively accepts its failure is flirting with an arbitrary and dangerous fatalism.

The administrator is accepting the status quo as God's will; she is fatalistically assuming that these events were meant to be. But in so doing she ignores the many human and natural factors that might very well have gone into the current status of the campaign. For example, she is ignoring the possible incompetency, disloyalty, or dishonesty in her staff. She is ignoring the possibility that various committees did not do their homework and hence were not aware of the most current fundraising strategies or had not anticipated the current recession. She may even be ignoring her own shortcomings as an administrator. Or the problem may lie in factors outside of the control of the institution. Perhaps there has been a sudden upswing in inflation or a serious recession. Perhaps would-be donors to the institution are not convinced that the institution is worth investing in and have chosen (either correctly or incorrectly) to invest their money elsewhere.

There are *many* possible reasons why a campaign might fail. To evoke God's sovereign will as the explanation and to act on this basis brackets out any consideration of such reasons and justifies the status quo. It establishes that what is ought to be and rules out the consideration that things could and/or should have been different. Thus at the very best, the administrator is ignoring possible factors that, if they had been corrected, could have made the campaign a success. As she evokes God's sovereign will, she ceases to be an administrator. At the very worst, the administrator's pious language leads her to ignore evils in the institution (incompetency, poor management, dishonesty, fraud, laziness). And those who are directly aware of the actual problems that contributed to the campaign's failure (or perhaps experienced them first hand by serving under an incompetent leadership and/or had their advice ignored) will find the pious remarks dangerously misleading—clouding rather than illuminating the issue.

There is also an arbitrariness in the administrator's position. She did not become an administrator by consistently deducing from her belief in God's sovereignty that what has occurred was meant to be. Administrators hire and fire, make plans, implement the most recent technology, lobby for more money, commission surveys, and at times even resign—all on the assumption that things can and should be different and that there are human and natural factors responsible for what occurs in reality. In other words, an administrator speaks and acts on the language and logic of human responsibility every day of his or her life. On what basis, then, does the administrator in our example suddenly switch to and act on the basis of the language of divine sovereignty at a certain point in campaign? Why not evoke God's will at the beginning of the campaign and not plan any strategy at all? The administrator's decision is arbitrary.

Moreover, the administrator certainly does not apply the language and logic of divine sovereignty in other areas of her life. If her daughter rode a tricycle on the porch against her mother's wishes and fell off, the administrator would hardly accept the child's claim that "it was God's will; it was meant to be." No fatalistic explanation would be admitted here, the mother would punish the child on the assumption that things could have been and should have been different. But why should the mother not accept the daughter's explanation? It is the same explanation she used to account for the failure of the campaign.

And of course the same sort of analysis could be made of the other examples given above. We conclude, then, that those who attempt to act on the position that God is in sovereign control of the events in their lives run into grave problems. At its best, this approach is unlivable. Why go to the doctor for anything? (If God wants us to be healthy, we will be healthy.) Why go to work? (If God wants us to have food and shelter, we will have food and shelter). Why teach our children not to play with matches? (If God wants our children to be burned, they will be burned.) While this approach is often applied to isolated events, those who verbally affirm this approach are not willing or able to apply it consistently to every event in their lives. We live, and we must do so, on the assumption that things *can* be different from what they in fact are.

Moreover, at its worst, this theology is morally suspect. Why work for a nuclear freeze? (If God wants nuclear war, there will be nuclear war.) Why work against racial injustice? (If God wants people to have a job, they will have a job.) Why work on scientific research to explore the relationship between radiation exposure and birth defects? (If God wants us to have a healthy baby, we will have a healthy baby.) If carried out consistently, this approach cuts the nerve of moral endeavor and leads the Christian into a passive life of moral resignation. What *is* will be what is right. Such a stance leads to the support of a status quo that is often evil and unjust. When we are at our moral best, we often do and often must act as though things *should* be different from the way they are.

If our analysis is sound, Christians—like those in the examples—who evoke and act on the basis of God's sovereignty are guilty of an arbitrary, unlivable, and dangerous fatalism. What implications does this have for the Calvinist/Arminian debate?

The lesson Arminians often draw from this line of argument is clear: The best way to avoid this dangerous and arbitrary fatalism is to avoid Calvinism—i.e., the assumption that God is exhaustively sovereign. While the fatalistic actions of the people in the above examples is to be lamented, some Arminians argue, it can be understood. For if God has decreed all events, then it must be that things *cannot* and *should* not be any different from what they are. And if this is the case, what sense does it make to try to make a difference? And hence a fatalistic attitude is bound to follow.

In contrast to this, the Arminian believes that what actually occurs in the world is, to an extent, consequent on the human will; God's exhaustive control over the world is denied. This means that things can occur that God does not will or want; things not only *can* be different but often *should* be different. And from all this follows our responsibility to work with God to bring about a better world.

But is there a logical connection between a belief in total sovereignty and a fatalistic lifestyle? Is denying God's exhaustive sovereignty the best (and perhaps only) way of avoiding fatalism? It certainly cannot be denied that some believers in divine sovereignty do from time to time fall into a fatalistic posture. The above examples capture how believers sometimes behave. Moreover, it cannot be denied that when Calvinists speak about such things as "a spirit of sweet resignation," they fuel the fire of the Arminian's challenge.[3] But it also cannot be denied that very few Calvinists are either professing or practicing fatalists.[4] Is this because, as Arminians often claim, that Calvinists are inconsistent—unwilling to carry their assumption about God to its logical and practical conclusion? Or is there a way that Calvinists can avoid fatalism?

BOTH/AND, NOT EITHER/OR

Richard Mouw, in a short and provocative editorial in the *Reformed Journal* offers one type of Calvinist response to these questions.[5] Mouw's comments are addressed to the problem the San Francisco Giants were having integrating religion and baseball. It seems that pitcher Bob Knepper explained a loss as "God's will." This apparently upset another player, who felt this predestinarian posture was making once-intense players very placid. This tension had the effect of dividing the team into two rival camps.

Mouw responds that "this is a false choice, as should be clear from the fact that the Canons of the Synod of Dort condemn both 'Stoicism' and 'Libertarianism' as equally despicable departures from the truth." He goes on to comment:

> If the born-again Christians on the Giants are indeed tempted by a placid predestinarianism, then they are in desperate need of some instruction in Reformed theology. The Belgic Confession clearly teaches that while nothing in the world happens without God's "appointment," God cannot be "charged with the sins which are committed." The application to baseball should be self-evident: to paraphrase the gun-lobby, God doesn't lose ball games, people do.

When it comes then to explaining just why Bob Knepper did lose the ball game, Mouw agrees with former Giants manager Dave Bristol, who explained: "I don't think religion was the problem—it was mechanics—dropping to a side-arm delivery."

The relevance of Mouw's comments to our present discussion should be obvious. To paraphrase Mouw's paraphrase: God does not cause graduate school rejections, school failures, insufficient funds, defective births, unemployment, or starvation—people do. In line with Dave Bristol's comment, one can almost hear Mouw give the following advice to the school administrator in the earlier example: "I don't think religion is your problem—it was a poor marketing strategy. Fire your director of development."

Mouw insists just as strongly as the Arminian that a fatalistic lifestyle (placid predestinarianism) must be avoided. However, unlike the Arminian, he does this without denying God's exhaustive sovereignty. Rather, he argues that Christians must reject either/or thinking and simultaneously affirm *both* the reality of divine sovereignty *and* the reality of human responsibility. Thus Bob Knepper, while sounding like a Calvinist is really not a Calvinist at all. For his affirmation of divine sovereignty leads him to deny, in practice, something that all good Calvinists recognize as equally true—human freedom and responsibility.

By the same token, Mouw would no doubt argue that Arminians, even though they avoid placid predestinarianism, are in error because their affirmation of human responsibility leads them to deny divine sovereignty. Thus those using Mouw's approach have grounds for rejecting both Bob Knepper's pseudo-Calvinistic fatalism and Arminianism because both falsely assume that one must choose between either divine sovereignty or human responsibility. According to Mouw's approach, believers must reject the heretical "either/or" for an orthodox Calvinistic "both/and."

But does this "both/and" approach provide the Calvinist with a basis for avoiding fatalism? The typical way of answering this question has been to ask the age-old question of whether God's sovereignty and human freedom can be simultaneously affirmed. Arminian's argue no; Calvinists argue yes. But fortunately this is not the only way of evaluating the "both/and" argument. For even if it be granted that divine sovereignty and human freedom are simultaneously true, the argument does not automatically succeed. The argument succeeds only if it can be shown that the truth of both rules out fatalism.

The question before us then is not, "Are divine sovereignty and human responsibility both true?" but rather, "If they are both true, is fatalism ruled out?" In short, does an affirmation of both necessitate that one live a nonfatalistic life? The answer to this last question is no.

Even if we grant that both divine sovereignty and human responsibility are true, why follow Mouw's advice to affirm human freedom and responsibility and hence live nonfatalistically, while at the same time continuing to affirm that God is sovereign? Could not a fatalist simply turn the tables and advise that we affirm God's sovereignty and hence live fatalistically but at the same time continue to affirm that humans are nonetheless free and responsible. If the Calvinist were to challenge the fatalist by claiming that surely we must pick between fatalism and human responsibility, could not the fatalist dismiss this challenge as "either/or" thinking. If the Calvinist can hold that belief in divine sovereignty is compatible with a nonfatalistic lifestyle, why can't the fatalist hold that belief in human responsibility is compatible with a fatalistic lifestyle? Or if the Calvinist were to ask whether it makes sense to affirm that we are responsible yet live fatalistically, could not the fatalist respond in kind: Does it make sense to deny fatalism yet go on to affirm that God is really sovereign?

It would appear that the Calvinist and the fatalist are at a stalemate, for the "both/and" technique works both ways. Thus even if we grant the Calvinist that both divine sovereignty and human responsibility are true, this gives us no reason for choosing one way of life over the other. It is not enough to argue for both divine sovereignty and human responsibility. One also has to argue why the truth of both leads to a nonfatalistic as opposed to a fatalistic lifestyle. It is here where the both/and approach seemingly fails.

THE TWO WILLS OF GOD

Another way some Calvinists attempt to avoid an arbitrary and dangerous fatalism hinges on the ambiguity in the notion of "God's will." All believers feel that it is important to seek and submit to God's will. But as R. C. Sproul warns, "When we seek the will of God, we must first ask ourselves which will are we seeking to discover."[6] It is common among Calvinists to distinguish between two distinct wills of God.

On the one hand, there is God's *sovereign* or decretive will, which unilaterally determines every event in the world. It refers to God's exhaustive, eternal, and immutable plan for the world. On the other hand, there is the *moral* or preceptive will of God, which refers to what God desires for his creation. This includes types of human actions that are pleasing in God's eyes and is captured in moral precepts (e.g., "Thou shalt not kill.") and also God's desires, wishes, or inner dispositions (e.g., "God is not willing that any should perish.").

An important distinction Calvinists make between these two wills concerns the degree to which these wills can be known. The moral will of God has been revealed to us, while the sovereign will of God remains primarily hidden. Thus Calvinists regularly refer to God's sovereign will as the secret will of God. In just what sense, however, is the sovereign will of God secret, and what is the practical consequence of this secrecy for how we live?

At first glance, it is not clear why God's sovereign will should be considered a secret. If it is true that God determines everything, then we can know that everything that has occurred is a part of God's plan and has occurred for a purpose. Thus anyone who believes in God's decretive will can know it by knowing the past. However, as Garry Friesen explains, while we can know that every event in the world that has happened is God's will, we do not and cannot know (apart from a special revelation) why it happened or what will happen next. By knowing the past we at best see only part of God's eternal plan. God's complete plan is hidden from our view.[7]

By way of illustration, let us take the case of Mary. If Mary applies to graduate school and is turned down, she can know with certainty that it was part of God's plan for the universe that she not be accepted. It is no secret, then, that God did not will her to be accepted. But from the fact that Mary was rejected *many* subsequent events are possible: She might reapply a second or even a third time and still be rejected; she might apply a second time and be accepted; she might change career, etc. Thus the event could be a means for bringing about any number of future events. There are many possible purposes God could have for her rejection; that is, there are a number of possible futures. Thus even if Mary believes in God's exhaustive sovereignty, the bare fact that she was rejected reveals nothing to her about what purposes this rejection will serve in her life or how it will plug into the future. God's actual purpose (and hence the future) remain an inpenetratable secret. Knowing *that* God has willed her rejection for a purpose does not shed any light on what will or should happen next in her life. Thus Friesen concludes, "The raw data of circumstances is mysterious to say the least."[8] God's sovereign will "has no direct bearing on the actual consideration of options or formulation of plans."[9] In fact, "for practical living, some things should simply be viewed as happening 'by chance'."[10]

If God's sovereign will is of no help, how then should Calvinists decide what course of action to take? Garry Friesen recommends "the way of wisdom."[11] While the decretive will of God is a secret, the moral will of God has been revealed in Scripture. Hence our decisions must be made in submission to God's *moral will*. Of course, Friesen argues, God's moral will is very general, hence the believer must exercise good judgment in making decisions in areas where God's moral will is not explicit.

Applying this method to the case of Mary, this would at the very least mean trying to figure out why she was rejected (e.g., was she prepared? Was she discriminated against?) and then plan an appropriate strategy of action (e.g., study harder, challenge the discrimination, seek another career, go for career counseling). Rather than fatalistically bracketing out these natural and human factors, Mary must take them into consideration if a wise career decision is to be made. Calvinists like Friesen, therefore, have much more in common with Mary's friend than with the pastor, even though it is the pastor who evokes the sovereignty of God.

Does Calvinism lead to an arbitrary and dangerous fatalism? Apparently not. R. C. Sproul warns his fellow Calvinists that "the secret counsel of God is none of our business!"[12] And those Calvinists who take Sproul seriously will no doubt agree with Friesen when he concludes, "For all practical purposes, *sovereign guidance has no direct bearing in the conscious considerations* of the decision maker."[13]

Calvinists can reach a similar conclusion through slightly different means. Berkhof, for example, argues:

> God's so ordering the universe that man will pursue a certain course of action, is . . . a quite different thing from His commanding him to do so. The decrees are not addresssed to man, and are not the nature of statute law; neither do they impose compulsion or obligation on the wills of men.[14]

What Berkhof suggests here is that God's decretive will is quite logically distinct from his moral will. The moral will of God is a standard that stands outside of and over against each individual. In other words, it is something in relation to which we can and must make a choice. The notions of freely seeking, submitting, and obeying are consistent with the inner logic of God's moral will. Consequently, even though humans should submit to God's moral will, they often do not. Sin and rebellion are real. In this sense, it is possible and proper to say that God's (moral) will is not always achieved.

The sovereign will of God, in contrast, establishes everything that happens; it cannot be frustrated. Consequently, as Berkhof puts it, the sovereign will of God is not "addressed to men as a rule of action."[15] It makes no sense to try to measure up, conform, or submit to the sovereign will of God.

By way of analogy, the Calvinists' God is much like an author of a novel. An author unilaterally determines that characters will make certain choices. And within the context of the play, characters obviously make real choices. But what a character in a novel does not and in fact cannot do is make choices about whether or not to submit to the author's will. It *makes no sense* to ask whether a character is within the sovereign will of the author. The fact that they are characters *means* that they are. There is no way a character of the story can somehow be outside the storyline determined by the author.

In the same way, to the Calvinist every human thought, decision, and subsequent action has, by definition, already been determined by God's sovereign will. In other words, it makes no sense to *try* to get into the sphere of God's sovereign will, for all events are by definition in it. We cannot help but be in it.

Consequently, those who believe in God's exhaustive sovereign will should not seek to submit to it. This is not because of its secret and mysterious nature. They should not because they cannot. The sovereign will of God is not something to which one can submit. It is not surprising, then, that those who try to involve God's sovereign will in their decision making and subsequent actions end up in inconsistent, arbitrary, and dangerous behavior. They have made a category mistake.

The practical implication of this is clear. While the Calvinist can believe that every event that occurs has been willed by God for a purpose, this cannot be the basis for our decision making. It is God's moral will that has relevance to our decision and subsequent behavior. Once again, it appears as though the Calvinist—by distinguishing between the two wills of God—can avoid a dangerous and arbitrary fatalism.

Of course whether either of these two moves is ultimately successful depends on whether the type of distinction the Calvinist wants to make between God's sovereign and moral wills can be meaningfully made. But at this point serious problems arise.

Just what is the relationship between God's two wills? They seem to be at cross purposes. For example, his moral will is that all be saved. Yet his sovereign will is that not all be saved. What is the *real* will of God? Obviously it must be the sovereign will, because this is what God ultimately brings about. But what then of the moral will? In what sense is it real; to what extent does it reveal something about God? The Calvinist appears to face an unresolvable dilemma. If God's moral will represents what God really wants to happen, then human sin really thwarts God's will. But then God is not sovereign. On the other hand, if God is sovereign, then the human will cannot be outside of the divine will. But then how can it be true that God really does not want humans to sin? Arminians escape this dilemma by denying that God has an exhaustive sovereign will and thereby they preserve both the reality of sin and the reality of God's moral will. Calvinists must try to have it both ways.

Calvinists are of course not unaware of this problem. John Murray wonders, "How can God say: this comes to pass by my infallible foreordination and providence, and also say to us: this thou shalt not bring to pass?"[16] And, as he elsewhere surmises, "If I am not mistaken it is at this point that sovereignty of God makes the human mind reel as it does nowhere else in connection with this topic."[17] And many Calvinists are willing to leave it an unresolved (or unresolvable) mystery—recognizing, however, that "it is the sanctified understanding that reels."[18]

Millard Erickson has attempted to resolve this tension between the two wills of God by distinguishing between what God "wills" (what he decides will actually occur) and what God "wishes" (God's general intention, the values he is pleased with). According to Erickson, God often wills to occur what he does not wish to occur. But this sort of distinction, he argues,

> is not as unique and foreign to us as we might at first think. It is not unlike the way parents sometimes treat their children. A mother may wish for her son to avoid a particular type of behavior, and may tell him so. Yet there are situations in which she may, unobserved by her son, see him about to engage in the forbidden action, yet choose not to intervene to prevent it. Here is a case in which the parent's wish is clearly that the child not engage in certain behavior, yet her will is that he do what he has willed to do. By choosing not to intervene to prevent the act, the mother is actually willing that it take place.[19]

Erickson certainly has a point. Parents do sometimes will what they do not wish or want to happen. And there are relevant similarities between parent/child and the God/human relationship. In both cases there is a relationship between moral agents in which one party has moral authority over the other and hence can give commands to the other. Moreover, in both instances one party has more power than the other and hence can control the actions of the other.

There is, however, a relevant dissimilarity between the two cases. The Calvinist God has total power over humans, while the parents do not have total power over the child. Thus parents give a moral command to their child. If the child obeys, then the parents will allow the child to carry out her act of obedience. There is a continuity between what the parents wish and will. On the other hand, if the child begins to disobey (or the parents have good reason to believe that the child will disobey), the parents might decide not to use their superior power to retrain the child from acting, and in this sense they have willed the event. The key here is that what the parents do depends on what the child decides to do. For the parents cannot control the will of the child. The distinction, then, between willing and wishing arises only as a reaction to what children choose. In other words, the distinction arises only in relationships in which no one party does not have total control over the other.

This, however, is not the case with the Calvinist's God, who is all-controlling. He not only controls human actions but also whether or not a human initially chooses to obey. He does not react to human choice; rather he determines it. Thus we can understand why there would at times be a difference between what finite human parents will and what they want, for they face circumstances they did not create and do not totally control. Parents are trying to salvage something good out of a bad situation. We cannot understand how this disparity could exist for the God who possesses exhaustive sovereignty.

We conclude, then, that, while it is hard (if not impossible) to imagine Calvinism without the distinction between God's sovereign will and his moral will, it is harder still to coherently conceive of a God in which this distinction really exists.

CONCLUSION

Our study began with two questions: (1) What practical difference does it make if one is a Calvinist or an Arminian? and (2) Does this difference tilt the evaluative scale toward either of these rival views? Arminians, we have seen, often claim that it does (or should) make a difference, for it is only the Arminian who can consistently avoid a dangerous and arbitrary fatalism. We also explored two ways Calvinists attempt to thwart the Arminian challenge. But we have seen that these attempts have problems. Hence we conclude that the evaluative scale is tipped toward the Arminian: Arminianism makes better sense of how we should and, in fact, do act in the world.

However, what if our criticisms of Calvinism have been off the mark? If this is the case, some interesting things follow. Even if we accept the Calvinist's claim that simultaneously affirming *both* divine sovereignty *and* human responsibility rules out fatalism, it is the truth that humans are free and responsible that affects how we live. Similarly, even if we accept that God indeed has two distinct wills, God's sovereign will is simply not something we can or should take into consideration in our decisions and actions. This consideration is reserved for God's moral will, which evokes but cannot determine action.

In a sense this essay is about two different languages Christians speak. On the one hand, we can speak the language of exhaustive sovereignty. On the other hand we can speak the language of human responsibility and God's moral will. As Arminians see it, we cannot speak both languages. And the Arminian of course speaks and lives the language of human freedom and God's moral will. Calvinists' in contrast, are theoretically committed to speaking both of these languages. However, when it comes to living, this theoretical "both/and" turns into a practical "either/or." It is the language of human responsibility and God's moral will that guides their lives.

Thus for all the theoretical differences between our rival views, practically speaking, it makes no difference in how we live. Even if the Calvinist can succeed in consistently avoiding fatalism, the Arminian has little to lose. For when Calvinists are at their self-proclaimed best, the fact that they believe that God is exhaustively sovereign does not affect how they live. When Calvinists are at their self-proclaimed best, they live and talk like Arminians. One wonders, then, what divine sovereignty really means. What is its practical importance? In a nutshell, the final Arminian challenge to the Calvinist view of exhaustive divine sovereignty is this: What difference does it make?

NOTES

[1] For example, see Murray's discussion of Calvin in John Murray, *Calvin on Scripture and Divine Sovereignty* (Grand Rapids: Baker, 1960), 66.

[2] See the discussion of the practical dimension of the divine-sovereignty/human-freedom debate in David Basinger and Randall Basinger, eds., *Predestination and Free Will* (Downers Grove: InterVarsity, 1986), 7–16.

[3] Arthur Pink, *The Sovereignty of God* (Grand Rapids: Baker, 1965), 272.

[4] See Roger R. Nicole, "Soli Deo Gloria," in James M. Boice, ed., *Our Sovereign God* (Grand Rapids: Baker, 1977), 172–74.

[5] 31 (June 1981): 5. See my discussion of Mouw in "What Difference Does It Make?" *Reformed Journal* 32 (December 1982): 15–18.

[6] R. C. Sproul, *God's Will and the Christian* (Wheaton: Tyndale, 1985), 32.

[7] Garry Friesen, *Decision Making and the Will of God* (Portland, Multnomah, 1982), 201–27.

[8] Ibid., 213.

[9] Ibid., 225.

[10] Ibid., 214.

[11] Ibid., 151–227.

[12] R. C. Sproul, "Discerning the Will of God," in Boice, *Our Sovereign God*, 110.

[13] Friesen, *Decision Making*, 233.

[14] L. Berkhof, *Systematic Theology*, 4th ed. (Grand Rapids: Eerdmans, 1949), 103.

[15] Ibid., 107.

[16] Murray, *Calvin on Scripture*, 69.

[17] Ibid., 68–69.

[18] Ibid., 69.

[19] Millard Erickson, *Christian Theology*, vol. 1 (Grand Rapids: Baker, 1983), 361.

THE BIBLICAL DOCTRINE
OF ELECTION

William G. MacDonald

INTRODUCTION

The history of the exposition of the doctrine of election[1] necessitates a polemical handling of this doctrine today. My method of clearing a path will be expositional rather than directly polemical. The most convincing polemic derives from a clear exposition of the basic biblical passages.

When doing theology, one always must ask the supreme question concerning God, *"What is his name?"* (Exod. 3:14). His true identity is ultimately the issue in every doctrine. What kind of God has manifested himself in history, culminating in the infallible revelation in Christ? What does a particular doctrine like election teach and imply about the nature of God? God's character is on the line in every doctrine and especially in the doctrine of election. Whom he chooses, how he chooses, and whether his criterion for choice is arcane or announced tell us much about God, even if we had no other doctrines to compare.

THE CONTINUUM OF GOD'S CHOICES IN HISTORY

When God answered for Moses and Israel the incisive question about his identity, he revealed himself as the consummate person: "I am who I am." His personhood is assured as an ongoing reality. We should expect this personal God to make decisions as to the recipients of his blessing and presence. Unlike the classical doctrine of election that made little reference to history, biblical history will be our starting point.[2]

Two great epochs demarcate biblical history: (1) from creation until Christ and (2) from Christ to the consummation. Another epoch prior to both of these is alluded to in Scripture as well. The apostle Paul cited a choice God made "before the creation of the world" (Eph. 1:4). God preplanned to grant grace, not abstractly, but "in Christ" to the church. He decided to do this "before the beginning of time" (2 Tim. 1:9). That unique epoch will be treated last, after having considered the two historical biblical epochs. In these later epochs God can be seen choosing in ordinary time according to his stated purpose of grace. There in the stream of time his self-revelation is concentrated.

Now this approach of treating the first epoch last may require some justification. We are committed by presupposition to know no more than the Bible divulges. Therefore we must begin with *historical* (inclusive of verbal) revelation, since it leads us to Christ Jesus, in and through whom we find the full revelation of what God is like. Were we to attempt to begin with eternity, the realm so dear to philosophical constructions, we would have no foundation outside ourselves against which to see and interpret the inspired words about what went on in the divine strategy of selection "before creation." We must not approach God's decisions from eternity as if we had footing there as his prepositive equal, and *on our own* were able to intuit the equivalent of the data of revelation.

The only safe way to approach this doctrine of the God who chooses according to his own wisdom is with awe and worship, and with both eyes on Jesus as seen in the open Bible. That Bible must not be pressed through a philosophical sieve. Many theologians would squeeze this doctrine to fit the shape of an inscrutable mystery. That procedure blocks out revelation and makes their pronouncements on the subject dubious. But it is precisely in reference to election/predestination/adoption that the apostle Paul reaches a crescendo in one of the thematic lines of his Ephesian symphony: *"He made known to us the mystery of his will according to his good pleasure"* (Eph. 1:9). We will later examine the full extent of this disclosure. Our task is to focus spiritual eyes on God's revelation, not to fill a void presumed to be otherwise inscrutable.

THE EPOCH FROM CREATION TO CHRIST

All God's words and acts as he relates to his creatures obviously reflect choices on his part. The "living God" plans, interacts, and also reacts (Gen. 6:5–8). So we will begin our consideration with certain instances in the Old Testament where God's choices of human beings to be special to him are featured:

1. God's choice to create the first man and his wife in his own image as the climax of creation;

2. God's choice of Abel and his sacrifice, over Cain and his sacrifice;
3. God's choice of Noah, "a righteous man," and his family over the rest of humanity, all of whom were "corrupt";
4. God's choice of Abraham to leave a nation of idolaters and to become in his posterity "a great nation" for God;
5. God's choice of Jacob over his twin Esau to be the patriarch of the Abrahamic nation, which would be called by his new name, Israel;
6. God's choice of David and his descendants over Saul and his descendants to rule over the Abrahamic nation in its kingdom phase;
7. God's choice of John the Baptizer before his conception to be the one to sensitize the Abrahamic people to their need for the Messiah's ministry.

THE EPOCH FROM CHRIST TO CONSUMMATION

The second historical epoch of divine choice commences with Christ, "the chosen one" (Matt. 12:18; Luke 9:35; 23:35; 1 Peter 2:4, 6), and includes his descendants by spiritual birth and adoption, who form "his body." Just as the first epoch of historical revelation featured *a chosen man and his descendants,* who became known as *the chosen ones,* so the second epoch features the same model. The "chosen one" par excellence was the distant son of David, from whom a new heavenly kingdom derives. He was also the deeper distant son of Abraham, from whom a new spiritual posterity descends; and he was also the remote son of, and "last," Adam, from whom [Christ] a new race of recreated people trace their lineage.

Jesus, the New Patriarch of the Chosen People

Jesus became to the kingdom of God what Abraham was to the Hebrew nation, the great patriarch (cf. Isa. 9:6; John 14:18) in whom all his offspring derive their identity and to whom they owe their allegiance. Early in his ministry Jesus was rejected on his first visit back to his hometown synagogue. He narrowly escaped assassination. Months later, after healing a handicapped man on the Sabbath in another synagogue, the religious authorities there jealously detested him to such a degree that they set themselves in an antichrist stance (Luke 6:11). It was right after this, and after a night of prayer (Luke 6:12–49), that Jesus reorganized believing Israel (his followers) to become symbolically a new nation submitted to God's rule.

In the place of the twelve sons of Israel, Christ chose twelve new patriarchs as "apostles" commissioned to represent him and to have a role of fruitfulness (John 15:16). Like Moses, he appointed another seventy men to multiply his ministry. Sent before him with a share of his power and authority, they subsequently reported extraordinary blessing. Jesus' next task then was to identify the constituents that would constitute the nonpolitical, theocratic people he was calling into formation.

Jesus' Basic Teachings—the Criteria of Selection

The anointed king-designate specified the requisite attitudes of those he sought to go with him into the arriving kingdom of God to be made up of God's select people. His conditions of participation were stated as the initial portion of his famous proverbs known traditionally as the Beatitudes. They were the forepart of his basic teaching given whenever he had a new audience, as, for instance, when he delivered the Sermon on the Mount. These prerequisites limited participation in God's kingdom to those kinds of people with whom he could work.

Being of Abrahamic descent through Jacob qualified the Jews to be members of Israel. Yet Jesus, who had no physical children, waited for a spiritual progeny to people his kingdom. Having wealth like Abraham would be of no advantage to a prospective participant; it could be a detriment if not shared. And those who, like the Pharisees, championed the law without a commensurate love of the mercy of God, or those who controlled the temple complex as did the Sadducees, without being in vital contact with the living God, would eliminate themselves from candidacy, because they would neither acknowledge the heaven-certified king nor accede to the attitudes he found acceptable.

To qualify for Christ's kingdom, one has to be humble and receptive, no stranger to sorrow, teachable, one who wants his life to be right all around, so much so that he values forgiveness and will not hide his motives. Such a one will promote social harmony but will not back down when persecution comes on account of his stand for Jesus and his teachings (Matt. 5:1–12).

What is important to note from the Beatitudes is that the Lord's criteria for selection are fully disclosed. There can be no guessing as to whom he will choose. Whole classes of people— the arrogant, the self-satisfied, the powerful men-of-the-world, and more—are automatically excluded. Fairness in spite of such divine discrimination is retained in the openness of the disclosure of his criteria of choice. Jesus will not arbitrarily choose favorites. Neither his whim, nor their outward appearances, nor popularity will condition his choices. Rather, he will select those citizens for whom the world generally has no use—such as the poor, the left-out, and the young.[3] What is important to him is their attitudes, motives, and outlooks, not their place in the world. It is not a question of good works either, but of values. Jesus, the master potter, was looking for the right kind of clay suitable to shape into kingdom-of-God citizenry.

Now this interpretation of the Beatitudes as containing entry-level requirements, rather than high-level virtues to be developed, cannot be sustained by the dubious method of counting supporters. There has been too much theological pressure on the Beatitudes, especially by those who would construe their conditional aspects as requiring a cluster of the fruit of the Spirit. But the master teacher did not even imply that. Some interpret the Beatitudes as if they were advanced levels of spirituality to be obtained somewhere deep in the Christian life, at least sometime before death. But if one does not *enter* with these necessary attitudes and pure motives, he gets nowhere at all with God! Nor can he grow into them.

The advanced virtues in which one can "grow" (2 Peter 3:18) are another matter altogether. Seven are specified by the apostle Peter to be added to faith (2 Peter 1:5–11). These are the virtues of a healthy, developing spirituality (goodness, knowledge, self-control, perseverance, godliness, brotherly kindness, and love) that combine to confirm that one belongs to God. They attest the believer's faith, serving to make that person's "calling and election sure" (2 Peter 1:10).

Now contrast these growing virtues that are spiritual fruit with the all-or-nothing quality of the Lord's teaching about blessable attitudes. Uncalibrated like honesty, each indispensable "condition" of the Beatitudes is integral: One is humble, or he is not. One is sorrowful, or he is not. One is teachable, or he is not. One is hungry for right relationships, or he is not. One will pass forgiveness on to others, or he will not. One has pure motives in responding to God, or he does not. One wants everyone to be at peace, or he does not. One is willing to suffer for his stand on God's side, or he is not. These all are *assumable* attitudes that type the person and the present state of his readiness to hear the Word of God. They do *not* qualify him with merit (i.e., pseudo-grace) so that he can stand on his own ground before God outside of Christ's call and redemption.

Note how the Beatitudes' conditions *correlate perfectly with Jesus' master parable*, which has become a conundrum to many interpreters because it collides with the notion that God would not be God if he did not determine absolutely the destiny of every human being without their consent. In the Parable of the Soils the divine constants—the planter, the seed, and the identity of weather conditions—contrast with the one variable—the difference in soils. "But the seed on good soil stands for those with *a noble and good heart* . . . " (Luke 8:15).

Jesus was always looking for people who had the kind of

attitudes, motives, and sensitivity to his values that would be suitable soil in which his word might take root and grow. The fact that all such people are assumed to be sinners (Luke 5:32) is beside the point here. They are not unlike those Gentiles who, although they have not been regenerated, "do *by nature* things required by the law" (Rom. 2:14). The point is this, and it is a major emphasis: the one and only determinant was the soil—not the planter, not the seed. Just as at the outset of this parable Jesus challenged those having ears "to hear," so in the great thrust of it he was in the same way challenging them to be the right kind of soil for his teachings.

Jesus, the Image of the Choosing God

The Good Shepherd chose his sheep (John 10:2–4, 16, 26–27; 21:16–17). He discriminated severely in his selections. But he was never capricious or mysterious as to the basis for his choosing. He divulged his criteria in proverbs and parables. He never extended any invitations tongue in cheek. He stuck by his sincere "whoevers." He identified himself with the people he was calling so as to make their responsive decisions easier. He personified grace and exhibited the ways of God. Jesus, like ideal parents, gave people freedom to reject him and his values. He knew grief and sorrow, and his tears (Luke 19:41–44) were revelatory of how God feels about those who reject his call. Jesus' tears are the guarantee that the *biblical* doctrine of election is pure, that it contains no trace of arbitrary damnation for anyone.

Many people who were greatly impressed by Jesus did not believe in him to the point of taking his invitation seriously or placing their lives at his disposal. In a parable he illustrated how the choice of one's destiny was one's own to accept or decline. The story of the Wedding Banquet for the King's Son has several memorable lines: "The wedding banquet is ready, but those [no-shows] I invited did not deserve to come. Go to the street corners and invite to the banquet anyone you find" (Matt. 22:8–9); and then after someone showed up not wearing a wedding garment and accordingly was bounced, this judgment was rendered: *"For many are invited, but few are chosen"* (Matt. 22:14).

All those called to the marriage banquet could become part of the in-group. That right was inherent in the call. Theirs was to dress fit for the wedding feast and to be there to honor the king's son. They were not *chosen*—as distinguished from being *called*—on the basis of their person (e.g., as being socially elite), but on the basis of their response of dressing properly and coming. Nor were they invited on the basis of their good works. They came as guests, not servants to be rewarded.

Notice how Jesus' audiences were coaxed by his storytelling

skill into great jury boxes, and time and again they would have to assess culpability in reference to the characters in his parables. Would they justify the ways of the divine figure represented, whether "king" in this case, or wealthy "estate owner" in some other, and were his people free to decide for themselves? Invariably the verdict would have to be that the king was fair, even gracious in his offers, and the subjects involved chose their own destiny.

The divine call was never coercive. Nowhere in all Jesus' parables and teaching does he portray a God-figure who *compels* compliance with his wishes, or overrides individual freedom to force his good will on anybody.[4] Only the great can afford to be vulnerable. The king in this parable could have sent his militia to put the ingrates under palace dining hall arrest until the wedding feast was finished so he would look good. But he did not. He suffered the embarrassment of having a hamper full of negative RSVP's. Thus he called and ultimately chose others who freely came. God is like that. Jesus made God's selective *modus operandum* transparent. The same calling and gift were offered to all, but individuals decided their own destiny. The king in his integrity was so secure he would not downgrade himself to an authoritarianism that would decide their destiny for them.

Jesus, the Source for the Doctrine of Election

One of the most enduring of the theses of Thomas Bernard's monumental Bampton Lectures of 1864 was this:

> The teaching of the Lord in the Gospels *includes the substance of all christian doctrine.* . . . In each case the later revelation may enlarge the earlier, may show its meaning and define its application. . . . There was nothing then on the lips of the first preachers of the Gospel, but what had "begun to be spoken" by its first preacher; and in following to their utmost the words of the Apostles we are still within the compass of the words of the Lord Jesus.[5]

The corollary of this great principle is evident. No *interpretation* of any passage in the Acts or the epistles that undercuts the revelations of the divine mind inculcated by Jesus can be accepted as valid. What he says and does is what God says and does. He had no hidden decrees to conceal, no dark side of his Father to protect from disclosure, no reason to be defensive about the way God chooses. Our doctrine of election must line up with the precedents Jesus set in his teaching and in his tears. Beware of any theology that treats Jesus as an embarrassment to be ignored—or worse—to be converted to a higher view in which God's supposed indomitable will (despite Matt. 18:14; 1 Tim. 2:4; 2 Peter 3:9) discounts grace and dries the tears of our Lord.

Jesus, the Center for the New Chosen People

The longer Jesus preached the kingdom of God, the more insistent became the question as to who would be the king of that realm. God would be its king, of course, as the phrase indicates. But did God have a man to represent him on earth? The evidence all pointed to Jesus. He then, on the one hand, purposefully escaped from all grass-roots attempts to acclaim him king prior to the cross; and on the other hand, he continued the process of laying the foundation for the new society that would emerge from his glorification. That new community would be "through Jesus Christ" (Eph. 1:5; Rom. 5:15–19) and especially "in him," not ἐν σαρκί (en sarki, "in the flesh") as Israel was in Abraham, but ἐν πνεύματι (en pneumati, "in the Spirit") by means of spiritual union with him (Rom. 8:9). That chosen community would experience "the sanctifying work of the Spirit, for obedience to Jesus Christ" (1 Peter 1:2), who became "head over everything for the church, which is his body, the fullness of him who fills everything in every way" (Eph. 1:22–23).

Jesus did not stand alongside of other Jews as the best of them all to be king. He stood in the likeness of the same human flesh as they, yet above them, not just morally as one who was holy, but he towered over them in terms of *privilege* and *power* and *knowledge*. Only he, the chosen one sent from God, could say, "All things have been committed to me by my Father" (Matt. 11:27). Only he would fit the description of Isaiah's prophecy (Isa. 42:1–4 quoted in Matt. 12:18–21) of the Lord's delightful Servant, destined certainly to win the nations and be their leader:

> Here is my servant whom I have chosen
>   the one I love, in whom I delight;
> I will put my Spirit on him,
>   and he will proclaim justice to the nations.
> He will not quarrel or cry out;
>   no one will hear his voice in the streets.
> A bruised reed he will not break,
>   and a smoldering wick he will not snuff out,
> till he lead justice to victory.
> In his name the nations will put their hope.

In the era prior to his crucifixion Jesus concentrated his ministry on Israel's lost sheep (Matt. 15:24). Yet he confidently anticipated the acquisition of "other sheep" (the nations) that he would someday lead (John 10:16). While Jews who had been dispersed to many nations were present for the first Christian Pentecost, it was Cornelius the Roman centurion at Caesarea who became the first non-Jewish national, together with his household, to trust in Jesus as the Savior of the whole world. To them the apostle Peter, after considerable celestial education, exclaimed under the Spirit's anointing: "I now realize how true it is that God does not show favoritism but accepts men from every nation who fear him and do what is right" (Acts 10:34–35). Even so, Peter was still "astonished that the gift of the Holy Spirit had been poured out even on the Gentiles" (Acts 10:45).

The remainder of Acts tells the story of the spread of the gospel among the nations, overcoming all national and sociological barriers. At the end of Acts this climactic statement about election occurs: "Therefore I want you [the Jews at Rome] to know that God's salvation has been sent to the Gentiles [i.e., "nations"], and they will listen!" (Acts 28:28). They did.

Thus the good news was "the power of God for the salvation of everyone who believes: first for the Jew, then for the Gentile" (Rom. 1:16). Jesus' "other sheep" were being brought under his leadership. God was calling and choosing nationals from the God-fearers who were exposed to the Word of God at the fringes of Jewish synagogues in various lands. Then pagans from many places and from a Greek city like Philippi—where there was no synagogue—were evangelized. It is clear from Acts that the extensive preaching of forgiveness of sins "in his name to all nations" (Luke 24:47) was being done just as Jesus had ordered.

THE HISTORICAL PEOPLE OF GOD VIS-À-VIS "THE MYSTERY"

Israel's calling to be a light to the nations (Isa. 49:6; Acts 13:47) was still waiting for implementation when Jesus was crucified. But God's purpose for the nations (Gen. 12:3) had not changed. By the third decade after Jesus' resurrection the overwhelming constituency of the church was internationals. At that time only a small remnant-sized percentage of his church was also descended from father Abraham. What we see, therefore, in the middle of the first century is the emergence of a new society polarized around the Lord Jesus Christ, who is seated in his ascended glory (Eph. 2:6). This "kingdom of God" (Acts 28:31) was known as "the church of God, which he bought with his own blood" (Acts 20:28).

Inevitable questions arise: Are there *two* "chosen" peoples? If affirmative, do they travel on different tracks to divergent destinies? If only *one*, which one is legitimate? Which had or has priority? Who, in fact, are *the chosen* of God?

Now the answer to these questions is to be found in *"the mystery"* that could be divulged only after Christ had been glorified. This mystery when unfolded is variously alluded to as "his [God's] will" (Eph. 1:9), "the manifold wisdom of God" (3:9–

10), "the gospel" (6:19), "the word of God in its fullness" (Col. 1:25–27), and concretely as "Christ" and his body (Eph. 5:32; Col. 1:25–2:2; 4:3).

The apostle is not saying that God's will, his Word, his wisdom, his good news, and his Christ are mysterious. He is saying that the mystery dissolved when God's will was revealed: "He made known to us the mystery of his will," and he was pleased to do this (Eph. 1:9). Thus he disclosed his wisdom in his Word, as the good news about *the comprehensiveness of Christ*, "who fills everything in every way" (1:23).

It cannot be stated too emphatically that this "mystery," *qua mysterium*, is limited to the Old Testament epoch. "This mystery, . . . for ages past was kept hidden in God" (Eph. 3:9), yes, "for long ages past" (Rom. 16:25), indeed, "for ages and generations" (Col. 1:26). After the resurrection and the formation of the church as "the fullness of him [i.e., Christ]" (Eph. 1:23), that which was once "mystery" became *revealed truth*, demonstrating the multidimensional wisdom of God. "The mystery . . . is now disclosed to the saints" (Col. 1:26).

Lest anyone infer that it was here reiterated and retained as a permanent mystery, let him note that the ages-long concealment was terminated in New Testament times: "To them [the saints] *God has chosen to make known among the Gentiles the glorious riches of this mystery*, which is Christ in you [or: "among you"], the hope of glory" (Col. 1:27). This text declares God's choice to make something rich and glorious known, and then he gives the gist of the disclosure.

One might legitimately inquire if this once-mysterious mystery featured in Ephesians (1:9; 3:9; 6:19) and Colossians (1:26; 4:3) is surely unveiled, since we are considering "the mystery of God, namely, Christ in whom *are hidden* all the treasures of wisdom and knowledge" (Col. 2:2–3). In "the mystery of Christ" (4:3) everything worth knowing is contained in the mind of Christ like a treasure chest *until* he decides to reveal it. An unopened treasure would be useless, however.

It is eminently characteristic of the Lord to reveal himself to believers: "The knowledge of the secrets of the kingdom of God has been given to you" (Luke 8:10). One must not stumble over the treasure-trove analogy in Colossians, for "God is light," and it is his nature to reveal his grace in appropriate circumstances. The twin epistles Colossians and Ephesians both state that "the mystery" has been revealed to the church. That is, knowledge possessed only by God has in New Testament times been shared with certain people. "The LORD confides in those who fear him; he makes his covenant known to them" (Ps. 25:14; cf. Prov. 3:32). "Surely the Sovereign LORD does nothing without revealing his plan to his servants the prophets" (Amos 3:7).

Now we must ask as to what specifically was revealed when the long-standing secret of election was declassified? After Paul's having expressed much sorrow about the destiny of contemporary Jews in Romans 9–11, he concludes his letter with a sublime doxology that features the once hidden mystery now revealed:

> Now to him who is able to establish you by my gospel and the proclamation of Jesus Christ, according to the revelation of the mystery hidden for long ages past, but now revealed and made known through the prophetic writings by the command of the eternal God, *so that all nations might believe and obey him*—to the only wise God be glory forever through Jesus Christ! Amen (Rom. 16:25–27).

In essence this passage says, as do so many other election texts, that God desires all the nations to be his chosen people. The eternal God in his superlative wisdom has commanded the church to proclaim Jesus Christ, in whose fullness all nations are meant to be included by faith. The apostle Paul in his letter to the Ephesians told how he came to understand this: "The mystery [was] made known to me by revelation . . . it has now been revealed by the Spirit to God's holy apostles and prophets" (Eph. 3:3, 5).

The subject matter of God's now divulged secret finds expression in the doctrine of election, which in turn is part of the larger doctrine of the abounding grace of God. Paul stated in Ephesians 3:1–6 what he "already [had] written briefly" (3:3)[6] about in chapter 1 (vv. 3–14) and touched on in chapter 2 (vv. 11–22). He spelled out the revelation with such clarity in chapter 3 that no one could misconstrue what he was saying: "*This mystery is that through the gospel the Gentiles are heirs together with Israel, members together of one body, and sharers together in the promise in Christ Jesus*" (v. 6).

Following this, Paul defined his own servant role for "the administration of this mystery, which for ages past was kept hidden in God who created all things" (Eph. 3:7–9). It is here that Paul characterizes it as "the manifold wisdom of God" (Eph. 3:10). It is God's "eternal purpose which he accomplished in Christ Jesus our Lord" (Eph. 3:11) now expressed as good news for all nations, including Israel.

The focus of election on Christ is schematic. Ephesians 3:6 quoted above said the nations and Israel were "members together of one body." This membership established the unity of the people of God by subsuming both groups—as everything else in Ephesians—"in Christ Jesus."[7] In chapter 2, for instance, Paul illustrated that unity by the fact that as only "one body" was put on the cross, so only one body of people benefit from the atonement by which he "*has made the two* [the Jews and the Gentiles] *one*" (Eph. 2:11–21). Thus there are three logically

possible centers for a new body politic, or rather, "body theocratic," but only one is valid according to the sublime wisdom of God:

1. Israel, the historic chosen nation
2. The believing nations, as a second-class parallel entity
3. Christ, according to the *corporate solidarity* principle

Taking these in order, we must remonstrate against the first
with Paul's own words: "not all who are descended from Israel are
Israel. Nor because they are his descendants are they all Abraham's children . . . only the remnant [of the numerous Israelites]
will be saved" (Rom. 9:6–7, 27). Although to Israel in the old
epoch belonged the blessings of adoption, glory, covenants,
institution of the law, cultus, and promises, all that was not
enough. They needed Christ. Those who remained loyal to God
followed Jesus and entered his sheepfold. "But not all the
Israelites accepted the good news" (Rom. 10:16).

Therefore, though the church in a metaphorical sense can be
called "the Israel of God" (Gal. 6:16) because believers all have the
faith of Abraham, it could no longer be said that nominal Israel
remained God's special people of favor. They are "loved on
account of the patriarchs" (Rom. 11:28), but not justified apart
from faith in Jesus (Gal. 2:15–16). Since they rejected God's *chosen
Servant* (Matt. 12:18), even his *chosen Son* (Luke 9:35), they could
not spurn "the Seed to whom the promise [to Abraham] referred"
(Gal. 3:19) and still maintain their historical Abrahamic status. For
God has indicated, beginning with Jesus' anointing beside the
Jordan River, the one "seed"—not "seeds"—that he had chosen
(Gal. 3:16). They could no longer be associated with Abraham
legitimately if they rejected Christ; any subsequent participation in
Abrahamic election would be valid only "if they do not persist in
unbelief" in Jesus (Rom. 11:23).

Second, it was unthinkable that God would choose many
nations, united or not, to stand on a par with ancient Israel as a
separate special people of God. Although the people of the other
nations were far more numerous, they would always be secondary, since Israel in the flesh of Abraham had historical priority.
That is, there is no way the Gentiles in and of themselves, though
loved of God on the basis of creation, could be certified en masse
as God's chosen people, in a second or parallel edition.

Furthermore, it would break with God's precedent of deriving
the chosen nation from the posterity of one man, Abraham (Gal.
3:8–9). On what basis would those nations then be united, and
what would keep one nation from asserting a higher status within
"the chosen"? The indispensable component here is missing—the
one on whom "God the Father has placed his seal of approval"
(John 6:27). God has not chosen the nations *as nations*. The same

unbelief that excludes the Jewish nation *as a nation* also applies to the Gentile nations: "The Scripture does not say 'and to seeds,' meaning many people, but 'and to your seed,' meaning one person, who is Christ" (Gal. 3:16).

ELECTION EXCLUSIVELY "IN CHRIST": EPHESIANS 1:3–14

The third logically possible focus of election, but the only *biblically* possible one is Christ, the predestined one: *"He was chosen before the creation of the world,* but was revealed in these last times for your sake"* (1 Peter 1:20).[8] Although he is in continuity with Abraham as his "Seed," he has become the originator of a new spiritual family. On the basis of his predestined atonement now completed (Acts 4:27–28), his descendants are sealed internally by the Spirit rather than being circumcised in their flesh (Rom. 2:29; Phil. 3:3). What has been said already about the exclusive position Christ holds as the one from whom God's chosen people get their identity need not be repeated. Suffice it to recall that *both Jews and Gentiles* are totally dependent on him for their status—if any—in God's family, and neither group could claim favored status *on its own*, no matter how ancient its calling, or however impressive the triumphalism of their numbers.

At this point there comes into view the most definitive passage on election in the New Testament, Ephesians 1:3–14. This hymn of glory is an integral grammatical unit held together by multiple repetitions of the relative pronoun in an interminably long sentence of two hundred and two Greek words. A further dimension of the one-time mystery is disclosed here: Election did not begin with the call of Abraham as everyone surmised from the historical scene. Election originated before anyone or anything was created. That is significant because it puts a new perspective on the position of the church, referred to three times as "us" in the most comprehensive statement about predestination in the New Testament:

> For he chose us in him before the creation of the world to be holy and blameless in his sight. In love he predestined us to be adopted as his sons through Jesus Christ, in accordance with his pleasure and will—to the praise of his glorious grace which he has freely given us in the One he loves (Eph. 1:4–6).

Three times in the three verses just quoted election/predestination is centered exclusively in Christ as the key figure. This is the *corporate solidarity* or *corporate personality* concept so easy for patriarchal societies to understand and so alien to the western tradition of individualism. In the textual transcription[9] of

The Choosing of the Church "in Christ"
A Textual Transcription Toward Exegesis of Ephesians 1:3–14

Εὐλογητὸς ὁ θεὸς καὶ πατὴρ τοῦ κυρίου ἡμῶν Ἰησοῦ Χριστοῦ,

ὁ εὐλογήσας   ἡμᾶς ἐν πάσῃ εὐλογίᾳ πνευματικῇ
                 ἐν τοῖς ἐπουρανίοις
          ἐν   Χριστῷ,

καθὼς ἐξελέξατο   ἐν   αὐτῷ   ἡμᾶς
                πρὸ καταβολῆς κόσμου
           εἶναι ἡμᾶς ἁγίους
           καὶ ἀμώμους κατενώπιον αὐτοῦ

ἐν ἀγάπῃ προορίσας   ἡμᾶς εἰς υἱοθεσίαν
              διὰ Ἰησοῦ Χριστοῦ   εἰς αὐτόν,
              κατὰ τὴν εὐδοκίαν τοῦ θελήματος αὐτοῦ,
         εἰς ἔπαινον δόξης τῆς χάριτος αὐτοῦ

ἐχαρίτωσεν   ἐν τῷ ἠγαπημένῳ,
        ἐν ᾧ ἔχομεν τὴν ἀπολύτρωσιν
        διὰ τοῦ αἵματος αὐτοῦ, τὴν ἄφεσιν τῶν παραπτωμάτων,

ἐπερίσσευσεν   καὶ πᾶσα σοφία ἐν πάσῃ ἡμᾶς διὰ
              φρονήσει,

γνωρίσας ...

τὸ · μυστήριον τοῦ · θελήματος αὐτοῦ,
κατὰ τὴν · εὐδοκίαν αὐτοῦ
ἣν

προέθετο
ἀνακεφαλαιώσασθαι τὰ πάντα ἐν αὐτῷ · αὐτῷ ἐν τῷ Χριστῷ, εἰς · οἰκονομίαν τοῦ πληρώματος τῶν καιρῶν,
τὰ · ἐπὶ τοῖς οὐρανοῖς
καὶ τὰ · ἐπὶ τῆς γῆς ·

ἐν αὐτῷ.
ἐν ᾧ · καὶ ἐκληρώθημεν
κατὰ · πρόθεσιν τοῦ · τὰ πάντα ἐνεργοῦντος
προορισθέντες κατὰ τὴν · βουλὴν τοῦ θελήματος αὐτοῦ

εἰς τὸ εἶναι ἡμᾶς
εἰς ἔπαινον δόξης αὐτοῦ,

τοὺς προηλπικότας ἐν τῷ Χριστῷ, ἐν ᾧ · καὶ ὑμεῖς ἀκούσαντες τὸν λόγον τῆς ἀληθείας,
τὸ · εὐαγγέλιον τῆς σωτηρίας ὑμῶν,
ἐν ᾧ · καὶ · πιστεύσαντες

ἐσφραγίσθητε τῷ πνεύματι τῆς ἐπαγγελίας τῷ ἁγίῳ,
ὅ ἐστιν
ἀρραβὼν τῆς κληρονομίας ἡμῶν,
εἰς ἀπολύτρωσιν τῆς · περιποιήσεως,
εἰς ἔπαινον τῆς δόξης αὐτοῦ.

Ephesians 1:3–14 one can trace in the left column the indispensability of Christ for every aspect of election:

"in Christ"	—every spiritual blessing descends (1:3)
"in him"	—the church was chosen before creation (1:4)
"through Jesus Christ"	—the church was predestined to adoption (1:5)
"in the One he loves"	—the church was given glorious grace (1:6)
"In him"	—the church was redeemed by blood in grace (1:7)
"in Christ"	—God's purpose and will were manifested (1:9)
"even [in] Christ"	—all in heaven and earth were brought together "under one head" (1:10)
[in him]	—Gr. [included in the reference above] (1:10)
"in him"	—the church was predestined in God's plan (1:11)
"in Christ"	—the Christian hope is centered (1:12)
"in Christ"	—the church was saved as it heard the gospel (1:13)
"in him"	—the believers are sealed with the Spirit (1:13)

The following observations on this pericope are made in the light of its exegesis:

1. In a unit of twelve verses (1:3–14) there are as many *foci on Christ* as there are verses. He is the one in whom or through whom "every spiritual blessing" proceeds. His diagrammatic centrality is evident and necessary to the doctrine. One must not talk about election without mentioning Christ in every breath—not mechanically—but in recognition of the truth that there is not a chance of being chosen outside of him.

2. A proper understanding of this passage turns on the Hebraic *corporate solidarity* principle.[10] The patriarch and his family, his possessions, his servants, and his descendants are one unit. This means that Christ and his people are inseparable: "*For he chose us in him. . . .*" Choice of the one (Christ) per se means choice of the other (the church). The church's destiny is based on him in eternity, derived from him in time, and actualized fully in union with him forever.

3. A startling revelation for one looking from a historical perspective is that *the church actually predates Israel!* It does so because the one "appointed . . . to be head over everything for the church, which is his body" (Eph. 1:22–23), preexisted in his deity.

That choice of the "one head" (1:10) was not of a severed head but the head in solidarity with the body that one day would materialize. The church has the distinction of having been chosen in its head eternally, while Israel, by contrast, was chosen in Abraham temporally. But this does not pit the church against Israel, for all Abraham's true children have his faith, inherit the promise made to him, and therefore now belong to Christ (Gal. 3:29). And by the same token, "those who believe [whoever they are, viz., the Gentiles—Gal. 3:8] are children of Abraham" (Gal. 3:7).

4. The truth of *eternal ecclesial election in Christ* is the key to unlock the mystery being explained throughout Ephesians (1:9; 3:3, 4, 9; 5:32; 6:19). Even the illustration of a husband's bodily oneness with his wife (Eph. 5:28–33) is an example of corporate solidarity that edges close to something more wonderful: "This is a profound mystery—but I am talking about *Christ and the church*" (Eph. 5:32). It is the eternal perspective of election that enables us to see that in the New Testament the "times will have reached their fulfillment—to bring all things in heaven and on earth together under one head, even Christ" (1:10). The mystery revealed not only dissolves the ethnic distinctions of Jews and Gentiles as being significant, but it also dissolves the vertical distance between heaven and earth so that "Christ and his body," like a colossus (Eph. 1:22) with head in heaven and body on earth, remains in corporate solidarity.

5. The terms for the doctrine of election used in this pericope are "chosen" (1:4, 11), "predestined" (1:5, 11), and by extension "adopted" (1:5). The last two of these are coordinated in the clause "he [God] predestined us to be adopted as his sons through Jesus Christ." Adoption accents choice for family membership. The Lord Jesus who filled the role of Messianic Father (Isa. 9:6; Luke 8:54; John 14:9–11; 14:18; 21:5–23) is now "bringing many sons to glory" (Heb. 2:10). The adoption is initiated by his giving us the family Spirit of sonship (Rom. 8:16), and it is to be consummated by our being given a glorious body like his (Rom. 8:23; Phil. 3:20–21). Adoption is a fitting metaphor for "placing a son" in God's family. Especially is it fitting for the majority of the believers like those Paul had in mind at Ephesus, "who are Gentiles by birth . . . excluded from citizenship in Israel and foreigners to the covenants of the promise" (Eph. 2:11–12). The Ephesians 1 sequence for the church is altogether appropriate: (1) chosen in Christ from eternity past; (2) "predestined according to the plan of him who works out everything in conformity with the purpose of his will" (1:11); and (3) "adopted as his sons through Jesus Christ" (1:5).[11]

6. The final cause of election eventuates in Christlikeness. That is, the church was destined to be "holy and blameless in his

sight" (1:4), "a radiant church, without stain or wrinkle or any other blemish, but holy and blameless" (Eph. 5:27). The parallel passage in Romans makes the cloning of Christ's nature in the church the desirable end toward which God's purpose works: "For those God foreknew he also predestined to be conformed to the likeness of his Son, that he might be the firstborn among many brothers" (Rom. 8:29). God preplanned to have a church of "Christians" (ones "like Christ").

7. The proper response to the doctrine of predestination in Christ is to offer a profusion of praise to God! Ephesians 1:3–14 opened with a wave of adoration (1:3), followed by another "to the praise of his glorious grace" (1:6), followed by another "for the praise of his glory" (1:12), and concluded with the same adoration (1:14). God's "glorious grace" (1:6), the ultimate source of every act on his part, was neither an abstraction floating in the ethereal realm, nor just a feeling of God toward his creation. It was a concrete expression and gift of himself "in the One he loves"; (1:6). Grace means God sacrifices himself, humbles himself, and gives himself (2 Cor. 8:9) so as to make it possible for human beings to reciprocate his love, for God is love. Grace is holy love in contact with and characterizing the object of that love. Grace is supremely personal, as seen in Jesus, who was "full of grace and truth" (John 1:14). The doctrine of election is just one of "the riches of God's grace" (Eph. 1:7), and those riches are "incomparable" to anything else in the world (2:7).

We must not be presumptuous about God's will. God is gracious, so when he exercises his will—as in his choice of the church to be the international body of Christ—it is "in love he predestined us" (1:4–5). Love issues in "the riches of God's grace" (1:7), which is the material cause of God's will to have a special, holy people. Now observe what happens if God's grace and his will are inverted so as to make the doctrine of grace subordinate to election. This gives theology greater respectability in the wide world of philosophy. For in philosophy grace, if addressed at all, is perceived to be an expression of weakness, a category of inevitable depletion. When grace is transmuted into a *power* category to achieve philosophical prestige, God can then be perceived to be an indomitable Will who needs to dominate others in order to actualize his nature, rather than a God of love who will sacrifice himself that his love might prevail where there is true freedom of response.

Attempts to make individualistic election the absolute of a theological system finally succeed in doing so by backing away from the contingencies of grace for the certainties of decrees that people are helpless against. God's love for the whole world is then called into question, and it becomes easy to conceive of him as a potentate like the Muslim God, who loves most to impose his will, and whose identity and image are conceptualized totally apart from Christ.

Moreover, it is a distortion of the doctrine of election to claim that God's will pertaining to salvation *still remains a mystery* after he has "made known to us the mystery of his will" (Eph. 1:9), and after "God has revealed it [his secret wisdom, hidden since time began] to us by his Spirit" (1 Cor. 2:7–10). It is theological tyranny of the worst kind (because it distorts God's image and Word) to assert that lying behind the open gospel of the grace of God there exists more important but inaccessible, supersecret knowledge never revealed to anyone during this age. This "mystery" is alleged to be the composite of billions of eternal decrees by which God determined exclusively within himself and absolutely what he willed to become of every human being one at a time before he created them, assigning a destiny of damnation to the overwhelming majority, and grace to certain others, all the while keeping two things secret: (1) what it was *in his nature* that kept all his decrees from going in the same direction and (2) who the lucky ones actually are.

The God revealed in Christ can afford to lavish the riches of his grace on his church "with all wisdom and understanding" (Eph. 1:8). He knows how important it is for us as children to know that the adoption is valid and we are chosen to be holy sons and daughters with the certainty that inheres in Christ's being the chosen one. And in response to our faith in Christ we are marked with the seal of his ownership, the Holy Spirit, promised in the Old Testament when the mystery was still on, and given now as the initial confirmation of election. It comes *after* faith (Eph. 1:11–14).

A certain man who believed that election remains a mystery today and that God's will in election is inscrutable, once announced to me strange words that no one, except a person of his theological background, would ever think of saying: "I will love God always," he said, "even if it should turn out in the end that his eternal decree was to send me forever to hell." There was no place for Christ in this statement, and not even Christ's cross had any bearing on the haunting question of his destiny. Whether out of fear or self-deception, he "loved" one who might be fooling him as to his real intentions for him. It seemed that he considered the quality of the love he professed for God superior to any his kind of God might have for him. Others have not been so charitable toward such an unpredictable will-over-love God as that.

But our only concern should be this: "Who shall separate us from the love of Christ?" (Rom. 8:35). It is ultimately a faithless question, arising out of false presuppositions about God, to ask, "*Am I elect?*" Faith focuses on Christ, and asks oneself only if one is trusting Christ fully and is therefore obedient to him (2 Cor. 13:5). Our election, like "every spiritual blessing," is secure "in Christ." We should not try to look beyond him.

Romans 8:28–30

This passage on predestination focuses on the church as a whole. Note the plurals: "those who love him," "[those] called," "those God foreknew," "many brothers," "those he predestined," "those he called," "those he justified." The near context, by contrast, focuses on "the people of Israel" (Rom. 9:4) and discourses on their plight as an unbelieving nation with a remnant of believers in Christ, and what the entry of the nations into faith means for both groups (chaps. 9–11).

Predestination is featured here as another term for the "purpose" of God that intends Christ to be the ruling Son in a great family of faith, the members of which are all like him in spiritual nature as if they had been cloned from him. Not his DNA, but "the Spirit of Christ" alluded to frequently in the earlier context (Rom. 8:9–27) will unite the community so as to fulfill the eternal purpose of God. The perspective is corporate and delineates the assured destiny of the church.

The perspective of God's foreknowledge is comprehensive:

$$
foreknowledge \begin{cases} glorification \\ justification \\ calling \\ predestination \end{cases}
$$

Two points need to be made: (1) Foreknowledge precedes predestination in the biblical formula. We dare not correct Paul and say that something has to be predetermined in order to be foreknown. God foresaw the actual situation with all its contingencies, interrelationships, and hidden motives of hearts. "Foreknow" cannot be construed to be "fix" without deep implications for the character of God. (2) God's foreknowledge brings assurance to the church that in the end God will have a family of "many brothers" whose experience of being *called, justified,* and finally *glorified* was preprogrammed (i.e., predestined) for the good of those who return his love and "to the praise of his glorious grace" (Eph. 1:6). Behind it all, as the context indicates, lies the love of Christ (Rom. 8:35), expressing the eternal "love of God" (8:39).

Acts 13:38–52

The doctrine of election, as we have seen, is inextricably tied to the transition of the people of God from headship in Abraham to headship in Christ, from being all Jewish to being indiscrimi-

nately "all nations," including a believing remnant of Jews. One of
the crises of that transition occurred while Paul was preaching
during a couple of Sabbaths in Pisidian Antioch. In the middle of
that episode there was recorded an explanatory word relative to
the great influx of Gentile God-fearers into the faith: καί
ἐπίστευσαν ὅσοι ἦσαν τεταγμένοι εἰς ζωὴν αἰώνιον (kai episteusan
hosoi ēsan tetagmenoi eis zōēn aiōnion—Acts 13:48b). The traditional
understanding of a "divine passive" for tetagmenoi makes an
interpretation of determinism inevitable.

The entire verse in the NIV reads this way: "When the Gentiles
heard this, they were glad and honored the word of the Lord; and
all who were appointed for eternal life believed" (Acts 13:48). If all that
was available to us were this English translation, we might deduce
that God alone fully determined this event and that the principals
were no more than chessmen being moved about on life's board
by the divine player. The key word that is misunderstood in this
context is tetagmenoi, perfect middle or passive participle from
τάσσω (tassō).

Before exploring the meaning of tassō here, a brief examination must be made of the context. As a prelude to his quoting
Habakkuk 1:5, Paul warned, "Take care that what the prophets
have said does not happen to you" (Acts 13:40). There is no hint of
determinism in such an admonition. The passage that follows
points up their recalcitrant unbelief. Such perfidy was foreknown,
all right, but it was not a phenomenon for which God was
responsible. For right here everyone is being called to faith, and all
hearers can "take care" to avoid a personal disaster. The story
continues: after many Jews followed Paul and Barnabas as
believers, the masses of the remaining Jews were filled with
jealousy against them and bad-mouthed them the following
Sabbath, when "almost the whole city gathered." Thereupon Paul
announced, "We had to speak the word of God to you first. Since
you reject it and do not consider yourselves worthy of eternal life, we now
turn to the Gentiles" (Acts 13:46).

Now we get the scene. The Jews were turning up their noses
at "eternal life," and the God-fearing Gentiles were moving in to
receive that eternal life God was offering freely. The verb tassō
means to "appoint" in the literal sense of "put in a position for,"
or "order," "determine." The voice of the perfect participle as we
have noted is ambiguous; tetagmenoi is best construed in this
context to be middle voice. The disputed sentence (Acts 13:48)
would look like this when the setting is fully honored and a divine
passive is not read into it: "When the Gentiles heard this, they
gloried in the Lord's Word, and as many as were putting themselves in
a position for eternal life believed."

This situation in Pisidian Antioch is similar to what might
occur if on registration day a seminary offered a super new course

called Theol. 777, "Eternal Life." Seniors would be given first opportunity to register for it, but most would pass it up, being satisfied with their present life as top dogs in the school and being skeptical of its worth. Then it would be opened to underclassmen, who would flock to it. So it could be said that the administration provided the great benefit, and as many as expressed their faith by getting in the registration line and signing up for it obtained "Eternal Life" in the ancient tradition of 1 Timothy 6:12. The pattern of faith being one's response to God, rather than something God does for a person is a consistent one seen throughout Acts and indeed the entire New Testament.[12]

CONCLUDING THESES

1. The doctrine of election features God's will, but even more it glorifies his grace supremely. In grace God takes the initiative in his call to obedience to Christ, and for those who believe, he confirms their election with the Spirit of Christ.

2. Christ is the chosen one in and through whom in corporate solidarity with him the church is selected to be God's own. No one is ever chosen *on his own*, that is, outside of Christ, or apart from incorporation into the church.

3. God's purpose in predestination is to have a vast holy society made up of those who are spiritually and, finally, physically transformed to model exactly the image of Christ. He is the omega of predestination.

4. God's choice of the church "in Christ" from eternity has become an open secret revealed fully now in the good news. The focus of faith is on Christ rather than on nonexistent secret decrees.

5. Whereas election appeared to be limited to Israel in Old Testament times, the eternal purpose of God to have in Christ an international family of all nations has been realized at last in the New Testament church, dissolving the ethnic dimension of the mystery.

6. Election and consequent predestination operate totally within the realm (and doctrine) of grace. It is pagan determinism that fabricates a parallel doctrine of foreordained damnation from eternity, where inexplicable hatred for certain ones replaces grace and Christ is excluded from the choosing transaction altogether. The tears of Jesus over Jerusalem dissolve determinism and preserve the true doctrine.

7. The biblical doctrine of election is transparent to the God who is holy love. He predestined himself to be the Savior. His will to sacrifice himself so that he might have mercy on all reveals his true nature. Grace has nothing to hide and everything to reveal—the heart of God!

"In love he predestined us to be adopted as his sons through Jesus Christ, in accordance with his pleasure and will—*to the praise of his glorious grace, which he has freely given us in the One he loves*" (Eph. 1:4–6).

NOTES

[1] A better word than election would be "selection," which is accurate and does not have the preponderant political connotations borne by "election." However, since there are such deep theological grooves cut in the term *election* by the literature, it will probably be the twenty-first century—when the new translations come into their own—that the nomenclature will catch up with the clearest English.

[2] Wolfhart Pannenberg, *Human Nature, Election, and History* (Philadelphia: Westminster, 1977), 46.

[3] The apostle to the nations would later write echoing the same theme that God delights to choose mostly those not considered wise by the world, nor influential, nor strong "so that no one may boast before him," but only "in Christ Jesus who has become for us wisdom from God" (1 Cor. 1:26–31). James confirms this by writing, "Has not God chosen those who are poor in the eyes of the world . . . to inherit the kingdom?" (James 2:5).

[4] The use of ἀναγκάζω, "invite (urgently)" or "urge (strongly," in the parallel account of Luke 14:23 for Matthew's καλέω, "call" or "invite" (Matt. 22:9) as instructions to the king's servants to procure replacement celebrants for the banquet does not alter this observation, even if the KJV's "compel" in Luke 14:23 continues to ring in older ears.

[5] Thomas D. Bernard, *The Progress of Doctrine in the New Testament*. 2nd ed., 1866. 63, 65–66.

[6] Markus Barth. *Ephesians: Commentary on Chapters 1–3*. Anchor Bible. (Garden City: Doubleday, 1974), 329.

[7] The letter to the Ephesians contains the following passages in which the "in Christ" terminology (using the preposition with his name, or with a pronoun, or with a synonymous allusion) occurs in the Greek text: 1:1,3,4,6,7,9,10[2],11,12,13 [2],15; 2:6,7,10,13[2],16[2],21[2],22; 3:6,11,12,21; 4:21[2],32; 5:8,20; 6:10,19,21.

[8] "Chosen" is also the translation of the TEV and LB; "predestined" in NEB, Moffatt, Goodspeed; "destined" in RSV and Phillips; "foreknown" in NASB, ASB, JB, and NBV.

[9] William G. MacDonald, *Greek Enchiridion* (Peabody, Mass.: Hendrickson, 1986), 139–52.

[10] Aubrey R. Johnson, *The Vitality of the Individual in the Thought of Ancient Israel* (Cardiff: University of Wales Press, 1949).

[11] Robert Shank, *Elect in the Son* (Springfield, Mo.: Westcott, 1970), 156.

[12] In my chapter, ". . . the Spirit of Grace (Heb. 10:29)" in *Grace Unlimited* (Minneapolis, Minn.: Bethany, 1975) all those passages that might be construed erroneously to teach that faith itself is the gift of God (on top of the gospel) are interpreted (Mark 11:22; Rom. 12:3; Gal. 5:22; Eph. 2:8–9), 87–89.

PREDESTINATION AND ASSURANCE

William J. Abraham

Debates between Calvinists and Arminians have sometimes been unseemly affairs. Both sides have been impatient to move in for the quick kill and have savored the sound of polemical victory. The result has too often been an unedifying spectacle that brings credit to no one, least of all the gospel of Jesus Christ. In more recent times, the noise of battle has abated considerably. Indeed attempts to rekindle old wars or to open up old wounds are bound to appear anachronistic and insensitive. To be sure, there are pockets within the modern evangelical subculture where one still hears heated conversations about predestination, free will, divine sovereignty, foreknowledge, election, perseverance and the like. However, modern, popular evangelicalism has become so theologically narrow and emaciated in recent times that these notions are not taken very seriously even by its own constituency. The only issue that still lingers in the popular mind is the question of "once saved always saved." This remains as a kind of hang-over from the days when Calvinists and Arminians debated the merits of two contrasting and competing systems of theology with enthusiasm and enormous dexterity.

In this chapter I want to quarry around afresh in the undergrowth of the debate between Calvinists and Arminians. I will focus specifically on the concepts of assurance and election. I have two aims overall. First, I want to suggest that the dispute about assurance has for the most part been a verbal one. In actual fact the two sides have been very close to each other in substance. Second, the protagonists in this dispute have much to offer each other in the development of a viable theological vision. Calvinists need a richer account of divine action and religious experience,

231

and Arminians need a deeper vision of the divine reality. We can begin by taking up the question of assurance.

On the surface, Calvinists find it odd that Arminians can seriously claim that the believer has any assurance of salvation. The reasons for this are not often made explicit. On a popular level Calvinists sometimes make fun of their opponents by suggesting that if Calvinists have their tulip as a reminder of their position then Arminians have their daisy. "He loves me; he loves me not; he loves me; he loves me not," is their natural state of mind. On a serious level I think that the argument at work here stems from the Arminian's claim that a believer can fall from grace. If a true believer can actually fall from grace, then there is no guarantee that one will remain a Christian and hence there is no guarantee that one will eventually be saved. Perhaps one will yield to temptation of various sorts, or one will fall because of trials of one kind of another, or one will be overwhelmed by internal and external pressures to abandon the faith. Whatever the case, it is entirely possible that the believer will fall away and, as many Arminians, albeit sadly, actually practice what they preach in these matters, this is not just a logical possibility but a practical possibility. Hence there cannot be any deep security for the believer who is sincerely committed to Arminian principles and who is aware of their logical consequences.

Arminians characteristically refuse to tackle the whole issue of assurance from this starting point. It is clear that Wesley, a paradigm of the tradition, does not begin with theoretical possibilities concerning the logical consequences of falling away; rather he begins with the marrow of the gospel and the explicit texts of Scripture on assurance. His two sermons on assurance make this abundantly clear.[1] Moreover the question for Wesley was not whether one would eventually be saved but whether one was actually saved now. The former issue does not seem to have bothered him very much. What mattered was that salvation is a present experience; it is not something we have to sit around and wait for in the future life; it is not something we are assured of because we hold the correct theory about the Christian life; it is something we experience here and now and which brings with it its own evidence of possession. In fact, Wesley is profoundly dissatisfied with purely inferential arguments as grounds for the assurance of the believer.

Like many in his day, he does, of course, quite happily allow the believer to appeal to inferential argument to secure assurance of salvation. He referred to this argument as the witness of our own spirit. This begins by summarizing the biblical material on the marks of the children of God. Thus Scripture teaches that the children of God love other Christians, they love God, they keep God's commandments, they exhibit the fruit of the Spirit in their

lives, and so on. The argument then moves to an examination of
our lives to see whether these marks are actually present. One
simply perceives or does not perceive these marks in one's own
life. Should one be skeptical about the reliability of our percep-
tions at this point, Wesley insists that such skepticism is generally
irrational. We simply become aware of such matters in the same
way as we are aware of our pains or of our own consciousness.

> How does it appear that you are alive? And that you are now in
> ease and not in pain? Are you not immediately conscious of it?
> By the same immediate consciousness you will know if your
> soul is alive to God; if you are saved from the pain of proud
> wrath, and have the ease of a meek and quiet spirit. By the
> same means you cannot but perceive if you love, rejoice, and
> delight in God. By the same you must be directly assured if you
> love your neighbour as yourself; if you are kindly affectioned to
> all mankind, and full of gentleness and longsuffering.[2]

Given the existence of such marks, one can then infer that one is
actually a child of God and thus arrive at a measure of assurance.
Wesley expressed the whole argument succinctly as follows:

> Strictly speaking, it [the testimony of our own spirit] is a
> conclusion drawn partly from the Word of God, and partly from
> our own experience. The Word of God says everyone who has
> the fruit of the Spirit is a child of God. Experience, or inward
> consciousness, tells me that I have the fruit of the Spirit. And
> hence I rationally conclude: therefore I am a child of God.[3]

What is fascinating about Wesley's position is that he
resolutely refuses to remain satisfied with rational arguments as a
foundation for the Christian's assurance. What really interested
him was the possibility of a logically distinct kind of evidence,
which he identified as the witness of the Holy Spirit in the heart of
the believer. In insisting on this, Wesley departed quite radically
from the standard interpretation of the language that was
common in his day, and he unwittingly helped pave the way for a
fresh visioning of the Christian life and ministry several generations down the road.

Conventional wisdom treated the witness of the Holy Spirit in
the life of the believer as just another way of providing rational
arguments for one's spiritual status of the kind already identified.
Taking his cue from Romans 8:16, Wesley suggested that there
was a witness that was "*immediate* and *direct*, not the result of
reflection or argumentation."[4] Such a testimony or experience was
beyond our ability to put into words. We just cannot adequately
describe the kind of experience the believer enjoys. The best that
Wesley could supply after twenty years of searching was this:

> By the "testimony of the Spirit" I mean an inward impression of
> the soul, whereby the Spirit of God immediately and directly

witnesses to my spirit that I am a child of God, that "Jesus Christ hath loved me and given himself for me"; that all my sins are blotted out, and I, even I, am reconcilied to God.[5]

It was this that was the foundation of the believer's certainty. We do not and cannot know how it is that God works, but we do know that as a result of this experience of God the believer "can no more doubt the reality of his sonship than he can doubt of the shining of the sun while he stands in the full blaze of the beams."[6] Perhaps the best way to construe this experience is as a matter of intimate, personal revelation, of hearing the voice of God within. Provided our "spiritual senses" are rightly disposed, we immediately and directly hear the voice of God within assuring us of our status as children. Beyond this we simply cannot go for a more bedrock foundation.

> To require a more minute and philosophical account of the *manner* whereby we distinguish these, and of the *criteria* or intrinsic marks whereby we know the voice of God, is to make a demand which cannot be answered; no, not by one who has the deepest knowledge of God. Suppose, when Paul answered before Agrippa, the wise Roman had said: "Thou talkest of hearing the voice of the Son of God. How dost thou know it was his voice? By what *criteria*, what intrinsic marks, dost thou know the voice of God? Explain to me the *manner* of distinguishing this from a human or angelic voice." Can you believe the Apostle himself would have once attempted to answer so idle a demand? And yet doubtless the moment he heard that voice he knew it was the voice of God. But *how* he knew this who is able to explain? Perhaps neither man nor angel.[7]

Likewise with forgiveness. God speaks to us that our sins are forgiven. There is nothing in God to prevent his bringing it about that we know that it is God who actually speaks. So he achieves this effect and we are absolutely assured that we are forgiven. Beyond that we cannot go, for there is no natural medium or natural method to explain the things of God to ordinary mortals. These things are spiritually discerned by spiritual senses, which God himself supplies as a matter of grace.

But may we not be deluded? May not our senses deceive us? Or may we not be led astray by the devil? At this juncture Wesley brings into play the appeal to standard rational arguments. We know we are not deluded, because we manifest the fruit of the Spirit, which is the mark of the children of God. This fruit cannot be produced by the devil, for he is not in the business of humbling us before God, softening our hearts in earnest mourning in God's presence, enabling us to love our neighbours, and so on. At this point the witness of the Holy Spirit in our hearts combines with the witness of our own spirit embodied in reflection on our lives to convince us that we truly are children of God. The former acts as the natural, psychological foundation for the latter in that we love God because He first loves us. So we are not relying on some inner voice alone; we are also appealing to phenomena that we, and presumably others, can actually perceive. In both cases there is an irreducible appeal to perceptual experience. This should not alarm us, for this is our normal epistemological state in cases of perceptual experience. In the end we have to trust our senses; there is nothing outside them or beyond them that we can rely on for additional evidence.

Such in broad outline is Wesley's treatment of assurance. Clearly it raises some fascinating epistemological questions, but we cannot pursue them here. Certainly for Wesley there was no intellectual tension between his commitment to the possibility of falling from grace and the possibility of genuine assurance. The former in no way precluded the latter. Indeed commitment to a doctrine of eternal security cannot in itself provide us with assurance; on the contrary when set in a classical Calvinist context, it can provide absolutely no help at all on this score. Wesley only hints at this possibility but it is worth pursuing in that it brings out how close Calvinists and Arminians are regarding assurance.[8]

The issue is this. Let us agree for the sake of the argument that true believers or the elect are eternally secure. Does this provide any warrant that any individual is actually, objectively secure here and now? Not at all. It provides assurance only if we know that we are one of the elect. Yet this is crucial information not vouchsafed to us. The elect are known only to God; in fact election depends entirely on God's arbitrary choice; only God knows those whom he has chosen to save. Clearly this is not something that has been revealed by God, hence we are left in the dark as to who the elect are. General propositions that tell us that the elect are secure are therefore ultimately vacuous when it comes to the question of our own personal assurance of our standing before God. It is Calvinists, not Arminians, who have a problem in providing adequate resources for a healthy doctrine of assurance. It is small wonder then that those who have meditated thoroughly on the doctrines of Calvinism in a personal and existential way have been driven at times to despair.

But should they be driven to despair? Is there a way out of this dilemma? A fruitful way to explore this is to turn to a paradigm of the Calvinist tradition and see how he or she attempts to resolve this issue. One of the obvious candidates for this role is Jonathan Edwards. In fact, Edwards provides a splendid response to this problem in his classic work on the religious affections.[9] The heart of Edwards' response is the setting out of a general theory that helps us to identify the elect but does not appeal to any kind of personal revelation. In short, what

Edwards does is develop an account of the signs of election that enables us to discern whether we are likely to be among the elect or not.

Edwards approaches this matter with exemplary caution. His first step is to argue that the elect are to be known by gracious affections, for it is these that are constitutive of true religion. His second step is to lay out negatively those signs that we cannot rely on in seeking to distinguish true from false affections. Thus he argues that we cannot rely on such considerations as the intensity of our affections or the impact of the affections on our bodies or on our tongues; we cannot appeal to the fact that the affections are not produced by ourselves as agents or that they are excited in us by Scripture or that they come dressed in an appearance of love or that they come in a certain number or a certain order or that they are accompanied by religious acts, such as worship, or that they lead us to praise God with our mouths or that they lead to confidence about our status before God or that they lead others to make favorable judgments about our spiritual status. All these considerations can mislead us in one way or another.

What, then, can we rely on? In our own case, but not in the case of others, we can know if we are elect if we display affections that manifest the following characteristics: Truly gracious affections arise from influences that are divine; they are grounded in the intrinsic nature of divine things as they are in themselves rather than because of the relation they bear to self-interest; they are founded on the moral beauty and excellence of divine realities; they arise from a mind that is properly enlightened to understand spiritual matters; they are accompanied by an inward conviction of the reality of divine things; they are attended by evangelical humiliation, by a genuine change of nature, by the spirit and temper of Jesus Christ, and by a Christian tenderness of spirit;   · they are expressed in a beautiful symmetry and proportion; they lead to an increase in spiritual appetite and a longing for spiritual attainments; above all, the truly gracious affections bear fruit in the full practice of the Christian life.

As it stands, this sounds like a wooden laundry-list of dry, medium-sized, spiritual goods. As spelled out in detail by Edwards, it represents one of the most outstanding expressions of the Christian tradition ever developed in North America. What interests us here is the inner logic of the proposal. In essence what we have is an extension of the witness of our own spirit already outlined above in reference to Wesley. What Edwards is suggesting is that we can decide in our own lives if we are elect or not by examining our consciousness, our inner motives, and our outer behavior and determining whether they manifest truly gracious affections. We have a typical case of rational argument in which we first of all determine the true marks of the religious affections as laid out in or inferred from the teaching of the Scriptures; we then examine our own lives to see what they look like; then, finally, we seek to determine if the results obtained in the second step match the conclusions arrived at in the first step; if they do match, we can deduce that we are among the elect. By this means, and by this means alone, we can know whether we have any right to assurance or not.

This whole approach to assurance raises some very serious problems. Notice that it seems to preclude any kind of appeal to religious experience as we find it in Wesley. In fact Edwards is quite explicit in his rejection of any appeal to personal revelation or the like in his analysis of the witness of the Holy Spirit. Aside from quoting with approval those divines who had treated the witness of the Spirit as a reflex act of the kind outlined above,[10] he says quite explicitly that it does not mean any kind of immediate impression, suggestion, or the like: "It appears that the witness of the Spirit the Apostle speaks of, is far from being any whisper, or immediate suggestion or revelation; but that gracious holy effect of the Spirit of God in the hearts of the saints, the disposition and temper of children, appearing in sweet childlike love to God, which casts out fear, or a spirit of a slave.[11] This appears to mean that one is relying fundamentally and entirely on rational arguments based on personal observation of one's behavior as the basis for one's assurance.

If so, it is surely a precarious enterprise. The tests that Edwards proposes are so stringent that only the most conspicuous saints are going to meet them and even then it is not entirely clear that they will know that they have met them; perhaps only God could determine who has satisfied the standards of behavior appropriate to the genuinely elect. It is small wonder that Edwards does not think that they are used with any degree of success by the beginning Christian or by those weak in faith. Such persons possess insufficient grace and inadequate capacities of discernment to know whether they really possess the relevant affections.[12] Indeed, in the end the only real test of the elect is whether they actually persevere or not in appropriate Christian living. This offers small comfort to the poor soul who wants to know now if she is elect or not; waiting to the end to see if God has taken her through the obstacle race of life is not going to be of much help.

This situation becomes even bleaker once we add in the possibility that one might be a temporary believer. I do not know that Edwards makes use of this notion but it has been central to much Calvinist theology. The issue of the temporary believer arises from a problem familiar to anyone who thinks seriously about the possibility of apostasy. What are we to make of those who seem to show some or even all the marks of the elect but then fall away and utterly reject the Christian gospel? For the Wesleyan this represents clear empirical confirmation of the possibility of falling away. In principle it cannot function in this way for the Calvinist, so the standard move made is to claim that they are not true believers; they are merely temporary believers who were never among the elect in the first place. They may even have been subject to the gracious activity of the Holy Spirit in much the same fashion as the elect, but God acted in this way merely for a season in order that ultimately fresh glory would come to his name.[13] Now if this possibility is seriously considered, the perplexity of the believer is bound to be increased and what little ground they may have had to start with is eroded considerably.

All this may explain why the kind of position developed by Edwards on assurance is absent from modern debates about this issue. There are very few who tackle the topic of assurance in the way he does. Perhaps this is why the question of "once saved always saved" is so emotional for many people. The grounds of their assurance are to be found neither in religious experience nor in rational arguments concerning the fruit of the Spirit in their lives. The matter is resolved by clinging to a doctrine of eternal security and applying it to oneself on the basis of a decision or conscious commitment to Christ. Thus many parents are anxious to see their children come to Christ, for they can then be at peace about their eternal destiny. They apply the logic of their doctrine: if x has accepted Christ, x is secure forever. No matter how far they roam into the world, they will always be secure, given that they can never fall from salvation. Hence it is only natural that many grow distinctly uncomfortable when they hear that it is possible to fall from grace. The foundations of their spiritual lives are being challenged in a very deep way. Perhaps this is why they think that the Arminian is constantly unsettled in his faith. They project their own phenomenology of certainty unto their opponent; they cannot conceive of any alternative vision of Christian certitude.

It should be conceded of course that this analysis may not do full justice to Edwards' account of assurance. It is clear, for example, that Edwards insists that rational arguments are utterly inadequate as grounds of certainty for the believer. The believer's faith does not rest merely on, say, probability arguments about this or that historical event. The Christian appears to have internal evidence of another sort to rely on, and thus one of the signs of the gracious affections is that it is accompanied by a conviction of the certainty of divine reality. So believers are not in the position of having an opinion, say, that Jesus is divine; "they see that it is really so: their eyes are opened, so that they see that really Jesus is the Christ, the Son of the living God."[14] As a result they behave in a radically different way from those who have not been enlightened by God. Yet I am not sure that this will really resolve the dilemma I have identified. For one thing, it may well be possible to have the kind of conviction that Edwards claims and yet not have the conviction or certainty that one is a child of God. Surely one can have a deep conviction that Jesus is the Son of God and yet be quite unconvinced about one's own personal salvation. It is this that is at stake in the debate about assurance. Moreover, the kind of rational argument Edwards is calling into question is the kind of argument open only to the learned; he is worried about having to rely on complex philosophical arguments or complicated historical research. But this does not overturn the fact that even the illiterate Christian still has to rely on a deductive argument to arrive at the certainty of his or her salvation. They have to go through a reflective process that moves from premise to conclusion. That in principle they have access to the relevant premises does not do away with the need to rely on deductive inference; without it they cannot reach the appropriate conclusion about their status before God. So they do have to rely on rational argument after all.

Be that as it may, I do not think that Calvinists should be particularly perturbed at this point. The obvious thing to do is to move in a Wesleyan direction on the issue of assurance. There is no reason Calvinists need sacrifice any of their basic doctrines if they incorporate into their account of assurance the appeal to the direct, immediate perception of God's graciousness to the individual, which we saw was primary in Wesley's analysis of the witness of the Holy Spirit. Certainly as it stands there seems to be enough in common to make this a plausible reconstruction of the Calvinist position. As far as assurance is an issue, the debate between the two positions is to a great extent a verbal one. The differences arise in part because the competing sides are interested in two different questions. The Arminian focuses on whether one can know *now* that one is a child of God; the Calvinist focuses on whether one will *ultimately* be saved in the future. The real equivalent to the Arminian focus in the Calvinist scheme of things is whether one can know *now* if one is numbered among the elect. When we look at the Calvinist treatment of this issue we find that the matters discussed parallel the issues taken up by the Arminian tradition. Wesley's appeal to perceptual as well as rational considerations offers a richer and more satisfactory solution to the problems at stake here. Crucial in it is his appeal to the immediate action of the Holy Spirit in the heart of the believer. Without this or some functional, intellectual equivalent it is difficult to see how anyone can begin to give an adequate account of assurance for the ordinary believer.

Decisions of this nature cannot, however, be made without paying a price. It may seem obtuse on the part of the Calvinist to refuse a friendly olive branch from a Wesleyan but maybe they are wise to refuse the offer graciously. In the final section of this chapter I would like therefore to reflect more broadly on the debate before us. Let us approach this by giving a brief account of the historical effects of the emphasis on religious experience and of the emphasis on the direct action of the Holy Spirit as it has been played out in the Wesleyan tradition. There is much more than meets the eye at first glance.

There is no doubt that Wesley's position is incipiently revolutionary. What he was doing was opening a door to divine intervention in the life of the believer. It is no wonder that he was accused of being an "enthusiast," for at stake is the possibility of a personal revelation that is logically distinct from past revelation. Wesley is open at this point in a way that was utterly impossible for Edwards. Edwards, in fact, astutely realized that to allow for the possibility of a direct, immediate "suggestion" or "whisper" of the Holy Spirit was to open the door to the extraordinary gifts of the Holy Spirit, a door he and his whole generation had kept firmly bolted and were determined to keep that way until doomsday. I suspect that Wesley did not fully realize what was happening, but it is surely no accident that some of his heirs eventually realised the full logic of his position and found themselves in the midst of a theological and practical revolution. Even yet most of Christendom does not know how to handle intellectually or pastorally the Pentecostal and charismatic developments of the original Wesleyan vision; perhaps it never will. In other words, Wesley really was an "enthusiast" of sorts in that he did believe in direct divine "impressions" on the soul, and this in a subtle but genuine way paves the way for the modern Pentecostal tradition.[15] For this reason alone many a sturdy Calvinist will resist the overture from Wesley.

They will be equally repelled by the other direction in which the Wesleyan tradition has developed. Again, it is surely no accident that the followers of Wesley have taken to classical forms of liberalism like the proverbial duck takes to water. The whole focus on religious experience when it is cut loose from the deeper theological framework in which it is embedded can very easily slide into an epistemology where the appeal to Scripture or to a solid conception of revelation is replaced by an appeal to religious experience *simpliciter*. The consequences of this for theology are there for all to see in the history of much modern Methodist theology.

In some respects I think that the focus on personal experience of God as it has worked itself out in Wesleyan theology has been an unmitigated disaster. In both conservative and liberal Wesleyanism it has led to an anthropocentrism that has drained the tradition of its fundamental resources and richness. On the one side it has led to a bland, moralistic activism that makes Christianity look as if it is an adult version of the Boy Scouts and the Girl Guides dressed up in the rhetoric of amateur sociology and moral theology. On the other side it has degenerated into a harsh legalism and a form of judgmental piety that suffocates the life of the soul and has nothing to offer but another sentimental appeal for Christians to dedicate their hearts to God once more. The full reasons for this state of affairs are thoroughly complex, but part of the fault lies with a disastrous turn to a focus not on God or on the gospel or the great truths of the classical tradition but on ourselves, our feelings and on our spiritual states and status. There are good reasons therefore for approaching the Wesleyan offer with considerable suspicion.

Yet I do not think that there can be any going back on the Wesleyan analysis if we are to provide an adequate theology of assurance. To be sure, there is work that needs to be done in clarifying both the phenomenology and the logic of the appeal to direct experience of the Holy Spirit. The philosophy of mind embraced by Edwards and Wesley sounds archaic in the wake of Wittgenstein and Ryle. Yet Wesley was fully aware of how mysterious the interaction between God and his children is, and he was keen to see the whole matter conceptualized as felicitously as possible. Recent work on the nature and epistemology of religious experience might be of some help here. My claim at this point is the simple one that Wesley was, at the very least, on to something which an adequate doctrine of the Christian life must incorporate. We simply should not forget that Wesley and others had to make a gigantic effort to retrieve a vital part of apostolic Christianity that is essential to evangelism and the pursuit of holiness.

If we are to succeed in the appropriation of Wesley, however, we will have to drink deeply at the wells of the Calvinist tradition and its sources in the Scriptures of the church. The serious errors of the past must be avoided, and we must not be afraid to follow through on the full logic of Wesley's proposals. We must find at all costs a way to rid us of the anthropocentrism that has ruined so much of the Arminian tradition. In other words, I am proposing an amicable arrangement where Calvinists and Arminians borrow lavishly from each other.

Especially pertinent in the present context is the whole Calvinist vision of the beauty and sovereignty of God. What may be ultimately at stake for the Calvinist tradition in the debate about assurance is not the status of this or that individual but the ultimate triumph of God's good and gracious intentions for creation. Its great exponents fear that Arminians introduce an element of contingency into the universe that puts at risk God's plans and purposes. Somehow if humans in any way act in the process of salvation, they introduce a weak link into the chain of events that may snap at any time and send the whole cosmos tumbling into chaos and darkness. Their concern is a legitimate one: if there is freedom, how can we be sure that God really will be able to fulfill his purposes for the universe? The answer proposed, of course, is that we can be sure only because God has determined the outcome from start to finish. We do not need to take this route to resolve this problem but I am convinced that any theological vision that takes our eyes off ourselves and our effort and redirects it into the fact of the transcendent, divine reality is worthy of sustained attention. It is this that meets one in Edwards. And Edwards has much else to give us. His analysis of the religious affections, his account of the pathology of revival, his devastating exposure of sin and idolatry, his love for the church and for good order within it, his passion for spiritual discernment, his commitment to clarity and rigor in theology—all these and much else deserve to be earnestly coveted by those who find the totality of his Calvinist vision profoundly mistaken and deeply unscriptural.[16]

NOTES

[1]Wesley's two sermons on the witness of the Spirit can be found in Albert C. Outler, ed., *The Works of John Wesley* (Nashville: Abingdon, 1984), 1:267–98.

[2]Ibid., 273.

[3]Ibid., 287–88.

[4]Ibid., 289.

[5]Ibid., 287.

[6]Ibid., 276.

[7]Ibid., 282.

[8]See his "Predestination Calmly Considered," in Albert C. Outler, ed. *John Wesley* (New York: Oxford University Press, 1964), 446.

[9]Jonathan Edwards, *Religious Affections* (New Haven: Yale University Press, 1959).

[10]Ibid., 235.

[11]Ibid., 238.

[12]Ibid., 195–96.

[13]Ibid., 304–5.

[14]Ibid., 292.

[15]There are, of course, other links between the Wesleyan tradition and modern Pentecostalism. See Vinson Synan, *The Holiness-Pentecostal Movements in the United States* (Grand Rapids: Eerdmans, 1972).

[16]One of the best discussions of the biblical material relevant to the issues discussed in this paper can be found in I. Howard Marshall, *Kept by the Power of God: A Study of Perseverance and Falling Away* (London: Epworth, 1969).

SOTERIOLOGY IN THE GOSPEL OF JOHN

Grant R. Osborne

In the companion volume to this book, *Grace Unlimited*, I wrote an article "Soteriology in the Epistle to the Hebrews," tracing the salvific purpose that lay behind that marvelous letter. Yet in a very real sense that epistle provides few problems for a Wesleyan-Arminian approach; it was tailor-made for arguments regarding apostasy and responsibility. If the position is to be supported properly, it must be studied with respect to the passages that center more on the sovereignty of God. Such is the Gospel of John. Few biblical books maintain a better balance between divine sovereignty and human responsibility than John, so it provides a perfect choice for our purpose.

Moreover, soteriology is at the heart of John's Gospel. Like Hebrews christology, so often called the core of the fourth Gospel, has a soteriological purpose, calling the reader to "believe" the Gospel.[1] In fact, John is an "encounter" Gospel, as Jesus forces every person he meets to consider the claims of God and to make a choice. The book is structured around a series of dramatic encounters (1:35–50; 3:1–15; 4:1–42; 9:1–41; 11:1–44), each salvific in its focus. As is well known, John's soteriology centers on several key terms that are used with multiple meanings from the perspective of the heavenly and the earthly dimensions: to know (οἶδα and γινώσκω used synonymously a total of 131 times in John's Gospel), to see (five verbs used, 114 times), to believe (98 times, always in verbal form to stress faith as a dynamic act), truth (48 times, combining the moral and intellectual connotations),[2] and life (66 times and parallel to the synoptic "kingdom" teaching). Often earthly scenes are given double meaning by using these terms, as in 1:35–40, where the disciples asked Jesus, "Where are you staying?" (μένω used of spiritual indwelling in

15:4–10 and found three times in 1:38–39), and Jesus responded, "Come and you will see" (both salvific terms in John). Behind the earthly scene a salvation drama was enacted, leading to their conversion (v. 41).

However, the exact delineation of the process of salvation in John, namely the interaction between divine sovereignty and human responsibility, is hotly debated. No New Testament book maintains a better balance, and both Calvinists and Arminians have extensively used the Fourth Gospel to support their positions. Only Romans 9–11 has a greater stress on divine predestination than does John in passages like 3:8, 27; 5:21; 6:35–40; 44–47; 10:29; 15:16, 19; or 17:6–9. At the same time John has the greatest stress on God's universal salvific love in such phrases as "Savior of the world" (4:42) and "Savior of all men" (1:7; 5:23; 11:48; 12:32). Is faith-decision an act of free will or the result of God's irresistible grace in drawing the elect to himself? This is the issue. There are two approaches: one could study John on these issues topically or in linear fashion, tracing the topic through the Gospel. I prefer the latter, because only in this way can we see these themes interact.

THE PROLOGUE (1:1–18)

Human responsibility is stressed in 1:4, 7, 9, 11. The interplay of light and life in verses 4–5 builds on Jewish Wisdom themes: as Rudolf Schnackenburg says, "Everything that is necessary for this end (of bringing men home to God's world of light), the giving of revelation and life, the banishment of the darkness of sin and guilt, the moral behavior which conquers evil works (cf. 3:19ff) and lusts (1 John 2:16f), is part of the light which the Logos radiates."[3] Moreover, this light enlightens "all men" (vv. 7, 9) who can participate in the life by "receiving" him (v. 12)—i.e., by coming to Jesus and believing that he is indeed God's envoy. At the very outset the stress is on God's universal salvific will in drawing "all men" to himself.

The debate is over verses 12–13, for, according to verses 9, 11, "every man" receives the light and is responsible to reject (v. 11) or accept (v. 12) it, yet those who do accept it are "born of God" (v. 13), clearly a sovereign act and not controlled by man's decision. How do we bring the two together? The one point to be stressed is that there is no hint of "irresistible grace," a doctrine that states that God's compassionate act of grace irresistibly draws the elect to himself.[4] To summarize the data, every person is enlightened and drawn toward the life that is in the Logos. Those who reject it are part of the "world," the realm of darkness. Those who accept it are "born of God"—i.e., they receive the new spiritual birth (see 3:3, 5) that comes from God alone. Clearly a person's faith decision does not produce salvation in and of itself: yet as the text says, salvation will not be wrought within a person without reception of the Logos. Sovereignty and responsibility exist side by side.

THE OPENING EVENTS (1:19–51)

Clearly christology and soteriology intertwine in the dramatic encounter of the first disciples. It begins with the Baptist's testimony that Jesus is "the lamb of God who takes away the sin of the world" (1:29, 36). Throughout John $\kappa\acute{o}\sigma\mu o\varsigma$ (105 times in the Johannine corpus) is primarily negative, dominated by sin and rebellion and controlled by the "prince of this world," Satan (12:31; 14:30; 16:11). However, the cosmos is also the object of Christ's sacrificial act (1:29, as the paschal lamb) and God's salvific love (3:16). It is under divine judgment and subject to death (8:24) because of unbelief (16:9), but all people are given the opportunity to repent (1:7, 9, 12). Yet there is still sovereignty; it is not the act of faith-decision but Jesus' sacrifice that removes sin. Nevertheless that decision is a necessary precursor, as enacted in the coming to faith of the early disciples in 1:35–51 (especially vv. 41, 45, 49–50).

THE EARLY SIGNS (2:1–4:42)

The consensus is that John's use of $\sigma\eta\mu\epsilon\hat{\imath}\alpha$ for miracles is part of his witness theme. In other words the miracles were "signs" sent to testify of Jesus' true significance. However, the extent of that testimony is strongly debated. James Montgomery Boice believes that they are self-authenticating, valid witnesses that call the nonbeliever to Christ.[5] However, this is problematic. In 2:11 the disciples do indeed "believe" because the signs manifested Jesus' glory. However, in 2:23–25 we see quite a different side. Here we see biased disciples who "believe" in Jesus on the basis of the "signs" (v. 23), but he does not "believe" (v. 24, with $\pi\iota\sigma\tau\epsilon\acute{\nu}\omega$ in both instances) in them. As Raymond E. Brown notes, Jesus' refusal was due to the incompleteness of their faith; these disciples were unable to see Jesus as anything other than a wonder-worker.[6] Jesus' omniscience in understanding "what was in a man" probably built on the Old Testament emphasis of Yahweh's knowledge of the hidden things of the heart (e.g., 1 Kings 8:39). This tells us that the signs encountered but did not guarantee a proper response. Without the eye of faith the theological significance of the signs cannot be perceived (see 4:48; 6:26–30).[7] Nevertheless, the presence of the signs-theology does favor a valid faith-decision on the part of the observer; a clear choice is demanded.

Furthermore, 2:23–25 prepares for the Nicodemus story of

3:1–15. In that episode the emphasis is on sovereignty, especially in verse 8 and then again in the Baptist's testimony in verse 27. Ancient people were always perplexed as to the origin and movements of wind, and this provides a natural metaphor for Jesus' point that one can never know or control the movement of the Spirit (note the word-play on $\pi\nu\epsilon\hat{\upsilon}\mu\alpha$) in salvation. It is God who is in control. This is the emphasis of the whole dialogue in 3:1–15, Nicodemus was probably one of those who misunderstood the nature of the signs in 2:23, and Jesus was telling him that God alone controlled the process of salvation: he had to be born "from above" (vv. 3, 7, lit. trans.). This is stressed even more in a major Johannine theme—that one can "receive only what is given him from heaven" (v. 27). Although this will be discussed in greater depth in connection with 6:35–40, note that once more God is seen as firmly in charge of the salvation process.

Responsibility is presented in the editorial excursus of 3:16–21.[8] The well-known verse 16 provides the clearest statement thus far that the divine love extends to the whole world and has faith-decision as its goal. The "whoever" who receive eternal life are obviously those among the world who believe. Moreover Christ's purpose is further specified as positive rather than negative, not to condemn ($\kappa\rho\acute{\iota}\nu\omega$) but to save (v. 17). There seems to be a contrast here, for verse 17 says Jesus does not come to judge, whereas 5:22–23, 30 and 9:39 say Jesus does come "for judgment." The solution probably can be found in 8:15–16—Jesus does not come to judge but his coming involves judgment because he forces people to come to decision, and this leads to judgment (3:19; 12:48) for those who reject his claims.

In Jesus' dramatic encounter with the Samaritan woman (4:1–42) faith-decision is the constant emphasis. Jesus speaks of the "gift of God" but links that gift of living water with asking. Although God controls the gift of eternal life, it is given on the basis of personal decision. Jesus gives the water but the person must drink it (vv. 13–14). The scene culminates in the confession of the Samaritans that Jesus is "Savior of the world" (v. 42; cf. 1 John 4:14), and indeed this is the high point of John's theme of universalistic salvation thus far. As Marshall points out, it is just this strain of universalism (i.e., that the gospel is for all men) that protects John from the charge of dualism, the charge that he divides mankind into two categories, the elect and the nonelect.[9] Rather, the fourth Gospel shows that Jesus came for everyone—Jew, Samaritan, Gentile—and that every person is brought to the point of decision.

JESUS AND THE JEWISH FEASTS (5:1–10:42)

In Jesus' discourse on the life and judgment given to the Son (5:19–47), sovereignty and responsibility are once more interspersed. Verses 19–24 look at the realized side of life and judgment, while verses 25–30 repeat this material in the final sense of the last judgment. Verse 21 is one of the strongest statements on election thus far. The Son emulates the Father in giving "life to whom he is pleased to give it." The stress in verses 19–20 is on the unity between Father and Son (v. 18) and there is double meaning in Jesus' use of "life" in verse 21, referring both to the miracle of 5:1–18 and to the bestowal of eternal life. There is no denying the strong predestinarian thrust of this verse. Yet how absolute is the statement? Does it demand a doctrine of irresistible grace (see above) and a denial of free will at the point of decision? It cannot, for Jesus states clearly, "Whoever hears my word and believes . . . has eternal life" (v. 24). The two sides—divine election and human decision—work together. Men and women cannot produce their own salvation, but they can "accept" God's act in Christ, and for those who do so Christ is "pleased to give" them "life" (vv. 21, 24). The key is οὓς θέλει ("whom he wishes"); does it refer to the process of salvation (= predestination in the Calvinist sense) or to sovereign control in general? Most commentators agree that the latter is the stress. As Morris says, "The Son gives life where He, not man, chooses."[10]

The marvelously deep "bread of life" discourse (chap. 6) provides the greatest challenge of this study of any section in the fourth Gospel. It is part of a larger section (chaps. 5–8) in which Jesus goes on the offensive against Jewish unbelief. The last half of chapter 5 centers on responsibility, detailing why the "witnesses" (the Father, the Baptist, his works, Moses) to Jesus' personhood are sufficient to lead any observer to faith (vv. 31–40); yet still the Jews reject him (vv. 41–47, acting out 1:11). This conflict escalates sharply in chapter 6, where Jesus labels himself "the bread of life" (v. 35) who "came down from heaven" (v. 41). The dissension caused by this manna theme and Jesus' teaching that he has fulfilled the Exodus and the ministry of Moses could hardly be ignored.[11] On the whole, the bread-of-life discourse speaks clearly of the divine revelation in Jesus, which alone is the path to life.[12]

The discourse itself (vv. 22–50) is the major focus of our study. There is inclusion between verses 26–27 and 57–58 centering on Jesus as the "eternal food," which must be ingested by an act of faith (v. 29). To the crowds' request for this new "bread," Jesus provided his interpretation (vv. 35–40). Here the sovereign control of salvation by God is given greater stress than anywhere else in John, and so we are at a critical point in our study. Following the "I am" statement in verse 35 concerning himself as the "bread of life."[13] Jesus recapitulates the responsibility of the Jews to "come" and "believe." As stated above, both are synonyms for faith decision and govern the whole of chapters 5–8. Next verses 36–37 look at the two sides of the issue, man's and God's. Negatively the Jews are responsible because of their disbelief (v. 36). Positively, all "given" by the Father will "come" and will "never be driven away." Obviously responsibility and predestination are again intertwined, yet here that relationship must be reexamined.

Carson states that the giving precedes the coming and that once believers come, their status as God's chosen is assured, arguing (1) that "cast out" in John always implies someone already "in," and (2) that verse 39 supports this by saying that Jesus will not "lose" any of those given.[14] Certainly there is a lot to be said for this view. The concepts of "given," "not cast out," and "eternal life" are all major concepts in John and together point to both the election and security of the believer in John. However, there is no hint of any chronological process here or anywhere else in John. In fact, as Léon-Dufour has argued,[15] there seems to be a chiastic arrangement here centering on verse 38.

36: seeing and not believing	40: looking and believing
37: not casting out what the Father gives	39: losing nothing of what the Father gives

38: I have come down from heaven

This arrangement makes eminent sense and tells us that responsibility (A = vv. 36, 40) and security (B = vv. 37, 39) stand alongside one another under the sovereign unity of the Father and Son in the process of salvation (v. 38). Whatever system we theorize must not make one subservient to the other, chronologically or otherwise.[16] Election there most certainly is, but does the "given" to Christ by God produce faith or does it work with that faith? The latter is much closer to the Johannine pattern as we have studied it thus far.

Similar thoughts are expressed in verses 44–47. The Jews grumbled about Jesus' claim to have descended from heaven (vv. 41–43) and Jesus responded by reiterating the point that no one can come unless drawn by the Father (v. 44: cf. v. 65). At first glance this supports the view that the drawing precedes and controls the coming. C. K. Barrett asserts that everyone given to Jesus will be drawn "with or without argument . . . " (and) those whom the Father does not give will not come."[17] Leon Morris adds, "There is not one instance in the New Testament of the use of this verb [to draw] where the resistance is unsuccessful."[18] In other words it provides an instance of irresistible grace. Certainly ἐλκύω is a very strong verb and implies a divine "drawing" or pull to salvation. However, it is to be doubted whether it is meant to be irresistible. If so, we are left with universalism in 12:32 ("I will draw all men to myself"). Moreover, Jesus did "lose" (cf. 6:39) one of his intimate followers, "the son of perdition" (17:12).

Jesus speaks here of God's control of salvation; the Jews have only themselves to blame for their unbelief. The quotation of Isaiah 54:13 in 'verse 45, "They will all be taught by God," is another instance of God's universal salvific will and as Kysar says implicitly provides an invitation to believe.[19] Yet it is more, for it tells the Jews that they are now in the time of fulfillment and in Jesus are being taught by God. If they reject that message, they are doubly guilty. God is drawing them, and only by faith-decision can they have eternal life (v. 47; cf. vv. 48–51). This is acted out in the two scenes of verses 60–66 and 67–71. In the first, many of his larger-circle of disciples questioned and then abandoned Jesus (v. 66, cf. 2:23–25). Yet his inner circle remained true (vv. 67–71). Again it is the "drawing" power of God that is the key (v. 65), placed in contrast to the apostasy of the partial disciples. The drawing of God leaves all without excuse for their unbelief.

Chapters 7–9 continue the emphasis on encounter and responsibility. In these chapters Jesus is presented as the fulfillment of the Feast of Tabernacles and indeed replaces first the water ceremony (7:37) and then the candle ceremony (8:12) of the feast, he himself providing the living water (7:37–39, cf. 4:13–14) and as the light of the world (8:12). In the water ceremony a priest carried water in a golden bowl each day from the pool of Siloam and poured it out at the side of the altar as a prayer for rain. This occurred every day except for the final day of that feast, and on that day Jesus stood and declared that he himself would provide the "living" water, namely the Holy Spirit (7:37–39). Note the emphasis on partaking and "belief" offered to anyone who would respond (v. 37). The result was division, as some made a faith-decision (see also vv. 17, 31), whereas others doubted, and still others wanted to arrest him (7:40–44).

This theme continues in 8:12–59. At the beginning of the feast they lit the golden candlesticks in the court of women, with the wicks fashioned from the priests' worn-out girdles (or sashes). It was said that all Jerusalem reflected the light of the procession. Jesus, speaking at the treasury (v. 20) in the court of women, declared himself "the light of the world," expanding the symbolism beyond Jewry to include all mankind. Again "whoever follows" Jesus will have "the light of life," combining both images from 1:3–5 (see above). Throughout the eighth chapter, Jesus' encounter with Jewish unbelief and call for faith-decision continued. He spoke of knowing him and the Father (vv. 9, 32), of believing (vv. 24, 30, 31, 45), of loving him (v. 42), of hearing (v. 47), and of keeping his Word (v. 51). Most of all, Jesus excoriates the Jews for their unbelief. There is a strong sense of the depravity of those who listened some of them being believers (v. 31).[20] They were guilty of unbelief and therefore were not "children of Abraham" but "of the devil" (vv. 39, 44).

Chapter 9 provides one of the great dramas of the book. The man born blind comes not only to physical sight but, in a series of dramatic steps, to spiritual sight. He is contrasted to the Pharisees, who claimed spiritual insight but progressively descended to spiritual blindness (culminating in vv. 40–41). In this way the meaning of Jesus as "light of the world" (see v. 5) is dramatically portrayed in contrast to the man and the Pharisees. Yet there is also a stress on sovereignty. The illness has as its ultimate purpose the glory of God, soon to be manifest in the miracle.[21]

Chapter 10 provides the strongest emphasis on sovereignty in this section. The Good Shepherd appears firmly in control in verses 1–5; he knows his sheep, and they follow him rather than a stranger, for they know his voice and belong to him. Jesus is both gate (v. 7) and shepherd (vv. 11, 14). He knows his sheep with the same salvific knowledge by which the Father knows him (v. 14). The "sheep that are not of this sheep pen" (v. 16) are future Gentile believers; they too will "listen and follow." These pastoral images were frequent throughout Jewish literature, often with a sense of election as "God's unlimited sovereignty over his flock" is combined with "the overwhelming consciousness of God's spontaneous love."[22]

On verse 26 Carson states, "Jesus does not say that his opponents are not among his sheep because they do not believe, but that they do not believe because they are not among his sheep."[23] This strong accent on Jewish guilt is followed by the famous declaration of security in verses 27–29, all built on Jesus' sovereign control ("I know them . . . I give them eternal life . . . no one can snatch them out of my hand") as anchored in the Father's sovereign control ("My Father, who has given them to me, is greater than all; no one can snatch them out of my Father's hand"). Election and security stand together in this magnificent chapter, and the two emphases are not to be denied.

However, while the chapter centers on God's work in predestination and assurance, we must define the emphases carefully. Neither one is absolute, i.e. accomplished apart from man's decision. The basic core of being given to Jesus by the Father, kept and protected from danger, not lost, and raised at the last day are all part of the Johannine theme of eternal life as a present possession. However, as Marshall says, "exegetical honesty compels us to ask whether the will of God can be frustrated by human sin."[24] In other words, are verses 27–29 a promise or a guarantee? Those who "snatch" the sheep are often identified (correctly) with the thieves and wolves (vv. 10, 12) of the allegory, and it is erroneous to read into this the impossibility of personal apostasy. On the other hand, some have tried to make listening and following in verse 27 a condition for the security of the believer: "If they follow, I give them eternal life."[25] However, these are statements rather than conditions, and this interpretation reads too much into the passage. Nevertheless the verbs are part of a larger Johannine pattern of faith-encounter and as in chapter 6 the two aspects—sovereignty and faith-decision—form two sides of the same coin. Election (in 10:1–18) and assurance (in 10:27–29) do not produce faith nor are they the result of faith; rather they work with faith-response. This is not emphasized in 10:1–30, where sovereignty is emphasized. However, in the larger sphere of Johannine thought as elucidated above it is the best interpretation of the data.

This is borne out in the immediately succeeding dialogue (10:31–39), in which Jesus calls the very listeners addressed in verses 22–30 (at the Feast of Dedication) to faith-response (vv. 37–38). There is no hint that it was made only for the sake of the elect or just to prove the guilt of the Jews. Rather Jesus desired that they "know" (note the repetitious aorist and present $\gamma\nu\hat{\omega}\tau\varepsilon$ $\kappa\alpha\grave{\iota}$ $\gamma\iota\nu\acute{\omega}\sigma\kappa\eta\tau\varepsilon$ to stress the beginning and continuing effects of the salvific "knowledge"[26]) him. The fact that this was a valid call to salvation is proven in verse 42, "and in that place many believed in Jesus." Election and faith-decision function together, the sheep hear and follow the voice of the Shepherd.

EVENTS PREPARING FOR THE PASSION (11:1–13:38)

There is not a great deal of material on this topic, as might be expected in a section centering more on the plane of christology and discipleship in light of the coming Passion. Yet it is obvious that the whole Gospel thus far has prepared for the culmination of God's revelation in Jesus' hour of glory. The raising of Lazarus is the miracle par excellence in John because it is an acted parable on Jesus' "life"-giving power. The central section is verses 25–26, "I am the resurrection and the life," and the hearers participate in that life via believing. The result, to be sure, is security ("never die") but in this passage "living" and "believing" (progressive presents denoting a continuous state) are necessary prerogatives. In other words, perseverance in the present life from God is necessary to maintain the future certainty of life in the next age; as stated above on 10:27-30, there is no conditional force: rather security and perseverance combine to produce life in the believer.

Chapters 12–13 culminate the divine preparation of events for that central point in salvation history. The scene in which Jesus was anointed for burial (12:1–11) ends with a statement of the many who were leaving Judaism on account of Jesus (v. 11). This is given as a major reason for the plot against Jesus' life. These were not half-hearted followers a la 2:23–25 or 6:60–66. As Brown says, this could actually be a message to partial believers of John's day to make this break and come over to the side of the church.[27] In the next scene, the vast crowd who came to meet Jesus in his triumphal entry caused the Pharisees to grumble that "the whole world has gone after" Jesus. Jesus then replied to the Greeks that one must "hate his life in this world" then follow and serve him in order to have eternal life (vv. 25–26). Jesus' purpose again is to save, not judge, the world (v. 46, cf. my discussion of 3:17, 19). In short, the universal proclamation of the gospel to whoever might believe continues even at the time of Jesus' "hour." Jesus continued to the very end to "draw *all men* to himself" (12:32) and the predestinarian passages must be balanced with such statements as this.

Chapter 13 centers on the sovereign control of salvation history. Two items of interest in v. 1 are (1) Jesus' knowledge and control of the time when he was to (voluntarily) leave this world and (2) the extent of his love for those disciples whom he had chosen (cf. 13:18). All that Jesus was to endure would be for the sake of those who were given to him. Yet this does not imply a limited atonement, for throughout John's Gospel Jesus' death is also for all, or for the world. Even Judas' defection was under divine control and should lead to belief (vv. 18–19) on the part of the disciples.[28]

THE FAREWELL DISCOURSE (14:1–17:26)

This is the high point of John's Gospel and is built on Old Testament farewell discourses like those of Moses (Deut. 32) or Joshua (Josh. 22–24). Again Jesus' sovereign control of the situation is stressed, and the basic theme is "I must depart so the Spirit might come." Unlike chapters 11–13 there is also a return to the strong balance and accent on sovereignty and responsibility. The promise to return for his followers (14:2–3) could refer to the coming of the Paraclete (the Holy Spirit as Jesus' "representative")[29] but almost certainly it is futuristic, referring to the parousia.[30] Jesus continues to work on behalf of his people; the stress here too is on their security in the Triune Godhead. There is no need for fear or anxiety (14:1, 27), for all three members of the Trinity—the Spirit-Paraclete (14:15–17), the Son (14:18–21), and the Father (14:22–24)—are at work on their behalf. Sovereignty is especially strong in 15:16, 19, where Jesus repeats, "You did not choose me, but I chose you. . . . " The language is very definitely that of election; however, we do not wish to overstate it theologically. The context speaks first of their new status with Jesus as "friends," and this is followed by reminding them that Jesus had the initiative from the beginning. In short, verses 16, 19 center on discipleship rather than on predestination.[31]

Those aspects that stress responsibility are exceedingly important. First there is the "abiding" theme, a major element in John's doctrine of perseverance. Yet here too there is a blend of sovereignty and responsibility, for the "dwelling" moves in both directions—Jesus "abides" in us, and this makes it possible for us to "dwell" in him (14:20; 15:4, 5, 7). This is the salvific counterpart of the mutual indwelling of the Father and Son (14:10; 15:9, 10). However,the emphasis is on responsibility, as seen in 15:4— "Remain in me, and I will remain in you." We should probably not interpret the first clause as conditional, "If you abide in me, I will abide in you," but rather we should take the two together as demanding mutual indwelling.[32] Nevertheless, there is a strong sense of perseverance. As Marshall says, "John thus uses the verb "abide" to express the need for disciples to continue in their personal commitment to Jesus; the abiding of Jesus in them is not an automatic process which is independent of their attitude to Him, but is the reverse side of their abiding in Him."[33]

The necessity of perseverance is stated unequivocally in the allegory of the vine in 15:1–6. Unlike the Good Shepherd allegory, where the interpretation followed the parable, allegory and meaning are intertwined in verses 1–6, with verses 7–17 forming a commentary on it. Building on Isaiah 5 and Ezekiel 17, teaching Israel's failure as the vine, Jesus is presented as the true vine, the Father as the gardener. The task of the branches (believers) is twofold: to abide in the vine, which in terms of the imagery means to draw one's sustenance completely from the vine; and to bear fruit, which in this context could refer to mission (note v. 16, "go and bear fruit") but probably refers more generally to all Christian responsibilities à la James 2:14–17 ("faith without works is dead") and the Christian characteristics of Galatians 5:22–23 ("the fruit of the Spirit"). The background helps to understand the options for interpreting the imagery. In February-March the vine is cultivated, with the dead branches cut away, and in August the fruit-bearing branches are cultivated or "pruned" so they will bear more fruit the following season. In both instances the demand of the text is for the perseverance of the branches in the vine.

The major issue is how far the allegory is to be taken. The rule when interpreting parables is to differentiate between those aspects that provide "local color" and thus have no theological significance and those allegorical elements that do bear theological weight. Here the debate centers on the fruitless branches, which are "cut off" (v. 2), "picked up, thrown into the fire and burned" (v. 6). If these are indeed allegorical, they provide a vivid picture of apostasy and its terrible results (cf. Heb. 6:4–6; 10:26–31). Yet they seem to contradict the many security promises that the believer will "never perish." (cf. John 3:15, 16; 10:28). Morris states, "We should not regard this as a proof that true believers may fall away. It is part of the viticultural picture, and no point could be made without it. The emphasis is on the bearing of fruit."[34] Yet Carson notes the "threat" of 15:16 ("*Then* the Father will give you . . .;" cf. 3:36; 5:29) and the seemingly real danger of apostasy in 16:1 ("All this I have told you so that you will not go astray") and exercises considerably more caution.[35] However, while 15:1ff. and 16:1 "sound like warnings of potentially real dangers," the many passages on security for Carson mean that the threats are hypothetical, "designed to foster persevering endurance . . . remove fears, increase faith, and remove all the posturings of self-sufficiency."[36] Certainly Carson's emphasis on divine sufficiency is correct; only the empowering presence of God makes it possible to overcome the pressures on the believer. Nevertheless, we must go one step further and recognize here the validity of the warning; John makes apostasy a real danger that can indeed occur. According to hermeneutical principles, there must be good *contextual* evidence before denying the theological force of a detail. If the purging of the branches is allegorical, the removal of dead branches must also possess theological meaning. What about the promises that the believer will "never perish"? They are true only to the extent to which the believer "abides" or "perseveres" in God. In other words, these are a present promise of future help but not an eternal guarantee. Security is conditional rather than unconditional.[37]

Chapter 17 provides major material for the priority of divine sovereignty. Christ's high-priestly prayer here is often said to prove the final perseverance of the elect. In it Jesus prays for glory, his own glory as well as that of his disciples (vv. 1–8), and then intercedes for his disciples (vv. 9–19) and for future believers (vv. 20–26). Gromacki finds four areas that stress the security of the believers: (1) they are gifts to the Son (vv. 2, 6, 9, 11, 12, 24); (2) they are possessions of the union of Father and Son (vv. 9–10); (3) they have eternal life (v. 2); and (4) Christ prays for their preservation (vv. 11, 24).[38] Again, much of this is true, but it does not provide a blanket guarantee of perseverance. Whatever one says about Judas' original position, he is an exception to Jesus' prayer for divine protection; in 17:12 Jesus says, "I protected them and kept them safe. . . . None has been lost *except* the one doomed to destruction. . . . " Apostasy is a valid possibility, but the power of God is exercised to keep the believer safe and secure.

THE PASSION AND RESURRECTION (18:1–21:25)

The passion and resurrection narratives do not contain a great deal of material directly relating to our topic. However, the major theme of John's passion story centers on Jesus' sovereign control of his destiny. This is seen in the opening account of the arrest. Jesus went to Gethsemane as a sovereign (the theological stress of 18:1), "knowing all that was going to happen" (v. 4). When Jesus responded to the query of the soldiers with the "I am" (v. 5, the major christological title in John), the soldiers "fell to the ground" (v. 6), the normal reaction to a theophany. So in the passion the soteriological purpose of the crucifixion is tied closely to Jesus' sovereignty. Even Caiaphas had been used of God when he prophesied unconsciously that one man should "die for the people" (11:49–50). This theme continues throughout the passion narrative, even in the crucifixion itself.[39]

There is a surprising reference to security in 18:9; when Jesus asked the soldiers to let his disciples go, this "fulfilled" his earlier promise, "I have not lost one of those you gave me." This gives great stress to the twin Johannine themes of security. He "will lose none" because Jesus' followers are "given" him by God. These two themes are combined also in 6:39 and 17:12; and in 18:9 is a summary of the teaching on assurance we have noted throughout John's Gospel. Moreover, by placing it in the fulfillment formula normally reserved for Old Testament citations, it is given canonical status. Again there is no question that security for believers is a major emphasis of the fourth Gospel.

Yet again we see this theme placed alongside responsibility. The trial before Pilate is set in a series of seven scenes juxtaposing those inside Pilate's palace (with Pilate's growing stress on Jesus' innocence) with those outside the palace (with the Jews' developing demand for Jesus' life).[40] Both the Jews and Pilate are seen as responsible for their actions. In 19:10–11 God's overarching sovereignty (Pilate's authority is "given from above") is placed alongside the guilt of Pilate and the greater guilt of the Jews.[41]

The resurrection narratives can be divided into separate scenes centering on soteriology (chap. 20) and ecclesiology (chap. 21).[42] John, like the other evangelists, has shaped the resurrection narratives to summarize his major themes.[43] Jesus' encounter with his disciples in the four scenes is a marvelous example of this. Each scene centers on a descending series of levels of faith and understanding. The "beloved disciple" was at the highest level, for he exemplifies a natural faith that leaps to the proper conclusion even though he and Peter did not yet understand the scriptural basis for Jesus' resurrection (20:8–9). From there the levels of faith drop sharply—Mary's was clouded by sorrow, the Eleven's by fear, and Thomas' by cynicism. Yet at each level Jesus encountered them and met their need. Mary's was overcome by the voice of the Good Shepherd (20:16; cf. 10:3–4), the disciples' by the physical sight of his hands and side (20:20), and Thomas' by touching his wounds (20:27). Throughout John's Gospel Jesus sovereignly encountered each one and called them to faith, in this case a persevering faith in Jesus as the risen Lord. Faith-decision, whether at the moment of conversion or later in the process of discipleship (as in chap. 20), is a blend of God's sovereign call and man's deliberate decision.

CONCLUSION

A current fad in academic circles is a preoccupation with "theology as story,"[44] which we will define as a narrative approach that redefines theology in terms of human drama. While many nonevangelicals use this to deny the propositional content of Scripture, it does not have to be so. We have seen in John a definite tendency to present theology in dramatic form, and this is exactly why this chapter has taken a narrative rather than a topical approach. There is no better way to see the true balance between supposedly opposite sides of the spectrum—namely sovereignty and free will—than to see them side by side in passage after passage. In fact the so-called "sovereignty-responsibility tension" for John is a balance as well as a tension. Therefore we must seek a solution that maintains this balance and does justice to the tension.

It is easy to see how both Calvinists and Arminians have used John to justify their positions. The text again and again sets sovereignty and faith-decision together in theological unity without attempting to resolve the dilemma. It assumes the balance without defining it for the reader. We are left to make sense of it for ourselves. As a result both systems—Calvinist and Arminian—are constantly tempted to read their philosophical solutions into the text and choose those proof-texts that support their own side over those that support the other. It is hoped that this narrative approach has avoided this error and allowed both sides to stand in that larger balance.

For John election is a reality; those who are Jesus' followers have been chosen and given to Christ. Their salvation is not due to their own efforts, for as part of the world, they once were totally depraved, in complete rebellion against God and without hope. Their conversion was an act of God, achieved through their encounter with Christ. Yet at the same time they came to Christ by way of faith-decision; they saw, believed, and thus knew Jesus as their Savior. Moreover, Christ came not just for the elect but as the "light of the world" and as "savior of the world." All people are equally drawn to the Father. Yet only some are saved. How do election and faith-decision interact in the narrative structure of John's Gospel?

The Calvinist approach begins with the doctrine of total depravity in the fourth Gospel. In 5:40 Jesus says, "You refuse to come to me to have life" and in 8:43–44 he says, "You are unable to hear what I say" because "you want to carry out your father's [the devil's] desires." The point then is that the "free will" of man turns always to sin and rejection, so that the only way for anyone to be saved is for God to predestine certain individuals out of the world for salvation. These, then, are irresistibly drawn by God and given to Christ. Christ gave himself as "Savior of the world" but his death is *efficient* only for the elect. To allow the human being a free decision (i.e., "absolute power to the contrary")[45] is to make God contingent and to deny his sovereignty.[46] Moreover this sovereignty must extend to the regenerate state as well and mean that God safeguards all believers, keeping them from apostasy.

However, other solutions are possible. One that must be rejected is that of Schnackenburg, who sees a strong dualism between those who disbelieve and those who commit themselves to Christ and thus are "chosen." He argues that the doctrine of predestination arose in the intertestamental period (e.g., with Qumran) to explain the unbelief of the Jewish people.[47] However, Schnackenburg has no real solution to the dilemma produced by such dualism, and I would argue that the error is in the rigidity of the dualism. Certainly there are two groups: the children of God and the children of Satan (e.g., 8:43–47), but there is no absolute dichotomy. The world is at one and the same time the scene of rejection and the scene of Jesus' saving activity. The Jews are called to faith and judged for their unbelief. Divine election and human decision are compatible and resolvable.

As argued elsewhere in this chapter, the Johannine solution is to be found in God's universal salvific will and "drawing" power. The world is indeed totally depraved and always chooses to reject Christ, but at the same time God seeks the salvation of all the world. How are we to reconcile these conflicting realities? God is an "equal opportunity" convicter who, in drawing all to himself, makes it possible to make a true decision to accept or reject Jesus. Those who accept are "chosen" and "given" to Christ. That decision is not possible without God's drawing power but it is a free moral decision without irresistible coercion. Election is still theologically true but is not absolute, i.e., apart from man's decision. Although foreknowledge is not emphasized by John, it is still part of the larger theological doctrine of predestination.[48] In Pauline terms (Rom. 8:29; cf. 1 Peter 1:2) it is part of this larger picture of predestination but is still distinguishable as the foundation of the doctrine. John does not attempt to harmonize the concepts of predestination and free will but merely assumes that larger unity and the validity of both. The means by which the two may be harmonized is afforded by Paul, and this is why it is included here. In conclusion John presents divine election as working with one's faith-decision rather than producing it. Every person is responsible to accept or reject the divine call.

The same balance is found regarding assurance and perseverance in John.[49] Of all New Testament books, the fourth Gospel contains the strongest emphasis on the believer's security. Yet we must ask whether that security is unconditional (guaranteeing final perseverance) or conditional (based on present perseverance). Due to the strong emphasis on the danger of apostasy and the theme of "abiding" in passages like 15:1–6 and 16:1 one must conclude that John teaches conditional security. Above all, we must state that both systems are coherent, consistent, and viable; each makes perfect sense of the Gospel of John. However, a modified Arminian theology that balances sovereignty and responsibility provides a better explanation of all the data regarding soteriology in the Gospel of John.

NOTES

[1] See D. A. Carson, "The Purpose of the Fourth Gospel: John 20:31 Reconsidered," *Journal of Biblical Literature* (1987), 106:4, in which he argues for an evangelistic purpose centering on the question "Who is the Messiah?"

[2] See I. de la Potterie, "L'arrière-fond du thème johannique de vérité," *Studia Evangelica I* (Berlin: Akademie-Verlag, 1957), 277–94, for the origin of this theme in the Jewish wisdom tradition rather than in Hellenistic thought. As such it is not merely intellectual but demands a moral response to the claims of Jesus.

[3] Rudolf Schnackenburg, *The Gospel According to St John*, trans. Kevin Smith, 3 vols. (New York: Seabury, 1980, 1982), 1:244.

[4] D. A. Carson, *Divine Sovereignty and Human Responsibility: Biblical Perspectives in Tension* (Atlanta: John Knox, 1981), 181–82, argues on the basis of parallel passages in 6:40–45, 66–70; 1 John 5:1 that faith "is the *evidence* of the new birth, not its *cause*" (italics mine). However, this is not demanded by the evidence and, as I will argue below, does not fit the other passages either. Rather, as in Ephesians 2:8–9 divine grace and human faith interact together in conversion.

[5] James Montgomery Boice, *Witness and Revelation in the Gospel of John* (Grand Rapids: Zondervan, 1970), 88–94.

[6] Raymond E. Brown, *The Gospel According to John*, 2 vols. (Anchor Bible: Garden City: Doubleday, 1966), 1:127.

[7] See Carson, *Divine Sovereignty*, 176–78; and Robert Kysar, *The Fourth Evangelist and His Gospel* (Minneapolis: Augsburg, 1975), 225–27.

[8] Nearly all commentators agree that at least 3:16–21 is an editorial clarification of the Nicodemus episode. Some would begin the editorial addition at verse 12 or at verse 14 (Brown, *Gospel According to John*, 1:136 sees tradition and homily interwoven into a single whole in vv. 12–21) but Leon Morris, *The Gospel According to John* (Grand Rapids: Eerdmans, 1971), 228, is certainly correct in stating that the third person style begins at verse 16.

[9] I. Howard Marshall, *Kept by the Power of God: A Study of Perseverance and Falling Away* (London: Epworth, 1969), 175–76.

[10] Morris, *John*, 315.

[11] See the summary of R. Alan Culpepper, *Anatomy of the Fourth Gospel* (Philadelphia: Fortress, 1983), 91–92, who says, "If it were not for the Prologue and the early chapters the reader would be fearful that the forces of unbelief were on the way to complete victory." Yet on the other hand Jesus is presented as in firm control. His destiny is that of suffering and rejection, but that is the path to victory.

[12] Brown, *John*, 1:272, provides a detailed discussion of the blend between sapiential (the bread = revelation) and eucharistic interpretations. I agree with him that both are found in verses 35–50 (with the sapiential being primary) but disagree that verses 51–58 are entirely eucharistic. Even there the sapiential is primary. In verses 51–58, Jesus uses the paschal image of eating the Lamb to say all must partake of him completely in order to have eternal life. See also Brown's defense of the placement of chapter 6 between chapters 5, 7 against Bultmann, et al., who believe it was an interpolation (pp. 235–36).

[13] Peder Borgen, *Bread from Heaven* (SNTS Supplements 10; Leiden: Brill, 1965), 154–58, points out the wisdom background to this section. Jesus is the divine wisdom, the final Torah, which alone can satisfy man's hunger and give life.

[14] Carson, *Divine Sovereignty*, 184. John Murray, *Redemption—Accomplished and Applied* (Grand Rapids: Eerdmans, 1955), 196–97, sees a progression here—they are not cast out, they are given, they will not be lost, they will be raised at the last day. Election and assurance are working together in this passage.

[15] Xavier Léon-Dufour, "Trois chiasmes johanniques," *NTS* 7 (1960–61), 251–53, as in Brown, *John*, 275–76. However, I do not agree with Léon-Dufour and Brown that verses 36–40 are a separate tradition from verse 35.

[16] Schnackenburg, *St. John*, 2:46–47, goes too far when he says, "Everyone the Father 'gives' Jesus will come to him, that is, if he follows God's 'pull' " (cf. 44). There is likewise no hint that coming precedes giving.

[17] C. K. Barrett, *The Gospel According to St. John* (Philadelphia: Westminster, 1978, 2nd ed.), 295.

[18] Morris, *John*, 371n.

[19] Robert Kysar, *John*, Augsburg Commentary (Minneapolis: Augsburg, 1986), 105.

[20] There is some disagreement as to the identity of these "believers," since they are not differentiated from those who sought to kill Jesus in verse 59. Some believe the "they" of verse 33 is a different group, others that the "believers" of verse 31 were different from those of verse 30. Neither has any basis in the text. Most likely this refers to the same levels of belief as 2:23–25 and is a warning to all readers to make certain their "belief" is solid. It appears to be a valid faith in verse 30 but by verses 39–59 they are no longer believing Jews. Perhaps there is implicitly a larger group containing those of verse 30 but with many unbelievers.

[21] See Carson, *Divine Sovereignty*, 127–28, who correctly sees this as a supreme example of God's control of events.

[22] E. Beyreuther, "Shepherd," in the *New International Dictionary of New Testament Theology*, ed. Colin Brown, 3 vols. (Grand Rapids: Zondervan, 1978), 3:565.

[23] Carson, *Divine Sovereignty*, 190.

[24] Marshall, *Kept by the Power*, 178. See also my "Exegetical Notes on Calvinist Texts," in Clark Pinnock, ed., *Grace Unlimited* (Minneapolis: Bethany, 1975), 172–73.

[25] E.g., Robert Shank, *Life in the Son* (Springfield, Mass.: Westcott, 1960), 208–9.

[26] See Barrett, *John*, 386.

[27] Brown, *John*, I, 459.

[28]As Morris, *John*, 623, points out, this is a full-fledged faith "that I am," i.e. in Jesus' deity. Even Judas' betrayal was under his complete control and was to be seen as the fulfillment of prophecy. When the disciples saw that, they would understand Jesus' deity, for only Yahweh could master a situation like that.

[29]See Robert Gundry, "In my Father's House are many *Monai* (John 14, 2)," *Zeitschrift für Neutestamentliche Wissenschaft* 58 (1967): 68–72.

[30]Among many others see Brown, *John*, 2:625–27; and Fernando F. Segovia, "The Structure, *Tendenz* and *Sitz im Leben* of John 13:31–14:31," *Journal of Biblical Literature* 104/3 (1985): 471–92 (especially 482n).

[31]See Schnackenburg, *St. John*, 3:111.

[32]See Barrett, *John*, 474. Brown, *John*, 2:661, states correctly that the options are not mutually exclusive.

[33]Marshall, *Kept by the Power*, 181.

[34]Morris, *John*, 669.

[35]Carson, *Divine Sovereignty*, 194–95.

[36]Ibid., 195–96.

[37]See Osborne, "Exegetical Notes," 184–85.

[38]Robert Glenn Gromacki, *Salvation Is Forever* (Chicago: Moody, 1973), 49–50.

[39]See my "Redactional Trajectories in the Crucifixion Narratives," *Evangelical Quarterly* 51/2 (1979): 80–96 (especially 91–96). The sovereignty theme is highlighted in the universal proclamation on the cross (in Hebrew, Latin, and Greek) of Jesus as "king of the Jews" (19:20–22).

[40]See Brown, *John*, 2:859, for the possibility that the seven inside-outside scenes are arranged in chiastic fashion.

[41]See F. F. Bruce, *The Gospel of John* (Grand Rapids: Eerdmans, 1983), 362, for the likelihood that those who handed Jesus over are the Jews rather than Judas.

[42]For arguments that John himself added chapter 21 as a later appendix, see B. de Solages, *Jean et les Synoptiques* (Leiden: Brill, 1979), 191–235; Grant R. Osborne, "John 21: Case Study for History and Redaction in the Resurrection Narratives," *Gospel Perspectives II: Studies of History and Tradition in the Four Gospels* ed. R. T. France and David Wenham (Sheffield: JSOT, 1981), 293–328 (especially 294–96).

[43]See Grant R. Osborne, *The Resurrection Narratives: A Redactional Approach* (Grand Rapids: Baker, 1984).

[44]See among others John J. Navone, *Toward a Theology of Story* (Slough: St. Paul, 1977); Terrance W. Tilley, *Story Theology* (Wilmington, Del.: Glazier, 1985).

[45]The definition of Carson, *Divine Sovereignty*, 220.

[46]For a recent presentation of this see John Feinberg, "God Ordains All Things" in David and Randall Basinger, eds., *Predestination and Free Will* (Downers Grove: InterVarsity, 1986), 17–43.

[47]Schnackenburg, *John*, 2:259–65; Barrett, "Paradox and Dualism," *Essays on John* (Philadelphia: Westminster, 1982), 98–115 (especially 113–14).

[48]See William Craig's discussion of foreknowledge in terms of "middle knowledge" in chapter 7.

[49]See also the excellent study of Gerald L. Borchert, *Assurance and Warning* (Nashville: Broadman, 1987), where he concludes, "For Christian interpreters to emphasize either of the dimensions and reduce the other is to misunderstand the marvelously balanced message of this Gospel" (see especially 86–152). It is regrettable that this work, so similar in style and approach to my own, arrived the very day I finished this study and I was unable to incorporate it further.

DIVINE COMMANDS, PREDESTINATION, AND MORAL INTUITION

Jerry L. Walls

I

The divine command theory of ethics maintains that morality depends, in some sense, on God. In its most explicit form, the theory holds that the very nature of moral rightness and wrongness derives from the will of God. Whatever God wills is right by virtue of His willing it; whatever he forbids is wrong by virtue of his forbidding it. God's will is thus the standard for right and wrong.

The theory enjoys at least two advantages over nontheistic theories. First, it provides an objective nonnatural account of the nature of right and wrong. It defines these in such a way that they do not depend on human attitudes, nor can they be reduced to natural facts about our world. Second, the theory is relatively clear, for we can grasp the essential claims it makes.

The divine-command theory is often attractive to religious believers, for they instinctively feel that morality is closely connected with the will of God. There are, however, serious difficulties to be faced by those inclined to embrace this theory. The most notorious of these is that it seems to entail that if God commanded us to do something that seemed to us clearly wrong, it would be wrong not to obey. For instance, if God were to command us to torture innocent persons just for the sake of torturing them, it would be wrong not to do so. In such cases, what is right or wrong would be in sharp conflict with our most deeply held sense of what is right and wrong. On the other hand, if we hold that it would be wrong to torture innocent persons just for the sake of torturing them, even if God commanded it, we seem to be admitting a standard of right and wrong that is independent of God's will. In this case, God's will becomes superfluous for determining what is right and wrong.[1]

Many critics have thought this dilemma represents an insurmountable difficulty and have been more than willing to lay the divine-command theory to rest. In recent years, however, the theory has received renewed attention and defense. One of the most interesting attempts to revive the theory comes from Robert Adams, who proposes what he calls a modified version of the divine-command theory. According to the modified theory, it is the commands of a *loving* God that are the standard of right and wrong.[2] A loving God, it is presumed, would not command things that seem obviously cruel or wicked.

In this chapter, I wish to explore the connection between divine-command ethics and a particular theological doctrine, namely, predestination. I will begin by sketching the views of Luther and Calvin in this regard and then turn to compare the views of Wesley. I will contend that the doctrine of predestination held by Luther and Calvin corresponds to, and shares the problems of, the traditional divine command theory. Wesley, by contrast, construes predestination in a way that parallels the modified theory. I will further argue that the position taken by Wesley is preferable to that of Luther and Calvin.

II

Martin Luther held a straightforward, uncompromising view of predestination. He stated his view most clearly in *Bondage of the Will*, the book he himself considered his best theological work.

As the title implies, the work is concerned to establish that the human will is not free. To the contrary, mankind is in bondage to sin and Satan. Consequently, no one is able to obey God or do the good. Fallen people are "free" only to sin. Because mankind is in this condition, moreover, no one is free to choose salvation.

It is this reality that forms the background of Luther's view of predestination. Since no one can choose salvation, it is entirely up to God to choose who will be saved, and who damned. Those who are chosen for salvation are freed from the bondage of sin by God's grace. The rest are chosen for damnation and are accordingly left in bondage.

Luther's doctrine in this regard is well known, and of course this brief sketch hardly captures its complexity and sophistication. It is sufficient, however, to point up a serious problem for Luther's view, namely, that it offends our sense of justice. On the face of it, it does not seem right that God should choose to damn persons who were never free either to choose good or to obey God. It does not seem right that salvation and damnation are distributed solely on the basis of God's arbitrary will, independent of anything human beings do or do not do.

Luther himself was quite sensitive to this difficulty, and he struggled profoundly in his efforts to resolve it. This is obvious from his following words.

> Doubtless it gives the greatest possible offence to common sense or natural reason, that God, Who is proclaimed as being full of mercy and goodness, and so on, should of His own mere will abandon, harden, and damn men, as though He delighted in the sins and great eternal torments of such poor wretches. It seems an iniquitous, cruel, intolerable thought to think of God; and it is this that has been a stumbling block to so many great men down the ages. And who would not stumble at it? I have stumbled at it myself more than once, down to the deepest pit of despair, so that I wished I had never been made a man.[3]

And yet, despite the powerful conflict between his view of predestination and his moral sensibilities, Luther maintained that there is no injustice in the way God metes out salvation and damnation. To those who thought otherwise, Luther replied:

> God is He for Whose will no cause or ground may be laid down as its rule and standard; for nothing is on a level with it or above it, but it is itself the rule for all things. If any rule or standard, or cause or ground, existed for it, it could no longer be the will of God. What God wills is not right because He ought, or was bound, so to will; on the contrary, what takes place must be right, because he so wills it.[4]

It is right, then, for God to predestine anyone he will to damnation simply because whatever God wills is right. God's will is the standard for right, so whatever He wills is right by definition.

Luther does not expect us to understand such mysteries as God's secret predestination. "It is not for us to inquire into these mysteries, but to adore them."[5] Nevertheless, Luther does not leave us with the prospect of being forever baffled by God's manner of dealing with human beings. Near the very end of his book, Luther claims that in the "light of glory," we will clearly see that God was just in his damnation of sinners. That is to say, we will ultimately perceive God's justice in this regard when confronted with God's fuller revelation of himself in the next life. It should not surprise us if this seems incomprehensible to us now. Since God is inaccessible to human understanding, it is inevitable that his justice eludes our grasp. To strengthen our faith in God's justice, Luther offers a parallel case. In the "light of nature" it is incomprehensible that there can exist a just God who governs the world, since the good often suffer while the wicked flourish. If a just God governs the world, it seems that the good should prosper while the wicked should suffer. This difficulty, however, is cleared up by the "light of grace." For in this light, we learn about a life that is to follow this life, in which the wicked will be judged and punished for the evil they have done. Since this life is only a precursor of the life to come, the difficulty involving the success of the wicked vanishes.

In a similar way, Luther claims the "light of glory" will dispel the seeming injustice of God's predestination. The light of glory will clear up what is incomprehensible in the light of grace, just as the light of grace cleared up what was incomprehensible in the light of nature.[6]

Let us turn now to Calvin. His view of predestination is essentially the same as Luther's, and for our purposes there is no need to be detained by the distinctions between them. What I want to emphasize is that he responded to the critics of his doctrine of predestination in much the same way that Luther did.

> It therefore seems to them that men have reason to expostulate with God if they are predestined to eternal death solely by his decision, apart from their own merit. If thoughts of this sort ever occur to pious men, they will be sufficiently armed to break their force even by the one consideration that it is very wicked merely to investigate the causes of God's will. For his will is, and rightly ought to be, the cause of all things that are. . . . For God's will is so much the highest rule of righteousness that whatever he wills, by the very fact that he wills it, must be considered righteous.[7]

Calvin and Luther share the conviction that it is improper, and even impious, to question whether God can be just, while choosing to damn anyone he will. Calvin agrees with Luther that it is not for us to inquire, but to adore. But more significant is the fact that Calvin also supports his view of predestination by appealing to the notion that whatever God wills is, by the very fact that He wills it, right.

Calvin goes on, a few lines later, to claim: "And now we do not advocate the fiction of 'absolute might'; because this is profane, it ought rightly to be hateful to us. We fancy no lawless god who is a law unto himself."[8] These lines are somewhat puzzling, to say the least, in view of his earlier remarks. He seems here to be denying that God has absolute authority over the moral law. It is obvious that Calvin wants to deny the apparent undesirable implication of his earlier claims. However, it is not at all clear how his two claims fit together.[9]

In any case, I hope it is clear that there is an interesting connection between divine-command ethics and the doctrine of predestination. Luther and Calvin attempt to vindicate their conception of predestination by appealing to the main principle of the traditional divine command theory of morality: that God's will is the ultimate standard for right and wrong.

As we noted above, the most serious problem with the divine-command theory is that it entails that if God were to command something that seems clearly wrong, it would be the right thing to do. The theory of predestination espoused by Luther and Calvin has the same sort of problem. It requires us to believe God is right in unconditionally damning whomever he will, even though this deeply offends our sense of justice.

In a sense, the problem is more pressing for Luther and Calvin. In traditional divine-command ethics, it is usually granted to be only a *possibility* that God might command something that seems obviously wicked to us. For Luther and Calvin, it is not a mere possibility, but an *actual fact*, that God is doing that which seems wicked to us, and is requiring us to believe it is just.

Or to put it another way, the problem that God might command something that seems wicked is not faced as a consequence of first embracing the claim that God's will is the standard for right and wrong. Rather, the claim that God is doing something that seems wicked is embraced first, and the notion that his will is the standard of right and wrong is invoked to justify the claim.

I want to stress, however, that I am not claiming that Luther and Calvin held a thoroughgoing divine-command theory of right and wrong. Other elements are present in their moral thought, such as the natural-law tradition.[10] Whether they are fully consistent in their moral thought is not my concern here. I only want to insist that the central concept in divine command ethics plays a prominent role in their defense of their doctrine of predestination.

III

John Wesley's view of predestination was fundamentally at odds with that of Calvin and Luther. Some of his sharpest polemics were directed against the doctrine of unconditional predestination. Indeed, his polemical concerns are so much at the forefront in his writings on predestination that it is easy to overlook the fact that he also expressed positive views on the subject. As opposed to Luther and Calvin, Wesley put forward a conditional view of predestination, according to which God extends his grace to all persons. God genuinely desires all persons to be saved, so none are damned because of God's choice to reject them. The essence of Wesley's view is stated in the following passage:

> I believe election means . . . a divine appointment of some men
> to eternal happiness. But I believe this election to be condition-
> al, as well as the reprobation opposite thereto. I believe the
> eternal decree concerning both is expressed in those words: "He
> that believeth shall be saved; he that believeth not shall be
> damned." And this decree, without doubt, God will not
> change, and men cannot resist.[11]

One of the main reasons Wesley was so opposed to the
doctrine of unconditional predestination was that he thought it
destroyed any meaningful attribution of love and justice to God.
Indeed, Wesley thought the doctrine represented "God as worse
than the devil; more false, more cruel, and more unjust."[12]

As we saw above, Luther, at least in some of his moments,
would sympathize with Wesley on this point. Ultimately, however, Luther resisted the force of his own convictions and accepted
the doctrine of unconditional predestination. He did so because he
believed the doctrine was taught in Scripture, and consequently
must be believed. The depth of the difference between Wesley on
the one hand and Luther and Calvin on the other is evident in
Wesley's response to the claim that Scripture proves unconditional
predestination:

> Whatever that scripture proves, it never can prove this;
> whatever its true meaning be, this cannot be its true mean-
> ing. . . . But this I know, better it were to say it had no sense at
> all, than to say it had such a sense as this. . . . Let it mean what
> it will, it cannot mean that the Judge of all the world is unjust.
> No scripture can mean that God is not love, or that his mercy is
> not over all his works; that is, whatever it prove beside, no
> scripture can prove [unconditional] predestination.[13]

For Wesley, that God is loving to all people was as certain as
anything he believed. As he put it at the very beginning of one of
his sermons: "Nothing is more sure, than that as 'the Lord is
loving to every man,' so 'his mercy is over all his works.'"[14]
Wesley was equally certain that a God who loved all people
would not unconditionally damn any of them. The very nature of
love is such that this is simply unthinkable. While Wesley thought
the doctrine of unconditional predestination clashed sharply with
God's truth and sincerity, it agreed "least of all with the scriptural
account of his love and goodness." And love is the "attribute
which God peculiarly claims, wherein he glories above all the
rest." But the whole notion of love is utterly perverted if it is held
that a loving God unconditionally damns some persons. "Is not
this such love as makes your blood run cold? . . . Can you think,
that the loving, the merciful God, ever dealt thus with any soul
which he hath made?"[15]

Now we are in a position to see how Wesley would answer

the claim that God can rightfully damn anyone he wishes to damn simply because whatever he wills is right by definition. To this he would respond that we cannot consider God's sovereign will in isolation from what we know of his justice and mercy.

> For Scripture nowhere speaks of this single attribute [sovereignty], as separate from the rest. Much less does it anywhere speak of the sovereignty of God as singly disposing the eternal states of men. No, no; in this awful work, God proceeds according to the *known* rules of his justice and mercy; but never assigns his sovereignty as the cause why any man is punished with everlasting destruction. (italics mine)[16]

If God cannot rightfully damn anyone he will, does this mean there is a standard of morality distinct from God to which he must conform? Wesley would firmly reject such a suggestion.

To see why this is so, let us consider Wesley's account of the relation between God's will and the moral law. While he held that there is "nothing arbitrary" in the moral law, he insisted that "the whole and every part thereof is totally dependent upon [God's] will." There is nothing arbitrary about the law because "it is adapted, in all respects, to the nature of things." So in a sense, the moral law depends on the nature of things. But it ultimately depends on God's will. For if the standard of right and wrong "depends on the nature and relations of things, then it must depend on God, or the will of God; because those things themselves, with all their relations, are the works of his hands."

These remarks represent the essence of Wesley's response to the question whether a thing is right because God wills it, or whether he wills it because it is right. Although he feared "this celebrated question is more curious than useful," he addressed it directly as follows.

> It seems then, that the whole difficulty arises from considering God's will as distinct from God: otherwise it vanishes away. For none can doubt but God is the cause of the law of God. But the will of God is God himself. It is God considered as willing thus or thus.[17]

It is not immediately clear how these remarks address the celebrated question. Which horn of the dilemma, if either, does Wesley select?

The key to answering this question, I think, is Wesley's affirmation that "God is the cause of the law of God." The law, in other words, is not autonomous. Since this is so, the bottom line for Wesley is that a thing is right because God wills it, and not the other way around.

Wesley hastens, however, to avoid the implication that God might—since his will is the standard of right and wrong—will something that seems clearly wicked. He does so by again refusing to consider the will of God in isolation. We can think of the will of God only in light of what we know of God himself. The possibility that God might will something that seems clearly wicked is ruled out because the fact about God of which we are *most certain* is that he is loving to all people. God is essentially loving, so to consider his will is to consider a loving God willing such and such. Nothing can be ascribed to the will of God that is incompatible with his nature as a loving Being.

God's creation of human beings with a certain nature was, to be sure, an act of his sovereign will. But because God created humans as he did, his will for them depends, in a sense, on the nature he gave them. As an essentially loving Being, God's will for people must fit their nature in the sense that it is conducive to their well-being and happiness. The moral law, Wesley emphasizes, flows from the fountain of God's love and goodness.[18]

Because God's moral law is adapted to our nature, it could not support our happiness if it were different. So given the nature we have, God could not will for us a different moral law. Such a different law could not be right, and we should reject the claim that such a law would be right if God willed it, simply because whatever God wills is right. Of course, this does not rule out the possibility that God might create beings who are essentially different from humans. If God were to create such beings, he would give them a law to fit *their* nature, and presumably this law would differ in certain respects from the moral law God has given us. This does not, however, affect the point that God could not, as an essentially loving Being, prescribe *for us* a different moral law than the one he has prescribed.

For analogous reasons, it would not be right for God to damn anyone unconditionally. If God were unconditionally to damn someone, it would be clear that he would not be treating that person in a way that fits his own nature as a loving God. Consequently, we know it would not be right for God to treat any person in such a way, and we can be sure that he in fact does not do so.

IV

Thus far I have tried to show that there are some interesting connections between divine command ethics and the doctrine of predestination. We have seen that Luther and Calvin defend a doctrine of unconditional predestination by appealing to the premise that whatever God does is right since God is the standard of right and wrong. They appealed to this principle because they recognized that their account of predestination was in conflict with the moral sensitivities of most persons, including, at times, themselves. Thus, their position illustrates the difficulty of traditional divine command ethics; namely, that if God were to will something that seems clearly wicked, it must be accepted as right.

Wesley, on the other hand insisted on a conditional view of predestination. He rejected outright the idea that it would be right for God to damn persons at will. Accordingly, Wesley defended a view of the relationship between God's will and the nature of right and wrong that differs significantly from that of Luther and Calvin. Both in his writings on predestination and in his more general account of the moral law, Wesley argued that God's will cannot be considered apart from what we know about God himself. Although God's will is the ultimate source of right and wrong, we cannot appeal to the will of God to justify something unless it is consistent with what we know of his character as a just and loving Being.

I want to suggest that Wesley's views parallel and accord with what Adams has called a "modified" divine-command theory of ethical wrongness.[19] Adams' essential modification, as we noted above, is the qualification that right and wrong are defined by the will of a *loving* God. Let us explore this more fully.

Adams introduces a number of considerations that indicate that his modification is a perfectly natural one. One such consideration is that the believer's obedient attitude toward the will of God is nurtured within the framework of a community in which it is assumed that God loves us. Without this assumption, the concept of the will of God would not have the function of giving meaning to the notions of right and wrong. As Adams puts it:

> But one of the reasons why the concept of the will of God can function as it does is that the love which God is believed to have toward man arouses in the believer certain attitudes of love toward God and devotion to His will. If the believer thinks about the unthinkable but logically possible situation in which God commands cruelty for its own sake, he finds that in relation to that kind of command of God he cannot take up the same attitude, and that the concept of the will or commands of God could not then have the same function in his life.[20]

These remarks are reminiscent of Wesley's claim that we cannot consider the will of God in isolation from our knowledge that God is loving to all men. Adams' suggestion that we could not have a proper attitude toward God's will if we thought of him as commanding cruelty for its own sake recalls Wesley's comment that the thought of God's unconditionally damning sinners makes "one's blood run cold." In the same vein, Wesley is doubtful that anyone can seriously think "the loving, the merciful God, ever dealt thus with any soul."

Another important element of Adams' modified theory is his conception that believers value some things independently of God's commands. "If the believer will not say that it would be wrong not to practice cruelty for its own sake if God commanded it, that is because he values kindness, and has a revulsion for cruelty, in a way that is at least to some extent independent of his belief that God commands kindness and forbids cruelty."[21]

The believer's positive feeling for kindness and revulsion for cruelty are independent of God in the sense that he instinctively forms these attitudes apart from any awareness that God commands the one and forbids the other. These attitudes are naturally present in normal persons and are fundamental components of their most basic moral intuitions. It is because the believer naturally values kindness that he readily resonates to the claim that God loves us. His fundamental moral intuitions are part of the background in his willing acceptance of the will of a loving God as the measure of right and wrong.

And yet the believer will ultimately say that his valuing kindness and abhorring cruelty is not independent of God. For God has created us and is the ultimate source of our moral sensibilities. It is reasonable to believe, as Adams puts it, that "God has created our moral faculties to reflect his commands."[22]

Now then, Wesley's emphatic rejection of unconditional predestination on the grounds that it depicts God as cruel and as worse than the devil suggests a similarly independent revulsion from cruelty and positive evaluation of kindness. The same may be said for his insistence that Scripture cannot prove unconditional predestination. His native sense of the nature of cruelty, love, and justice apparently played a decisive role in his interpretation of Scripture. Scripture simply could not mean that God was not loving to all people. It could not mean that God would treat anyone in a way that seems clearly cruel and unjust to us.

Those unfamiliar with Wesley's writings may be tempted to conclude from this that the ultimate authority in Wesley's theology was not Scripture, but his own judgment. This charge, however, will not stick, for Wesley's theology is thoroughly biblical and it is clear that Scripture functioned as his primary authority. He offered extensive scriptural support for his doctrine of conditional predestination while maintaining that unconditional reprobation is "utterly irreconcilable to the whole scope and tenor both of the Old and New Testament."[23] Of course, it can be debated whether or not Wesley correctly discerned the "tenor" of the Old and New Testaments. But it cannot be seriously doubted that he felt as much compelled by Scripture as by his moral sensibilities to reject the doctrine of unconditional predestination.

V

We have seen that Wesley's view of predestination is similar in interesting ways to the modified divine-command theory of ethics, just as Luther and Calvin's account of predestination corresponds to a more traditional theory of divine command ethics. Both Wesley and the modified-divine command theory rely heavily on God's love to block difficulties that otherwise arise. Now, then, is this appeal to love a legitimate move? One critic of the move has argued that the appeal to love is not an option for a truly consistent divine-command theory. For such an appeal produces a deep tension at the heart of the theory. John Chandler writes as follows:

> I would further suggest that the [Divine Command Theory] has traditionally been associated with a particular conception of God's nature, one which emphasizes His absolute power and freedom, and consequently the unknowability of His will by human reason. . . . Theories which emphasize God's love on the other hand suppose a greater grasp of His nature by analogy with human nature, and a lesser gulf between world and God. If this is correct, the modified [Divine Command Theory] yokes together fundamentally alien conceptions of God, the world, and morality.[24]

I think Chandler has correctly identified the major line of division between the two positions. The issue is not only what God is like, but also, what we can know about God. It is, in other words, an epistemological issue.

Chandler is mistaken, however, in his charge that the modified divine-command theory yokes together fundamentally alien conceptions of God. It is rather that the former conception of God he describes is rejected in favor of the latter. It is not that the modified theory tries to have it both ways.

Chandler seems to assume it is meaningless to appeal to God's *will* unless we allow that God could will things that altogether violate our sense of what is right and wrong. But it must be remembered that the appeal is to *God's* will, and that assumes we know something about God. The appeal is not simply to an unattached, abstract will, but to the will of a personal God who is believed to be not only just but also loving.

So the questions are these: (1) Do we know that God is loving as well as just? (2) Is our intuitive sense of love and justice sufficiently reliable that we can have some knowledge of the kinds of things God would not do?

I take it as uncontroversial among Christians that God is both loving and just. The real question seems to be the second one, namely, whether we have a reliable grasp of the nature of love and justice. Notice, however, that our affirmative answer to the first question will not have much substance unless we also give an affirmative answer to the second. For if we do not have a sufficiently reliable grasp of the nature of love and justice to be sure that God would not treat us in certain ways, then there seems to be little meaning to the claim that God is both loving and just. If we believe God treats some of us in ways that we would normally judge to be cruel or wicked, then it is simply unclear what we mean when we say he is loving and just. In this case, we are not assuming we have a sound grasp of God's nature "by analogy with human nature." God's love and justice are one thing; our understanding of these notions is quite another. On the other hand, those who assume we have a sound grasp of the nature of God's love and justice will be certain that God will not treat us in ways that seem clearly cruel or wicked.

It does not follow, however, if our fundamental grasp of the nature of love and justice is sound, that God's commands are superfluous. For we do not have detailed knowledge of the nature and relations of all things, and consequently, we do not have a full understanding of what is loving and just in many cases. God is the author of all creaturely natures and the designer of the relations obtaining among creatures. We must rely on God's commands to know fully what we ought to do in order to act in accordance with love and justice.

Moreover, our native moral faculties have been affected by the fall and are thus not *wholly* reliable. We need the benefit of revelation to refine our moral intuitions. What we learn from Scripture deepens, enhances, and modifies our intuitive grasp of love and justice.[25] Nevertheless, if we assume we have a sound grasp of God's nature by analogy with human nature, there should not be a fundamental clash between our sense of love and justice, and God's actual love and justice. For our sense of love and justice in some sense remains a reflection of God's moral nature.

Those who hold that God could will something that to us seems utterly wicked do so on the assumption that our moral intuitions, even operating at their best, are not an accurate reflection of God's moral nature. The above quote from Luther is a good example of this notion. As we recall, he admitted that God's justice does not seem like justice to us, and indeed, God's unconditional predestination of some to damnation seems cruel to us. But both Luther and Calvin insist that our moral judgments are mistaken and are not to be trusted on this matter. We are to believe God is loving and just because we have been assured that he is, even though it seems evident to us that he is not.

In maintaining this, Luther and Calvin represent a view we could call "moral fideism." They are willing to grant that the deliverances of the Christian faith may be sharply at odds with even our clearest moral judgments, but they insist that we are to believe those deliverances anyway.

By contrast, we could call the view that we do have a basically sound grasp of God's love and justice "moral reliabilism." Wesley is a good representative of this view, for it was axiomatic for him that our clearest moral intuitions are reliable. He forcefully rejected the suggestion that our most deeply rooted moral judgments may be deceptive. This is quite obvious in his critical discussion of some of the theories of determinism that were popular in his day. Those defenders of determinism conceded that we have a deeply ingrained sense that we are free, and that freedom is an essential presupposition of moral blame and commendation. Nevertheless, they maintained, we are not really free, for all our actions are determined, down to the last detail. If this is the case, Wesley charged, God is " 'the father of lies!' Such you doubtless represent him, when you say . . . that the feelings which he has interwoven with our inmost nature are . . . illusive!"[26] It is simply unthinkable for Wesley that God has created us in such a way that our strongest moral feelings cannot be trusted. Such a thought, as he put it (in words also used elsewhere), "makes one's blood run cold."

But what about Luther's suggestion that in "the light of glory" we will see the justice of unconditional predestination? Luther's suggestion, remember, is that this will be analogous to the way in which "the light of grace" resolved the seeming injustice perceived in "the light of nature." In the light of grace, we understand that the wicked will be punished in the next life, and this resolves the apparent injustice that arises from the fact that the wicked often prosper in this life.

It is hard to see how this analogy gives us reason to believe unconditional predestination can be just. The point of the analogy seems to be that the revelation of the afterlife provides us with new information that gives us a new perspective on the injustice apparently discerned by the "light of nature." In other words, we come to understand that the prosperity of the wicked in this life is not the final word.

However, one's salvation or damnation *is* the final word, so to speak. There is nothing beyond eternal salvation and damnation that can redress the seeming injustice of some simply being chosen for damnation. So there does not appear to be a fitting analogy between the light of grace and the light of glory.

Luther is correct, however, to maintain that it is not always easy to discern God's justice, and indeed, that on the surface God's ways may appear unjust. Such cases do try our faith. In maintaining that a loving God would not will things that seem clearly wicked to us, I do not mean to imply that there is never any tension between God's ways and our moral judgments.

But there is a difference between the difficulty of seeing how God could be either loving or just while willing a certain thing and the certainty that he would be neither loving nor just if he willed that thing. In the former, we can think of at least some possible reason why a good God might so will, but in the latter we cannot.

Consider in this light God's command to sacrifice Isaac. This certainly tried Abraham's faith. The New Testament informs us, however, that Abraham's faith remained intact because he believed God would raise Isaac from the dead if he sacrificed him (Heb. 11:17–19). He believed God would do something to keep his promise to give him descendants through Isaac. If he had to sacrifice Isaac, Isaac's death would not be the final word. God would do something to rectify the matter.

But again, with respect to God's choice to damn at will certain persons, there is no conceivable way to rectify the seeming injustice of the situation. We have no reason at all to hope that God might choose in the end to spare such persons, as he did Isaac, or raise them from the death of damnation to eternal life. So the point remains that unconditional damnation is not like the cases in which faith is tried. The seeming injustice is not such that we have any reason to hope it will eventually be rectified. The injustice is not merely on the surface but seems to be intractable, for damnation is the ultimate, irreparable tragedy.

But perhaps Luther's suggestion can be interpreted another way. Perhaps what he is saying is that the light of glory will reveal, not new information concerning the fate of the damned, but rather a new understanding of the information we already have. Maybe it is only the corrupting influence of sin that prevents us from seeing how God can be perfectly just while unconditionally predestining some people for damnation. Once our moral faculties are corrected by the removal of sin, we will see things in a fundamentally different way. It will then be clear that creatures could not possibly have legitimate grounds for complaint against their Creator, no matter how he treated them. It was only our sinful pride that ever inclined us to think otherwise. In this light, the justice of God's predestination will be clear to us.

Some may find this plausible; I do not. While I do not deny the corrupting influence of sin on our moral faculties, I would argue nevertheless that our moral faculties are part of the remaining image of God in man. As such they are a basically reliable reflection of God's love and justice. It is not sinful rebellion but sound moral insight to insist that a just God, not to mention a loving one, would not unconditionally damn anyone.[27]

VI

So a parting of the ways between the two views is finally inevitable. The disagreement over whether our revulsion against the doctrine of unconditional predestination registers a sound moral judgment, or whether it is to be attributed to sin is yet another instance of the fundamental differences between what I have called moral reliabilism on the one hand and moral fideism on the other.

The differences between the two views are obviously deep and there is no simple means of resolving the conflict. In the end, perhaps the best we can do is lay out clearly the two views with the differences in full view in order to allow the undecided a fair opportunity to determine which is more convincing. Neither side should be under the illusion that there is a knockdown argument that will carry the day. Exegetical considerations are important, but they will not fully resolve the issue. There are competent exegetes on both sides, and part of what is at issue is the correct interpretation of several controversial passages of Scripture. To me it seems clearly preferable to go with the reliabilists in adopting an understanding of Scripture that is compatible with our clear moral intuitions. Since God is the source of both, I would urge, the two should mesh. But this claim will hardly persuade those with fideistic inclinations.

Or to put it another way, I think most persons who engage this controversy will admit that the doctrine of unconditional predestination "makes one's blood run cold." Yet it must be recognized that only those who find positive moral significance in such a reaction will have a reason to follow Wesley on the doctrine of predestination, rather than Luther and Calvin.[28]

NOTES

[1] In the foregoing summary, I largely follow Robert Merrihew Adams, "Moral Arguments for Theistic Belief," in C. F. Delaney, ed., *Rationality and Religious Belief* (Notre Dame: University of Notre Dame Press, 1979), 117–20.

[2] Adams has laid out his theory in his paper "A Modified Divine Command Theory of Ethical Wrongness," in Paul Helm, ed., *Divine Commands and Morality* (Oxford: Oxford University Press, 1981), 83–108. See also Edward Wierenga, "A Defensible Divine Command Theory," *Noûs* 17 (1983): 387–407. For a full statement and defense of the divine-command theory, which does not appeal to God's love, see Philip L. Quinn, *Divine Commands and Moral Requirements*, (Oxford: Clarendon, 1978).

[3] Martin Luther, *Bondage of the Will*, trans. J. I. Packer and O. R. Johnston, (Revell, 1957), 217.

[4] Ibid., 209.

[5] Ibid., 208.

[6] Luther espouses this in ibid., 314–18.

[7] John Calvin, *Institutes of the Christian Religion,* trans. Ford Lewis Battles, ed. John T. McNeill (Philadelphia: Westminster, 1961), 3.23.2.

[8] Ibid.

[9] In his translation of the *Institutes* (London: Clarke, 1949), Henry Beveridge rendered the last line of the quote just cited as follows: "We do not imagine God to be lawless. He is a law to himself"; this translation removes some of the puzzlement.

[10] See John T. McNeill, "Natural Law in the Teaching of the Reformers," *Journal of Religion* 26 (1946): 168–82.

[11] John Wesley, *Works* 1872; reprint (Grand Rapids: Baker, 1979), 10:210. See also Wesley's sermon "On Predestination." *Works,* 6:225–30.

[12] Ibid., 7:382.

[13] Ibid., 7:383.

[14] Ibid., 6:241. The Scripture verse in this passage is one that Wesley often cited. It is from Psalm 145:9.

[15] All quotes in this paragraph are from ibid., 10:227, 229.

[16] Ibid., 10:220; cf. 235, 362.

[17] This quote, as well as those in the previous paragraph, are from ibid., 5:440–41. They appear in his sermon "The Origin, Nature, Property, and Use of the Law." This question, of course, has been with us since Plato. See *Euthyphro,* 10a.

[18] *Works,* 5:441–42.

[19] Adams calls his theory a theory of "wrongness" for convenience. He says it could also be developed as a theory of ethical obligatoriness or permittedness. See Quinn, *Divine Commands,* 83.

[20] Ibid., 88.

[21] Ibid., 93.

[22] Ibid., 115; cf. also 91.

[23] Wesley, *Works,* 10:211; For Wesley's interpretation of some of the passages often used to support unconditional predestination, see 217ff.

[24] John Chandler, "Divine Command Theories and the Appeal to Love," *American Philosophical Quarterly,* 22/3 (July 1985): 238.

[25] For a suggestive discussion of the interplay between our basic moral insights and what we learn from revelation, see Basil Mitchell, *Morality: Religious and Secular* (Oxford: Clarendon, 1980), 145–56.

[26] Wesley, *Works,* 10:471. I should emphasize that Wesley believed we are free only by grace. God extends to fallen man grace that enables him to believe, do the good, and so on.

[27] Some of the material in this section expands on arguments originally presented in my article, "The Free Will Defense, Calvinism, Wesley and the Goodness of God," *Christian Scholar's Review,* 13/1:19–33.

[28] I am grateful to Philip Quinn, William Abraham, and Edward Wierenga for helpful comments on an earlier draft of this paper.

FREEDOM, JUSTICE, AND MORAL RESPONSIBILITY

Bruce R. Reichenbach

John Calvin's description of the human predicament evokes a wide range of human emotions—from the heights of a humility that derives from the recognition that we are particularly God-blessed to the shattering depths of despair because we are totally depraved. "First, [a person] should consider the end of his being created and endued with such estimable gifts [reason, intelligence, will]; a reflection which may excite him to the consideration of Divine worship, and of a future life. Secondly, he should examine his own ability, or rather his want of ability, the view of which may confound and almost annihilate him."[1] We have, for all intents and purposes, lost our original abilities. Particularly in regard to that which has to do with our moral and spiritual life, we can do nothing good, but instead are surrounded by "miserable necessity" (2.2.1)—we cannot but sin.

The present human predicament results, in part, from the heinous sin of our first parents. Their infidelity to God, disobedience to his command, and rebellion against his rule not only plunged themselves into misery, but dragged down their posterity with them, endowing their successors with the awful legacy of original sin.[2]

The effects of the fall are staggering. The fall obliterated the divine image, resulting in "loss of wisdom, strength, sanctity, truth, and righteousness" (2.1.5). We are so "totally over-whelmed" that "no part is free from sin" (2.1.9). The abilities with which the Creator originally endowed us are either hopelessly disfigured or totally destroyed. Our reason is partly, if not largely, debilitated. Only through the general assistance of the Spirit can reason arrive at truth about temporal things. God graciously endows people with the talents needed to know the liberal sciences, the mechanical arts, mathematics, civil politics, domestic economy, and logic. Only by divine illumination can we know God, ascertain his favor and grace toward us, and regulate our lives according to God's laws. Without it, we are "blinder than moles" (2.2.18). The will likewise is affected, so that we are "bound with the firmest bonds" (2.2.27). The fall destroyed our liberty of will[3] and has so polluted and depraved us that without divine grace we cannot do any good thing (2.2.27; 2.3.5; 2 Cor. 3:5; John 15:5).

This state of fallenness leaves us convicted and condemned. "Our nature being so totally vitiated and depraved, we are, on account of this very corruption, considered as convicted and justly condemned in the sight of God" (2.1.8). We are involved in Adam's sin, not only in terms of its polluting consequences, but also in terms of his guilt and punishment. This condition extends to all, even newborns, for "though they have not yet produced the fruits of their iniquity, yet they have the seed of it within them" (which is accounted as sin in God's sight) and therefore are "odious and abominable to God" (2.1.8).

But if this accurately describes the human condition, cannot we plead guiltlessness? Our plea is not based on any alleged sinlessness, for "all have sinned and fall short of the glory of God" (Rom. 3:23). Rather, it is based on our being determined to sin, on our inability not to sin. If we cannot but do evil, if we are impotent from the moment of our birth, are we not guiltless and hence unjustly condemned for the evil we do? If we sin because of our totally depraved nature, and if we did not create or choose that nature but unwillingly and unwittingly inherited it from our first parents, are we not excused from the moral reprobation accruing to the acts that derive from that nature? Cannot we charge our predicament and liability to another?

Calvin says no. We are all *deservedly* involved in Adam's guilt. "This liableness to punishment arises not from the delinquency of another. . . . It is not to be understood as if we, though innocent, were undeservedly loaded with the guilt of his sin; but, because we are all subject to a curse, in consequence of his transgression, he is therefore said to have involved us in guilt" (2.1.8).

But where is the justice in this? First, why do we deserve the guilt that derives from Adam's act? Calvin suggests that we deserve it because we are all subject to the curse resulting from Adam's transgression. But why do we deserve the curse? It cannot be because we share in his guilt, for that would be arguing in a circle. Is it because we sinned in Adam? But in what way have we so sinned? Calvin agrees that we did not participate as individuals in his personal guilt. He sees original sin more in terms of something that is transmitted ("communicated," "transfused," "infected"). Is it then simply because we are human? Calvin writes that we, as Adam's descendants, are infected by his sin. Since we are formed of flesh (carnally generated from corrupted nature), we are flesh (of the sinful world) (2.1.6; John 3:5–6). But if we inherit the curse and guilt in this manner, the original problem remains, namely, how can we be held accountable for it, for it is merely a dimension of our procreated humanness.[4] We are no more morally responsible for our human predicament of original sin than we would be responsible for the color of our eyes, a genetic deformity, or our gender.

Second, if we are guilty from birth, so that even without doing anything else we are justly condemned by God, what have we contributed to that guilt? If you say, "We contributed additional wrong acts," ["depravity never ceases in us, but is perpetually producing new fruits, those works of the flesh" (2.1.8)] that does not relieve the problem, for not only is the guilt already determined and the sentence passed, but those additional wrong acts result from our impotence to do any good, a condition that likewise arises from our inherited nature. Again, the problem remains: how can we be justly condemned if our evil deeds are necessitated by a nature about which we could and can do nothing?

But there is more to the story. The fall of Eve and Adam was no accident, no unexpected event. It was predetermined by God, part of his eternal plan. "For the first man fell because the Lord had determined it was so expedient. The reason for this determination is unknown to us. Yet it is certain that he determined thus, only because he foresaw it would tend to the just illustration of the glory of his name. . . . Man falls, therefore, according to the appointment of Divine Providence; but he falls by his own fault" (3.23.8; also 3.23.4).

Not only did God foreordain the fall of our first parents, he also foreordained our own sins. God ordains and commands each event. "All events are governed by the secret counsel of God" (1.16.2).[5] He regulates and directs the actions of each individual creature to the specific and proper end by his will, so that each person's every action is disposed by his deliberate will, ultimately to achieve the divine purpose.

This is not to be understood in the sense that God is merely the first cause of motion, or that he only influences nature, which then on its own achieves its end. Calvin argues that when foreordination is coupled with omnipotence, God exerts his power and efficacy in both the inanimate and animate world. He is "vigilant, efficacious, operative, and engaged in continual action" (1.16.3). God actively governs the world; he is causally effective in bringing about the events he has foreordained. "The whole may be summed up thus; that, as the will of God is said to be the cause of all things, his providence is established as the governor in all the counsels and works of men, so that it not only exerts its power in the elect, who are influenced by the Holy Spirit, but also compels the compliance of the reprobate" (1.18.2).[6]

But if we are foreordained to sin, and if God in his omnipotence is causally efficacious in bringing this about, it is impossible for us to not sin. If God foreordained that Cain slay Abel, that David seduce Bathsheba, that Judas betray Jesus, these persons could not have performed other than that ordained role. But can the God who predetermined that we and they act thus hold us morally accountable? To do so seems unjust. Is not he, in so foreordaining events, equally, if not more or entirely, culpable?

Calvin says no, for although we do evil according to God's determinate will, we "do not serve the will of God. For we cannot say, that he who is influenced by a wicked heart, acts in obedience to the commands of God, while he is only gratifying his own malignant passions" (1.17.5). The sinner is not obeying the will— or better, the precepts—of God, but only his own passions, and is thereby culpable.[7]

It is true that the sinner is not obeying the command of God as found in his revealed will. He is not responding to God's obligation-creating will, which tells him that he *ought to* act in a certain way. Yet the sinner's very passions and desires are directed by the secret inspiration of God (1.18.2). God operates on the mind, desires, and will, directing human deliberations and endeavors as he pleases. What a person desires is directed by and ultimately serves God's foreordaining will. But if it serves his foreordaining will, though it does not accord with his obligation-creating will, and if it occurs because actuated by the divine, omnipotent will, how can the sinner be held morally accountable? He is not obeying God's obligation-creating will because in his foreordination God has efficaciously willed the sinner not to.[8]

In short, original sin, which removes our free agency and which soils beyond any self-hope our reason and character, and foreordination, which efficaciously condemns us to do wrongful acts, conspire to remove our moral accountability. How can humans be held accountable if they are not free to do good, if their sin is necessitated, both by original sin and divine foreordination and omnipotence? If we cannot but sin, we cannot be held morally accountable for our actions. Whence then is human moral accountability and divine justice?

Behind his individual arguments and excoriations at what he terms these cavils, Calvin gives two fundamental replies to these objections: (1) being actuated by God is compatible with the person acting voluntarily, so that even though we are caused to act in a certain way, the moral accountability derives not from the cause of the action, but from the character of the actor and his voluntary action, and (2) since we are sinners in the eyes of God, whatever the cause of our sinful character, we rightly are subject to his retributive justice. Let us consider these replies in turn.

FREEDOM AND NECESSITY

Calvin argues that although our debilitated nature enslaves us to do nothing but evil and although God has preordained that those not elect do nothing but evil and causally governs the world to this end, we are still morally accountable for the evil we do. The reason is that we *voluntarily* follow our evil desires and passions into evil ways. We, of our own accord, act wrongfully because we want to. If we do wrong because we want to, then we can be held accountable for those actions. Necessitation by God and by original sin are compatible with moral accountability.

We must, he argues, distinguish between an act that is done out of necessity and one that is done under constraint or compulsion (2.3.5; 2.5.1).[9] On the one hand, acting out of necessity (or its opposite, free will) refers to the causal structure of our acts. An act that is necessary has a sufficient causal antecedent, either in terms of a specific set of causal conditions or, more relevant for our purposes, in terms of God's foreordination and continuing omnipotent intervention, whereas an act that is done out of free will has no such determining antecedents. That is, a person with free will has the power to discern good and evil and is undetermined, so as to be able to choose either. On the other hand, acting under constraint (or its opposite, acting voluntarily) refers to whether we are able to do what we want. If someone holds a pistol to my head and tells me to remove money from another person's pocket, and if I do so, I am acting under constraint. If I am acting against what I want to do, I am acting involuntarily.

For Calvin, the freedom presupposed by moral accountability does not refer to the necessitating conditions of our actions. It is not the ability to do otherwise than we do, given a certain set of causal conditions. "Freedom is not an equal power to do or to think either good or evil" (2.2.6–7).[10] Rather, it arises in relation to the second distinction above. In those cases in which we can be held morally accountable we must be able to act voluntarily. We must be able to act unconstrained and unrestrained by external forces operating against our will. To be free is not to be prevented from doing what we want to do.

Thus it is perfectly possible (indeed, subsequent to the fall, actually the case) for a person to be determined to or necessarily sin and yet be held morally accountable for that sin. Calvin mentions God and the devil as examples of the compatibility of being determined and morally accountable. God is necessarily good. "There is such a close connection between the goodness of

God and his Deity, that his being God is not more necessary than his being good." Thus God, as God, cannot do anything but that which is good; his doing good is necessitated by his very nature. God does not stand neutral between good and evil, loftily deliberating indeterminately about what he should do. He acts, and it is, indeed must be, good. Yet God is to be praised for his good deeds, for he does good voluntarily, out of the liberty of his will (2.3.5).

Similarly with the devil. "The devil is by his fall so alienated from communion with all that is good, that he can do nothing but what is evil." Not only does his nature necessitate his doing evil, but his actions are foreordained and governed by God. God arms the devil for his tasks, causally instigating him as his agent. "God often actuates the reprobate by the interposition of Satan, but in such a manner that Satan himself acts his part by the Divine impulse, and proceeds to the extent of the Divine appointment" (1.18.2).[11] Yet the devil is to be condemned for his evil deeds, for he does evil voluntarily—i.e., because he wants to.

The same applies to human persons. We sin under the necessity imposed by the evil and perverse nature we have inherited from Adam. We likewise sin under the necessity of divine foreordination and a causally efficacious divine will. We cannot but sin when God has so foreordained. Only with divine assistance can we think or do good. Yet we, "having been corrupted by the fall, sin voluntarily, not with reluctance or constraint; with the strongest propensity of dispositions, not with violent coercion; with the bias of [our] own passions, not with external compulsion: yet such is the [de]pravity of [our] nature, that [we] cannot be excited and biased to anything but what is evil" (2.3.5). And since we sin voluntarily, we stand under the judgment of God for those sins. We can be held accountable for them, for we did them freely.

In sum, Calvin teaches a compatibilist doctrine of freedom. *Necessity* deals with the causal conditions under which a person acts. Causally, the will is bound by the slavery of sin and by the directing act of God, who moves our will and deliberations wherever and however he pleases. Although this necessity speaks to the origins of our desires, beliefs, and choices, it says nothing about the character of our desires, beliefs, or choices, or the actions that follow from them. As such, it says nothing about moral responsibility. A person's character, desires, and volitions are worthy of praise or blame, irrespective of how they are acquired. *Freedom*, on the other hand, is not the contradictory of necessity. A free act is one that a person does voluntarily, under no external coercion or compulsion. It stems from—or, better, accords with—his wants and desires. Only for free acts can the person be held morally responsible (2.5.1–2).

But is Calvin's compatibilist doctrine true? According to him, God not only foreordains every event but also is the active cause behind each event. This applies not only to events in the external world, but also to events in what might be termed our internal world. God operates on the human mind, controlling desires and beliefs,[12] hardening and renewing as he wills. And he operates on our acts of choosing, so that our very choices (acts of will) are caused by God himself.[13] He is thus the author (cause) of both our willing and our doing. Since our choosing, believing, and desiring are caused by one who exists and foreordains all things prior to our existence, we cannot will, choose, believe, or desire other than we are caused to do.

But then the freedom asserted by Calvin and the compatibilist is an illusion, for the coercion that controls our acts when we are not free here extends to our desires and choices. When our actions are coerced, we are prevented from doing what we want, i.e., from doing anything other than it is determined that we do. When our will is coerced, we are prevented from making any choices other than it is determined that we make. We will what we must will, and cannot will or choose otherwise (unless the causal conditions be different). But the causal conditions cannot be different from what they are, for their nature and order is part of God's predetermined plan.

Thus there is no instance in which we can desire other than decreed by God. Should we will, believe, or desire other than decreed by God, that very will, belief or desire is itself decreed by God. Freedom as voluntary action becomes an empty notion, for divine coercion extends into the depths of our choosing.

To put it another way, it is true that a free act is one that is done by a free agent not acting under constraint or restraint. But what the compatibilist fails to recognize is that constraints can be causal as well as restrictive of action. That is, the constraints can act on agents, determining their beliefs, desires, and intentions, so that they cannot will at all or are unable to will in any fashion other than they do.

Jonathan Edwards, in defense of the Calvinist view, replies that this is an uncommon use of the words *constraint* and *unable*. To be unable to do what one wants presupposes that the agent already has a "present will or inclination to the things, with respect to which [he] is said to be unable."[14] That is, if the person is unable to do something, it means that he has already willed to do it and that circumstances have prevented or now prevent his acting on his choice. In this case it makes sense to say that the agent was not free. But to speak of the agent as unable to make a decision other than he is determined to make does not presuppose that he has a "present will or inclination." Here, then, it does not make sense to say the agent was not free, for there is no choice to be countermanded. Hence, whether his particular act of will was causally determined is irrelevant to his being unable to do the act. Whatever the source of the strongest motive, that motive or inclination will determine the action taken. Thus what is significant for determining issues of freedom and moral accountability is not the source of the volition or its causal status, but whether the agent was able to act in accord with his volition.

Now it is true that being unable to carry out one's will is one sense of the word *unable*. I am not free if I am unable to act on my choices because of some external constraint. However, there is another sense of the word that is also relevant to the freedom required for moral responsibility. I am not free if I am unable to choose to do other than I did. We say, for example, that a person acting under the influence of strong drugs or hypnosis or who is insane is not free. By this we do not mean that these persons cannot carry out their choices. Rather, we mean that they are in such a position that they are unable to will or choose other than they are determined to do by certain factors beyond their control. And as such, they cannot properly be held morally accountable for their acts (even if their acts are not constrained by another person).[15]

To this Edwards might respond that such persons, though capable of actions that are either harmful or beneficial, are not moral agents, not because they are determined to act as they do by factors beyond their present control, but because they cannot be influenced by moral inducements or motives. Their reason or understanding is so affected by drugs, insanity, or whatever that it cannot guide their choice concerning what is morally proper or improper.

This response, however, will not work because of Edward's theory of motivation. Edwards holds that the strongest motive causes or determines the choice made (the act of the will). That is, the agent always and necessarily acts for what he deems apparently good, i.e., most agreeable or pleasing. It is not that the person evaluates his inducements or selects between competing motives. If the agent selected between motives, he would then have to have a stronger or strongest motive according to which he would select, and if he in turn had to select this motive, this would lead to an infinite regress. Rather, the strongest motive determines the action chosen. Consequently, that which causes the motive is what causes our choice, and this in turn causes our action. The agent, then, is determined to act as he does by whatever motive determines the volition.

But this has the devastating consequence of precluding moral agents. For Edwards, a moral agent is not only a being "capable of those actions that have a moral quality" and having a "moral faculty, or sense of moral good and evil," but also one who possesses a capacity "of being influenced in his actions by moral inducements or motives, exhibited to the view of understanding and reason, to engage in a conduct agreeable to the moral faculty."[16] But as we have seen, according to him, moral agents do not consider the motives and choose which they will accept as determinative of their actions, and reason does not guide choice but only registers it. Rather, actions necessarily follow from the strongest motive. That is, when it comes to the determining power of motives, reason and understanding are irrelevant; the strongest motive necessarily determines the act, whatever it is and whatever its source. But this means that Edwards assimilates being influenced by motives being determined by them. If the influences are not the strongest, they are powerless to motivate action; if they are the strongest, the volition necessarily occurs as they dictate. The agent has had no say in the affair. But then there is no room for the self to be influenced in its actions by moral inducements, and hence the self is not a moral agent.

Edwards contrasts moral agents (human persons) with "brute creatures." The latter are not moral agents because they have no moral faculty and because they do not "act from choice guided by understanding, or with a capacity of reasoning and reflecting, but only from instinct, and are not capable of being influenced by moral inducements."[17] But if the strongest motive that determines the volition and act is not a product of an agent's choices or preferences, but follows from certain antecedent causes beyond the control of the agent, then persons are not different in their actions from animals, for both persons and brutes necessarily act according to the strongest motive (whatever its origin). But if animals are not moral agents, since reason does not guide their choice nor can they act other than in accordance with the strongest desires or preferences supplied by their instincts, neither are persons who act under similar restraints or conditions moral agents. Persons are unique only in their ability to recognize good and evil, reward or punishment. People praise, cows moo. But this difference in ability is not sufficient to make the former moral *agents*.

Contrary to Edwards, the freedom necessitated by our concept of moral agency applies to more than simply our actions (where we are free when we can carry out what we have chosen to do). It also applies to our choices. An agent is free when he could have chosen to do otherwise than he did.[18] What the Calvinist has failed to grapple with is the very nature of choice. To choose means to select from among alternatives what one is going to do. If that selection process is not genuine, there is no genuine choice. For example, if there are no alternatives available to the agent, there can be no choice, only the implementation in action. If the alternatives are apparent only, in that we (mistakenly) think there is more than one alternative available to us, we have only the illusion of choice, not genuine choice. Choice, then, implies that persons can select among genuine alternative courses of action, and agents are free when they are not necessitated, either by external or internal coercion, in their choice and action.

Calvin's compatibilist doctrine of freedom, then, will not suffice to account for moral responsibility. If we are to be free, not only must we be able to *act* according to our choices, but we must also be able to *choose* to act otherwise than we did. We are not compelled by external forces to choose or act as we do, external forces here including God as well as other persons. Likewise, we are not compelled to choose or act as we do by internal forces, such as a given or inherited nature or bias. We must be under no compulsion, either external or internal, to choose or act in a given way. In short, a person is free only if, given a certain set of circumstances or causal conditions, the person (to put it in the past tense) could have chosen and done otherwise than he did.

This does not mean that there are no causal conditions operative on the agent. Nor does it mean that the agent will have no biases, dispositions, or tendencies to act in certain ways. I am not describing or advocating a radical or perfect[19] freedom, where our choices are made completely independent of causal conditions or where no restraints whatsoever are placed on us. Freedom is not the absence of influences, either external or internal. Here Calvin, Augustine, and other theologians of their convictions are correct in their description of the freedom-removing aspects of sin. The more we sin, the more we are bound in the slavery of sin. It becomes a disposition or bias in us. And we do, in fact, often act out of this bias. Our biases are part of the causal conditions that influence our decisions. But although we do not act in our freedom from complete neutrality or in a dispositionless state (though we are influenced by these [sinful] desires and biases), we still can act contrary to those dispositions and choose not to follow their leading. Doing good might not be in our individual power, but one might attribute its possibility to the general work of the Holy Spirit, in the same way that Calvin attributes general rationality or the restraining of evil to the general work of the Spirit.

Genuine freedom means that the causal conditions do not determine the person's choice or action. Freedom, as actually found in our experience, is a relative notion: it is relative to the context and the causal conditions operative in it. There are degrees of freedom. But where we are free (to some extent), given the extant causal conditions, we could have done other than we did, even though it might have been very difficult to do so.

It should be clear that this libertarian or incompatibilist notion of freedom is incompatible with either a total depravity that determines our moral character and actions or with divine foreordination (not based on foreknowledge) and divine causation of all events.[20] If we are necessitated to evil by either of these, our morally significant freedom is removed.

This of course is not to say that we are not fallen. All have sinned, but the sinning is the result of the conscious decisions that we, like our first parents, have made. It does not deny that we have a sinful bias or disposition, only that this bias does not necessitate our actions. Neither does this remove divine foreordination. What it does require, however, is that divine foreordination be based on divine foreknowledge (Rom. 8:29).[21]

RETRIBUTIVE AND DISTRIBUTIVE JUSTICE

In his second response to our original criticism that his view cannot account for human moral responsibility, Calvin appeals to divine justice. He argues that since we share in the guilt of Adam's sin, and since we cannot but sin ourselves, so that "every inclination of [our] heart is evil from childhood" (Gen. 8:21), God is just in holding us morally accountable. Indeed, God's justice *requires* that we as sinners be held accountable for our deeds and punished appropriately.

Calvin's emphasis is clearly on *retributive* justice. According to retributive justice, the person who does wrong deserves to be punished. It does not tell us how much that person is to be punished. Other principles, such as *lex talionis*, provide that guidance. However, it does tell us *who* is to be held accountable and punished (the guilty, not the innocent) and *that* they are to be held accountable and punished. Not to treat the guilty as accountable and punishable is an affront to justice.

In both the Old and New Testaments God is pictured as dispensing retributive justice, both in the present and in the future (for example, at the final Judgment). But although Calvin has properly focused on retributive justice, he has overlooked another aspect or type of justice, namely, *distributive* justice. Insofar as, on Calvin's view, humans cannot save themselves, let alone think the good or do the good, God's mercy is necessary for this to occur. God distributes the ability to think and do good. There is good ground, then, for considering how justice relates to this divine distribution. Of course, God distributes more than this. There is the rain, which he sends on the just and the unjust (Matt. 5:45); the care he takes of sparrows and humans (Matt. 10:29–31); the protection he affords and the provisions he supplies (Ps. 23). God is a merciful and bountiful God, and his justice cannot be isolated from that mercy and bounty.

In most applications of distributive justice, when one dispenses goods or opportunities to other individuals, either because one wants to or is under some obligation to do so, one takes care to treat equals equally and unequals according to or in relation to their relevant inequalities.[22] There is considerable debate concerning the nature and relevance of these inequalities or grounds for distribution.

Distributive Justice According to Merit

Some, such as Thomas Aquinas, have argued that distributive justice is to be dispensed according to an individual's merits or worth.[23] Each is to be given according to his due. There are instances in which this would be most appropriate. For example, it would be unjust for a teacher to hand out the grades at the end of the term on the basis of anything other than merit. If she dispensed them on the basis of mere equality (everyone gets the same grade) or need (for example, Susie deserves a D but she has had personal problems or has not had an A yet this year and needs an A to pass, so the teacher will give her an A) she would be unjust. A similar case for dispensing goods based on merit can be made in athletic contests. We crown the winner, not an individual who lost but who has not won for a number of years and needs to (to boost morale or qualify for future races).

However, in matters having to do with divine dispensation of favors or grace, Scripture tells us that God dispenses grace independent of merits. God selected Israel to be the medium of his activity and the locus of his blessing, not because it was a great nation, but because it was no nation. We are saved, "not by works, so that no one can boast" (Eph. 2:9). Hence a theory of justice based on merit is irrelevant to our considerations of God's salvific and good-producing grace.[24]

Distributive Justice According to Needs

A second view is found in those who suggest that distributive justice should be dispensed according to needs.[25] Those who have the greater needs deserve the greater favors. It would seem that the ideal goal would be total equality of wealth and opportunity. But this is not so, for there will always be inequalities of wealth and station. Complete equality of status, position, and opportunity is impossible, if for no other reason than that we are born into different contexts or circumstances. Rather, the goal of justice is that there be no social and economic inequalities except those that result from maximizing the good for those who are deprived. That is, justice demands that goods and services be distributed so that those who are worst off are no worse off than the most needy would be under any other form of distribution.

A current government practice amply illustrates this basis for just distribution. For example, when the government distributes its excess cheese, it would be unjust to give it to all citizens, rich and poor, equally. The wealthy can purchase cheese with their own resources. Neither would it be just for it to dispense the cheese according to merit, so that those who contribute most to society or have acquired merit in some other way get the cheese, while others do not. Rather, the cheese is distributed, justly, to those who cannot afford it, to the needy on the basis of their need. The needs of the needy are claims on us, claims the fulfillment of which persons are entitled to because they are persons.

If we use need as the relevant inequality. it is clear that Calvin's view of divine justice is woefully lacking. Although God is just when justice is considered retributively, he is unjust when considered distributively. According to Calvin, because of the drastic consequences of original sin, we are capable only of doing evil acts. It is God who works in and through us in every good deed (Phil. 2:13). This means that unless God gives us the grace to do good, we are doomed to think or do nothing but evil. We might rightly say that all persons are desperately needy: we all are sinners and need God's grace.

It is true that God gives grace to do good and repent of our sins. He inclines the heart and transforms the human will to the end that those moved are saved. But, according to Calvin, he gives saving grace only to some, not all. God will have mercy on whom he will have mercy, we are repeatedly told. But is such a God just? If he could give grace to all (he has it to give) so that all will be saved, and if he can do this (it does not conflict with his omnipotence), and if he truly wants that all should be saved (1 Tim. 2:4; 2 Peter 3:9), why then does he not? Is not a God who abandons the needy to perdition by not giving them his Spirit and who can distribute grace at no cost to himself but does not unjust? Since his grace is the only means by which needy sinners can be saved, and since God alone is the source of that grace, justice demands that if he gives it to humans, he distribute it in such a way that those who still are needy are no more needy in their human predicament than the needy would have been under any other system of distribution. "Will not the Judge of all the earth do right?" (Gen. 18:25).[26]

It is important to note that for Calvin, the sins of the wicked are not simply the results of their own wills. Pharaoh's heart was not simply hardened by himself. Rather, the sins of the wicked are due to God's deliberate abandonment of them to their depravity, "They have been raised up, by a just but inscrutable judgment of God, to display his glory in their condemnation" (3.24.14). The God who hardened their hearts is capable of softening or, better, transforming and also renewing them. The problem with Calvin's view is that God does not do so, "because his immutable decree had predestinated them to destruction" (3.24.14). But where is his distributive justice in this account? Where is his just concern for the spiritually needy? It is said that he wills that all be saved. If he can show irresistible grace to all without harming his omnipotence and goodness, why then does he not? Does not distributive justice demand it? Calvin suggests three replies to this "caviling".

1. He argues that if God by mercy would relieve the sins of all persons, he would abandon his position as the just judge who inflicts punishment for human sinfulness. "Justice requires that he should likewise show himself to be a just judge in the infliction of punishment" (3.23.11). Our objection tempts God to abandon his justice. None would be judged, and none would be punished; where, then, would be his (retributive) justice?

Calvin's response reveals a dilemma of divine roles. On the one hand, God is the precondition of doing right; without his action we can do only evil. If he desires more good, he can provide more grace. On the other hand, he is the dispenser of punishment for evil done; if all persons do right, there is no punishment. If God desires more punishment (retributive justice), he can withhold greater portions of distributive grace. Thus which role God chooses to emphasize will lead to a diminishing of the alternative role. Calvin's choice of retributive over distributive justice clearly shows where his affections lie. Love plays second fiddle to punishment.

Beyond this ambiguity of roles, however, one must wonder whether the consequences regarding justice foreseen by Calvin would occur. Does God's showing greater mercy mean that retributive justice must be dispensed with? For one thing, retributive justice still holds in that it compels discernment of the guilty. It demands that *only the guilty* be punished. If there are no guilty, if all are forgiven, justice is not foregone. It still is in force; there is simply no one to whom to apply it. If justice is not abandoned in the saving of one sinner, it is not dispensed with in saving all sinners.[27] There is an absurdity in Calvin's demand that someone *must* do evil, else there is no justice. In making justice require performance of evil he has stood justice on its head.

Furthermore, even for those whose sins are forgiven, the judgment on their sins has been made and the penalty imposed. The innocent will be acquitted (Rom. 2:6–7, 10). But there are none: all have sinned. What has happened is that God has acted on our behalf. Christ has committed an act of obedience. In doing so, he is innocent, yet he both takes on himself our sinfulness (making us righteous) (Rom. 5:19) and pays the penalty for our sin through his death on the cross (Rom. 3:25). By his action we are acquitted, justified before God.

Retributive justice was invoked. We were, as it were, tried and found guilty. The punishment of death for our sins was imposed. But Christ has taken on himself our sins and punishment; "while we were still sinners, Christ died for us" (Rom. 5:8). Justice is served, but by the mercy of God and not our own innocence we are justified. Christ's love and obedience provide the means of justification and absorption of the penalty. Thus, even were no person ever punished, even if all were saved, retributive justice would still stand, for the judicial drama already has been played out in Christ's atoning death.

2. Calvin appeals to examples from both the Old and New Testaments where God selects nations and individuals for his mercy. From the thousands in Mesopotamia God selected Abraham to be the father of his people. "When the Most High gave the nations their inheritance, when he divided all mankind, he set up boundaries for the peoples. . . .For the Lord's portion is his people, Jacob his allotted inheritance" (Deut. 32:8–9; cf. Ps. 64:4). Even within this select band of Abraham's seed God chose some and rejected others. Ishmael was driven out; Isaac was retained. "Jacob have I loved; Esau have I hated" (Mal. 1:2–3). Similarly, "he chose us in him before the creation of the world to be holy and blameless in his sight. . .in accordance with his pleasure and will" (Eph. 1:4–5; cf. 2 Tim. 1:9). It is not that we have chosen him, but that he has chosen us (John 15:16; cf. 13:18).

Now there can be no doubt that God is active in selecting certain persons or groups of persons to achieve his ends. Joseph's brothers sold him into slavery in Egypt, yet at the same time it was God who sent him on ahead to preserve his family and the Egyptians (Gen. 45:8; 50:20). Similarly, as punishment for Solomon's idolatry and departure from the law, God gives part of the kingdom to Jeroboam. The division is made possible by Rehoboam's obstinacy, which God had a hand in bringing about (1 Kings 11:29–38; 12:15). Again, after the Exile, God stirred up the people to obey his voice to rebuild the temple (Hag. 1:12–14).[28] Jeremiah was chosen as a prophet to deliver the word of the Lord (Jer. 1:5–9); Peter was selected to feed Christ's flock (John 21:15–17); Saul was chosen to be God's apostle to the Gentiles and to Israel (Acts 9:15–16).

Nevertheless, this selection should not be misunderstood. There are insufficient grounds in these instances of selection for concluding to a divine determinism of all human actions. Neither should divine selection be assimilated to a single model. Just as our own actions intersect with those of others in various ways, so God's actions intersect with ours in diverse ways. Several models, by no means exhaustive of the possibilities, might be suggested.

First, God's action is sometimes co-action with human free agency. This might be understood in at least two different ways: (1) The human agent freely brings about the particular action and can be held morally accountable for it. At the same time, God works through that action, achieving through it a purpose that is perhaps contrary to or transcendent to that of the human agent. The Joseph example might be a case in point. God was active in the mercantile transaction of Joseph's brothers, not in the sense that he determined that they sell Joseph to the traders, but that by their free action the consequences he desired were realized. Similar things might be said about his use of foreign nations such as Assyria and Egypt to punish disobedient Israel. (2) Both God and the human agent brought about the event, though each by himself was sufficient to do so. This is an example of what might be termed overcausation. Suppose, for example, that you and I, unknown to each other, decide to blow up a building at precisely the same time. I lay in enough explosives to demolish the building, as do you. By chance we both set our detonators to the same time, and at the appointed second the building explodes. In this case of co-action, since both of us blew up the building, both are responsible for doing so, though each was sufficient in himself to accomplish the end. An example of this might be the hardening of Pharaoh's heart. God is said to have done it, but so did Pharaoh himself (Exod. 4:21; 7:3; 8:15, 32; 9:12, 34; 1 Sam. 6:6). Since each willed it so as to bring it about, each can be properly said to have caused it.

Second, God acts through persuasion to realize his purposes. His stirring up of Zerubbabel and the people, though an action on God's part, is consonant with their freedom. Similar persuasive powers, this time accompanied by direct physical action, were used to convert Saul (Acts 9:3–5).

As we sometimes compel others to act in a certain way, so God too at times acts directly, in a manner that limits human freedom.[29] Yet it cannot be the case that God always, or perhaps even frequently, works to achieve his purposes in ways that remove human freedom. It is through persuasion that his intentions are most often realized, for it is persuasion that is most consistent with human freedom and with the moral and spiritual development it makes possible. Indeed, in each case it is necessary that the selectee respond to the divine selection. The story of Jonah provides the case of a selectee who said no, though it also illustrates the lengths to which God will go to persuade people to follow his will. However, that he persuades does not imply that he persuades successfully in every case, as the history of Israel aptly demonstrates.

Third, his selection is often conditional. Jeroboam was selected to start another dynasty, conditional upon his own continued obedience. Israel's selection, too, was conditional. Not all who are natural descendants of Abraham truly belong to him. For many of the natural seed, the blessings of selection have been squandered, to the point where God calls them "not my people, and I am not your God" (Hos. 1:9). Yet he promises continued action so as to save out a remnant. This action is persuasive ("I will allure her"), co-active ("I will plant her for myself in the land"), and direct ("I will make a covenant for them").

It is true that Scripture emphasizes that the work of salvation comes through the auspices of God. "No one comes to me unless the Father who sent me draws him" (John 6:44). "A man can receive only what is given him from heaven" (3:27). It is by grace that we are saved, through faith. Yet in the matter of grace, Paul himself writes that "God has bound all men over to disobedience so that he may have mercy on them all" (Rom. 11:32; cf. Titus 2:11). God's grace extends to all, so that in Christ all who by faith receive his grace are justified (Rom. 5:15–19). God's distributive justice, especially as seen in Christ's justificatory act (1 Tim. 2:6; 1 John 2:2), extends and is made available to all persons, not to a select few.

3. When all else fails, Calvin retreats to the unfathomableness of divine grace. Quoting Augustine, he writes, " 'God could convert to good the will of the wicked, because he is omnipotent. It is evident that he could. Why, then, does he not? Because he would not. Why he would not, remains with himself.' For we ought not to aim at more wisdom than becomes us" (3.24.13; cf. 2.1.10). The curtain of ignorance descends when we approach the mystery of God's reasons. "Let us be content with some degree of ignorance where the wisdom of God soars into its own sublimity" (3.24.14).

Yet in this matter we cannot escape by appeals to an unfathomable, transcendent will of God. For one thing, it leads Calvin onto dangerous grounds. For example, his contention that God wills it because he wills it leads to his view that something is considered just simply because God wills it. There is nothing "greater and higher than the will of God, . . the highest standard of perfection, even the law of all laws" (3.23.2). Although Calvin denies that this makes the standard of right and justice arbitrary, so that anything that God willed—including murder, rape, and torture—would be good by virtue of his having willed it, his argument (that it is right and just because the will of God is "pure from every fault") either begs the question in that it presupposes a prior notion of moral goodness by which we can measure divine faultlessness, or is guilty of equivocation in that it makes the ontological goodness or perfection characteristic of God's nature the ground for moral goodness.[30] Further, even here, regarding the charge of arbitrariness, he pleads *nolo contendere*, since we are not proper judges of the right and good.

For another, if Calvin is so sure of the character of God's retributive justice, to the extent that he affirms that God abandons people so that his justice is preserved and his glory magnified, surely distributive justice cannot remain a mystery when it is invoked as a difficulty within Calvinism. Indeed, there is good evidence that God's distributive justice accords, at least in part, with human need. For example, when Jesus is questioned about the company he keeps, about his association with tax collectors and sinners, he replies, "It is not the healthy who need a doctor, but the sick. I have not come to call the righteous, but sinners" (Mark 2:17). It is the needy to whom Jesus directly ministers, who are the recipients of the abundant grace of Christ Jesus, who "came into the world to save sinners" (1 Tim. 1:14–15; cf. Luke 19:10). A similar theme echoes through Jesus' announcement of his mission. He has come "to preach the good news to the poor . . . to proclaim freedom for the prisoners, and recovery of sight for the blind, to release the oppressed" (Luke 4:18–19).[31] His ministry of grace is specifically directed toward the needy, to those oppressed and downtrodden in ways spiritual, social, political, economic, and physical. There lies behind this announcement the concept of the Jubilee Year, when debts are forgiven, when the Israelite bond-servants are given their liberty, when the just order is reintroduced.

God's most significant act of grace is his sending and sacrificing his only Son. The justificatory act is available for all who in faith appropriate it. The eternal life that comes through the Son is available to all, to whoever believes in him (John 3:15–18, 36).

Distributive Justice According to Entitlement

Others have suggested that distributive justice is not a recipient notion, as in the considerations that invoke merit or need, so much as an entitlement notion. For example, Robert Nozick argues that people are entitled to hold and disperse at their pleasure (so long as they do not violate anyone else's rights or entitlements) those assets justly derived.[32] This means that in the dispersion of goods or assets, no one can be compelled to dispense those assets justly derived or held in any way contrary to their desires (given the above qualification about not violating the rights of others).[33]

The application of this theory, at first glance, seems irrelevant to the question at hand, namely, how to understand divine distributive justice, for one might argue, as we did with merit, that the biblical view is that we have no natural assets to which we are entitled. Naked we came into this world, and naked we shall depart (Job 1:21). However, we should look at this theory, not from the perspective of the recipients of distributive favor (as we did in the two theories above), but rather from the perspective of God, the holder of all assets. Using Nozick's account, one might argue that since God is the creator and source of everything, all assets are justly his from their beginning. Consequently, he is under no obligation to dispense his assets or grace in any particular way. According to this classic libertarian theory, he is at liberty, and he is completely just to say, "I will have mercy on whom I have mercy, and I will have compassion on whom I have compassion" (Rom. 9:15, quoting Exod. 33:19).

Nozick's individualistic account seems to accord well with Calvin, who frequently quotes this and similar passages (e.g., John 6:44–45; 15:16, in 3.22.6–8). God chooses whomever he wills, and he does it as it fits his pleasure and purposes. He selected Isaac and rejected Ishmael, chose Jacob but not Esau, and elevated Ephraim over Manasseh. These decisions were based, not on any deserts of these individuals, but on God's own good pleasure. And can anyone complain of God's justice in this matter? No, for God can dispose of his assets as suits him, and this disposition is just (Rom. 9:19–29).[34]

But is this an adequate account of distributive justice? I have serious qualms. For one thing, it ignores the community of humankind and the interdependence between humans and that between humans and the environment that makes individual existence, well-being, and wealth possible. Granted that we have entitlements, entitlements without ownership of what we are entitled to are empty. (A legitimate king in exile might be entitled to the throne, but his entitlement is empty unless he sits on the throne.) That which fulfills my entitlements is not solely personally derived, but is made possible by the activities and efforts of many in the community, working with a shared environment. I may be entitled to the food in my refrigerator, but the food would not be there for me to justly own unless farmers had grown it, food companies packaged it, and merchants sold it. Its very availability for me to buy it depends on the social network of which I am a part. At the same time, this larger community creates relationships and ensuing social obligations that limit my entitlements. The strict individualism that underlies this account of justice cannot be sustained.[35] In addition, this account of distributive justice ignores other, human dimensions of the transfer of goods from one person to another. For example, I might *justly* (in Nozick's sense) purchase with my *justly* derived wealth an item that another is entitled to sell, and thus be *justly* entitled to it. Yet there might be an injustice in the purchase because, though I paid the price asked, it was not a *fair* price, for the person selling it (suppose it be an heirloom or their last personal possession) might be doing so simply to subsist and are taking whatever they can get. There are determinants of fairness other than a person selling a justly held item, the bidding or asking price and free market considerations of supply and demand. Finally, though all humans have entitlements, they also have needs, and there seems no good reason for giving priority to the former over the latter as a matter of course. To put it another way, we are entitled to have our basic needs met just as much as to acquire, have, and dispose of property, and there is no reason to think that the latter will always (or even usually) take priority.

These are hints of directions an evaluation might take, but it would lead us much too far afield to attempt to provide a detailed evaluation of this view of justice.[36] What I would like to do, however, is ask whether it is adequate when applied in the case at hand. That is, will it provide a satisfactory account of distributive justice in a Calvinist system, which allows, indeed, requires, God to hold individuals morally responsible for their state and actions? The answer, I believe, is no. And the reason has not to do with the acceptability or adequacy of the entitlement theory of justice, but with the particular connection to retributive justice that Calvin gives it. In particular, he wants to hold not only that God is just in dispensing his grace (assets) as he pleases, but that he likewise is just in holding those to whom they are not dispensed guilty and condemnable for not possessing or having received those assets. To return to our cheese example, it is like saying that the government is entitled to dispense the excess cheese to whomever it wants in whatever quantity it desires, and that likewise it can prosecute those who do not have this cheese for their failure to possess it.

Now this scenario might be acceptable if it could be shown that those who lack the divinely given grace and faith do not have them because they have squandered them (though prosecution for squandering is incompatible with the entitlement theory, for on this account one is free to dispense, even squander, those assets as one sees fit). But people are held accountable because they do evil, and they do evil because they have not received divine enabling grace. Furthermore, the situation is so structured that it is impossible for them to take any action to acquire what they lack. Unless God distributes his grace to them, there is no way they can do good or be saved, or even want to do good or be saved. Thus those who are judged because they are not saved and do not do right are punished for not having the asset they cannot get (saving faith and the ability to do right).

But surely, if God is entitled to distribute his grace however he wills and if this is just, it is not just to punish those who have not received that grace and cannot get it, for not having it. To hold persons accountable, it must be possible for them to avoid that for which they are being held accountable. They must have been able not to have done the deed. But if people cannot do unless God gives them the desire and power to do, they cannot do other than they have done. God can hold them accountable only with respect to what he has given them.

It might be objected that this entitlement view of justice is embodied in Jesus' parable of the workers in the vineyard. The landowner hired workers at different times during the day. The first people hired agreed to a just wage, whereas the others agreed to be paid whatever was right. When the day ended and the payments were made, the landowner gave all the same wage, regardless of the time spent working in the vineyard. When the first workers, who expected more because they labored all day, complained, the landowner replied that they should be satisfied with what he paid them, for their wages accorded with to what they had agreed. It is simply that he wanted to give the same wage to the others. "Don't I have the right to do what I want with my own money?" (Matt. 20:15).

This right might be his, given Nozick's account. However, it is important to note that this entitlement claim is used by Jesus to support generosity ("Or are you envious because I am generous?"), not judgment. Where possession and use is judged, the distribution has been to all. In another parable, the estate owner who went on a journey gave to all his servants (though in varying amounts) and expected a return from them according to what was entrusted to them. When one was judged because he had failed to invest his talents, the judgment was fair, for he was given the opportunity, as were the others, to invest the graciously given money (Matt. 25:14–30). Our point is not to deny that God (or we, for that matter) possesses entitlements to his (justly held) goods and services. Rather, it is to claim that this entitlement is inconsistent with holding in judgment those to whom no benefits are given.

A second objection to a Calvinist employment of the entitlement view of distributive justice might be raised along a different line. To defend Calvin's view of God's sovereignty we have invoked an uncompromising interpretation of the entitlement theory of justice. But even those who hold this individualistic account of distributive justice realize that the right to acquire, hold, use, and dispense what one is entitled to must be balanced to some degree by considerations related to the basic rights of people. That is, the rights to property can be overridden by concerns dealing with individual rights to survival or to some baseline good. Nozick recognizes this when he restricts the acquisition by one person of all of a limited resource previously utilized freely by the community. Acquisition is not just if the overall position of those who previously had access to the resource is worsened. This does not absolutely rule out acquisition, but in those cases where the resource is acquired, the others must be compensated with equivalent resources and opportunities for their lost liberties.[37]

Although this particular type of case does not apply to our considerations (since we are not dealing with something previously available to all), Nozick suggests one that does. He argues that "a person may not appropriate the only water hole in a desert and charge what he will. Nor may he charge what he will if he possesses one, and unfortunately it happens that all the water holes in the desert dry up, except for his. The unfortunate circumstance, admittedly no fault of his, brings into operation the Lockean proviso (not to make the situation of others worse than their baseline situation) and limits his property rights."[38] Applying this last case to the matter of God's distribution of his grace, one might argue that with the fall, the water holes of doing good and being saved have dried up. Since God alone has access to the remaining source, though our loss of the water of life is no fault of his, it would be unjust for God not to share his grace so as to improve people to the baseline condition. His right to whatever he possesses is overridden by the basic rights of his creation to (eternal) life. It might be disputed what that baseline condition is (Nozick never delineates it), but one can reasonably suggest that, for our purposes here, it refers to a condition where life (eternal) is made possible to all who, following the catastrophe of the fall, face only certain (eternal) death. That is, it is a state where death can be avoided by receiving what God can make available. And on Calvin's view, whatever God can make possible he can make actual by his willing of it and the granting of irresistible grace. Thus, even on an entitlement theory of justice, God is not justified in holding to himself what in full measure belongs to him, but justice demands that it be shared, at least to the extent of making possible to all the baseline condition of salvation.

In reply, Calvin might press his case in a more individualistic fashion. For example, Nozick holds that "the situation would be different if his water hole didn't dry up, due to special precautions he took to prevent this."[39] Here individualism and the relation of labor to property win out, for apparently, since the other persons forfeited their property rights by not doing what they could to save their wells, the owner of the producing well is no longer obligated to relinquish his right to his well, despite their dire need. It is not the end-state that matters, but the particular way that the dire calamity has arisen and the relevant property-related actions or procedures taken or not taken by the populus. In a similar vein, Calvin might reply that God has his property (his goodness and power) because of his own precautions (he did not fall), whereas we lost ours by our first parents' carelessness in the fall and subsequently in our sinning. Thus God is not obligated to restore us to any baseline condition. It is not the end-state of our dire need that matters, but the fact that historically we (through our first parents) have forfeited the right to baseline maintenance.

But can our ancestors forfeit our rights to baseline maintenance? One can surmise that Nozick would say that since our ancestors squandered what they had, the person who has got what he has justly owes us nothing. It is the history, not the end-state, that determines whether distribution is required. If this applied to what is over and above the baseline, there might be some justice in it. I am under no obligation to restore the son of a bankrupt exmillionaire to a status of wealth. But if the baseline is to have any meaning at all, it comes into play not only at the time when one seeks to appropriate a commonly held good, but also when one can without cost assist another who has fallen below that line.

Further, even if this last point be rejected on the ground that it illicitly introduces end-state considerations, Calvin still would be hard-pressed to forego all end-state considerations, for it is precisely those considerations that are used in the judgment God assesses on us all. It is not because Adam sinned that we are condemned. It is because we lack goodness of character and the deeds stemming from that that we are justly condemned. But once end-state considerations are introduced, as they are here with retributive justice, since in the divine plan retributive justice is so closely linked with distributive justice, God's entitlement rights must be correlated with the deprived state of the needy. Baseline considerations having to do with our present need and the prospects of (eternal) death if no help is forthcoming demand a justice that gives all of us as needy that which makes possible our salvation. But it is this justice that Calvin's concept of God cannot supply.

CONCLUSION

In short, neither Calvin's appeal to a compatibilist view of freedom nor his restrictive appeal to retributive justice or, more broadly, to an entitlement view of distributive justice, suffices to answer the contention that the determinism that arises from his view of original sin and divine foreordination removes moral accountability. Our objection is more than a cavil. It requires the abandonment of necessitarian views of divine sovereignty and opens the door to the view that the human drama is a real one— that God has given us genuine freedom to accept or reject the grace offered to all.

NOTES

[1] John Calvin, *Institutes of the Christian Religion*, trans. John Allen (Philadelphia: Presbyterian Board of Publication, 1843), 2.1.3. References in the text are to this edition.

[2] "Original sin . . . appears to be an hereditary pravity and corruption of our nature, diffused through all the parts of the soul, rendering us obnoxious to the Divine wrath, and producing in us those works which the Scripture calls 'works of the flesh.' " (2.1.8).

[3] This loss, according to Calvin, is not so great as we might imagine, since Adam's example shows us "how miserable free will is, unless God give us both will and power" (2.3.10).

[4] Our perdition therefore proceeds from the sinfulness of our flesh, not from God; it being only a consequence of our degenerating from our primitive condition" (2.1.10).

[5] "He governs heaven and earth by his providence, and regulates all things in such a manner that nothing happens but according to his counsel" (1.16.3).

[6] "For when God is said to harden or show mercy to whom he pleases, men are taught by this declaration to seek no cause beside his will" (3.23.11).

[7] Calvin's reply hinges on an equivocation on "will." He denies that the thief, murderer, or adulterer is doing the will of God, for they are not obeying God's precepts but are acting out of the contumacy of their own hearts. Thus, since they are not doing God's will but acting according to their own, they, not God, are morally accountable for their actions. On the other hand, he goes on to argue that "thieves, and homicides, and other malefactors, are instruments of Divine providence." But as instruments of God, they act according to his will. "Nothing can happen but what is subject to his knowledge, and decreed by his will" (1.16.3). In the first case, "will" refers to the *oughts* that God commands; in the latter it refers to God's determination of all events, i.e., to what *is* or will be the case.

[8] Calvinists have subsequently distinguished between these two wills, the decretive will (which determines that events will happen) and the preceptive will (which embodies the prescriptions concerning what we should do). This distinction, though it sharpens the terminology, solves no problems, for it still leaves unresolved how God can decretively will what he preceptively forbids, and preceptively command what his decretive will makes impossible.

[9] Jonathan Edwards makes a similar distinction between what he terms the common sense of necessity (where something stands against our wills and frustrates our endeavor or desires) and metaphysical or philosophical necessity ("the full and fixed connection between the things signified by the subject and predicate of a proposition, which affirms something to be true"). According to the former, an agent is free when he is not acting under constraint or restraint, but can do as he chooses. This is the sense of necessity involved in evaluating whether a moral agent is acting freely. Causal necessity, which is one type of metaphysical necessity, is irrelevant to the freedom necessary for someone to be a moral agent. *Freedom of the Will* (New Haven: Yale University Press, 1957), 1:3–4.

[10] Edwards too argues that we cannot act in a state of motivational equilibrium. "In every act . . . of the will, there is some preponderation of the mind or inclination, one way rather than another. . . . It is the strongest motive which determines the will" (1:1–2). Since motives are the cause of and hence necessitate the act of the will, the cause cannot be located in any self-determining power in the will that, "acting in a state of indifference and equilibrium, determines itself to a preference" (2:10).

Edwards, however, goes on to clarify his position. Since it is tautologous to say that people choose what they are inclined to choose or prefer ("for the mind to will something, and for it to go after something by an act of preference and inclination, are the same thing" [2:10]), he holds, not that the will is *determined* by the greatest apparent good (which forms the strongest motive), but that the will "always is as the greatest apparent good is, . . . because an appearing most agreeable or pleasing to the mind, and the mind's preferring and choosing, seem hardly to be properly and perfectly distinct" (1:2; 2:9). Thus it becomes more proper to say that the *act* is determined by the strongest motive than to say that the *will* is so determined. But then Edwards has not shown that the will cannot be self-determining, for his argument to this end depended on the thesis that the cause of the act of the will was already located, namely, in the motives. The "causation *of* such 'motives' (whatever that may mean) is not a causation of the act of will *by* motives, and it was in this latter connection that the necessary determination of the will was said to consist." Arthur E. Murphy, "Jonathan Edwards on Free Will and Moral Agency," *Philosophical Review* 68 (April 1959), 194. In short, if Edwards understands the relation of the strongest motives to the act of the will as being a relation of identity rather than causation, then his appeal to the way motives function does not exclude, contradict, or negate an appeal to self-determination.

11 Among numerous other passages in Calvin, see 1.17.8; 1.18.1. This reflects Calvin's analysis of such passages as Job 1; 1 Sam. 16:14; 1 Kings 22:20–23; 2 Cor. 4:4.

12 "Whatever conceptions we form in our minds, they are directed by the secret inspiration of God" (1.23.2). From the context, it is clear that "directed" is not to be understood in any passive or permissive sense, but in an active or causal sense.

13 God "moves the will . . . by an efficacious influence" (2.3.10). "The hand of God no less rules the internal affections than it precedes the external acts, and that God does not perform by the hand of men those things which he has decreed without first working in their hearts the very will which precedes their acts." John Calvin, *The Eternal Predestination of God*, quoted in John Murray, *Calvin on Scripture and Divine Sovereignty* (Grand Rapids: Baker, 1960), 56.

14 Edwards, *Freedom of the Will*, 1:4.

15 This way of putting it is not entirely correct. This contention must be qualified to distinguish, for example, between the person who knowingly and willfully puts himself under the power of drugs and someone who does not do so either knowingly or willingly. Although the former does not act freely at the time, he is still morally accountable for his actions because he freely and knowingly put himself in that state. Freedom at the time of the act, then, might not be a necessary condition for moral accountability, though freedom understood in a broader time span—e.g., one that includes a historical relationship between a prior free act and the state out of which the agent acted—is necessary.

16 Edwards, *Freedom of the Will*, 1:5.

17 Ibid.

18 Calvin, when pressed to explain how a person can deliberate when his actions follow from and hence are determined by God's providence, retreats to the contention that deliberation is possible because the future is unknown to us. He writes, "Therefore it has pleased God to conceal from us all future events, that we may meet them as doubtful contingencies, and not cease to oppose to them the remedies with which we are provided, till they shall have been surmounted, or shall have overcome all our diligence" (1.17.4). This seems to ground freedom, which deliberation presupposes, on our ignorance of the future. Freedom as related to our deliberations becomes illusory. The irony is that Calvin rejects the notion of freedom based on reason (where reason reflects on the options) and will (choosing between alternatives, selecting one path but perfectly capable of choosing another) in favor of a freedom based on ignorance. We can deliberate about future choices because God has hidden the future (and of course much of the past and present) from us. Apparently if we knew what was, is, and will be, there would be no contingencies, only necessities, and the illusion of deliberation and the freedom it presupposes would escape from our grasp. And this is because

deliberations and their presupposed freedom deal only with contingencies, and there are no contingencies.

[19] Richard Swinburne, *The Coherence of Theism* (Oxford: Oxford University Press, 1977), 145–48, sees this kind of freedom as characteristic only of God.

[20] Interestingly enough, Calvin seems not to have realized this. On the one hand, only to our first parents does he grant freedom in a libertarian sense. "In this integrity man was endued with free will, by which, if he had chosen, he might have obtained eternal life. . . . Adam, therefore, could have stood if he would, since he fell merely by his own will. . . . Yet his choice of good and evil was free" (1.15.8). On the other hand, since the fall was preordained, indeed caused, by God, Adam could have been free only in a compatibilist sense. "Nor should it be thought absurd to affirm that God not only foresaw the fall of the first man, and the ruin of his posterity in him, but also arranged all by the determination of his own will" (3.23.7). His attempt to reconcile them by excluding considerations of predestination in the consideration of Adam's falling of his own (libertarian) free will (1.15.8) is arbitrary and misleading, especially since he introduces considerations of predestination into the fall elsewhere (3.18.7).

[21] For a more extensive discussion of this, see my article, "God Limits His Power," in David and Randall Basinger, eds., *Predestination and Free Will* (Downers Grove: InterVarsity, 1986).

[22] My statement here applies only to what Robert Nozick, *Anarchy, State and Utopia* (New York: Basic Books, 1974), 155–60, terms patterned theories of distributive justice, as over against unpatterned theories, which do not assign shares of resources in proportion to an individual's ranking on some scale. Our third characterization of distributive justice below will investigate his nonpatterned formulation.

[23] Thomas Aquinas, *Summa Theologica*, 1, Q.21, Art.1.

[24] However, Scripture at times portrays God as distributing benefits (e.g., talents, abilities, or added responsibilities) based on merit, past performance, or obedience. Although these benefits are not held to concern salvation, their presence or absence can have eternal consequences. For example, note what happens to the foolish investor in the parable of the talents in Matthew 25:14–30.

[25] For example, John Rawls, *A Theory of Justice* (Cambridge, Mass.: Harvard University Press, 1971).

[26] This passage is interesting in that in a context of retributive justice, Abraham challenged God to be just in his distribution of protection to the righteous innocent.

[27] The fallacy of composition is not committed here, for the same kinds of considerations that apply in forgiving one person apply also in forgiving all other persons.

¼&AND OTHER Old Testament, New Testament, and intertestamental passages from a compatibilist viewpoint can be found in D. A. Carson *Divine Sovereignty and Human Responsibility* (Atlanta: John Knox, 1981).

[29] Some of the more difficult passages are those that relate God's moving or inciting people to wrong actions to achieve his purposes—as with Samson (Judges 14:1–4), or with David (2 Sam. 24:1)—and yet is not held even in part morally responsible. It is interesting to note that the Old Testament authors themselves had difficulty with the concept of God inciting to sin, so that in a later account of David's numbering of the army they changed the inciter from God to Satan (1 Chron. 21:1).

[30] I have discussed this issue in my *Evil and a Good God* (New York: Fordham University Press, 1982), chap. 7. I have suggested some possible solutions in "The Divine Command Theory and Objective Good," in Rocco Porreco, ed., *The Georgetown Symposium on Ethics* (Washington, D.C.: University Press of America, 1984), 219–33.

[31] This same theme runs through the beatitudes, spiritualized in Matthew 5, socialized in Luke 6.

[32] Nozick, *Anarchy, State, and Utopia*, 150–51, 225.

[33] Nozick suggests the maxim, "From each as they choose, to each as they are chosen." Ibid., 160.

[34] It might be suggested that a Calvinist interpretation is even stricter than a Nozickean one, for whereas Nozick restricts a just dispensing of one's goods to instances where the rights of other persons are not violated, Calvin would seemingly allow the rights by primogeniture of Esau and Manasseh to be violated without any censure of God's justice. In effect, the lump of clay (Rom. 9:19–21) has no rights whatsoever over against the potter.

[35] I will have more to say about this shortly.

[36] For a substantial start in this direction, see Jeffrey Paul, ed., *Reading Nozick* (Totowa, N.J.: Rowman and Allanheld, 1983), 305–411.

[37] Nozick, *Anarchy, State, and Utopia*, 175–80. Strangely enough, the compensation is not in terms of rights or freedoms, but in terms of the material gain made possible in the long run by capitalism. This seems to go against his rejection of end-state considerations. See Cheyney C. Ryan, "Yours, Mine and Ours: Property Rights and Individual Liberty," in Paul, ed., *Reading Nozick*, 338–39.

[38] Nozick, *Anarchy, State, and Utopia*, 180. His individualism quickly reemerges when he considers resources not previously accessed freely. "A medical researcher who synthesizes a new substance that effectively treats a certain disease and who refuses to sell except on his terms does not worsen the situation by depriving them of whatever he has appropriated. The others easily can possess the same materials he appropriated; the researcher's appropriation or purchase of chemicals didn't make those chemicals scarce in a way so as to violate the Lockean proviso" (181).

[39] Ibid., 180.

INDEX OF PERSONS

(References to Biblical authors are generally placed in the Scripture index. Thus to find references to the views of Paul, for example, one would look for references to the various Pauline epistles.)

INDEX OF SUBJECTS

INDEX OF SCRIPTURE REFERENCES